Here is a book which records in the very words of Jesus answers to questions raised by all of us, especially non-believers. Some of these are: "Who or what is God?" "Is the Son of God the Son of Man?" "Was it necessary for Jesus to be crucified for our sins?" "Are non-believers condemned to ever-lasting 'fire'?" "Is there life everlasting after death?" "Must we believe in Jesus to have life everlasting in Heaven with God?"

Each chapter is a life cycle of Jesus in that it follows His life chronologically. Its seventeen chapters form a cycle of thought beginning with "Jesus said of God the Father" and ending with "Jesus said of Life Everlasting."

The book has a concordant index of some 61 pages. Aside from being an excellent reference to the contents of the book, its every page is a source of deep reflection and many a meditation.

It's the type of book to have near at hand.

Reproduced from a Painting by the Author

Jesus Said

† JESUS

SAID . . .

by Lydia N. Ratzlaff

> God is Spirit, and they who
> worship Him must worship
> in Spirit and in Truth.
>
> JOHN 4:24

> I am the Way, and the
> Truth, and the Life.
>
> JOHN 14:6

BRUCE   PUBLISHING   COMPANY
SAINT   PAUL   •   MINNESOTA

First printing

Library of Congress
catalog card number:
63-20369

The Bruce Publishing Company
Saint Paul, Minnesota

Printed in the United States of America

NIHIL OBSTAT:

Rev. Walter H. Peters, S.T.L, Ph.D.,
Censor Librorum

IMPRIMATUR:

Rt. Rev. Msgr. John J. Cullinan, V.G.,
Archdiocese of St. Paul

October 26, 1962

Preface

WHAT IS the purpose of this book titled JESUS SAID?

It answers in the very words of Jesus Himself questions raised by all of us, and especially by non-believers as to:

Who or what is God? Why is God called the Father? Is there such a Divine Being as the Son of God? Did Jesus ever call Himself Jesus Christ? Did He ever call Himself the Messias? Did He ever refer to Himself as the Son of Man? Is the Son of Man the Son of God? Did God send His Son from Heaven to man on earth? Why? Was it necessary for Jesus to be crucified for our sins? Did Jesus ever foretell His crucifixion or His resurrection from the dead? Did He speak of the resurrection of man from the dead? Did Jesus foretell His own ascension into Heaven? Just what is meant by belief in God? What is meant by the word faith? Must we believe in Jesus Christ to have everlasting life in Heaven with God after death? Are non-believers condemned to everlasting "fire?" Is there a Holy Spirit, also called Holy Ghost? If so, what is the work of the Holy Spirit in God's divine plan? Does Jesus tell us much about the human soul, *per se?* Do angels exist? What is the Kingdom of God? What is the Kingdom of Heaven? Does the Kingdom of God mean the Kingdom of Heaven? Is there a devil called Satan? Does Satan have evil spirits or bad angels? What is hell? What is the judgment? What is Judgment Day? Is there Everlasting Life after death? And answers to many, many more questions.

Also JESUS SAID is a book of reference and meditation.

In a true sense, each chapter is a life cycle of Jesus. For example,—in Chapter I "of GOD the FATHER," the first reference is made to the answer which Jesus made to His holy mother after having been "lost" for three days. His parents

7

"found" Him discoursing with the Scribes in the Temple in Jerusalem. His mother said to Him, "Son, why hast Thou done so to us? Behold, in sorrow Thy father and I have been seeking Thee." The boy Jesus replied, *Did you not know that I must be about My Father's business?* The last reference in the chapter are the words of Jesus dying on the infamous cross, *Father, into Thy hands I commend My spirit.*

Often the same or similar quotations by Jesus are found in more than one Gospel. When this occurs, with but few exceptions, only one quotation is placed in the text, the other or others are footnoted at the bottom of the page.

For clarification, the very words of Jesus are italicized.

Table of Contents

CHAPTER: PAGE:

I   of God, the Father 13- 53

II   of the Son of God, Jesus Christ 54- 83

III   of the Son of Man 84-114

IV   of the Crucifixion 115-131

V   of the Resurrection of Jesus 132-139

VI   of the Resurrection of Man 140-148

VII   of the Ascension of Jesus 149-156

VIII   of Faith, Belief in God 157-177

IX   of the Holy Spirit 178-184

X   of the Soul 185-189

XI   of the Good Angels 190-194

XII   of the Kingdom of God 195-205

XIII   of Heaven and the Kingdom of Heaven 206-228

XIV   of Satan and the Bad Angels 229-239

XV   of Hell 240-248

XVI   of Judgment 249-272

XVII   of Life Everlasting 273-294

The Nicene Creed

I believe in one GOD, *the* FATHER ALMIGHTY,
Maker of Heaven and earth, and of all things
visible and invisible.
And in one Lord, JESUS CHRIST, *the Only-*
begotten Son of God.
Born of the Father before all ages. God of
God; Light of Light; true God of true God.
Begotten not made; of one being with the
Father; by Whom all things were made.
Who for us men, and for our salvation,
came down from Heaven. AND WAS MADE FLESH
OF THE VIRGIN MARY BY THE HOLY SPIRIT
AND WAS MADE MAN.
He was also crucified for us, suffered under
Pontius Pilate and was buried.
And on the third day He rose again according
to the Scriptures.
And ascending into Heaven, He sitteth
at the right hand of the Father.
And He shall come again in glory to judge
the living and the dead;
And of His Kingdom there shall be no end.
And I believe in the HOLY GHOST,
Lord and Giver of Life,
Who proceeds from the Father and the Son.
Who together with the Father and the Son
is no less adored, and glorified;
Who spoke by the Prophets.
And I believe in ONE, HOLY, CATHOLIC
and APOSTOLIC CHURCH.
I confess one Baptism for the remission of sins.
And I look for the resurrection of the dead,
And the LIFE *of the* WORLD *to come.*

AMEN!

CHAPTER I

JESUS SAID
of God, the Father

1. EVERY YEAR Jesus' parents, Mary and His foster-father, Joseph, went to Jerusalem at the Feast of the Passover. Therefore, when He was twelve years old, they went up to Jerusalem. After the Feast they joined the caravan returning to Nazareth. They had come a day's journey when it occurred to Mary and Joseph to look for the boy Jesus among their relatives and acquaintances. Not finding Him, they returned to Jerusalem. Three days later, they found Him in the Temple, sitting in the midst of the teachers, listening to them and asking questions. All who were listening to Him were amazed at His understanding and His answers. When Mary and Joseph saw Jesus, they were astonished. His mother said to Him, "Son, why hast Thou done so to us? Behold, in sorrow, Thy father and I have been seeking Thee." The boy Jesus said to them, *How is it that you sought Me? Did you not know that I must be about My Father's business?* Mary and Joseph did not understand these words that Jesus spoke to them. Luke 2:49

2. YEARS LATER, Jesus came from Galilee to John, at the Jordan, to be baptized. Soon after, Jesus was led into the nearby desert by the Holy Spirit to be tempted by the devil. Fasting forty days and forty nights, He was hungry. The tempter came and said to Him, "If Thou art the Son of God, command that these stones become loaves of bread." Jesus answered, *It is written, "Not by bread alone does man live, but by every word that comes forth from the mouth of God."* Then he took Him into Jerusalem and set Him on the pinnacle of the Temple, and said, "If Thou art the Son of God, throw Thyself down"; for it is written, "He will give His angels charge concerning thee; and upon their hands they shall bear thee up, lest thou dash thy foot against a stone." Jesus said to him, *It is written further, "Thou shalt not tempt the Lord thy God."* Again the devil took Him to a very high mountain, and showed Him all the kingdoms of the world and the glory of them, saying, "All these things will I give Thee, if Thou wilt fall down and worship me." Jesus said to him, *Begone, Satan! for it is written, "The Lord thy God shalt thou worship and Him only shalt thou serve."* Then the devil left Him; and angels came to minister to Him.[1] Matthew 4:1-11

3. YOU RECALL the scene at the River Jordan, how Andrew, the first disciple, was led by his brother, Simon Peter, to Jesus. Then as Jesus was about to depart He came upon Philip, who in turn called Nathanael. When Jesus saw Nathanael coming toward Him, He said, *Behold a true Israelite in whom there is no guile!* Nathanael asked, "Whence knowest Thou me?" Jesus replied, *Before Philip called thee, when thou wast under a fig tree, I saw thee.* Nathanael said, "Rabbi, Thou art the Son of God, Thou art King of Israel." Jesus said, *Because I said that I saw thee under the fig tree, thou dost believe. Amen, amen, I say to you, you shall see Heaven opened, and the angels of God ascending and descending upon the Son of Man.* John 1:40-51

1. *Luke 4:1-12*

14

4. IT WAS after the marriage feast at Cana where Jesus had performed His first miracle of changing water into wine that He went up to Jerusalem for the Passover. In the Temple Jesus found men selling oxen, sheep and doves, and money-changers at their tables. Making a kind of whip of cords, He drove them all out of the Temple, also the sheep and the oxen. Then He poured out the money of the changers and overturned the tables. To them, who were selling doves He said, *Take these things away, and do not make the House of My Father a house of business.* John 2:13-17

5. Now THERE WAS a certain man among the Pharisees, Nicodemus by name, a ruler of the Jews, who came to Jesus at night. Jesus said to him, *Amen, amen, I say to thee, unless a man be born again of water and the Spirit, he cannot enter into the Kingdom of God.* Nicodemus asked, "How can these things be?" Continuing Jesus said, *For God so loved the world that He gave His only-begotten Son, that those who believe in Him may not perish, but may have Life Everlasting. For God did not send His Son into the world in order to judge the world, but that the world might be saved through Him. He who believes in Him is not judged; but he who does not believe is already judged, because he does not believe in the name of the only-begotten Son of God. Now this is the judgment: The Light has come into the world, yet men have loved the darkness rather than the Light, for their works were evil. For everyone who does evil hates the Light, and does not come to the Light, that his deeds may not be exposed. But he who does the truth comes to the Light that his deeds may be made manifest, for they have been performed in God.* John 3:5-21

6. JESUS LEFT JUDEA and went again into Galilee, and had to pass through Samaria. He came to a town called Sichar, near the field that Jacob gave to his son, Joseph. Jacob's well was there. Jesus wearied from the journey, was sitting at the well. A Samaritan woman came to draw water. She was amazed when Jesus asked her for a drink of water, for Jews did not associate with Samaritans. But He said to her, *If thou didst know the gift of God, and Who it is Who says to thee, "Give Me to drink," thou, perhaps, wouldst have asked of Him, and He would have given thee living water. . . .* The Samaritan woman said to Jesus, "Our fathers worshipped on this mountain (Gerizim) but you say that at Jerusalem is the place where one ought to worship." Jesus replied, *Woman, believe Me, the hour is coming when neither on this mountain nor in Jerusalem will you worship the Father. You worship what you do not know; we worship what we know, for Salvation is from the Jews. But the hour is coming, and is now here, when the true worshippers will worship the Father in Spirit and in Truth. For the Father also seeks such to Him. God is Spirit, and they who worship Him must worship in Spirit and in Truth. . . .* Jesus' disciples, who had gone into the town to buy food, returned. They were perplexed that He was speaking to a Samaritan woman. However, knowing that He was hungry, they said "Rabbi, eat." Jesus replied, *My food is to do the will of Him Who sent Me, to accomplish His work.* John 4:10-34

7. AFTER JESUS had been baptized in the Jordan by John the Baptist and fasted forty days and nights in the desert, He returned in the power of the Holy Spirit into Galilee. His fame went out through the whole country. He taught in their synagogues and was honored by all. He came to Nazareth, where He had been brought up. According to His custom, He entered the synagogue on the Sabbath, and stood up to read. The volume of Isaias the Prophet was handed to Him. After He opened the volume, He found the place where it was written and read, *"The Spirit of the Lord is upon Me because He has anointed Me; to bring good news to the poor He has sent Me, to proclaim to the captives release, and sight to the blind; to set at liberty the*

oppressed, to proclaim the acceptable year of the Lord, and the day of recompense." Closing the volume, He gave it back to the attendant and sat down. The eyes of all in the synagogue were gazing on Him. Then He said to them, *Today this Scripture has been fulfilled in your hearing.* Luke 4:14-21

8. WHO SHALL SEE GOD? In the eighth beatitude at the beginning of His Sermon on the Mount, Jesus taught His disciples, saying, *Blessed are the clean of heart, for they shall see God. . . .* and, *blessed are the peacemakers, for they shall be called the children of God. . . . Even so let your light shine before men, in order that they may see your good works and give glory to your Father in Heaven. . . .* Also in this same Sermon Jesus instructed the people concerning oaths. *Again, you have heard that it was said to the ancients, "Thou shalt not swear falsely, but fulfill thy oaths to the Lord." But I say to you not to swear at all: neither by Heaven, for it is the Throne of God, nor by the earth, for it is His footstool; nor by Jerusalem, for it is the City of the King. . . .* Then Jesus told them why they should love their enemies. *You have heard it was said, "Thou shalt love thy neighbor, and shalt hate thy enemy." But I say to you, love your enemies, do good to those who hate you, and pray for those who persecute and calumniate you, so that you may be children of your Father in Heaven, Who makes His sun to rise on the good and the evil, and sends rain on the just and the unjust. For if you love those that love you, what reward shall you have? Do not even the publicans do that? And if you salute your brethren only, what are you doing more than others? Do not even the Gentiles do that? You therefore are to be perfect, even as your Heavenly Father is perfect.* Matthew 5:8-48

9. MATTHEW CONTINUES the Sermon on the Mount in his sixth chapter. Here Jesus tells us of the great love of the Father for us and what our love should be to Him and to our neighbor for the love of God. *Take heed not to do your good before men, in order to be seen by them; otherwise you shall have no reward with your Father in Heaven. Therefore when thou givest alms, do not sound a trumpet before thee, as the hypocrites do in the synagogues and streets, in order that they may be honored by men. Amen, I say to you, they have received their reward. But when thou givest alms, do not let thy left hand know what thy right hand is doing, so that thy alms may be given in secret; and thy Father, Who sees in secret, will reward thee. Again, when you pray, you shall not be like the hypocrites, who love to pray standing in the synagogues and at the street corners, in order that they may be seen by men. Amen I say to you, they have received their reward. But when thou prayest, go into thy room, and closing thy door, pray to thy Father in secret; and thy Father, Who sees in secret, will reward thee. But in praying, do not multiply words, as the Gentiles do; for they think that by saying a great deal, they will be heard. So do not be like them; for your Father knows what you need before you ask Him. In this manner therefore shall you pray:*[2]

Our Father Who art in Heaven,
Hallowed be Thy name.
Thy Kingdom come
Thy will be done on earth
As it is in heaven.
Give us this day our daily bread.
And forgive us our debts,
As we also forgive our debtors.
And lead us not into temptation,
But deliver us from evil.

For if you forgive men their offenses, your Heavenly Father will also forgive you your offenses. But if you do not forgive men neither will your Father forgive you your offenses. And when you fast do not look gloomy like the hyprocrites, who dis-

---

2. *Luke 11:2-4*

18

figure their faces in order to appear to men as fasting. Amen I say to you, they have received their reward. But thou, when thou dost fast, anoint thy head and wash thy face, so that thou mayest not be seen fasting by men, but by thy Father, Who is in secret; and thy Father, Who sees in secret, will reward thee. Do not lay up for yourselves treasures on earth, where rust and moth consume, and where thieves break in and steal; but lay up for yourselves treasures in Heaven, where neither rust nor moth consume, nor thieves break in and steal. For where thy treasure is, there also will thy heart be. The lamp of the body is thy eye. If thy eye be sound, thy whole body will be full of light. But if thy eye be evil, thy whole body will be full of darkness. Therefore if the light that is in thee is darkness, how great is the darkness itself! No man can serve two masters; for either he will hate the one and love the other, or else he will stand by the one and despise the other. You cannot serve God and mammon.[3] Therefore I say to you, do not be anxious for your life, what you shall eat; nor yet for your body, what you shall put on. Is not the life a greater thing than the food, and the body than the clothing? Look at the birds of the air: they do not sow, or reap, or gather into barns; yet your Heavenly Father feeds them. Are not you of much more value than they? But which of you by being anxious about it can add to his stature a single cubit? And as for clothing, why are you anxious? Consider how the lilies of the field grow; they neither toil nor spin, yet I say to you that not even Solomon in all his glory was arrayed like one of these. But if God so clothes the grass of the field, which flourishes today but tomorrow is thrown into the oven, how much more you, O you of little faith! Therefore do not be anxious, saying, "What shall we eat?" or, "What shall we drink?" or, "What are we to put on?" (for after all these things the Gentiles seek); for your Father knows that you need all these things. But seek first the Kingdom of God and His justice,

---

3. *Luke 16:13*

and all these things shall be given you besides. Therefore do not be anxious about tomorrow; for tomorrow will have anxieties of its own. Sufficient for the day is its own trouble. Matthew 6:1-34

10. FINALLY, nearing the conclusion of His Sermon on the Mount, Jesus reminds us, *Not everyone who says to Me, "Lord, Lord," shall enter the Kingdom of Heaven; but he who does the will of My Father in Heaven shall enter the Kingdom of Heaven.* Matthew 7:21

11. BE MERCIFUL, *therefore, even as your Father is merciful.* Luke 6:36

12. AFTER THE STORM on the Sea of Galilee, Jesus and His disciples continued by boat southward to a town called Gerasa where Jesus cured a man who had been possessed by devils from his birth. The man entreated Jesus that he might follow Him but He said, *Return to thy house, and tell all that God has done for thee.*[4] Luke 8:39

13. JESUS SUMMONED His twelve Apostles and instructed them about their mission to preach the Gospel of the Kingdom of God. He gave them power and authority over devils, and to cure diseases. Jesus said, *The harvest is great, but the laborers are few. Pray therefore the Lord of the harvest to send forth laborers into His harvest.*[5] Matthew 9:37-38

14. CONTINUING HIS INSTRUCTIONS to the Twelve, Jesus stressed that when they instructed the people about the Kingdom of God, *it is not you who are speaking, but the Spirit of your Father Who speaks through you. . . . Do not be afraid of those who kill the body but cannot kill the soul. But rather*

4. *Matthew 8:28-34, Mark 5:1-20;* 5. *Luke 10:1-2*

be afraid of Him Who is able to destroy both soul and body in hell. . . . Therefore, everyone who acknowledges Me before men, I also will acknowledge him before My Father in Heaven. But whoever disowns Me before men, I in turn will disown him before My Father in Heaven.[6] Matthew 10:20-33

15. SOON AFTER Jesus appointed seventy-two others instructing them as He had the Twelve to go forth into every town telling the people about the Kingdom of God. Jesus rejoicing in the Holy Spirit said, *I praise Thee, Father, Lord of Heaven and earth, that Thou didst hide these things from the wise and prudent, and didst reveal them to little ones. Yes, Father, for such was Thy good pleasure. All things have been delivered to Me by My Father; and no one knows the Son except the Father; nor does anyone know the Father except the Son, and him to whom the Son chooses to reveal Him.*[7] Matthew 11:25-27

16. ONE SABBATH DAY Jesus and His disciples were passing through a field of grain. They were hungry. And as they walked along they plucked the grain and rubbed it between their hands and ate it. The Pharisees who were always watching Jesus to see if they could snare Him, said, "Why is it that the disciples of John and the Pharisees fast, while your disciples do not and are doing what is not lawful on the Sabbath?" Jesus said, *Have you never read what David did when he entered the House of God, when Abiathar was high priest, and ate the proposition, which he could not lawfully eat, but only the priests? and how he gave them to those who were with him? The Sabbath was made for man, and not man for the Sabbath. Therefore the Son of Man is Lord even of the Sabbath.*[8,9] Mark 2:25-27

17. ONE DAY Jesus was in Jerusalem and cured a man at the Pool of Bethsaida not far from the Temple. It was on the

---

6. *Luke 12:4-9;* 7. *Luke 10:21-22;* 8. *Matthew 12:4;* 9. *Luke 6:4*

Sabbath. This is one reason why the Jews kept persecuting Jesus because He healed the sick on the Sabbath. Jesus, however, had an answer for them. *My Father works even until now, and I work.* This made the Jews even more anxious to put Him to death, because He not only broke the Sabbath, but also called God His own Father, making Himself equal to God. Jesus, knowing their evil thoughts, said to them, *Amen, amen, I say to you, the Son can do nothing of Himself, but only what He sees the Father doing. For whatever He does, this the Son also does in like manner. For the Father loves the Son, and shows Him all that He Himself does. And greater works than these He will show Him, that you may wonder. For as the Father raises the dead and gives them Life, even so the Son also gives Life to whom He will. For neither does the Father judge any man, but all judgment He has given to the Son, that all men may honor the Son even as they honor the Father. He who does not honor the Son, does not honor the Father Who sent Him. Amen, amen, I say to you, he who hears My word, and believes Him Who sent Me, has Life Everlasting, and does not come to judgment, but has passed from death to Life. Amen, amen, I say to you, the hour is coming, and now is here, when the dead shall hear the voice of the Son of God, and those who hear shall live. For as the Father has Life in Himself, even so He has given to the Son also to have Life in Himself; and He has granted Him power to render judgment, because He is Son of Man. Do not wonder at this, for the hour is coming in which all who are in the tombs shall hear the voice of the Son of God. And they who have done good shall come forth unto resurrection of Life; but they who have done evil unto resurrection of judgment. Of Myself I can do nothing. As I hear, I judge, and My judgment is just because I seek not My own will, but the will of Him Who sent Me. . . . The witness, however, that I have is greater than that of John. For the works which the Father has given Me to accomplish, these very works that I do, bear witness to Me, that the Father has sent Me. And the*

Father Himself, Who sent Me, has borne witness to Me. But you have never heard His voice, or seen His face. And you have not His word abiding in you, since you do not believe Him Whom He has sent. You search the Scriptures, because in them you think that you have Life Everlasting. And it is they that bear witness to Me, yet you are not willing to come to Me that you may have Life. I do not receive glory from men. But I know that you have not the love of God in you. I have come in the name of My Father, and you do not receive Me. If another come in his own name, him you will receive. How can you believe who receive glory from one another, and do not seek the glory which is from the only God? Do not think that I shall accuse you to the Father. There is one who accuses you, Moses, in whom you hope. For if you believed Moses you would believe Me also, for he wrote of Me. But if you do not believe his writings, how will you believe My words? John 5:17-45

18. WHEREVER JESUS WENT He drew vast crowds. This caused the people of Nazareth who thought of Jesus only as the son of Joseph, the carpenter, much concern and they tried to lay hold of Him. They even went so far as to say, "He has gone mad!" Someone came to tell Jesus that His mother was seeking Him and He replied, *Who are My mother and My brethren?* And looking round on those who were sitting about Him He said, *Behold My mother and My brethren! For whoever does the will of My Father in Heaven, he is My brother and sister and mother.*[10,11] Matthew 12:47-50

19. THE PHARISEES and some of the Scribes, when they heard of the numerous miracles that Jesus performed and how the multitudes were following Him, came down from Jerusalem to the shores of the Sea of Galilee. Always they were on the watch to snare Him. One day they saw the disciplines eating with defiled (unwashed) hands and they found fault. The Jews did

---

10. *Mark 3:35;* 11. *Luke 8:21*

not eat without frequent washing of the hands. The Pharisees asked Jesus, "Why do not thy disciples walk according to the tradition of the ancients, instead of eating bread with defiled hands?" Jesus replied, *Well did Isaias prophecy of you hypocrites, as it is written, "This people honors Me with their lips, but their heart is far from Me; and in vain do they worship Me, teaching as doctrine the precepts of men." For, letting go the commandment of God, you hold fast the tradition of men, the washing of pots and of cups; and many other things you do like these. Well do you nullify the commandment of God, that you may keep your own tradition! For Moses said, "Honor thy father and thy mother;" and "Let him who curses father or mother be put to death." But you say, "Let a man say to his father or his mother, 'Any support thou mightest have had from me is Corban' (that is given to God). And you do not allow him to do anything further for his father or mother. You make void the commandment of God by your tradition, which you have handed down; and many such like things you do.*[12] Mark 7:6-13

20. THE DISCIPLES became fearful, and came up to Jesus, saying, "Dost Thou know that the Pharisees have taken offense at what Thou hast been saying?" Jesus replied, *Every plant that My Heavenly Father has not planted will be rooted up. Let them alone; they are blind guides of blind men. If a blind man guide a blind man, both fall into a pit.* Matthew 15:13-14

21. AFTER JESUS had performed the miracle of making five barley loaves and two fish more than enough food to feed five thousand persons, the crowds persued Him relentlessly. Jesus observing this, said, *Amen, amen, I say to you, you seek Me, not because you have seen signs, but because you have eaten of the loaves and have been filled. Do not labor for the food that perishes, but for that which endures unto Life Ever-*

---

12. *Matthew 15:3-9*

24

lasting, which the Son of Man will give you. For upon Him the Father, God Himself, has set His seal. And they asked Him, "What are we to do that we may perform the works of God?" In answer Jesus said, *This is the work of God, that you believe in Him Whom He has sent.* The crowds clamored for further signs from Jesus that they might believe in Him, to which He replied, *Amen, amen, I say to you, Moses did not give you the Bread from Heaven, but My Father gives you the true Bread from Heaven. For the Bread of God is that which comes down from Heaven and gives Life to the world.* They said therefore to Him, give us always of this bread." Then Jesus said to them, *I am the Bread of Life. He who comes to Me shall not hunger, and he who believes in Me shall never thirst. But I have told you that you have seen Me and you do not believe. All that the Father gives to Me shall come to Me, and him who comes to Me I will not cast out. For I have come down from Heaven, not to do My own will, but the will of Him Who sent Me. Now this is the will of Him Who sent Me, the Father, that I should lose nothing of what He has given Me, but that I should raise it up on the last day. For this is the will of My Father Who sent Me, that whoever beholds the Son, and believes in Him, shall have Everlasting Life, and I will raise him up on the last day.* The Jews were perplexed by this and said, "Is this not Jesus, whose father and mother we know? How, then, does he say, 'I have come down from heaven?' " Jesus, knowing their thoughts, said, *Do not murmur among yourselves. No one can come to Me unless the Father Who sent Me draw him, and I will raise him up on the last day. It is written in the Prophets, "And they all shall be taught of God." Everyone who has listened to the Father, and has learned, comes to Me; not that anyone has seen the Father except Him Who is from God, He has seen the Father. Amen, amen, I say to you, he who believes in Me has Life Everlasting. . . . As the living Father has sent Me, and as I live because of the Father, so he who eats Me, he also shall live because of Me. . . .* From this time many of Jesus' disciples, who said, "This is a hard saying. Who can listen to it?", turned away and no longer went about with Him. Jesus said, *This is why I have said to you, "No one can come to Me unless he is enabled to do so by My Father."* John 6:26-66

22. WHEN JESUS ASKED His disciples, *Who do men say the Son of Man is?*, they replied, "Some say John the Baptist; others, Elias or Jeremias or one of the Prophets." Pushing the question still further, Jesus asked, *But Who do you say that I am?* Simon Peter spoke up, "Thou art the Christ, the Son of the living God." Jesus blessed him, saying, *Blessed art thou, Simon Bar Jona, for flesh and blood has not revealed this to thee, but My Father in Heaven. And I say to thee, thou art Peter, and upon this rock I will build My Church, and the gates of hell shall not prevail against it. And I will give thee the keys of the Kingdom of Heaven; and whatever thou shalt bind on earth shall be bound in Heaven, and whatever thou shalt loose on earth shall be loosed in Heaven.* Matthew 16:17-19

23. JESUS CHARGED His disciples not to tell anyone that He was Jesus the Christ. Now He began to show his disciples that He must go to Jerusalem and suffer many things from the elders and Scribes and chief priests, and be put to death, and on the third day rise again. Peter chided Him, saying, "This will never happen to Thee." Jesus turned to him and said, *Get behind Me, satan, thou art a scandal to Me; for thou dost not mind the things of God, but those of men. . . . The Son of Man is to come with His angels in the glory of His Father, and then He will render to everyone according to his conduct.*[13,14] Matthew 16:20-27

24. ONE DAY on the way to Capharnaum the disciples began arguing with one another as to which was the greatest among them. Jesus knowing the reasoning in their hearts, called the Twelve to Him. Taking a little child into His arms, He said,

---

13. *Mark 8:31-38;* 14. *Luke 9:21-26*

Whoever humbles himself as this little child, he is the greatest in the Kingdom of Heaven. . . . See that you do not despise one of these little ones; for I tell you, their angels in Heaven always behold the face of My Father in Heaven. . . . It is not the will of your Father in Heaven that a single one of these little ones should perish. . . . And then Jesus instructed the Twelve on the power of united prayer, *I say to you further, that if two of you shall agree on earth about anything at all for which they ask, it shall be done for them by My Father in Heaven. For where two or three are gathered together for My sake, there I am in the midst of them. . . .* Then Peter asked Jesus how many times he should forgive his brother who had sinned against him. Jesus replied, *Seventy times seven.* And then He told them the parable of the unmerciful servant, who although his master had shown him mercy, was unmerciful toward his fellow-servant. The master learning of this behavior of the unmerciful servant handed him over to the torturers. Concluding Jesus said, *So also My Heavenly Father will do to you, if you do not each forgive your brothers from your hearts.* Matthew 18:13-35

25. Now AFTER these teachings Jesus went about in Galilee. He did not wish to go in Judea because the Jews were seeking to put Him to death. The Jewish Feast of the Tabernacles was at hand. Jesus' disciples begged Him to go up to Jerusalem to manifest Himself to the world. But Jesus said, *Go up to the feast, but I do not go, for My time is not yet fulfilled.* However, as soon as they had departed, Jesus also went up, but privately. When the feast was half over, Jesus went into the Temple and began to teach. The Jews marvelled, saying, "How does this man come by learning, since he has not studied?" Then Jesus revealed to them the source of His teachings, saying, *My teaching is not My own, but His Who sent Me. If anyone desires to do His will, he will know of the teaching whether it is from God, or whether I speak on My own authority. He who speaks on his own authority seeks his own glory. But He Who seeks the glory* *of the One Who sent Him is truthful, and there is no injustice in Him. Did not Moses give you the Law, and none of you observes the Law? Why do you seek to put Me to death?* John 7:1-20

26. MANY OF THE PEOPLE who listened to Jesus in the Temple believed in Him. Others were confused, saying, "Is not this the man they seek to kill? And behold, he speaks openly and they say nothing to him? Can it be that the rulers have really come to know that this is the Christ? Yet we know where this man is from; but when the Christ comes, no one will know where He is from." Jesus therefore, while teaching in the Temple, cried out and said, *You both know Me, and know where I am from. Yet I have not come of Myself, but He is true Who has sent Me, Whom you do not know. I know Him because I am from Him, and He has sent Me.* They wanted to seize Him, but no one laid hands on Him because His hour had not yet come. Jesus then said, *Yet a little while I am with you, and then I go to Him Who sent Me. You will seek Me and will not find Me; and where I am you cannot come.* John 7:25-34

27. ON THE LAST, the great day of the Feast of Tabernacles, Jesus stood up and cried out, saying, *If anyone thirst, let him come to Me and drink. He who believes in Me, as the Scripture says, "From within him there shall flow rivers of living waters."* Some of the crowd when they heard these words, said, "This is truly the Prophet. This is the Christ." Others said, "Search the Scriptures and see that out of Galilee arises no prophet." Thus there arose a division among the crowd. Again some of them wanted to seize Him but no one laid hands on Him. John 7:37-44

28. SAINT JOHN tells us that Jesus went to the Mount of Olives (Most likely it was to the grotto at the foot of the Mount beside the Garden of Gethsemani. The Franciscans call it the "Grotto of the Betrayal." Here daily they celebrate Holy Mass.) At daybreak Jesus came again to the Temple and preached there. When He said, *I am the Light of the world, he who follows Me does not walk in darkness, but will have the Light of Life,* the Pharisees said to Him, "Thou bearest witness to thyself. Thy witness is not true." Jesus answered, *Even if I bear witness to Myself, My witness is true, because I know where I came from and where I go. But you do not know where I came from or where I go. You judge according to the flesh; I judge no one. And even if I do judge, My judgment is true, because I am not alone, but with Me is He Who sent Me, the Father. And in your Law it is written that the witness of two persons is true. It is I Who bear witness to Myself, and He who sent Me, the Father, bears witness to Me.* They therefore said to Him, "Where is thy father?" Jesus answered, *You know neither Me nor My Father. If you knew Me, you would then know My Father also.* Jesus spoke these words in the treasury, a room off the Court of the Women in the Temple, while teaching there. And no one seized Him, because His hour had not yet come. John 8:1-20

29. CONTINUING, JESUS SAID to the Pharisees, *You will die in your sins; for if you do not believe that I am He* (i.e., the Messias) ; *you will die in your sin.* They therefore said to Him, "Who art thou?" Jesus replied, *Why do I speak to you at all! I have many things to speak and to judge concerning you; but He Who sent Me is true, and the things that I heard from Him, these I speak in the world.* And they did not understand that He was speaking to them about the Father. Jesus, therefore, said to them, *When you have lifted up the Son of Man, then you will know that I am He, and that of Myself I do nothing: but that I preach only what the Father has taught Me. And He Who sent Me is with Me; He has not left Me alone, because I do always the things that are pleasing to Him.* John 8:23-29

30. JESUS SAID TO THE JEWS, *I know that you are the children of Abraham; but you seek to kill Me because My word takes* *no hold among you. I speak what I have seen with the Father; and you do what you have seen with your father.* They said, "Abraham is our father." To which Jesus replied, *If you are the children of Abraham, do the works of Abraham. But as it is, you are seeking to kill Me, One Who has spoken the truth to you which I have heard from God. That is not what Abraham did. You are doing the works of your father. . . . If God were your Father, you would surely love Me. For from God I came forth and have come; for neither have I come of Myself, but He sent Me. Why do you not understand My speech? Because you cannot listen to My word. The father from who you are is the devil, and the desires of your father it is your will to do. He was a murderer from the beginning, and has not stood in the truth because there is no truth in him. When he tells a lie he speaks from his very nature, for he is a liar and the father of lies. But because I speak the truth you do not believe Me. Which of you can convict Me of sin? If I speak the truth, why do you not believe Me? He who is of God hears the words of God. The reason why you do not hear is that you are not of God.* John 8:37-47

31. THE JEWS therefore in answer said to Jesus, "Are we not right in saying that thou art a Samaritan, and hast a devil?" Jesus answered, *I have not a devil, but I honor My Father, and you dishonor Me. Yet I do not seek My own glory; there is One Who seeks and Who judges. Amen, amen, I say to you, if anyone keep My word, he will never see death.* John 8:48-51

32. THE UNBELIEVING JEWS taunted Jesus, saying, "Now we know that thou hast a devil. . . . Whom dost thou make thyself?" Jesus answered, *If I glorify Myself, My glory is nothing. It is My Father Who glorifies Me, of Whom you say that He is your God. And you do not know Him, but I know Him. And if I say that I do not know Him, I shall be like you, a liar. But I know Him, and I keep His word. Abraham your father rejoiced* *that he was to see My day. He saw it* (Abraham can be said to have seen Christ's day either in faith and prophetic vision, or from his place in limbo when Christ was born) *and was glad.* The Jews therefore said to Him, "Thou art not yet fifty years old, and hast thou seen Abraham?" Jesus said to them, *Amen, amen, I say to you, before Abraham came to be, I AM* (Jesus' eternal existence). They therefore took up stones to cast at Him; but Jesus hid Himself, and went out from the Temple. John 8:52-59

33. AND AS HE WAS PASSING BY, He saw a man blind from birth. His disciples asked Him, "Rabbi, who has sinned, this man or his parents, that he should be born blind?" Jesus answered, *Neither has this man sinned, nor his parents, but the works of God were to be made manifest in him. I must do the works of Him Who sent Me while it is day; night is coming, when no one can work. As long as I am in the world I am the Light of the world.* When He had said these things, He spat on the ground and made clay with the spittle, and spread the clay over his eyes, and said to him, *Go, wash in the pool of Siloe.* So he went away, and washed, and returned seeing. John 9:1-7

34. I AM *the Good Shepherd, and I know Mine and Mine know Me, even as the Father knows Me and I know the Father; and I lay down My life for My sheep. And other sheep I have that are not of this fold. Them also I must bring, and they shall hear My voice, and there shall be One Fold and One Shepherd. For this reason the Father loves Me, because I lay down My life that I may take it up again. No one takes it from Me, but I lay it down of Myself. I have the power to lay it down, and I have the power to take it up again. Such is the command I have received from My Father.* John 10:14-18

35. Now THERE TOOK PLACE at Jerusalem the Feast of the Dedication. It was winter. Jesus was walking in the Temple, in Solomon's portico. The Jews gathered round Him, and said to Him, "How long dost thou keep us in suspense? If thou art the Christ, tell us openly." Jesus answered them, *I tell you and you do not believe. The works that I do in the name of My Father, these bear witness concerning Me. But you do not believe because you are not of My sheep. My sheep hear My voice, and I know them and they follow Me. And I give them Everlasting Life; and they shall never perish, neither shall anyone snatch them out of My hand. What My Father has given Me is greater than all; and no one is able to snatch anything out of the hand of My Father. I and the Father are one.* The Jews, who said, "He has a devil and is mad," took up stones to stone Him. Jesus said, *Many good works have I shown you from My Father. For which of these works do you stone Me?* The Jews replied, "Not for a good work do we stone thee, but for blasphemy, and because thou, being a man, makest thyself God." Jesus answered them, *Is it not written in your Law, "I said you are gods?" If he called them gods to whom the word of God was addressed (and the Scripture cannot be broken), do you say of Him Whom the Father has made holy and sent into the world, "Thou blasphemest," because I said, "I am the Son of God"? If I do not perform the works of My Father, do not believe Me. But if I do perform them, and if you are not willing to believe Me, believe the works, that you may know and believe that the Father is in Me and I in the Father.* They sought therefore to seize Him; but He went forth out of their hands. John 10:22-39

36. SAINT LUKE in his eleventh chapter relates Jesus' lessons on prayer stating five of the seven petitions of the "Lord's Prayer" found in the fifth chapter of the Gospel according to Saint Matthew. Then he quotes Jesus, speaking to the Jews, *If you, evil as you are, know how to give good gifts to your children, how much more will your Heavenly Father give the Good Spirit to those who ask Him!* Luke 11:1-13

37. THE PHARISEES never ceased tormenting Jesus. One day when He had cast out a devil, they said, "By Beelzebub, the prince of devils, he casts out devils." And others, to test Him, demanded from Him a sign from Heaven. Jesus seeing their thoughts, said to them, *Now, if I cast out devils by Beelzebub, by whom do your children cast them out? Therefore they shall be your judges. But if I cast out devils by the finger of God, then the Kingdom of God has come upon you.* Luke 11:14-20

38. As JESUS WAS SAYING these things, a woman cried out, "Blessed is the womb that bore Thee, and the breasts that nursed Thee." He answered her, *Rather, blessed are they who hear the word of God and keep it.* "Jesus does not forbid this woman to praise His mother, but He stresses the point that spiritual is above physical relationship and, at least implicitly, states that Mary is to be felicitated more for keeping the word of God than for being chosen to be His mother."[15] Luke 11: 27-28

39. Now AFTER JESUS HAD SPOKEN, a Pharisee asked Him to dine with him. The Pharisee wondered why He had not washed before dinner as was the custom of the Jews. Jesus said, *You Pharisees clean the outside of the cup and the dish, but within you are full of robbery and wickedness. . . . Woe to you Pharisees! because you pay tithes on mint and rue and every herb, and disregard justice and the love of God. . . .* A lawyer present said to Him, "Master, in saying these things, thou insultest us also." Jesus replied, *Woe to you lawyers, also! because you load men with oppressive burdens and you yourselves with one of your fingers do not touch the burdens. Woe to you! for you build the tombs of the Prophets, whereas your fathers killed them. You are witnesses and approve the deeds of your fathers; for they indeed killed them, and you build their*

---

15. COMMENTARY ON THE NEW TESTAMENT *(Washington: The Catholic Biblical Association, 1942)* 263

tombs. For this reason also the wisdom of God has said, "I will send them prophets and apostles; and some of them they will put to death and persecute, that the blood of all the prophets that has been shed from the foundation of the world may be required of this generation, from the blood of Abel unto the blood of Zacharias, who was slain between the altar and the Temple." Luke 11:37-51

40. AFTER JESUS HAD SAID these things, the Pharisees and the lawyers set traps for Him and plotted to seize upon something out of His mouth that they might accuse Him. Knowing this, He said to His disciples, *I say to you, My friends: Do not be afraid of those who kill the body, and after that have nothing that they can do. But I will show you Whom you shall be afraid of: be afraid of Him Who, after He has killed, has power to cast into hell. Yes, I say to you, be afraid of Him. Are not five sparrows sold for two farthings? And yet not one of them is forgotten before God?*[16] Luke 12:4-9

41. JESUS WARNED HIS DISCIPLES against avarice. He spoke a parable to them of the man who had very abundant crops. This rich man said to his soul, "Soul, thou hast many good things laid up for many years; take thy ease, eat, drink, be merry." *But God said to him, "Thou fool, this night do they demand thy soul of thee; and the things that thou hast provided, whose will they be?" So is he who lays up treasure for himself, and is not rich as regards God.* Luke 12:20-21

42. HE TOLD them to put their trust in God. *Consider the ravens: they neither sow nor reap, they have neither storeroom nor barn; yet God feeds them. Of how much more value are you than they! ... Consider how the lilies grow; they neither toil nor spin, yet I say to you that not even Solomon in all his glory was arrayed like one of these. But if God so clothes the*

---

16. *Matthew 10:20-33*

grass which flourishes in the field today but tomorrow is thrown into the oven how much more you, O you of little faith! And as for you, do not seek what you shall eat, or what you shall drink; and do not exalt yourselves (for after all these things the nations of the world seek); but your Father knows that you need these things. But seek the Kingdom of God, and all these things shall be given you besides. Do not be afraid, little flock, for it has pleased your Father to give you the Kingdom.[17] Luke 12: 22-32

43. SOME OF THE PHARISEES came up to Jesus, saying, "Depart and be on thy way, for Herod wants to kill thee." And He said to them, *Go and say to that fox, "Behold, I cast out devils and perform cures today and tomorrow, and the third day I am to end My course. Nevertheless, I must go My way today and tomorrow and the next day, for it cannot be that a Prophet perish outside Jerusalem". Jerusalem, Jerusalem, thou who killest the Prophets, and stonest those who are sent to thee! how often would I have gathered thy children together, as a hen gathers her young under her wings, but thou wouldest not! Behold, your house is left to you. And I say to you, you shall not see Me until the time comes when you shall say, "Blessed is He Who comes in the name of the Lord!"*[18] Luke 13:31-35

44. THE PUBLICANS and sinners were drawing near to Jesus to listen to Him. When the Pharisees and the Scribes saw this, they murmured, saying, "This man welcomes sinners and eats with them." Then Jesus spoke to them the parable of the lost sheep and how the shepherd rejoiced when he found it. Also of the woman who having ten drachmas, lost one of them. Great was her joy when she found it again. *Even so, I say to you, there will be joy among the angels of God over one sinner who repents.*[19] Luke 15:1-10.

---

17. *Matthew 6:25-34;* 18. *Matthew 23:37-39;* 19. *Matthew 18:14*

45. No SERVANT *can serve two masters; for either he will hate the one and love the other, or else he will stand by the one and despise the other. You cannot serve God and mammon.*[20] Luke 16:13

46. Now THE PHARISEES, who were fond of money, were listening to all these things, and they began to sneer at Jesus. But He said to them, *You are they who declare yourselves just in the sight of men, but God knows your heart; for that which is exalted in the sight of men is an abomination before God.* Luke 16:14-15

47. JESUS WAS ON HIS WAY to Jerusalem, passing between Samaria and Galilee. As He was entering a certain village, ten lepers met Him, standing afar off, and crying, "Jesus, master, have pity on us." When He saw them, He said simply, *Go, show yourselves to the priests.* As they were on their way, they were made clean. One of them, seeing that he had been made clean, returned, glorifying God. He fell on his face at Jesus' feet, giving thanks. He was a Samaritan. Jesus asked, *Were not ten made clean? Where are the nine? Has no one been found to return and give glory to God except this foreigner?* Luke 17: 11-18

48. JESUS INSTRUCTED HIS DISCIPLES that they must always pray to God and not lose heart. He told them a parable of a judge who was continuously being bothered by a widow who wanted justice done her against an adversary. The judge wearied of her, saying, "Although I do not fear God, nor even respect man, I will do her justice, lest by her continual coming she finally wear me out." Jesus concluded, *Hear what the unjust judge says; and will not God avenge His elect, who cry to Him day and night? And will He be slow to act in their case? I tell you that He will avenge them quickly.* Luke 18:1-8

---

20. *Matthew 6:24*

OF GOD, THE FATHER

49. JESUS SPOKE THIS PARABLE to some who trusted in themselves as being just and despised others. *Two men went up to the Temple to pray, the one a Pharisee and the other a publican. The Pharisee stood and began to pray thus within himself: "O, God, I thank Thee that I am not like the rest of men, robbers, dishonest, adulterers, or even like this publican. I fast twice a week; I pay tithes of all that I possess." But the publican standing afar off, would not so much as lift up his eyes to Heaven, but kept striking his breast, saying, "O God, be merciful to me the sinner!" I tell you, this man went back to his home justified rather than the other; for everyone who exalts himself shall be humbled, and he who humbles himself shall be exalted.* Luke 18:9-14

50. ONE DAY THE PHARISEES came to Jesus about the question of divorce, "Is it lawful for a man to put away his wife for any cause?" Jesus said, *Have you not read that the Creator, from the beginning, made them male and female, and said, "For this cause a man shall leave his father and mother, and cleave to his wife, and the two shall become one flesh?" Therefore now they are no longer two, but one flesh. What therefore God has joined together, let no man put asunder.*[21] Matthew 19:3-6

51. A YOUNG RULER who had great possessions came to Jesus, asking Him, "Good Master, what good work shall I do to have eternal life?" Jesus said to him, *Why dost thou ask Me what is good? One there is Who is good, and He is God. . . .* When Jesus told him to sell what he had and give to the poor, the young man went away sad. Jesus looking round said to His disciples, *Amen I say to you, with difficulty will a rich man enter the Kingdom of Heaven.* The disciples hearing this, said, "Who then can be saved?" Jesus said, *With men this is impossible, but with God all things are possible.*[22,23] Matthew 19:16-26

---

21. *Mark 10:2-9;* 22. *Mark 10:17-27;* 23. *Luke 18:18-27*

52. In Bethany, a short distance to the eastward of Jerusalem, lived Mary, who had anointed Jesus' feet and wiped them with her hair; and her sister, Martha; and her brother, Lazarus. All of them were beloved by Jesus. Lazarus became very ill. The sisters were greatly alarmed and sent word to Jesus, "Lord, behold, he whom Thou lovest is sick." When Jesus heard this, He said, *This sickness is not unto death, but for the glory of God, that through it the Son of God may be glorified.* . . . Jesus came to Bethany. When Martha saw Him, she said, "Lord, by this time he is already decayed, for he is dead four days." Jesus said to her, *Have I not told thee that if thou believe thou shalt behold the glory of God?* . . . They therefore removed the stone in front of the cave. Jesus raising His eyes, said, *Father, I give Thee thanks that Thou always hearest Me, but because of the people who stand around, I spoke, that they may believe that Thou hast sent Me.* When He said this, He cried out, *Lazarus, come forth!* Immediately Lazarus, bound with bandages, came out of the cave. Jesus said to them, *Unbind him, and let him go.* John 11:4-42

53. The mother of James and John came to Jesus and said to Him, "Command that these my two sons may sit, one at Thy right hand and one at Thy left hand, in Thy Kingdom." . . . Jesus said, *As for sitting at My right hand and at My left, that is not Mine to give you, but it belongs to those for whom it has been prepared by My Father.*[24] Matthew 20:20-23

54. It was the hour when Jesus should make His triumphal entry into Jerusalem. He was coming up from Jericho and came to Bethphage, not far from the Mount of Olives. He sent two disciples, saying to them, *Go into the village opposite you, and immediately you will find an ass tied, and a colt with her; loose them and bring them to Me, And if anyone say anything*

---

24. *Mark 10:35-40*

38

to you, you shall say that the Lord has need of them, and immediately he will send them.[25,26,27] Matthew 21:1-3

55. JESUS ENTERED THE TEMPLE of God. As He had done once before He cast out all those who were selling and buying in the Temple, and overturned the tables of the money-changers and the seats of those who sold the doves. He said to them, *It is written, "My House shall be called a House of prayer"; but you have made it a den of thieves.*[28,29] Matthew 21:12-14

56. THE DISCIPLES WERE AMAZED when they saw the fig tree, which Jesus had cursed the day previous, actually all withered up from the roots. (This must have taken place at the foot of the Mount of Olives near the bank of the Brook Cedron which they were to cross before entering the Temple in Jerusalem.) Jesus said, *Have faith in God. Amen I say to you, whoover says to this mountain, "Arise, and hurl thyself into the sea," and does not waver in his heart, but believes that whatever he says will be done, it shall be done for him. Therefore I say to you, all things whatever you ask for in prayer, believe that you shall receive, and they shall come to you. And when you stand up to pray, forgive whatever you have against anyone, that your Father in Heaven may also forgive you your offenses. But if you do not forgive, neither will your Father in Heaven forgive you your offenses.*[30] Mark 11:22-26

57. THE CHIEF PRIESTS and the elders of the people asked Jesus by what authority He did all the miracles. He told them of the parable of the two sons and also of the parable of the vine-dressers, saying in conclusion to them, *Did you never read in the Scriptures, "The stone which the builders rejected has become the corner stone: by the Lord this has been done, and it is wonderful in our eyes?" Therefore I say to you, that the*

---

25. *Mark 11:1-3;* 26. *Luke 19:29-31;* 27. *John 12:12-15;* 28. *Mark 11:15-17;* 29. *Luke 19:45-46;* 30. *Matthew 21:21-22*

Kingdom of God will be taken away from you and will be given to a people yielding its fruits.[31,32] Matthew 21:42-43

58. THE CHIEF PRIESTS and the Scribes sent forth spies, who should pretend to be just men, that they might trap Jesus in His talk and then deliver Him to the authorities. They said, "Master, we know that thou art truthful, and that thou teachest the way of God in truth, . . . Tell us, what dost thou think: Is it lawful to give tribute to Caesar, or not?" Jesus, knowing their wickedness, said, *Why do you test Me, you hypocrites? Show Me the coin of tribute.* So they offered Him a denarius. Jesus asked, *Whose are this image and the inscription?* They answered, "Caesar's." Then He said to them, *Render, therefore, to Caesar the things that are Caesar's, and to God the things that are God's.*[33,34] Matthew 22:15-21.

59. ON THAT SAME DAY some of the Sadducees, who said there is no resurrection, came to Jesus. They presented to Him this problem: A married woman becomes a widow and re-marries. The second husband dies and she re-marries again. And so on up to the seventh husband. "At the resurrection, therefore, of which of the seven will she be the wife? Jesus replied, *You err because you know neither the Scriptures nor the power of God. For at the resurrection they will neither marry nor be given in marriage, but will be as angels of God in Heaven. But as to the resurrection of the dead, have you not read what was spoken to you by God, "I am the God of Abraham, and the God of Isaac, and the God of Jacob?" He is not the God of the dead, but of the living.*[35,36] Matthew 22:23-32

60. THE PHARISEES, hearing that Jesus had silenced the Sadducees, gathered together. And one of them, a doctor of the Law, putting Him to the test, asked Him, "Master, which

---

31. *Mark 12:10-11;* 32. *Luke 20:17;* 33. *Mark 12:13-17;* 34. *Luke 20:20-25;* 35. *Mark 12:18-27;* 36. *Luke 20:27-38*

is the great commandment in the Law?" Jesus said to him, *"Thou shalt love the Lord thy God with thy whole heart, and with thy whole soul, and with thy whole mind." This is the greatest and the first commandment. And the second is like it, "Thou shalt love thy neighbor as thyself." On these two commandments depend the whole Law and the Prophets.*[37] Matthew 22:34-40

61. Now WHILE the Pharisees were gathered together, Jesus questioned them, saying, *What do you think of the Christ? Whose son is He?* They said to Him, "David's". Jesus said to them, *How then does David in the Spirit call Him Lord, saying, "The Lord said to my Lord: Sit thou at My right hand, till I make Thy enemies, Thy footstool?" If David, therefore, calls him, "Lord", how is He his son?* No one answered Him, and no one dared ask any more questions of Him.[38,39] Matthew 22:41-45

62. IN THE TWENTY-THIRD CHAPTER of the Gospel according to Saint Matthew, Jesus denounces the Scribes and Pharisees in very much the same manner as is related by Saint Luke in his eleventh chapter. Jesus warned the people and His disciples to beware of the hypocrisy of the Scribes and the Pharisees. How they love to be called by men "Rabbi." Jesus said, *But do not you be called "Rabbi"; for One is your Master, and all you are brothers. And call no one on earth your father; for One is your Father, Who is in Heaven. . . . Woe to you, blind guides, who say . . . whoever swears by the Temple, it is nothing; but whoever swears by the gold of the Temple, he is bound."* Jesus said, *He who swears by the Temple swears by it, and by Him Who dwells in It. And he who swears by Heaven swears by the Throne of God, and by Him Who sits upon It.* Matthew 23:9-22

---

37. *Mark 12:28-31;* 38. *Mark 12:35-37;* 39. *Luke 20:41-44*

63. JESUS SAT DOWN opposite the treasury of the Temple, and
observed how the people were putting money into the
treasury. Many rich were putting in large sums. A poor widow
came and she put in two mites. (which is about one half of our
cent.) Jesus called His disciples together, and said to them,
*Truly, I say to you, this poor widow has put in more than all.
For all these out of their abundance have put in as gifts to God;
but she out of her want has put in all that she had to live on.*
Luke 21:3-4

64. AS JESUS WAS LEAVING the Temple and going away, the
disciples called His attention to the great buildings of the
Temple adorned as they were with beautiful stones and offerings. Then Jesus prophesied that the days were coming in which
there would not be left one stone upon another that would not
be thrown down. Therefore, a little later, as Jesus was sitting
on the Mount of Olives, opposite the Temple, Peter and James
and John and Andrew asked Him privately, "Tell us, when
are these things to happen, and what will be the sign when all
these things will begin to come to pass?" Jesus then told them
of the impending destruction of Jerusalem and the signs of
the last day of the world. *But of that day or hour no one knows,
neither the angels of Heaven, nor the Son, but the Father only.*[40]
Mark 13:32

65. THEN JESUS TOLD THEM of the last judgment. *But when
the Son of Man shall come in His majesty, and all the angels
with Him, then He will sit on the throne of His glory; and
before Him will be gathered all the nations, and He will separate
them one from another, as the shepherd separates the sheep
from the goats; and He will set the sheep on His right hand,
but the goats on the left. Then the King will say to those on
His right hand, "Come, blessed of My Father, take possession*

---

40. *Matthew 24:36*

42

of the Kingdom prepared for you from the foundation of the world." Matthew 25:31-34

66. Now THE DAY of the Unleavened Bread came, on which the passover had to be sacrificed. The disciples came to Jesus, asking Him, "Where dost Thou want us to prepare for Thee to eat the passover?" He said to Peter and John, *Go into the city to a certain man, and say to him, "The Master says, 'My time is near at hand; at thy house I am keeping the Passover with My disciples.'"* The disciples did as Jesus bade them and prepared the passover. . . . While they were at supper, Jesus took bread, and blessed and broke, and gave it to His disciples, and said, *Take and eat; this is My body.* And taking the cup, He gave thanks and gave it to them, saying, *All of you drink of this; for this is My blood of the New Covenant, which is being shed for many unto the forgiveness of sins. But I say to you, I will not drink henceforth of this fruit of the vine, until that day when I shall drink it new with you in the Kingdom of My Father.*[41,42] Matthew 26:17-29

67. ONCE AGAIN contention arose among the Apostles as to which one of them was reputed to be the greatest. Jesus said, *You are they who have continued with Me in My trials. And I appoint to you a Kingdom, even as My Father has appointed to Me, that you may eat and drink at My table in My Kingdom; and you shall sit upon thrones, judging the twelve tribes of Israel.* Luke 22:24-30

68. JESUS KNEW that soon the hour had come for Him to suffer, to die, and to be glorified. In His last words to the people, He said, *If anyone serves Me, let him follow Me; and where I am there also shall My servants be. If anyone serves Me, My Father will honor him. Now My soul is troubled. And what shall*

---

41. *Mark 14:12-25;* 42. *Luke 22:7-18*

I say? Father, save Me from this hour! No, this is why I came to this hour. Father, glorify Thy name! John 12:23-28

69. HE WHO BELIEVES *in Me, believes not in Me but in Him Who sent Me. And he who sees Me, sees Him Who sent Me. I have come a Light into the world, that whoever believes in Me may not remain in the darkness. And if anyone hears My words, and does not keep them, it is not I Who judge him; for I have not come to judge the world, but to save the world. He who rejects Me, and does not accept My words, has One to condemn him. The word that I have spoken will condemn him on the last day. For I have not spoken on My own authority, but He Who sent Me, the Father, has comanded Me what I should declare. And I know that His commandment is Everlasting Life. The things, therefore, that I speak, I speak as the Father has bidden Me.* John 12:44-50

70. AMEN, AMEN, *I say to you, he who receives anyone I send, receives Me; and he who receives Me, receives Him Who sent Me.* John 13:20

71. WHEN JESUS HAD SAID these things He was saddened, and said solemnly, *Amen, amen I say to you, one of you will betray Me.* John, the Apostle whom Jesus loved, said to Him, "Lord, who is it?" Jesus answered, *It is he for whom I shall dip the bread, and give it to him.* And when Jesus had dipped the bread, He gave it to Judas Iscariot, the son of Simon. And after the morsel, Satan entered into Judas. Jesus said to him, *What thou dost, do quickly.* . . . It was night. When Judas had gone out, Jesus said, *Now is the Son of Man glorified, and God is glorified in Him. If God is glorified in Him, God will also glorify Him in Himself, and will glorify Him at once.* John 13:26-32

72. LET NOT YOUR HEART *be troubled. You believe in God, believe also in Me. In My Father's house there are many* *mansions. . . . I am the Way, and the Truth, and the Life. No one comes to the Father but through Me. If you had known Me, you would also have known the Father. And henceforth you do know Him, and you have seen Him.* Philip said to Him, "Lord, show us the Father and it is enough for us." Jesus said to him, *Have I been so long a time with you, and you have not known Me? Philip, he who sees Me sees also the Father. How canst thou say, "Show us the Father"? Dost thou not believe that I am in the Father and the Father in Me? The words that I speak to you I speak not on My own authority. But the Father dwelling in Me, it is He Who does the works. Do you believe that I am in the Father and the Father in Me? Otherwise believe because of the works themselves. Amen, amen, I say to you, he who believes in Me, the works that I do he also shall do, and greater than these he shall do, because I am going to the Father. And whatever you ask in My name, that I will do, in order that the Father may be glorified in the Son. If you ask anything in My name, I will do it. If you love Me, keep My commandments. And I will ask the Father and He will give you another Advocate to dwell with you forever, the Spirit of Truth Whom the world cannot receive, because it neither sees Him nor knows Him. But you shall know Him, because He will dwell with you, and be in you. I will not leave you orphans; I will come to you. Yet a little while and the world no longer sees Me. But you see Me, for I live and you shall live. In that day you will know that I am in My Father, and you in Me, and I in you. He who has My commandments and keeps them, he it is who loves Me. But he who loves Me will be loved by My Father, and I will love him and manifest Myself to him.* Judas, not the Iscariot, said to Him, "Lord, how is it that Thou are about to manifest Thyself to us, and not to the world?" Jesus answered, *If anyone love Me, he will keep My word, and My Father will love him, and We will come to him and make Our abode with him. He who does not love Me does not keep My words. And the word that you have heard is not Mine, but the Father's Who sent Me. These things*

45

I have spoken to you while yet dwelling with you. But the Advocate, the Holy Spirit, Whom the Father will send in My name, He will teach you all things, and bring to your mind whatever I have said to you. Peace I leave with you. My peace I give to you; not as the world gives do I give you. Do not let your heart be troubled, or be afraid. You have heard Me say to you, "I go away and I am coming to you." If you loved Me, you would indeed rejoice that I am going to the Father, for the Father is greater than I. And now I have told you before it comes to pass, that when it has come to pass you may believe. I will no longer speak much with you, for the prince of the world is coming, and in Me he has nothing. But he comes that the world may know that I love the Father, and that I do as the Father has commanded Me. Arise, let us go from here. John 14:1-31

73. I AM *the true Vine, and My Father is the vine-dresser. Every branch in Me that bears no fruit He will take away; and every branch that bears fruit He will cleanse that it may bear more fruit. . . . If you abide in Me, and if My words abide in you, ask whatever you will and it shall be done to you. In this is My Father glorified, that you may bear very much fruit, and become My disciples. As the Father has loved me, I also have loved you. Abide in My love. If you keep My commandments you will abide in My love, as I also have kept My Father's commandments, and abide in His love. . . . I have called you friends, because all things that I have heard from My Father I have made known to you. You have not chosen Me, but I have chosen you, and have appointed you that you should go and bear fruit, and that your fruit should remain; that whatever you ask the Father in My name He may give you. These things I command you, that you may love one another. . . . If they* (the Jews) *have persecuted Me, they will persecute you also. . . . because they do not know Him Who sent Me. . . . He who hates Me hates My Father also. If I had not done among them works such as no one else has done, they would have no sin. But now* *they have seen, and have hated both Me and My Father; but that the word written in their Law may be fulfilled, "They have hated Me without cause." But when the Advocate has come, Whom I will send you from the Father, He will bear witness concerning Me. And you also bear witness, because from the beginning you are with Me.* John 15:1-27

74. JESUS PREDICTS the persecution of His Apostles, saying, *They will expel you from the synagogues. Yes, the hour is coming for everyone who kills you to think that he is offering worship to God. And these things they will do because they have not known the Father nor Me. . . . These things, however, I did not tell you from the beginning, because I was with you.* John 16:2-4

75. ONCE MORE JESUS tells the Apostles that He will send them the Advocate, the Holy Spirit, and why. *And now I am going to Him Who sent Me. . . . It is expedient for you that I depart. For if I do not go, the Advocate will not come to you; but if I go, I will send Him to you. And when He has come He will convict the world of sin, . . . because they do not believe in Me; of justice, because I go to the Father, and you will see Me no more.* John 16:5-10

76. ALL THINGS *that the Father has are Mine. That is why I have said that He will receive of what is Mine, and will declare it to you. A little while and you shall see Me no longer; and again a little while and you shall see Me, because I go to the Father.* John 16:15-16

77. AMEN, AMEN, *I say to you, if you ask the Father anything in My name, He will give it to you. Hitherto you have not asked anything in My name. Ask, and you shall receive. . . . the hour is coming when I will no longer speak to you in parables, but will speak to you plainly of the Father. In that day you shall* *ask in My name; and I do not say to you that I will ask the Father for you, for the Father Himself loves you because you have loved Me, and have believed that I came forth from God. I came forth from the Father and have come into the world. Again I leave the world and go to the Father.* John 16:23-28

78. Now THAT JESUS no longer spoke in parables but plainly of the Father His disciples said, "Now we know that Thou knowest all things, . . . and we believe that Thou camest forth from God." Jesus hastens to warn them that their faith is to be put to further test. *Behold, the hour is coming, and already has come, for you to be scattered, each one to his own house, and to leave Me alone. But I am not alone, because the Father is with Me. These things I have spoken to you that in Me you may have peace. In the world you will have affliction. But take courage, I have overcome the world.* John 16:29-33

79. THEN IN BEHALF of His beloved Apostles, Jesus pours out His soul to the Father, God. *Father, the hour has come! Glorify Thy Son, that Thy Son may glorify Thee, even as Thou hast given Him power over all flesh, in order that to all Thou hast given Him, He may give Everlasting Life. Now this is Everlasting Life, that they may know Thee, the only true God, and Him Whom Thou hast sent, Jesus Christ. I have glorified Thee on earth; I have accomplished the work that Thou hast given Me to do. And now do Thou, Father, glorify Me with Thyself, with the glory that I had with Thee before the world existed. I have manifested Thy name to the men whom Thou hast given Me out of the world. They were Thine, and Thou hast given them to Me, and they have kept Thy word. Now they have learnt that whatever Thou hast given Me is from Thee; because the words that Thou hast given Me I have given to them. And they have received them, and have known of a truth that I came forth from Thee, and they have believed that Thou* *didst send me. I pray for them; not for the world do I pray, but for those whom Thou hast given Me, because they are Thine; and all things that are Mine are Thine, and Thine are Mine; and I am glorified in them. And I am no longer in the world, but these are in the world, and I am coming to Thee. Holy Father, keep in Thy name those whom Thou hast given Me, that they may be one even as We are. While I was with them, I kept them in Thy name. Those whom Thou hast given Me I guarded; and not one of them perished except the son of perdition, in order that the Scripture might be fulfilled. But now I am coming to Thee; and these things I speak in the world, in order that they may have My love made full in themselves. I have given them Thy word; and the world has hated them, because they are not of the world, even as I am not of the world. I do not pray that Thou take them out of the world, but that Thou keep them from evil. They are not of the world, even as I am not of the world. Sanctify them in the Truth. Thy word is Truth. Even as Thou hast sent Me into the world, so I also have sent them into the world. And for them I sanctify Myself, that they also may be sanctified in Truth. Yet not for these only do I pray, but for those also who through their word are to be-lieve in Me, that all may be one, even as Thou, Father, in Me and I in Thee; that they also may be one in Us, that the world may believe that Thou hast sent Me. And the glory that Thou hast given Me, I have given to them, that they may be one, even as We are one: I in them and Thou in Me; that they may be perfected in unity, and that the world may know that Thou hast sent Me, and that Thou hast loved them even as Thou hast loved Me. Father, I will that where I am, they also whom Thou hast given Me may be with Me; in order that they may behold My glory, which Thou hast given Me, because Thou hast loved Me before the creation of the world. Just Father, the world has not known Thee, but I have known Thee, and these have known that Thou hast sent Me. And I have made known to them Thy name, and will make it known, in order that the love with which*

Thou hast loved Me may be in them, and I in them. John
17:1-26

80. WHEN JESUS and His Apostles left the Supper Room (the
Cenacle) of the house on Mount Sion, most likely they
descended the long series of stone steps leading to the pool of
Siloe below. Then crossing the Brook Cedron and following along
its eastern bank they came to the large cave near the Garden
of Gethsemani at the foot of the Mount of Olives. This cave was
very familiar to all of them. It must have been here that Jesus
asked His Apostles to rest but took Peter and James and John
with Him to the Garden. Jesus became very sad. After asking
them to wait and watch with Him, Jesus went forward a little,
fell prostrate on the ground and prayed, *Father, if it is possible,
let this cup pass away from Me; yet not as I will, but as Thou
willest.* Then He came to the Apostles and found them sleeping.
. . . A second time He went away and prayed, *My Father, if this
cup cannot pass away unless I drink it, Thy will be done.* And
Jesus came again and found the three asleep. He went back and
prayed a third time, saying the same words over.[43,44] Matthew
26:36-44

81. JUDAS ISCARIOT, who betrayed Jesus, also knew this cave
since Jesus had often met there together with His disciples.
So taking Roman soldiers, and attendants from the chief priests
and Pharisees, Judas came there with lanterns, and torches, and
clubs, and weapons. Simon Peter having a sword, drew it, and
struck the servant of the high priest cutting off his right ear.
Even at this hour Jesus performed a miracle: by touching the
ear, He healed it. Then He said to Peter, *Put back thy sword into its place; for all those who take the sword will perish by the
sword. Or dost thou suppose that I cannot entreat My Father,
and He will even now furnish Me with more than twelve legions*

---

43. *Mark 14:32-39;* 44. *Luke 22:39-46*

of angels? How then are the Scriptures to be fulfilled, that thus it must take place?[45] Matthew 26:47-54

82. AFTER JUDAS had betrayed Jesus, they seized Jesus and took Him to the house of the high priest, Caiphas. Then as day broke, the chief priests and the Scribes and the elders of the people gathered together, and led Him away into their Sanhedrin. Caiphas said, "I adjure thee by the living God that thou tell us whether thou art the Christ, the Son of God." Jesus said to him, *Thou hast said it. Nevertheless I say to you, hereafter you shall see the Son of Man sitting at the right hand of the Power and coming upon the clouds of Heaven.* Then Caiphas tore his gaments, saying "He has blasphemed; what further need have we of witnesses?"[46,47] Matthew 26:57-65

83. THEN THEY LED JESUS from Caiphas to Pilate in the praetorium. Pilate questioned Jesus and sent Him to Herod, who in turn returned Him to Pilate. Pilate said to the chief priests, "You have brought before me this man, as one who perverts the people; and behold, I upon examining him in your presence have found no guilt in him as touching those things of which you accuse him. Neither has Herod." But the whole mob cried out, "Crucify him! Crucify him!" Pilate went back into the praetorium and said to Jesus, "Where art thou from?" Jesus made no answer. Pilate therefore said to Him, "Dost thou not know that I have power to crucify thee, and that I have power to release thee?" Jesus answered, *Thou wouldst have no power at all over Me were it not given thee from above.* John 19:8-11

84. THEN PILATE pronounced sentence that what they asked for should be done. They led Jesus out to the place called Golgotha, which translated, is the Place of the Skull. There they crucified Him. As they nailed Him to the infamous cross Jesus

---

45. *John 18:1-11;* 46. *Mark 14:53-63;* 47. *Luke 22:63-71*

said, *Father, forgive them, for they do not know what they are doing.* Luke 23:34

85. JESUS, tortured body and soul, now hung on the cross. It was about the sixth hour (noon our time), and there was darkness over the whole land until the ninth hour (three o'clock). About the ninth hour Jesus cried out with a loud voice, saying, *Eli, Eli, lema sabacthani,* that is, *My God, My God, why hast Thou forsaken Me?*[48] Matthew 27:45-46

86. THE SUN DARKENED, and the curtain of the Temple was torn in two from the top to the bottom. The earth quaked, the rocks were rent, and the tombs opened. Jesus cried out, *Father, into Thy hands I commend My spirit.* And having said this He expired. Luke 23:45-46

87. NEAR GOLGOTHA where Jesus was crucified there was a garden and in the garden a new tomb in which no one had yet been laid. There they laid Jesus. Now on the first day of the week Mary Magdalene came early to the tomb, while it was still dark. She saw the stone had been taken away from the entrance to the tomb and the tomb empty. Standing beside the tomb she wept. Then she turned round and beheld someone standing there. She did not know that it was Jesus. Thinking that he was the gardener, she said to him, "Sir, if thou hast removed Him, tell me where thou hast laid Him and I will take Him away." Jesus said to her, *"Mary!"* She said to Him, "Rabboni!" ("Master!") Jesus said, *Do not touch Me, for I have not yet ascended to My Father, but go to My brethren and say to them, "I ascend to My Father and your Father, to My God and your God".* John 20:17

88. So MARY MAGDALENE went to the disciples and announced, "I have seen the Lord". They did not believe her. Then late

---

48. *Mark 15:33-34*

that same day, the first day of the week, though the doors where the disciples gathered had been closed for fear of the Jews, Jesus came and stood in their midst, saying to them, *Peace be to you! As the Father has sent Me, I also send you.* When He had said this, He breathed upon them, and said to them, *Receive the Holy Spirit; whose sins you shall forgive, they are forgiven them; and whose sins you shall retain, they are retained.* John 20:21-23

89. AND I SEND FORTH *upon you the promise of My Father. But wait here in the city, until you are clothed with power from on high.* Luke 24:49

90. THEN THE ELEVEN APOSTLES went into Galilee, to the mountain to which Jesus had directed them to go. And when they saw Him they worshipped Him. Yet some doubted! Jesus spoke to them saying, *All power in Heaven and on earth has been given to Me. Go, therefore, and make disciples of all nations, baptizing them in the name of the Father, and of the Son, and of the Holy Spirit, teaching them to observe all that I have commanded you; and behold, I am with you all days, even unto the consummation of the world.* Matthew 28:16-20

CHAPTER II

JESUS SAID
of the Son of God,
Jesus Christ

91. NICODEMUS, the Pharisee who finally became a disciple of Jesus, learned from Him the great mystery of the love of God for man. Jesus said, *For God so loved the world that He gave His only-begotten Son, that those who believe in Him may not perish, but may have Life Everlasting. For God did not send His Son into the world in order to judge the world, but that the world might be saved through Him. He who believes in Him is not judged; but he who does not believe is already judged, because he does not believe in the name of the only-begotten Son of God. Now this is the judgment: The Light has come into the world, yet men have loved the darkness rather than the Light, for their works were evil. For everyone who does evil hates the Light, and does not come to the Light, that his deeds may not be exposed. But he who does the truth comes to the Light that his deeds may be made manifest, for they have been performed in God.* John 3:16-21

92. AFTER THE SERMON on the Mount, Jesus performed many miracles. The disciples of John the Baptist brought him word of these miracles. So John summoned two of them to go to Jesus and ask Him, "Art Thou He Who is to come, or shall we look for another?" Jesus answering them, said, *Go and report to John what you have heard and seen: the blind see, the lame walk, the lepers are cleansed, the deaf hear, the dead rise, and the poor have the Gospel preached to them.* Matthew 11:4-5

93. BESIDES THE TWELVE APOSTLES, Jesus had many disciples. He sent seventy-two of them into every town and place where He Himself was about to come. They returned to Him with joy, saying, "Lord, even the devils are subject to us in Thy name." Jesus, too, rejoiced in the Holy Spirit, saying, *I praise Thee, Father, Lord of Heaven and earth, that Thou didst hide these things from the wise and prudent, and didst reveal them to little ones. Yes, Father, for such was Thy good pleasure. All things have been delivered to Me by My Father; and no one knows the Son except the Father; nor does anyone know the Father except the Son, and him to whom the Son chooses to reveal Him. Come to Me, all you who labor and are burdened, and I will give you rest. Take My yoke upon you, and learn from Me, for I am meek and humble of heart; and you will find rest for your souls. For My yoke is easy, and My burden light.*[49] Matthew 11:25-30

94. THE LEADERS OF THE JEWS kept persecuting Jesus and even sought to put Him to death not only because He healed the sick on the Sabbath, but also because He called God His own Father. In their opinion Jesus made Himself equal to God, when He said, *My Father works even until now, and I work.* Then Jesus declared His claim to divinity. *Amen, amen, I say to you, the Son can do nothing of Himself, but only what He sees the Father doing. For whatever He does, this the Son also*

---

49. *Luke 10:21-22*

does in like manner. For the Father loves the Son, and shows Him all that He Himself does. And greater works than these He will show Him, that you may wonder. For as the Father raises the dead and gives them Life, even so the Son also gives Life to whom He will. For neither does the Father judge any man, but all judgment He has given to the Son, that all men may honor the Son even as they honor the Father. He who does not honor the Son, does not honor the Father Who sent Him. Amen, amen, I say to you, he who hears My word, and believes Him Who sent Me, has Life Everlasting, and does not come to judgment, but has passed from death to Life. Amen, amen, I say to you, the hour is coming, and now is here, when the dead shall hear the voice of the Son of God, and those who hear shall live. For as the Father has Life in Himself, even so He has given to the Son also to have Life in Himself; and He has granted Him power to render judgment, because He is Son of Man. Do not wonder at this, for the hour is coming in which all who are in the tombs shall hear the voice of the Son of God. And they who have done good shall come forth unto resurrection of Life; but they who have done evil unto resurrection of judgment. Of Myself I can do nothing. As I hear, I judge, and My judgment is just because I seek not My own will, but the will of Him Who sent Me. If I bear witness concerning Myself, My witness is not true. There is another who bears witness concerning Me, and I know that the witness that he bears concerning Me is true. You have sent to John, and he has borne witness to the Truth. I however do not receive the witness of man, but I say these things that you may be saved. He was the lamp, burning and shining; and you desired to rejoice for a while in his light. The witness, however, that I have is greater than that of John. For the works which the Father has given Me to accomplish, these very works that I do, bear witness to Me, that the Father has sent Me. And the Father Himself, Who has sent Me, has borne witness to Me. But you have never heard His voice, or seen His face. And you have not His word abiding in you, since you do not believe Him Whom He has sent. You search the Scriptures, because in them you think that you have Life Everlasting. And it is they that bear witness to Me, yet you are not willing to come to Me that you may have Life. I do not receive glory from men. But I know that you have not the love of God in you. I have come in the name of My Father, and you do not receive Me. If another come in his own name, him you will receive. How can you believe who receive glory from one another, and do not seek the glory which is from the only God? Do not think that I shall accuse you to the Father. There is one who accuses you, Moses, in whom you hope. For if you believed Moses you would believe Me also, for he wrote of Me. But if you do not believe his writings, how will you believe My words? John 5:16-47

95. THE CROWDS FOLLOWED JESUS everywhere in Galilee. One day they asked Him, "What are we to do that we may perform the works of God?" In answer He said to them, *This is the work of God, that you believe in Him Whom He has sent. . . . I am the Bread of Life. He who comes to Me shall not hunger, and he who believes in Me shall never thirst. But I have told you that you have seen Me and you do not believe. All that the Father gives to Me I will not cast out. For I have come down from Heaven, not to do My own will, but the will of Him Who sent Me. Now this is the will of Him Who sent Me, the Father, that I should lose nothing of what He has given Me, but that I should raise it up on the last day. For this is the will of My Father Who sent Me, that whoever beholds the Son, and believes in Him, shall have Everlasting Life, and I will raise him up on the last day. . . . Do not murmur among yourselves. No one can come to Me unless the Father Who sent Me draw him, and I will raise him up on the last day. It is written in the Prophets, "And they all shall be taught of God."*[50] *Everyone*

---

50. *Isaias 54:13; Jeremias 31:33*

who has listened to the Father, and has learned, comes to Me; not that anyone has seen the Father except Him Who is from God, He has seen the Father. Amen, amen, I say to you, he who believes in Me has Life Everlasting. I am the Bread of Life. Your fathers ate the manna in the desert, and have died. This is the Bread that comes down from Heaven, so that if anyone eat of it he will not die. I am the Living Bread that has come down from Heaven. If anyone eat of this Bread he shall live forever; and the Bread that I will give is My flesh for the Life of the world. John 6:28-52

96. Now JESUS, having come into the district of Caesarea Philippi to the north of Capharnaum, asked His disciples, *Who do men say the Son of Man is?* In answer to His question, they said, "Some say, John the Baptist; and others, Elias; and others, Jeremias, or one of the Prophets." Jesus asked them, *But who do you say that I am?* Simon Peter spoke up, "Thou art the Christ, the Son of the living God." Jesus said, *Blessed art thou, Simon Bar-Jona, for flesh and blood has not revealed this to thee, but My Father in Heaven. And I say to thee, thou art Peter, and upon this rock I will build My Church, and the gates of hell shall not prevail against it. And I will give thee the keys of the Kingdom of Heaven; and whatever thou shalt bind on earth shall be bound in Heaven, and whatever thou shalt loose on earth shall be loosed in Heaven.* Then He strictly charged His disciples to tell no one that He was Jesus the Christ (the Messias). Matthew 16:13-20

97. A DISCUSSION AROSE among the disciples, which of them was the greatest. Jesus took a little child and set him at His side, and said to them, *Whoever receives this little child for My sake, receives Me; and whoever receives Me, receives Him Who sent Me. He who is the least among you, he is the greatest.*[51,52] Luke 9:46-48

---

51. *Matthew 18:5;* 52. *Mark 9:36*

98. To THE PEOPLE gathered in Jerusalem, Jesus said, *I am the
Light of the world. He who follows Me does not walk in
the darkness, but will have the Light of Life.* The Pharisees
therefore said to Him, "Thou bearest witness to thyself. Thy
witness is not true." Jesus replied, *Even if I bear witness to
Myself, My witness is true, because I know where I came from
and where I go. But you do not know where I came from or
where I go. You judge according to the flesh; I judge no one.
And even if I do judge, My judgment is true, because I am not
alone, but with Me is He Who sent Me, the Father. And in
your Law it is written that the witness of two persons is true. It
is I Who bear witness to Myself, and He Who sent Me, the
Father, bears witness to Me.* They therefore said to Him,
"Where is thy father?" Jesus answered, *You know neither Me
nor My Father. If you knew Me, you would then know My
Father also.* Jesus spoke these words in the treasury, a room off
the Court of the Women, while teaching in the Temple. No one
seized Him, because His hour had not yet come. John 8:12-20

99. JESUS CONTINUED, *I go, and you will seek Me, and in your
sin you will die. Where I go you cannot come. You are
from below, I am from above. You are of this world, I am not
of this world. Therefore I said to you that you will die in your
sins; for if you do not believe that I am He* (the Messias), *you
will die in your sin.* They therefore said to Him, "Who art
thou?" Jesus replied, *Why do I speak to you at all! I have
many things to speak and to judge concerning you; but He Who
sent Me is true, and the things that I heard from Him, these I
speak in the world. . . . When you have lifted up the Son of
Man, then you will know that I am He, and that of Myself I
do nothing: but that I preach only what the Father has taught
Me. And He Who sent Me is with Me; He has not left Me
alone, because I do always the things that are pleasing to Him.*
When Jesus was speaking these things, many believed in Him.
John 8:21-30

100. Jesus therefore said to the Jews who had come to believe in Him, *If you abide in My word, you shall be My disciples indeed, and you shall know the Truth, and the Truth shall make you free. . . . Amen, amen, I say to you, everyone who commits sin is a slave of sin. . . .If therefore the Son makes you free, you will be free indeed.* John 8:31-36

101. To others who did not believe in Him, Jesus said, *If God were your Father, you would surely love Me. For from God I came forth and have come; for neither have I come of Myself, but He sent Me. . . . If I speak the Truth, why do you not believe Me? He who is of God hears the words of God. The reason why you do not hear is that you are not of God. . . .* They taunted Him, saying, "Are we not right in saying that thou art a Samaritan, and hast a devil?" Jesus answered, *I have not a devil, but I honor My Father, and you dishonor Me. . . . Amen, amen, I say to you, if anyone keep My word, he will never see death. . . . If I glorify Myself, My glory is nothing. It is My Father Who glorifies Me, of Whom you say that He is your God. And you do not know Him, but I know Him. And if I say that I do not know Him, I shall be like you, a liar. But I know Him, and I keep His word. Abraham, your father, rejoiced that he was to see My day.* (Abraham can be said to have seen Christ's day either in faith and prophetic vision, or from his place in limbo when Christ was born). *He saw it, and was glad. . . . Amen, amen, I say to you, before Abraham came to be, I AM.* They took up stones to cast at Him. Jesus hid Himself. Then He left the Temple. John 8:42-59

102. As Jesus and His Apostles went out from the Temple, they saw a man blind from birth. They asked Him, "Rabbi, who has sinned, this man or his parents, that he should be born blind?" Jesus answered, *Neither has this man sinned, nor his parents, but the works of God were to be made manifest in him. I must do the works of Him Who sent Me while it is* *day; night is coming, when no one can work. As long as I am in the world I am the Light of the world.* When He had said these things, He spat on the ground and made clay with the spittle, and spread the clay over his eyes, and said to him, *Go, wash in the pool of Siloe.* So he went away, and washed, and returned seeing. . . . Later Jesus saw this man, and asked him, *Dost thou believe in the Son of God?* The man asked Him, "Who is He, Lord, that I may believe in Him?" Jesus replied, *Thou hast both seen Him, and He it is Who speaks with thee.* And he said, "I believe, Lord." And falling down on his knees, he worshipped Jesus. John 9:1-38

103. *I AM the Good Shepherd. The Good Shepherd lays down His life for His sheep. But the hireling who is not a shepherd, whose own the sheep are not, sees the wolf coming and leaves the sheep and flees. And the wolf snatches and scatters the sheep; but the hireling flees because he is a hireling, and has no concern for the sheep. I am the Good Shepherd, and I know Mine and Mine know Me, even as the Father knows Me, and I know the Father; and I lay down My life for My sheep. And other sheep I have that are not of this Fold. Them also I must bring, and they shall hear My voice, and there shall be One Fold and One Shepherd. For this reason the Father loves Me, because I lay down My life that I may take it up again. No one takes it from Me, but I lay it down of Myself. I have the power to lay it down, and I have the power to take it up again. Such is the command I have received from My Father.* John 10:11-18

104. IT WAS DECEMBER AND WINTER. Saint John reminds us that the Feast of the Dedication was taking place in the Temple at Jerusalem. This Feast was instituted by Judas Macabeus in 64 B.C. to be celebrated yearly in commemoration of the restoration and purification of the Temple which had been polluted by the heathens. It was observed for eight days midst manifestations of joy.[53] Jesus was walking in the Temple, in Solomon's portico, a covered walk along the eastern side of the court which surrounded the Temple. The Jews gathering around Him, asked, "How long dost thou keep us in suspense? If thou art the Christ, tell us openly." Jesus replied, *I tell you and you do not believe. The works that I do in the name of My Father, these bear witness concerning Me. But you do not believe because you are not of My sheep. My sheep hear My voice, and I know them and they follow Me. And I give them Everlasting Life; and they shall never perish, neither shall anyone snatch them out of My hand. What My Father has given Me is greater than all; and no one is able to snatch anything out of the hand of My Father. I and the Father are one.* The unbelieving Jews took up stones to stone Him. Jesus said, *Many good works have I shown you from My Father. For which of these works do you stone Me?* The Jews answered Him, "Not for a good work do we stone thee, but for blasphemy, and because thou, being a man, makest thyself God." Jesus asked them, *Is it not written in your Law, "I said you are gods?"*[54] *If he called them gods to whom the word of God was addressed (and the Scripture cannot be broken), do you say of Him Whom the Father has made holy and sent into the world, "Thou blasphemest", because I said, "I am the Son of God"? If I do not perform the works of My Father, do not believe Me. But if I do perform them, and if you are not willing to believe Me, believe the works, that you may know and believe that the Father is in Me and I in the Father.* They sought therefore to seize Him; but He went forth out of their hands. John 10:22-39

105. CERTAIN PHARISEES came to Jesus, saying to Him, "Depart and be on thy way, for Herod wants to kill thee." Jesus said to them, *Go and say to that fox, "Behold, I cast out devils*

---

53. *I Macabeus 4:41-64; II Macabeus 6:2*
54. *Psalm 81:6 Scholars tell us that the judges who administered the Law were called gods, because they represented God.*

and perform cures today and tomorrow, and the third day I am to end My course. Nevertheless, I must go My way today and tomorrow and the next day, for it cannot be that a Prophet perish outside Jerusalem." Luke 13:31-33

106. JESUS MUST HAVE BEEN on the Mount of Olives and possibly on His way to Bethany to the home of His beloved friends, Mary and Martha and their brother Lazarus, when He looked back at the City of God, and with sadness cried out, *Jerusalem, Jerusalem! thou who killest the Prophets, and stonest those who are sent to thee! How often would I have gathered thy children together, as a hen gathers her young under her wings, but thou wouldst not! Behold, your house is left to you desolate. For I say to you, you shall not see Me henceforth until you shall say, "Blessed is He Who comes in the name of the Lord!"*[55] Matthew 23:37-39

107. LAZARUS BECAME VERY ILL. His sisters, Mary and Martha, sent word to Jesus saying, "Lord, behold, he whom thou lovest is sick." When Jesus heard this, He said, *This sickness is not unto death, but for the glory of God, that through it the Son may be glorified.* And yet Jesus said plainly to His disciples, *Lazarus is dead; and I rejoice on your account that I was not there, that you may believe. But let us go to him.* Lazarus had been dead four days and had been laid in a tomb. Jesus said to Martha, *Thy brother shall rise. . . . I am the Resurrection and the Life; he who believes in Me, even if he died, shall live; and whoever lives and believes in Me, shall never die. Dost thou believe this?* She replied, "Yes, Lord, I believe that Thou art the Christ, the Son of God, Who hast come into the world." Jesus asked that the stone placed against the entrance of the tomb be removed. Speaking again to Martha, He said, *Have I not told thee that if thou believe thou shalt behold the glory of God?* Then raising His eyes, He said, *Father, I give Thee thanks that*

---

55. *Luke 13:34-35*

Thou always hearest Me; but because of the people who stand round, I spoke, that they may believe that Thou hast sent Me. When He had said this, He cried out with a loud voice, *Lazarus, come forth!* And at once he who had been dead came forth, bound feet and hands with bandages, and his face was tied up with a cloth. Jesus said to them, *Unbind him, and let him go.* John 11:1-44

108. THE PHARISEES had been questioning Jesus in order to trap Him. Then Jesus put to them this question, *What do you think of the Christ? Whose Son is He?* they said to Him, "David's" He said to them, *How then does David in the Spirit call Him Lord, saying, "The Lord said to my Lord: Sit Thou at My right hand, till I make Thy enemies Thy footstool?" If David, therefore, calls Him "Lord", how is He his son?* And no one could answer Him a word; neither did anyone dare from that day forth to ask Him any more questions.[56,57] Matthew 22:41-46

109. JESUS WAS ON HIS WAY out of the temple as one of His disciples said to Him, "Master, look, what wonderful stones and buildings!" Jesus said, *Dost thou see all these great buildings? There will not be left one stone upon another that will not be thrown down.* Then soon after as He was sitting on the Mount of Olives, opposite the Temple, Peter and James and John and Andrew asked Him privately, "Tell us, when are these things to happen, and what will be the sign when all these things will come to pass?" In answer Jesus said, *Take care that no one leads you astray. For many will come in My name, saying, "I am He"; and they will lead many astray. . . . But be on your guard. For they will deliver you up to councils, and you will be beaten in synagogues, and you will stand before governors and kings for My sake, for a witness to them. . . . And you will be hated by all for My name's sake; but he who has per-*

---

56. *Mark 12:35-37*; 57. *Luke 20:41-44*

severed to the end will be saved. . . . And then if anyone say to you, "Behold, here is the christ; behold, there he is," do not believe it. For false christs and false prophets will arise, and will show signs and wonders, so as to lead astray, if possible, even the elect. Be on your guard, therefore; behold, I have told you all things beforehand. . . . Heaven and earth will pass away, but My words will not pass away. But of that day and hour no one knows, neither the angels in Heaven, nor the Son, but the Father only. Take heed, watch and pray, for you do not know when the time is.[58] Mark 13:1-33

110. THEN JESUS TOLD His disciples of the signs of the last day, and of His coming again. *As the lightning comes forth from the east and shines even to the west, so also will the coming of the Son of Man* (the Son of God, Jesus Christ) *be. . . . But immediately after the tribulation of those days, the sun will be darkened, and the moon will not give her light, and the stars will fall from Heaven, and the powers of Heaven will be shaken. And then will appear the sign of the Son of Man in Heaven; and then will all tribes of the earth mourn, and they will see the Son of Man coming upon the clouds of Heaven with great power and majesty. And He will send forth His angels with a trumpet and a great sound, and they will gather His elect from the four winds, from one end of the heavens to the other. . . . Watch therefore, for you do not know at what hour your Lord is to come.*[59] Matthew 24:27-42

111. JESUS ALSO TOLD His disciples of the last judgment. *But when the Son of Man shall come in His majesty, and all the angels with Him then He will sit on the Throne of His glory; and before Him will be gathered all the nations, and He will separate them one from another, as the shepherd separates the sheep from the goats; and He will set the sheep on His right hand, but the goats on the left. Then the King will say to those on*

58. *Matthew 24:1-25;* 59. *Mark 13:24-27*

His right hand, "Come, blessed of My Father, take possession of the Kingdom prepared for you from the foundation of the world; for I was hungry and you gave Me to eat; I was thirsty and you gave Me to drink; I was a stranger and you took Me in; naked and you covered Me; sick and you visited Me; I was in prison and you came to Me." Then the just will answer Him, saying, "Lord, when did we see Thee hungry, and feed Thee; or thirsty, and give Thee drink? And when did we see Thee a stranger, and take Thee in; or naked, and clothe Thee? Or when did we see Thee sick, or in prison, and come to Thee?" And answering the King will say to them, "Amen I say to you, as long as you did it for one of these, the least of My brethren, you did it for Me." Then He will say to those on His left hand, "Depart from Me, accursed ones, into the everlasting fire which was prepared for the devil and his angels. For I was hungry, and you did not give Me to eat; I was thirsty and you gave Me no drink; I was a stranger and you did not take Me in; naked, and you did not clothe Me; sick, and in prison, and you did not visit Me." Then they also will answer and say, "Lord, when did we see Thee hungry, or thirsty, or a stranger, or naked, or sick, or in prison, and did not minister to Thee?" Then He will answer them, saying, "Amen I say to you, as long as you did not do it for one of these least ones, you did not do it for Me." And these will go into everlasting punishment, but the just into Everlasting Life. Matthew 25:31-46

112. WHEN JESUS had finished these words of counsel and prophesy of the last days and the last judgment, He reminded His disciples of the approaching feast, saying, *You know that after two days the Passover will be here; and the Son of Man will be delivered up to be crucified.* Matthew 26:1-2

113. SEVERAL DAYS BEFORE when Jesus was in Bethany, in the house of Simon the leper, Mary Magdalene came with an alabaster jar of precious ointment, and poured it on His head, as He reclined at table. Then one of His disciples, Judas Iscariot, he who was about to betray Him, said, "Why was this ointment not sold and the money given to the poor?" Jesus said, *Let her be. Why do you trouble the woman? She has done Me a good turn. For the poor you have always with you, but you do not always have Me. For in pouring this ointment on My body, she has done it for My burial. Amen, I say to you, wherever in the whole world this Gospel is preached, this also that she has done shall be told in memory of her.*[60,61] Matthew 26:6-13

114. IT WAS EARLY SPRING. The Feast of the Unleavened Bread, which is also called the Feast of the Passover,[62] was drawing near. What was this unleavened bread? The Jews called it "matzah", a kind of flat bread having no special flavor as it contained neither salt nor yeast. It was compulsory to eat some of this unleavened bread on the first two nights of the Passover. This matzah was symbolic of the haste with which the Jews departed from their captivity in Egypt taking with them as food unleavened dough. Jesus was in Judea. The day of the Unleavened Bread came, on which the passover (a lamb) had to be sacrificed. Jesus, observing the Law, sent Peter and John into Jerusalem to prepare this Feast. They asked Him, "Where dost Thou want us to prepare it?" Jesus said to them, *Behold, on your entering the city, there will meet you a man carrying a pitcher of water; follow him into the house into which he goes. And you shall say to the master of the house, "The Master says, 'My time is near at hand. Where is the guest chamber, that I may eat the passover there with My disciples?'"* and he will show you a large upper room furnished; there make ready. And they went, and found just as He had told them; and they prepared the passover.[63,64] Luke 22:7-13

---

60. *Mark 14:3-9;* 61. *John 12:1-8;* 62. *Luke 22:1;* 63. *Matthew 26:17-19* 64. *Mark 14:12-16*

115. Now WHEN EVENING ARRIVED, Jesus came with the Twelve to the Upper Room. While they were at table, Jesus said, *Amen I say to you, one of you will betray Me. . . . He who dips his hand into the dish with Me, he will betray Me. The Son of Man indeed goes His way, as it is written of Him; but woe to that man by whom the Son of Man is betrayed! It were better for that man if he had not been born.*[65,66,67] Matthew 26:20-25

116. WHEN JUDAS ISCARIOT had gone out from the Upper Room, Jesus said, *Now is the Son of Man glorified, and God is glorified in Him. If God is glorified in Him, God will also glorify Him in Himself, and will glorify Him at once. Little children, yet a little while I am with you. You will seek Me, and, as I said to the Jews, "Where I go you cannot come," so to you also I say it now. A new commandment I give you, that you love one another: that as I have loved you, you also love one another. By this will all men know that you are My disciples, if you have love for one another.* John 13:31-35

117. AND WHILE THEY WERE EATING, Jesus said, *I have greatly desired to eat of this passover with you before I suffer; for I say to you that I will eat of it no more, until it has been fulfilled in the Kingdom of God.* Then Jesus took bread, and blessed and broke, and gave it to His disciples, saying, *Take and eat; this is My body.* And taking a cup, He gave thanks and gave it to them, saying, *All of you drink of this; for this is My blood of the New Covenant, which is being shed for many unto the forgiveness of sins.*[68,69] Matthew 26:26-29

118. AFTER RECITING A HYMN, Jesus and His eleven (Judas had gone to carry out his act of betrayal) Apostles went from the Cenacle on Mount Sion to the Garden of Gethsemani at the foot of the Mount of Olives. Then Jesus said, *You will all be*

---

65. *Mark 14:17-21;* 66. *Luke 22:21-23;* 67. *John 13:21-26;* 68. *Mark 14:22-25;* 69. *Luke 22:14-20*

scandalized this night because of Me; for it is written, "I will smite the Shepherd, and the sheep of the flock will be scattered." But after I have risen, I will go before you into Galilee.[70] Matthew 26:30-32

119. Simon Peter said to Jesus, "Lord, where art Thou going?" Jesus answered, *Where I am going thou canst not follow Me now, but thou shalt follow later.* Peter said to Him, "Why can I not follow Thee now? I will lay down my life for Thee." Jesus said to him, *Wilt thou lay down thy life for Me? Amen, amen, I say to thee, the cock will not crow before thou dost deny Me thrice.*[71,72,73] John 13:36-38

120. After Jesus had predicted that Peter would deny Him three times, He spoke words of comfort to the saddened Apostles: *Let not your heart be troubled. You believe in God, believe also in Me. In My Father's house there are many mansions. Were it not so, I should have told you, because I go to prepare a place for you. And if I go and prepare a place for you, I am coming again, and I will take you to Myself; that where I am, there you also may be. And where I go you know, and the way you know.* Thomas said to Him, "Lord, we do not where Thou art going, and how can we know the way?" Jesus said to Him, *I am the Way, and the Truth, and the Life. No one comes to the Father but through Me. If you had known Me, you would also have known My Father. And henceforth you do know Him, and you have seen Him.* Philip said to Him, "Lord, show us the Father and it is enough for us." Jesus said to him, *Have I been so long a time with you, and you have not known Me. Philip, he who sees Me sees also the Father. How canst thou say, "Show us the Father?" Dost thou not believe that I am in the Father and the Father in Me? The words that I speak to you I speak not on My own authority. But the Father*

---

70. *Mark 14:26-31;* 71. *Matthew 26:34;* 72. *Mark 14:30;* 73. *Luke 22:34*

dwelling in Me, it is He Who does the works. Do you believe that I am in the Father and the Father in Me? Otherwise believe because of the works themselves. Amen, amen, I say to you, he who believes in Me, the works that I do he also shall do, and greater than these he shall do, because I am going to the Father. And whatever you ask in My name, that I will do, in order that the Father may be glorified in the Son. If you ask Me anything in My name, I will do it. If you love Me, keep My commandments. And I will ask the Father and He will give you another Advocate to dwell with you forever, the Spirit of Truth Whom the world cannot receive, because it neither sees Him nor knows Him. But you shall know Him, because He will dwell with you, and be in you. I will not leave you orphans; I will come to you. Yet a little while and the world no longer sees Me. But you see Me, for I live and you shall live. In that day you will know that I am in My Father, and you in Me, and I in you. He who has My commandments and keeps them, he it is who loves Me. But he who loves Me will be loved by My Father, and I will love him and manifest Myself to him. Judas, not the Iscariot, said to Him, "Lord, how is it that Thou art about to manifest Thyself to us, and not to the world?" Jesus answered and said to him, *If anyone love Me, he will keep My word, and My Father will love him, and We will come to him and make Our abode with him. He who does not love Me does not keep My words. And the word that you have heard is not Mine, but the Father's Who sent Me. These things I have spoken to you while yet dwelling with you. But the Advocate, the Holy Spirit, Whom the Father will send in My name, He will teach you all things, and bring to your mind whatever I have said to you. Peace I leave with you, My peace I give to you; not as the world gives do I give to you. Do not let your heart be troubled, or be afraid. You have heard Me say to you, "I go away and I am coming to you." If you loved Me, you would indeed rejoice that I am going to the Father, for the*

Father is greater than I. And now I have told you before it comes to pass, that when it has come to pass you may believe. I will no longer speak much with you, for the prince of the world is coming, and in Me he has nothing. But he comes that the world may know that I love the Father, and that I do as the Father has commanded Me. Arise, let us go from here. John 14:1-31

121. HAVING SAID, *Arise, let us go from here,* Jesus and the Eleven must have gone from the Supper Room toward the Garden of Gethsemani at the foot of the Mount of Olives. According to the fifteenth chapter of Saint John, Jesus continued His discourse, saying, *I am the true Vine, and My Father is the Vine-dresser. Every branch in Me that bears no fruit He will take away; and every branch that bears fruit He will cleanse that it may bear more fruit. You are already clean because of the word that I have spoken to you. Abide in Me, and I in you. As the branch cannot bear fruit of itself unless it remain on the vine, so neither can you unless you abide in Me. I am the Vine, you are the branches. He who abides in Me, and I in him, he bears much fruit; for without Me you can do nothing. If anyone does not abide in Me, he shall be cast outside as the branch and wither; and they shall gather them up and cast them into the fire, and they shall burn. If you abide in Me, and if My words abide in you, ask whatever you will and it shall be done to you. In this is My Father glorified, that you may bear very much fruit, and become My disciples. As the Father has loved Me, I also have loved you. Abide in My love. If you keep My commandments you will abide in My love, as I also have kept My Father's commandments, and abide in His love. These things I have spoken to you that My joy may be in you, and that your joy may be made full. This is My commandment, that you love one another as I have loved you. Greater love than this no one has, that one lay down his life for* *his friends. You are My friends if you do the things I command you. No longer do I call you servants, because the servant does not know what his master does. But I have called you friends, because all things that I have heard from My Father I have made known to you. You have not chosen Me, but I have chosen you, and have appointed you that you should go and bear fruit, and that your friut should remain; that whatever you ask the Father in My name He may give you. These things I command you, that you may love one another.* John 15:1-17

122. THEN JESUS PREDICTED the world's hatred and persecution of the disciples because they believed in Him. *If the world hates you, know that it has hated Me before you. If you were of the world, the world would love what is its own. But because you are not of the world, but I have chosen you out of the world, therefore the world hates you. Remember the word that I have spoken to you: No servant is greater than his master. If they have persecuted Me, they will persecute you also; if they have kept My word, they will keep yours also. But all these things they will do to you for My name's sake, because they do not know Him Who sent Me. If I had not come and spoken to them, they would have no sin. But now they have no excuse for their sin. He who hates Me hates My Father also. If I had not done among them works such as no one else has done, they would have no sin. But now they have seen, and have hated both Me and My Father; but that the word written in their Law may be fulfilled, "They have hated Me without cause." But when the Advocate has come, Whom I will send you from the Father, the Spirit of Truth Who proceeds from the Father, He will bear witness concerning Me. And you also bear witness, because from the beginning you are with Me.* John 15:18-27

123. JESUS CONTINUES HIS PREDICTION. *These things I have spoken to you that you may not be scandalized. They will*

72

expel you from the synagogues. Yes, the hour is coming for everyone who kills you to think that he is offering worship to God. And these things they will do because they have not known the Father nor Me. But these things I have spoken to you, that when the time has come you may remember that I told you. These things, however, I did not tell you from the beginning, because I was with you. John 16:1-4

124. JESUS THEN EXPLAINS the role of the Advocate, the Holy Spirit, Who will come to the disciples when He has gone to the Father. *And now I am going to Him Who sent Me, and no one of you asks Me, "Where art Thou going?" But because I have spoken to you these things, sorrow has filled your heart. But I speak the truth to you; it is expedient for you that I depart. For if I do not go, the Advocate will not come to you; but if I go, I will send Him to you. And when He has come He will convict the world of sin, and of justice, and of judgment: of sin, because they do not believe in Me; of justice, because I go to the Father, and you will see Me no more; and of judgment, because the prince of this world has already been judged. Many things yet I have to say to you, but you cannot bear them now. But when He, the Spirit of Truth, has come, He will teach you all the truth. For He will not speak on His own authority, but whatever He will hear He will speak, and the things that are to come He will declare to you. He will glorify Me, because He will receive of what is Mine and declare it to you. All things that the Father has are Mine. That is why I have said that He will receive of what is Mine, and will declare it to you. A little while and you shall see Me no longer; and again a little while and you shall see Me, because I go to the Father.* John 16:5-16

125. THE DISCIPLES WERE PERPLEXED when Jesus said, *A little while and you shall not see Me, and again a little while and you shall see Me;* and, *I go to the Father.* They kept saying therefore, "What is this 'little while' of which He speaks? We do not know what He is saying." Jesus knew that they wanted to ask Him, so He said to them, *You inquire about this among yourselves because I said, "A little while and you shall not see Me, and again a little while and you shall see Me." Amen, amen, I say to you, that you shall weep and lament, but the world shall rejoice; and you shall be sorrowful, but your sorrow shall be turned into joy. A woman about to give birth has sorrow, because her hour has come. But when she has brought forth the child, she no longer remembers the anguish for her joy that a man is born into the world. And you therefore have sorrow now; but I will see you again, and your heart shall rejoice, and your joy no one shall take from you. And in that day you shall ask Me nothing. Amen, amen, I say to you, if you ask the Father anything in My name, He will give it to you. Hitherto you have not asked anything in My name. Ask, and you shall receive, that your joy may be full. These things I have spoken to you in parables. The hour is coming when I will no longer speak to you in parables, but will speak to you plainly of the Father. In that day you shall ask in My name; and I do not say to you that I will ask the Father for you, for the Father Himself loves you because you have loved Me, and have believed that I came forth from God. I came forth from the Father and have come into the world. Again I leave the world and go to the Father.* His disciples said to Him, "Behold, now Thou speakest plainly, and utterest no parable. Now we know that Thou knowest all things, and dost not need that anyone should question Thee. For this reason we believe that Thou camest forth from God." Jesus answered them, *Do you now believe? Behold, the hour is coming, and has already come, for you to be scattered, each one to his own house, and to leave Me alone. But I am not alone, because the Father is with Me. These things I have spoken to you that in Me you may have peace. In the world you will have affliction. But take courage, I have overcome the world.* John 16:17-33

74

126. IN THE SEVENTEENTH CHAPTER of Saint John, Jesus no longer speaks directly to the Eleven, but raising His eyes to Heaven, He implores and prays to God the Father. *Father, the hour has come! Glorify Thy Son, that Thy Son may glorify Thee, even as Thou hast given Him power over all flesh, in order that to all Thou hast given Him He may give Everlasting Life. Now this is Everlasting Life, that they may know Thee, the only true God, and Him Whom Thou hast sent, Jesus Christ. I have glorified Thee on earth; I have accomplished the work that Thou hast given Me to do. And now do Thou, Father, glorify Me with Thyself, with the glory that I had with Thee before the world existed. I have manifested Thy name to the men whom Thou hast given Me out of the world. They were Thine, and Thou hast given them to Me, and they have kept Thy word. Now they have learnt that whatever Thou hast given Me is from Thee; because the words that Thou hast given Me I have given to them. And they have received them, and have known of a truth that I came forth from Thee, and they have believed that Thou didst send Me. I pray for them; not for the world do I pray, but for those whom Thou hast given Me, because they are Thine; and all things that are Mine are Thine, and Thine are Mine; and I am glorified in them. And I am no longer in the world, but these are in the world, and I am coming to Thee. Holy Father, keep in Thy name those whom Thou hast given Me, that they may be one even as We are. While I was with them, I kept them in Thy name. Those whom Thou hast given Me I guarded; and not one of them perished except the son of perdition, in order that the Scripture might be fulfilled. But now I am coming to Thee; and these things I speak in the world, in order that they may have My joy made full in themselves. I have given them Thy word; and the world has hated them, because they are not of the world, even as I am not of the world. I do not pray that Thou take them out of the world, but that Thou keep them from evil. They are not of the world, even as I am not of the world.*

Sanctify them in the Truth. Thy word is Truth. Even as Thou hast sent Me into the world, so I also have sent them into the world. And for them I sanctify Myself, that they also may be sanctified in Truth. Yet not for these only do I pray, but for those also who through their word are to believe in Me, that all may be one, even as Thou, Father, in Me and I in Thee; that they also may be one in Us, that the world may believe that Thou hast sent Me. And the glory that Thou hast given Me, I have given to them, that they may be one, even as We are one: I in them and Thou in Me; that they may be perfected in unity, and that the world may know that Thou hast sent Me, and that Thou hast loved them even as Thou hast loved Me. Father, I will that where I am, they also whom Thou hast given Me may be with Me; in order that they may behold My glory, which Thou hast given Me, because Thou hast loved Me before the creation of the world. Just Father, the world has not known Thee, but I have know Thee, and these have known that Thou hast sent Me. And I have made known to them Thy name, and will make it known, in order that the love with which Thou hast loved Me may be in them, and I in them. John 17:1-26

127. THEN JESUS WENT with His Apostles to the Garden of Gethsemani at the foot of the Mount of Olives. He said to them, *Sit down here, while I go yonder and pray.* He took Peter, James and John with Him. He withdrew a short distance from them, and fell prostrate upon the ground and prayed, *Father, if it is possible, let this cup pass away from Me; yet not as I will, but as Thou willest.* He arose and came to the three Apostles and found them asleep. . . . Again a second time He went aside and prayed, *My Father, if this cup cannot pass away unless I drink it, Thy will be done.* Jesus came again to them and found them asleep. Leaving them He went back again and prayed a third time, saying the same words over again. Returning to His Apostles, He said, *Sleep on now, and take your rest! Behold, the hour is at hand when the Son of*

Man will be betrayed into the hands of sinners. Rise, let us go. Behold, he who betrays Me is at hand.[74,75] Matthew 26:36-46

128. AND WHILE HE WAS STILL SPEAKING, Judas Iscariot, one of the Twelve, now turned traitor, came and with him a great mob brought together by the unbelieving chief priests and the Scribes and elders. One of the Apostles (Peter) struck the servant of the high priest with a sword, cutting off his ear. But Jesus, even at this late hour, touched the ear and healed it, saying to Peter, *Put back thy sword into its place; for all those who take the sword will perish by the sword. Or dost thou suppose that I cannot entreat My Father, and He will even now furnish Me with more than twelve legions of angels? How then are the Scriptures to be fulfilled, that thus it must take place?*[76] Matthew 26:47-54

129. JUDAS DREW NEAR to Jesus to kiss Him. Jesus said, *Judas, dost thou betray the Son of Man with a kiss?* ... Then to the mob He said, *As against a robber you have come out with swords and clubs, to seize Me. I was daily with you in the Temple teaching, and you did not lay hands on Me. But it is so that the Scriptures may be fulfilled.*[77,78] Luke 22:47-53

130. THOSE WHO HAD TAKEN Jesus prisoner, now led Him away to the Sanhedrin where Caiphas the high priest, the Scribes and the elders had gathered together. .... Caiphas said to Him, "I adjure thee by the living God that thou tell us whether thou art the Christ, the Son of God." Jesus said to him, *Thou hast said it. Nevertheless, I say to you, hereafter you shall see the Son of Man sitting at the right hand of the Power* (of God) *and coming upon the clouds of Heaven.* Then Caiphas tore his garments, saying, "He has blasphemed; what further need have we of witnesses?" ... "He is liable to death."[79,80] Matthew 26:57-66

---

74. *Mark 14:32-42;* 75. *Luke 22:39-46;* 76. *John 18:1-11;* 77. *Matthew 26:55;* 78. *Mark 14:43-49;* 79. *Mark 14:60-62;* 80. *Luke 22:66-71*

131. THEN THE JEWS LED JESUS from the house of Caiphas to Pilate's praetorium. It was early morning. The Jews themselves did not enter, because if they did they would be defiled and unable to eat the passover. Therefore Pilate summoned Jesus inside and asked Him, "Art thou the king of the Jews?" Jesus asked, *Dost thou say this of thyself, or have others told thee of Me? . . . My Kingdom is not of this world. If My Kingdom were of this world, My followers would have fought that I might not be delivered to the Jews. But, as it is, My Kingdom is not from here.* Pilate therefore said to Him, "Thou art then a king?" Jesus answered, *Thou sayest it; I am a King. This is why I was born, and why I have come into the world, to bear witness to the Truth. Everyone who is of the Truth hears My voice.* Pilate said to Him, "What is truth?" John 18:28-38

132. PILATE QUESTIONED JESUS FURTHER but could find nothing unlawful upon which to convict Him to death. So he went out to the mob gathered in front of the praetorium and proclaimed, "I find no guilt in him. Do you wish, therefore, that I release to you the king of the Jews?" The Jews shouted, "Not this man!" Pilate then gave Jesus over to the torturers and they scourged Him. Then the soldiers made sport of Him by putting a crown of plaited thorns upon His head and a robe of purple over His shoulders. . . . Even after the scourging and the crowning of thorns, Pilate had misgivings, for he went again back into the praetorium, and asked Jesus, "Where art thou from?" Jesus made no answer. Pilate therefore said to Him, "Dost thou not speak to me? Dost thou not know that I have power to crucify thee, and that I have power to release thee?" Jesus answered, *Thou wouldst have no power at all over Me were it not given thee from Above. Therefore, he who betrayed Me to thee has the greater sin.* John 19:1-11

133. WHEN THE EXECUTIONERS CAME to the Place of the Skull, also called Golgotha, beyond the city wall, they crucified

Jesus with the two robbers, one on His right hand and the other on His left. In His torment, nailed to the infamous cross, the compassionate Son of God, implored, *Father, forgive them, for they do not know what they are doing.* Luke 24:33-34

134. ONE OF THOSE ROBBERS who were hanged was abusing Jesus, saying, "If thou art the Christ, save thyself and us!" But the other in answer rebuked him and said, "Dost not even thou fear God, seeing that thou art under the same sentence? And we indeed justly, for we are receiving what our deeds deserved; but this man has done nothing wrong." And he said to Jesus, "Lord, remember me when Thou comest into Thy Kingdom." And Jesus said to him, *Amen I say to thee, this day thou shalt be with Me in Paradise,* that is, the abode of the just souls under the old dispensation, who were waiting in limbo for the coming of the Messias to lead them to Heaven. Luke 23:39-43

135. THERE WAS DARKNESS over the whole land on that first Good Friday from the sixth hour (noon) until the ninth hour (three o'clock). But about the ninth hour Jesus cried out with a loud voice, *Eli, Eli, lema sabacthani,* that is, *My God, My God, why hast Thou forsaken Me?*[81] Matthew 27:45-46

136. THE CURTAIN of the Temple was torn in two from top to bottom. Jesus cried out, *Father, into Thy hands I commend My spirit.* And having said this, He expired. Then the earth quaked; the rocks were rent; the tombs were opened, and many bodies of the saints who had fallen asleep arose. . . . Now when the centurion, and those who were with him keeping guard over Jesus, saw the earthquake and the things that were happening, became very frightened, saying, "Truly He was the Son of God."[82,83] Luke 23:45-46

---

81. *Mark 15:33-34;* 82. *Matthew 27:51-54;* 83. *Mark 15:38-39*

137. As the first day of the week began to dawn, Mary
Magdalene, Mary the mother of James, and Salome, came
to the tomb. They found that an angel of the Lord had rolled
away the stone in front of the tomb, and was sitting upon it. He
said to the women, "Do not be afraid; for I know that you seek
Jesus, Who was crucified. He is not here, for He has risen even
as He said. Come, see the place where the Lord was laid. Go
quickly, tell His disciples that He has risen." And they
departed quickly from the tomb in fear and great joy, and ran
to tell the disciples. And behold Jesus met them, saying, *Do not
be afraid; go, take word to My brethren that they are to set out
for Galilee; there they shall see Me.*[84,85,86] Matthew 28:1-10

138. Saint John in his twentieth chapter renders his account
of the resurrection of Jesus. When Mary Magdalene came
early to the tomb and saw the stone had been rolled away from
its entrance, she became alarmed and rushed to tell the Apostles,
crying, "They have taken the Lord from the tomb, and we do
not know where they have laid Him." Hearing this, Simon Peter
and John ran to the tomb. When they saw that it was empty,
they believed what Mary Magdalene had told them. Then they
departed. But Mary was standing outside weeping at the tomb.
. . . When Mary turned around she saw a man standing there.
She did not know that it was Jesus. . . . Then He said to her,
Mary! She said to Him, "Rabboni!" (that is to say "Master!")
Jesus said to her, *Do not touch Me, for I have not yet ascended
to My Father, but go to My brethren and say to them, "I ascend
to My Father and your Father, to My God and your God."*
John 20:1-17

139. When it was late that same day, the first of the week,
though the doors where the disciples gathered had been
closed for fear of the Jews, Jesus came and stood in the midst

---

84. *Mark 16:1-8;* 85. *Luke 24:1-11;* 86. *John 20:12*

and said to them, *Peace be to you!* And when He had said this, He showed them His hands and His side. The disciples therefore rejoiced at the sight of Jesus. He said to them again, *Peace be to you! As the Father has sent Me, I also send you.* When He had said this, He breathed upon them, and said to them, *Receive the Holy Spirit; whose sins you shall forgive, they are forgiven them; and whose sins you shall retain, they are retained.*[87] John 20:19-23

140. TWO OF THE DISCIPLES were returning from Jerusalem that very day (the Resurrection) to a village named Emmaus. While in their perplexity they were discussing the crucifixion and pondering the news of the resurrection, Jesus Himself also drew near and went along with them. But their eyes were held, that they should not recognize Him. . . . Finally Jesus said to them, *O foolish ones and slow of heart to believe in all that the Prophets have spoken! Did not the Christ have to suffer these things before entering into His glory?* . . . Jesus went home with them. At the table He took bread and blessed and broke and began handing it to them. Suddenly their eyes were opened and they recognized Him. Then He vanished from their sight. . . . Rising up that very hour, they returned to Jerusalem. They found the Eleven gathered together and those who were with them said, "The Lord has risen indeed, and has appeared to Simon." Then they themselves began to relate what had happened on the journey, and how they recognized Him in the breaking of the bread. Luke 24:13-35

141. Now THOMAS, one of the Twelve, called the Twin, was not with them when Jesus came. The other disciples therefore said to him, "We have seen the Lord." But he said to them, "Unless I see in his hands the print of the nails, and put my finger into the place of the nails, and put my hand into his

87. *Luke 24:36-43*

side, I will not believe." After eight days, the disciples were again inside, and Thomas with them. Jesus came, the doors being closed, and stood in their midst, and said, *Peace be to you! He said to Thomas, *Bring here thy finger, and see My hands; and bring here thy hand, and put it into My side; and be not unbelieving, but believing.* Then Thomas said to Him, "My Lord and My God!" Jesus replied, *Because thou hast seen Me, thou hast believed. Blessed are they who have not seen, and yet have believed.* John 20:24-29

142. JESUS MANIFESTED HIMSELF again at the Sea of Galilee. Simon Peter, Thomas, Nathanael, James and his brother, John, and two other disciples had gone out to fish. It was night. When day was breaking, Jesus stood on the beach. It was John who recognized Him, exclaiming, "It is the Lord." How overwhelmed with joy they must have been to behold Him! When, therefore, they had landed, they saw a fire ready, and a fish upon it. And there was bread also. . . . Jesus said to them, *Come and breakfast.* Breakfast over, Jesus said to Simon Peter, *Simon, son of John, dost thou love Me more than these do?* He said to Him, "Yes, Lord, Thou knowest that I love thee." Jesus said to him, *Feed My lambs.* He said to him a second time, *Simon, son of John, dost thou love Me?* Simon Peter said to Him, "Yes, Lord, Thou knowest that I love Thee." Jesus said to him, *Feed My lambs.* A third time He said to him, *Simon, son of John, dost thou love Me?* Peter was grieved because Jesus said to him for the third time, *Dost thou love Me?* And he said to Him, "Lord, Thou knowest all things, Thou knowest that I love Thee." Then Jesus said to him, *Feed My sheep.* . . . And *follow Me.* What further proof do we need for the primacy of Saint Peter, or what further sign from God is needed for Christians to believe that on that day beside the northern shore of the Sea of Galilee, Jesus Christ made Simon Bar-Jona the first vicar of what is called today the Roman Catholic Church? John 21:1-19

143. Jesus Christ, the risen Lord, instructed His beloved Eleven further, saying, *These are the words which I spoke to you while I was yet with you, that all things must be fulfilled that are written in the Law of Moses and the Prophets and the Psalms concerning Me.* Then He opened their minds, that they might understand the Scriptures. And He said to them, *Thus it is written; and thus the Christ should suffer, and should rise again from the dead on the third day; and that repentance and remission of sins should be preached in His name to all nations, beginning from Jerusalem. And you yourselves are witnesses of these things. And I send forth upon you the promise of My Father. But wait here in the city* (Jerusalem), *until you are clothed with power from On High.* Luke 24:44-49

144. Jesus also commanded and said to His followers, *Go into the whole world and preach the Gospel* (of the Kingdom of God) *to every creature. He who believes and is baptized shall be saved, but he who does not believe shall be condemned. And these signs shall attend those who believe: in My name they shall cast out devils; they shall speak in new tongues; they shall take up serpents; and if they drink any deadly thing, it shall not hurt them; they shall lay hands upon the sick and they shall get well.* Mark 16:15-18

145. Saint Matthew closes his last chapter of the first Gospel with these words which the Son of God, Jesus Christ, uttered when He commissioned His chosen Apostles: *All power in Heaven and on earth has been given to Me. Go, therefore, and make disciples of all nations, baptizing them in the name of the Father, and of the Son, and of the Holy Spirit, teaching them to observe all that I have commanded you; and behold, I am with you all days, even unto the consummation of the world.* Matthew 28:16-20.

CHAPTER III

JESUS SAID
of the Son of Man

THE EXPRESSION, SON OF MAN, is found in Daniel.[88] Jesus used the expression Himself when He wanted to allude to Himself as the Messias not manifestly but in a veiled manner. "Jesus used it deliberately and gave it a new significance. It was singularly fitted both to draw attention to Himself, to bring out His human nature, and to insinuate the fulfillment of the prophecies concerning His Passion and Death."[89]

146. TO THE ALREADY ASTONISHED yet believing *true Israelite in whom there is no guile,* Nathanael, Jesus said of Himself, *Amen, amen, I say to you, you shall see Heaven opened, and the angels of God ascending and descending upon the Son of Man.* John 1:51

147. NICODEMUS, ALTHOUGH A PHARISEE, believed in Jesus. He wanted to learn more from Him about the Kingdom of God. So he came at night fearing that the Pharisees who hated

88. *Daniel 7:13-14;* 89. *Richard T. Murphy, O.P., Book Review of Henry B. Sharman, "Son of Man and Kingdom of God,"* Catholic Biblical Quarterly, *VIII (1943), 249*

Jesus might see him. He said to Jesus, "Rabbi, we know that Thou hast come a teacher from God, for no one can work these signs that Thou workest unless God be with Him." . . . Jesus said, *Amen, amen, I say to thee unless a man be born again, he cannot see the Kingdom of God.* Nicodemus was confused. . . . Jesus continued, *If I have spoken of earthly things to you, and you do not believe, how will you believe if I speak of Heavenly things? And no one has ascended into Heaven except Him Who has descended from Heaven: the Son of Man Who is in Heaven. And as Moses lifted up the serpent in the desert, even so must the Son of Man be lifted up, that those who believe in Him may not perish, but may have Everlasting Life. For God so loved the world that He gave His only-begotten Son, that those who believe in Him may not perish, but may have Life Everlasting. For God did not send His Son into the world in order to judge the world, but that the world might be saved through Him.* John 3:12-17

148. THE FOXES *have dens, and the birds of the air have nests; but the Son of Man has nowhere to lay His head.* Matthew 8:20

149. JESUS WAS IN THE REGION of the Sea of Galilee performing one miracle after the other. Then He returned by boat to Capharnaum. This was known as His own town although He had been raised in Nazareth. Four men brought to Him a paralytic lying on a pallet. Jesus, seeing their faith, said to the paralytic, *Take courage, son; thy sins are forgiven thee.* Now the Scribes and Pharisees sitting there began to argue, saying, "Why does this man speak thus? He blasphemes. Who can forgive sins, but only God?" Jesus knowing their thoughts, said to them, *Why do you harbor evil thoughts in your hearts? For which is easier, to say, "Thy sins are forgiven thee," or to say, "Arise, and walk?" But that you may know that the Son of Man has power on earth to forgive sins.* Then He said to the paralytic, *Arise,*

85

take up thy pallet and go to thy house. He arose and went away to his house.[90,91] Matthew 9:1-7

150. JESUS, EARLY IN HIS MINISTRY, foretold the opposition which His Apostles would encounter because they believed in Him. He said, *You will be hated by all for My name's sake. But he who has persevered to the end will be saved. When they persecute you in one town, flee to another. Amen I say to you, you will not have gone through the towns of Israel before the Son of Man comes.* Matthew 10:16-23

151. ONE SABBATH DAY in northern Galilee, Jesus and His disciples went through a field of ripened grain. The disciples being hungry, plucked ears of grain as they walked along, rubbed them with their hands and ate the grain. Some of the Pharisees said to them, "Why are you doing what is not lawful on the Sabbath?" Jesus answered for them, saying, *Have you not, then, read what David did when he and those with him were hungry? How he entered the House of God, and took, ate, and gave to those who were with him, the loaves of proposition, which no one may lawfully eat except the priests?* He concluded, *The Son of Man is Lord even of the Sabbath.*[92,93] Luke 6:1-5

152. JESUS SAID TO THOSE who were listening to Him when He gave His Sermon on the Mount, *Blessed shall you be when men hate you, and when they shut you out, and reproach you, and reject your name as evil, because of the Son of Man. Rejoice on that day and exult, for behold your reward is great in Heaven. For in the self-same manner their fathers used to treat the Prophets.* Luke 6:22-23

153. JESUS LIKENS THE MEN of His generation to stubborn *children sitting in the market place, calling to one another and saying, "We have piped to you and you have not danced;*

---

90. *Mark 2:1-12;* 91. *Luke 5:18-25;* 92. *Matthew 12:1-8;* 93. *Mark 2:23-28*

we have sung dirges, and you have not wept." For John the Baptist came neither eating bread nor drinking wine, and you say, "He has a devil." The Son of Man came eating and drinking, and you say, "Behold, a man who is a glutton, and a winedrinker, a friend of publicans and sinners!" And wisdom is justified by all her children.[94] Luke 7:31-35

154. THROUGHOUT HIS WHOLE MINISTRY, the Scribes and the Pharisees and the elders blasphemed Jesus. When He cast out devils, they said He did it by Beelzebub, the prince of the devils. To this, Jesus replied, *But if I cast out devils by the Spirit of God, then the Kingdom of God has come upon you. . . . Whoever speaks a word against the Son of Man, it shall be forgiven him; but whoever speaks against the Holy Spirit, it will not be forgiven him, either in this world or in the world to come.*[95,96] Matthew 12:27-32

155. DESPITE THE FACT that Jesus performed miracle after miracle, the Scribes and the Pharisees kept asking Him, "Master we would see a sign from thee." Jesus said, *An evil and adulterous generation demands a sign, and no sign shall be given it but the sign of Jonas the Prophet. For even as Jonas was in the belly of the fish three days and three nights, so will the Son of Man be three days and three nights in the heart of the earth.*[97] Matthew 12:38-40

156. JESUS SPOKE to the crowds in parables. After a parable on weeds, His disciples came to Him, saying, "Explain to us the parable of the weeds in the field." Answering them, He said, *He Who sows the good seed is the Son of Man. The field is the world; the good seed, the sons of the Kingdom; the weeds, the sons of the wicked one; and the enemy who sowed them is the devil. But the harvest is the end of the world, and the*

---

94. *Matthew 11:16-19;* 95. *Mark 3:28-29;* 96. *Luke 11:20;* 97. *Luke 11:29-30*

reapers are the angels. Therefore, just as the weeds are gathered up and burnt with fire, so will it be at the end of the world. The Son of Man will send forth His angels, and they will gather out of his Kingdom all scandals and those who work iniquity, and cast them into the furnace of fire, where there will be the weeping, and the gnashing of teeth. Then the just will shine forth like the sun in the Kingdom of their Father. He who has ears to hear, let him hear. Matthew 13:36-43

157. IN HIS CLAIM TO DIVINITY, Jesus Christ said to the unbelieving Jews, *Amen, amen, I say to you, the hour is coming, and now is here, when the dead shall hear the voice of the Son of God, and those who hear shall live. For as the Father has Life in Himself, even so He has given to the Son also to have Life in Himself; and He has granted Him power to render judgment, because He is Son of Man. Do not wonder at this, for the hour is coming in which all who are in the tombs shall hear the voice of the Son of God. And they who have done good shall come forth unto resurrection of Life; but they who have done evil unto ressurection of judgment. Of Myself I can do nothing. As I hear, I judge, and My judgment is just because I seek not My own will, but the will of Him Who sent Me.* John 5:25-30

158. AFTER JESUS HAD MIRACULOUSLY fed five thousand men with five loaves and two fish, He went apart to the mount near Capharnaum, Himself alone. But the crowds who were seeking Him, found Him. He said to them, *Amen, amen, I say to you, you seek Me, not because you have seen signs, but because you have eaten of the loaves, and have been filled. Do not labor for the food that perishes, but for that which endures unto Life Everlasting, which the Son of Man will give you. For upon Him the Father, God Himself, has set His seal.* John 6:26-27

159. WHEN JESUS TOLD THE PEOPLE that they should believe in Him because He had been sent by God, they said, "What sign, then, dost thou, that we may see and believe thee? Our fathers ate the manna in the desert, even as it is written, 'Bread from heaven He gave them to eat.'" Then Jesus said to them, *Amen, amen, I say to you, Moses did not give you the Bread from Heaven, but My father gives you the true Bread from Heaven. For the Bread of God is that which comes down from Heaven and gives Life to the world.* They said therefore to Him, "Lord, give us always this bread." Then Jesus said to them, *I am the Bread of Life. He who comes to Me shall not hunger, and he who believes in Me shall never thirst. But I have told you that you have seen Me and you do not believe. All that the Father gives to Me shall come to Me, and him who comes to Me I will not cast out. For I have come down from Heaven, not to do My own will, but the will of Him Who sent Me. Now this is the will of Him Who sent Me, the Father, that I should lose nothing of what He has given Me, but that I should raise it up on the last day. For this is the will of My Father Who sent Me, that whoever beholds the Son, and believes in Him, shall have Everlasting Life, and I will raise him up on the last day.* . . . The unbelieving Jews said, "How can he say that he has come down from heaven?" Jesus answered, *Do not murmur among yourselves. No one can come to Me unless the Father Who sent Me draw him, and I will raise him up on the last day. It is written in the Prophets, "And they all shall be taught of God."*[98] *Everyone who has listened to the Father, and has learned, comes to Me; not that anyone has seen the Father except Him Who is from God, He has seen the Father. Amen, amen, I say to you, he who believes in Me has Life Everlasting. I am the Bread of Life. Your fathers ate the manna in the desert, and have died. This is the Bread that comes down from Heaven, so that if anyone eat of it he will not die. I am the*

---

98. *Isaias 54:13; Jeremias 31:33*

Living Bread that has come down from Heaven. If anyone eat of this Bread he shall live forever; and the Bread that I will give is My flesh for the Life of the world. The Jews said, "How can this man give us his flesh to eat?" Jesus therefore said to them, *Amen, amen, I say to you, unless you eat the flesh of the Son of Man, and drink His blood, you shall not have Life in you. He who eats My flesh and drinks My blood has Life Everlasting and I will raise him up on the last day. For My flesh is food indeed, and My blood is drink indeed. He who eats My flesh, and drinks My blood, abides in Me and I in him. As the living Father has sent Me, and as I live because of the Father, so he who eats Me, he also shall live because of Me. This is the Bread that has come down from Heaven; not as your fathers ate the manna, and died. He who eats this Bread shall live forever.* These things He said when teaching in the synagogue at Capharnaum. . . . *Does this scandalize you? What then if you should see the Son of Man ascending where He was before?*[99] John 6:28-65

160. JESUS CAME INTO THE DISTRICT of Caesarea Philippi, which is some distance to the north of the Sea of Galilee. Jesus asked His disciples, *Who do men say the Son of Man is?* They replied, "Some say, John the Baptist; and others, Elias; and others, Jeremias, or one of the prophets." He asked them, *But Who do you say that I am?* Simon Peter responded, "Thou art the Christ, the Son of the living God." Jesus answered, *Blessed art thou, Simon Bar-Jona, for flesh and blood has not revealed this to thee, but My Father in Heaven. And I say to thee, thou art Peter, and upon this rock I will build My Church, and the gates of hell shall not prevail against it. And I will give thee the keys of the Kingdom of Heaven; and whatever thou shalt bind on earth shall be bound in Heaven, and whatever thou shalt loose on earth shall be loosed in Heaven.* Then He

99. *Matthew 16:1-4*

strictly charged His disciples to tell no one that He was Jesus Christ.[100,101] Matthew 16:13-20

161. FROM THAT TIME JESUS told His Apostles that He would suffer much from the Scribes and Pharisees and even be put to death. Then He said to them, *If anyone wishes to come after Me, let him deny himself, and take up his cross, and follow Me. For he who would save his life will lose it; but he who loses his life for My sake will find it. For what does it profit a man, if he gain the whole world, but suffer the loss of his own soul? Or what will a man give in exchange for his soul? For the Son of Man is to come with His angels in the glory of His Father, and then He will render to everyone according to his conduct. Amen I say to you, there are some of those standing here who will not taste death, till they have seen the Son of Man coming in His Kingdom.*[102,103] Matthew 16:24-28

162. JESUS RETURNED AGAIN to the environs of Nazareth. Passing through a vast fertile valley, the Plain of Esdraelon, He came to the foot of a high mountain, known to us as Mount Thabor. Leaving His disciples in the village at its foot, He took with Him Peter, James and John, and climbed to its summit. It was here that Jesus was transfigured: His face shone as the sun, and His garments became white as snow. Moses and Elias appeared and talked with Him. And as a bright cloud overshadowed them, a voice out of the cloud said, "This is My beloved Son, in Whom I am well pleased; hear Him." Coming down from the mountain, Jesus cautioned His Apostles, saying, *Tell the vision to no one, till the Son of Man has risen from the dead.* Matthew 17:1-9

163. PETER, JAMES AND JOHN pondered what the words *till the Son of Man has risen from the dead* might mean. And they asked Jesus, "Why then do the Pharisees and the Scribes say that Elias must come first?" He answered them, *Elias indeed is to come and will restore all things. But I say to you that Elias has come already, and they did not know him, but did to him whatever they wished. So also shall the Son of Man suffer at their hands.* Then they understood that He had spoken to them of John the Baptist.[104] Matthew 17:10-13

164. THEY WERE PASSING THROUGH GALILEE and Jesus did not want anyone to know it. For He was teaching His disciples, and saying to them, *The Son of Man is to be betrayed into the hands of men, and they will kill Him; and on the third day He will rise again.* But they did not understand this saying, and were afraid to ask Him.[105,106] Matthew 17:21-22

165. JESUS AND HIS APOSTLES entered a town in Samaria, and the townspeople would not receive them. When James and John saw this, they said, "Lord, wilt Thou that we bid fire come down from Heaven and consume them?" Jesus rebuked them, saying, *You do not know of what manner of spirit you are; for the Son of Man did not come to destroy men's lives, but to save them.* Luke 9:51-55

166. THE FOXES *have dens, and the birds of the air have nests, but the Son of Man has nowhere to lay His head.* Luke 9:58

167. JESUS CAME TO JERUSALEM and was teaching in the Temple. He said to the Jews, *I go, and you will seek Me, and in your sin you will die. Where I go you cannot come. . . . You are from below, I am from above. You are of this world, I am not of this world. Therefore I said to you that you will die in your sins; for if you do not believe that I am He, you will die in your sin. . . . Why do I speak to you at all! I have many things to speak and to judge concerning you; but He Who*

104. *Mark 9:9-12;* 105. *Mark 9:29-31;* 106. *Luke 9:44-45*

*sent Me is true, and the things that I heard from Him, these
I speak in the world.* And they did not understand that He was
speaking to them about the Father. Jesus therefore said to them,
*When you have lifted up the Son of Man, then you will know
that I am He* (the Messias) *and that of Myself I do nothing:
but that I preach only what the Father has taught Me. And He
Who sent Me is with Me; He has not left Me alone, because I
do always the things that are pleasing to Him.* John 8:21-29

168. THIS GENERATION *is an evil generation: it demands a sign,
and no sign shall be given it but the sign of Jonas. For even
as Jonas was a sign to the Ninevites, so will also the Son of Man
be to this generation. The queen of the South will rise up in
the judgment with the men of this generation and will condemn
them; for she came from the ends of the earth to hear the
wisdom of Solomon, and behold, a greater than Solomon is here.
The men of Nineve will rise up in the judgment with this
generation and will condemn it; for they repented at the
preaching of Jonas, and behold a greater than Jonas is here.*
Luke 11:29-32

169. AND I SAY TO YOU, *everyone who acknowledges Me before
men, him will the Son of Man also acknowledge before the
angels of God. But whoever disowns Me before men will be
disowned before the angels of God. And everyone who speaks
against the Son of Man, it shall be forgiven him; but to him who
blasphemes against the Holy Spirit, it will not be forgiven.* Luke
12:8-10

170. JESUS CAUTIONS HIS FOLLOWERS to be like watchful servants, who, having everything in readiness, await their
master's return: *Let your loins be girt about and your lamps
burning, and you yourselves like men waiting for their master's
return from the wedding; so that when he comes and knocks,
they may straightway open to him. You also must be ready,*

because at an hour that you do not expect, the Son of Man is coming. Luke 12:40

171. THE DAYS WILL COME *when you will long to see one day of the Son of Man, and will not see it. And they will say to you, "Behold, here he is; behold, there he is." Do not go or follow after them. For as the lightning when it flashes from one end of the sky to the other, so will the Son of Man be in His day. But first He must suffer many things and be rejected by this generation. And as it came to pass in the days of Noe, even so will it be in the days of the Son of Man. They were eating and drinking, they were marrying and giving in marriage, until the day when Noe entered the ark, and the flood came and destroyed them all. Or as it came to pass in the days of Lot: they were eating and drinking, they were buying and selling, they were planting and building; but on the day that Lot went out from Sodom, it rained fire and brimstone from Heaven and destroyed them all. In the same wise will it be on the day that the Son of Man is revealed.*[107] Luke 17:22-30

172. AMEN, I SAY TO YOU *who have followed me, in the regeneration when the Son of Man shall sit on the Throne of His glory, shall also sit on twelve thrones, judging the twelve tribes of Israel.* Matthew 19:28

173. ALTHOUGH JESUS COUNSELED His Apostles that they must always pray and not lose heart, He said, *Yet when the Son of Man comes, will He find, do you think, faith on the earth?* Luke 18:8

174. JESUS AND HIS DISCIPLES were on their way to Jerusalem. Jesus was walking on in front. The Apostles were in dismay and afraid because now Jesus told them for the third

---

107. *Matthew 24:36-38*

time of His Passion, saying, *Behold, we are going up to Jerusalem, and all things that have been written by the Prophets concerning the Son of Man will be accomplished. For He will be delivered to the Gentiles, and will be mocked and scourged and spit upon; and after they have scourged Him, they will put Him to death; and on the third day He will rise again.* The disciples understood none of these things and this saying was hidden from them, neither did they get to know the things that were being said.[108,109] Luke 18:31-34

175. THE MOTHER OF JAMES AND JOHN asked Jesus to place her two sons one at His right hand and the other at His left in His Kingdom. When the ten Apostles heard of this, they became very indignant. Jesus said to them, *Whoever wishes to become great among you shall be your servant; and whoever wishes to be first among you shall be your slave; even as the Son of Man has not come to be served but to serve, and to give His life as a ransom for many.*[110] Mark 10:35-45

176. JESUS WAS PASSING THROUGH JERICHO. Here lived a man named Zacchaeus who was a leading publican and very rich. He wanted to get a look at Jesus but could not, on account of the crowd in front of him, because he was small of stature. So he ran on ahead and climbed into a sycamore tree. When Jesus came to the place, He looked up at him and said, *Zacchaeus, make haste and come down; for I must stay in thy house today.* The little man slid down, rushed home, and welcomed Jesus with great joy. Then he said to Him, "Lord, I give one-half of my possessions to the poor, and if I have defrauded anyone of anything, I restore it four-fold." Jesus said to Zacchaeus, *Today salvation has come to this house, since he, too, is a son of Abraham. For the Son of Man came to seek and to save what was lost.* Luke 19:1-10

---

108. *Matthew 20:17-19;* 109. *Mark 10:32-34;* 110. *Matthew 20:20-28*

177. THE PHARISEES WERE BENT on asking Jesus tricky questions. Then Jesus asked them one, *What do you think of the Christ? Whose Son is He?* They said to Him, "David's." He said to them, *How then does David in the Spirit call Him Lord, saying, "The Lord said to my Lord: Sit Thou at My right hand, till I make Thy enemies Thy footstool?" If David, therefore, calls Him "Lord," how is He his son?* And no one could answer Him a word; neither did anyone dare from that day forth ask Him any more questions. [111,112] Matthew 22:41-46

178. JESUS FORETOLD SIGNS of the last day, saying, *For as the lightning comes forth from the east and shines even to the west, so also will the coming of the Son of Man be. Wherever the body is, there will the eagles be gathered together. But immediately after the tribulation of those days, the sun will be darkened, and the moon will not give her light, and the stars will fall from Heaven, and the powers of Heaven will be shaken. And then will appear the sign of the Son of Man in Heaven; and then will all the tribes of the earth mourn, and they will see the Son of Man coming upon the clouds of Heaven with great power and majesty. And He will send forth His angels with a trumpet and a great sound, and they will gather His elect from the four winds, from one end of the heavens to the other.*[113,114] Matthew 24:27-31

179. WATCH THEREFORE, *for you do not know at what hour your Lord is to come. But of this be assured, that if the householder had know at what hour the thief was coming, he would certainly have watched, and not have let his house be broken into. Therefore you also must be ready, because at an hour that you do not expect, the Son of Man will come.* Matthew 24:42-44

---

111. *Mark 12:35-37;* 112. *Luke 20:41-44;* 113. *Mark 13:26;* 114. *Luke 21:25-27*

180. BUT WHEN THE SON OF MAN *shall come in His majesty, and all the angels with Him, then He will sit on the Throne of His glory; and before Him will be gathered all the nations, and He will separate them one from another, as the shepherd separates the sheep from the goats; and He will set the sheep on His right hand, but the goats on the left. Then the King will say to those on His right hand, "Come blessed of My Father, take possession of the Kingdom prepared for you from the foundation of the world."* Matthew 25:31-34

181. JESUS WAS SITTING on the Mount of Olives, opposite the Temple. Peter, James, John and Andrew asked Him, "Tell us, when are these things to happen?" Of the last judgment, Jesus said, *But of that day or hour no one knows, neither the angels, nor the Son, but the Father only.*[115] Mark 13:32

182. THE FEAST OF THE PASSOVER was drawing near. That great feast commemorating the time when God sent the final plague upon Egypt after which the Jews were released from captivity. That time when God spoke to Moses telling him to instruct the Jews to take a lamb without blemish, a male of one year, and sacrifice it; to put its blood on both side posts and upper door posts of the houses where the Jews were to eat the pascal lamb. Then when the angel of the Lord came to strike the Egyptians with the plague, he would pass over the Jewish houses on which he saw the sign of the blood. This day was to be a memorial and kept as a feast to the Lord in all generations with everlasting observance.[116] At this time Jesus went up to Jerusalem and taught daily in the Temple to the masses gathered there. To His Apostles, He said, *You know that after two days the Passover will be here; and the Son of Man will be delivered up to be crucified.* Matthew 26:2

183. IN HIS WARNING of Jerusalem's impending destruction and the ultimate end of the world, Jesus impressed upon His

---

115. *Matthew 24:36;* 116. *Exodus XII, 1-14*

disciples the need of watchfulness, saying, *But take heed to your-selves, lest your hearts be overburdened with self-indulgence and drunkenness and the cares of this life, and that day come upon you suddenly as a snare. For come it will upon all who dwell on the face of all the earth. Watch, then, praying at all times that you may be accounted worthy to escape all these things that are to be, and to stand before the Son of Man.* Luke 21: 34-36

184. *The hour has come for the Son of Man to be glorified*
Amen, amen, I say to you, unless the grain of wheat falls into the ground and dies, it remains alone. But if it dies, it brings forth much fruit. John 12:23-25

185. JESUS SAID TO THE PEOPLE, *If I be lifted up from the earth,*
I will draw all things to Myself. Now He said this signi-fying by what death He was to die. The crowd answered Him "We have heard from the Law that the Christ abides forever And how canst thou say, 'The Son of Man must be lifted up'? Who is this Son of Man"? Jesus therefore said to them, *Yet a little while the Light is among you. Walk while you have the Light, that darkness may not overtake you. He who walks in the darkness does not know where he goes. While you have the Light, believe in the Light, that you may become sons of Light* These things Jesus spoke, and He went away and hid Himself from them. John 12:31-36.

186. Now AT EVENTIDE on the day of the Unleavened Bread
when the Passover had to be sacrificed and eaten, Jesus was at table with the Twelve in the Upper Room of one of His disciples. Jesus said to them, *The Son of Man indeed goes His way, as it is written of Him; but woe to that man by whom the Son of Man is betrayed: It were better for that man if he had not been born.*[117,118] Matthew 26:24

---

117. *Mark 14:21;* 118. *Luke 22:22*

187. JESUS KNOWING that one of His chosen Apostles was ready to betray Him, became troubled in spirit, and as He sat there at the supper table, He said solemnly, *Amen, amen, I say to you, one of you will betray Me.* The Apostles therefore looked at one another, uncertain of whom He was speaking. John, who was sitting next to Jesus, said to Him, "Lord, who is it?" Jesus answered, *It is he for whom I shall dip the bread, and give it to him.* Jesus gave it to Judas Iscariot, the son of Simon, saying to him, *What thou dost, do quickly.* When he had gone out, Jesus said, *Now is the Son of Man glorified, and God is glorified in Him. If God is glorified in Him, God will also glorify Him in Himself, and will glorify Him at once.* John 13:21-32

188. AND WHILE THEY WERE EATING, Jesus said, *I have greatly desired to eat of this passover with you before I suffer; for I say to you that I will eat of it no more, until it has been fulfilled in the Kingdom of God.* Then Jesus took bread, and blessed and broke, and gave it to His disciples, saying, *Take and eat; this is My body.* And taking a cup, He gave thanks and gave it to them, saying, *All of you drink of this; for this is My blood of the New Covenant, which is being shed for many unto the forgiveness of sins.*[119,120] Matthew 26:26-29

189. AFTER RECITING A HYMN, Jesus and His Apostles went out of the Upper Room on Mount Sion to the Mount of Olives. Then Jesus said, *You will all be scandalized this night because of Me; for it is written, "I will smite the shepherd, and the sheep of the flock will be scattered." But after I have risen, I will go before you into Galilee.*[121] Matthew 26:30-32

190. SIMON PETER SAID TO JESUS, "Lord, where art Thou going?" Jesus answered, *Where I am going thou canst not follow Me now but thou shalt follow later.* Peter said to Him, "Why can I not follow Thee now? I will lay down my life for

---

119. *Mark 14:22-25;* 120. *Luke 22:14-20;* 121. *Mark 14:26-31*

Thee." Jesus answered him, *Wilt thou lay down thy life for Me?*
Amen, amen, I say to thee, the cock will not crow before thou
dost deny Me thrice.[122,123,124] John 13:36-38

191. AFTER JESUS HAD PREDICTED that Peter would deny Him
three times, He spoke words of comfort to the saddened
Apostles: *Let not your heart be troubled. You believe in God,*
believe also in Me. In My Father's House there are many
mansions. Were it not so, I should have told you, because I go
to prepare a place for you. And if I go and prepare a place for
you, I am coming again, and I will take you to Myself; that
where I am, there you also may be. And where I go you know,
and the way you know. Thomas said to Him, "Lord, we do not
know where Thou art going, and how can we know the way?"
Jesus said to Him, *I am the Way and the Truth, and the Life.*
No one comes to the Father but through Me. If you had known
Me, you would also have known My Father. And henceforth
you do know Him, and you have seen Him. Philip said to Him,
"Lord, show us the Father and it is enough for us." Jesus said
to him, *Have I been so long a time with you, and you have not*
known Me. Philip, he who sees Me sees also the Father. How
canst thou say, "Show us the Father"? Dost thou not believe
that I am in the Father and the Father in Me? The words that
I speak to you I speak not on My own authority. But the Father
dwelling in Me, it is He Who does the works. Do you believe
that I am in the Father and the Father in Me? Otherwise
believe because of the works themselves. Amen, amen, I say
to you, he who believes in Me, the works that I do he also shall
do, and greater than these he shall do, because I am going to
the Father. And whatever you ask in My name, that I will do,
in order that the Father may be glorified in the Son. If you ask
Me anything in My name, I will do it. If you love Me, keep My
commandments. And I will ask the Father and He will give
you another Advocate to dwell with you forever, the Spirit of

122. *Matthew 26:34;* 123. *Mark 14:30;* 124. *Luke 22:34*

ruth Whom the world cannot receive, because it neither sees Him nor knows Him. But you shall know Him, because He will dwell with you, and be in you. I will not leave you orphans; I will come to you. Yet a little while and the world no longer sees Me. But you see Me, for I live and you shall live. In that day you will know that I am in My Father, and you in Me, and I in you. He who has My commandments and keeps them, he it is who loves Me. But he who loves Me will be loved by My Father, and I will love him and manifest Myself to him. Judas, not the Iscariot, said to Him, "Lord, how is it that Thou art about to manifest Thyself to us, and not to the world?" Jesus answered and said to him, *If anyone love Me, he will keep My word, and My Father will love him, and We will come to him and make Our abode with him. He who does not love Me does not keep My words. And the word that you have heard is not Mine, but the Father's Who sent Me. These things I have spoken to you while yet dwelling with you. But the Advocate, the Holy Spirit, Whom the Father will send in My name, He will teach you all things, and bring to your mind whatever I have said to you. Peace I leave with you, My peace I give to you; not as the world gives do I give to you. Do not let your heart be troubled, or be afraid. You have heard Me say to you, "I go away and I am coming to you." If you loved Me, you would indeed rejoice that I am going to the Father, for the Father is greater than I. And now I have told you before it comes to pass, that when it has come to pass you may believe. I will no longer speak much with you, for the prince of the world is coming, and in Me he has nothing. But he comes that the world may know that I love the Father, and that I do as the Father has commanded Me. Arise, let us go from here.* John 14:1-31

2. HAVING SAID, *Arise, let us go from here,* Jesus and the Eleven must have gone from the Upper Room toward the Garden of Gethsemani at the foot of the Mount of Olives.

According to the fifteenth chapter of Saint John, Jesus continued His discourse, saying, *I am the true Vine, and My Fathe*
is the Vine-dresser. Every branch in Me that bears no fruit H
will take away; and every branch that bears fruit He will cleans
that it may bear more fruit. You are already clean because o
the word that I have spoken to you. Abide in Me, and I in yot
As the branch cannot bear fruit of itself unless it remain on th
vine, so neither can you unless you abide in Me. I am the Vine
you are the branches. He who abides in Me, and I in him, h
bears much fruit; for without Me you can do nothing. If anyon
does not abide in Me, he shall be cast outside as the branch an
wither; and they shall gather them up and cast them into th
fire, and they shall burn. If you abide in Me, and if My word
abide in you, ask whatever you will and it shall be done to yot
In this is My Father glorified, that you may bear very muc
fruit, and become My disciples. As the Father has loved M
I also have loved you. Abide in My love. If you keep M
commandments you will abide in My love, as I also have kef
My Father's commandments, and abide in His love.   The.
things I have spoken to you that My joy may be in you, and the
your joy may be made full. This is My commandment, that yc
love one another as I have loved you. Greater love than this r
one has, that one lay down his life for his friends. You are M
friends if you do the things I command you. No longer do I cc
you servants, because the servant does not know what his mast
does. But I have called you friends, because all things that
have heard from My Father I have made known to you. Yc
have not chosen Me, but I have chosen you, and have appointe
you that you should go and bear fruit, and that your fruit shou
remain; that whatever you ask the Father in My name He me
give you. These things I command you, that you may love ot
another. John 15:1-17

193. THEN JESUS PREDICTED the world's hatred and persecuti
of the disciples because they believed in Him. *If the wor*

hates you, know that it has hated Me before you. If you were of the world, the world would love what is its own. But because you are not of the world, but I have chosen you out of the world, therefore the world hates you. Remember the word that I have spoken to you: No servant is greater than his master. If they have persecuted Me, they will persecute you also; if they have kept My word, they will keep yours also. But all these things they will do to you for My name's sake, because they do not know Him Who sent Me. If I had not come and spoken to them, they would have no sin. But now they have no excuse for their sin. He who hates Me hates My Father also. If I had not done among them works such as no one else has done, they would have no sin. But now they have seen, and have hated both Me and My Father; but that the word written in their Law may be fulfilled, "They have hated Me without cause."[125] But when the Advocate has come, Whom I will send you from the Father, the Spirit of Truth Who proceeds from the Father, He will bear witness concerning Me. And you also bear witness, because from the beginning you are with Me. John 15:18-27

194. JESUS CONTINUES HIS PREDICTION. *These things I have spoken to you that you may not be scandalized. They will expel you from the synagogues. Yes, the hour is coming for everyone who kills you to think that he is offering worship to God. And these things they will do because they have not known the Father nor Me. But these things I have spoken to you, that when the time has come you may remember that I told you. These things, however, I did not tell you from the beginning, because I was with you.* John 16:1-4

195. JESUS THEN EXPLAINS THE ROLE of the Advocate, the Holy Spirit, Who will come to the disciples when He has gone to the Father. *And now I am going to Him Who sent Me, and no one of you asks Me, "Where art Thou going?" But because*

25. *Psalms 34:19; 68:5*

I have spoken to you these things, sorrow has filled your heart. But I speak the truth to you; it is expedient for you that I depart. For if I do not go, the Advocate will not come to you; but if I go, I will send Him to you. And when He has come He will convict the world of sin, and of justice, and of judgment: of sin, because they do not believe in Me; of justice, because I go to the Father, and you will see Me no more; and of judgment, because the prince of this world has already been judged. Many things yet I have to say to you, but you cannot bear them now. But when He, the Spirit of Truth, has come, He will teach you all the Truth. For He will not speak on His own authority, but whatever He will hear He will speak, and the things that are to come He will declare to you. He will glorify Me, because He will receive of what is Mine and declare it to you. All things that the Father has are Mine. That is why I have said that He will receive of what is Mine, and will declare it to you. A little while and you shall see Me no longer; and again a little while and you shall see Me, because I go to the Father. John 16:5-16

196. The disciples were perplexed when Jesus said, *A little while and you shall not see Me, and again a little while and you shall see Me;* and, *I go to the Father.* They kept saying therefore, "What is this 'little while' of which He speaks? We do not know what He is saying." Jesus knew that they wanted to ask Him, so He said to them, *You inquire about this among yourselves because I said, "A little while and you shall not see Me, and again a little while and you shall see Me." Amen, amen, I say to you, that you shall weep and lament, but the world shall rejoice; and you shall be sorrowful, but your sorrow shall be turned into joy. A woman about to give birth has sorrow, because her hour has come. But when she has brought forth the child, she no longer remembers the anguish for her joy that a man is born into the world. And you therefore have sorrow now, but I will see you again, and your heart shall rejoice, and your joy no one shall take from you. And in that day you shall ask*

Me nothing. Amen, amen, I say to you, if you ask the Father anything in My name, He will give it to you. Hitherto you have not asked anything in My name. Ask, and you shall receive, that your joy may be full. These things I have spoken to you in parables. The hour is coming when I will no longer speak to you in parables, but will speak to you plainly of the Father. In that day you shall ask in My name; and I do not say to you that I will ask the Father for you, for the Father Himself loves you because you have loved Me, and have believed that I came forth from God. I came forth from the Father and have come into the world. Again I leave the world and go to the Father. His disciples said to Him, "Behold, now Thou speakest plainly, and utterest no parable. Now we know that Thou knowest all things, and dost not need that anyone should question Thee. For this reason we believe that Thou camest forth from God." Jesus answered them, *Do you now believe? Behold, the hour is coming, and has already come, for you to be scattered, each one to his own house, and to leave Me alone. But I am not alone, because the Father is with Me. These things I have spoken to you that in Me you may have peace. In the world you will have affliction. But take courge, I have overcome the world.* John 16:17-33

197. IN THE SEVENTEENTH CHAPTER of Saint John, Jesus no longer speaks directly to the Eleven, but raising His eyes to Heaven, implores and prays to God, the Father. *Father, the hour has come! Glorify Thy Son, that Thy Son may glorify Thee, even as Thou hast given Him power over all flesh, in order that to all Thou hast given Him He may give Everlasting Life. Now this is Everlasting Life, that they may know Thee, the only true God, and Him Whom Thou hast sent, Jesus Christ. I have glorified Thee on earth; I have accomplished the work that Thou hast given Me to do. And now do Thou, Father, glorify Me with Thyself, with the glory that I had with Thee before the world existed. I have manifested Thy name to the men* *whom Thou hast given Me out of the world. They were Thine, and Thou hast given them to Me, and they have kept Thy word. Now they have learnt that whatever Thou hast given Me is from Thee; because the words that Thou hast given Me I have given to them. And they have received them, and have known of a truth that I came forth from Thee, and they have believed that Thou didst send Me. I pray for them; not for the world do I pray, but for those whom Thou hast given Me, because they are Thine; and all things that are Mine are Thine, and Thine are Mine; and I am glorified in them. And I am no longer in the world, but these are in the world, and I am coming to Thee. Holy Father, keep in Thy name those whom Thou hast given Me, that they may be one even as We are. While I was with them, I kept them in Thy name. Those whom Thou hast given Me I guarded; and not one of them perished except the son of perdition, in order that the Scripture might be fulfilled. But now I am coming to Thee; and these things I speak in the world, in order that they may have My joy made full in themselves. I have given them Thy word; and the world has hated them, because they are not of the world, even as I am not of the world. I do not pray that Thou take them out of the world, but that Thou keep them from evil. They are not of the world, even as I am not of the world. Sanctify them in the Truth. Thy word is Truth. Even as Thou hast sent Me into the world, so I also have sent them into the world. And for them I sanctify Myself, that they also may be sanctified in truth. Yet not for these only do I pray, but for those also who through their word are to believe in Me, that all may be one, even as Thou, father, in Me and I in Thee; that they also may be one in Us, that the world may believe that Thou hast sent Me. And the glory that Thou hast given Me, I have given to them, that they may be one, even as We are one: I in them and Thou in Me; that they may be perfected in unity, and that the world may know that Thou hast sent Me, and that Thou hast loved them even as Thou hast loved Me. Father, I will that where I am, they also whom Thou hast given Me may be with Me; in order that they may behold My glory, which Thou hast given Me, because Thou hast loved Me before the creation of the world. Just Father, the world has not known Thee, but I have known Thee, and these have known that Thou hast sent Me. And I have made known to them Thy name, and will make it known, in order that the love with which Thou hast loved Me may be in them, and I in them.* John 17:1-26

198. THEN JESUS WENT WITH HIS APOSTLES to the Garden of Gethsemani at the foot of the Mount of Olives. He said to them, *Sit down here, while I go yonder and pray.* But He took Peter and James and John with Him. Withdrawing a short distance from them, He fell prostrate upon the ground and prayed, *Father, if it is possible, let this cup pass away from Me; yet not as I will, but as Thou willest.* He arose and came to the three Apostles and found them asleep. . . . Again a second time He went aside and prayed, *My Father, if this cup cannot pass away unless I drink it, Thy will be done.* Jesus came again to the three and found them asleep. Leaving them He went back and prayed a third time, saying the same words over again. Returning to them, He said, *Sleep on now, and take your rest! Behold, the hour is at hand when the Son of Man will be betrayed into the hands of sinners. Rise, let us go. Behold, he who betrays Me is at hand.*[126,127] Matthew 26:36-46

199. AND WHILE HE WAS STILL SPEAKING, Judas Iscariot, one of the Twelve, now turned traitor, came and with him a great mob brought together by the unbelieving chief priests and the Scribes and elders. One of the Apostles (Peter) struck the servant of the high priest with a sword, cutting off his ear. But Jesus, even at this late hour, performed a miracle by touching the ear and healing it. To Peter He said, *Put back thy sword*

126. *Mark 14:32-42;* 127. *Luke 22:39-46*

into its place; for all those who take the sword will perish by the sword. Or dost thou suppose that I cannot entreat My Father, and He will even now furnish Me with more than twelve legions of angels? How then are the Scriptures to be fulfilled, that thus it must take place?[128] Matthew 26:47-54

200. JUDAS DREW NEAR TO JESUS to kiss Him. Jesus said, *Judas, dost thou betray the Son of Man with a kiss? . . .* Then to the mob He said, *As against a robber you have come out with swords and clubs, to seize Me. I was daily with you in the Temple teaching, and you did not lay hands on Me. But it is so that the Scriptures may be fulfilled.*[129,130] Luke 22:47-53

201. THOSE WHO HAD TAKEN JESUS PRISONER, now led Him away to the Sanhedrin where Caiphas the high priest, the Scribes and the elders had gathered together. . . . Caiphas said to Him, "I adjure thee by the living God that thou tell us whether thou art the Christ, the Son of God." Jesus said to him, *Thou hast said it. Nevertheless, I say to you, hereafter you shall see the Son of Man sitting at the right hand of the Power* (of God) *and coming upon the clouds of Heaven.* Then Caiphas tore his garments, saying, "He has blasphemed; what further need have we of witnesses?" . . . "He is liable to death."[131,132] Matthew 26:57-66

202. THEN THE JEWS LED JESUS from the house of Caiphas to Pontius Pilate's praetorium. It was early morning. The Jews themselves did not enter, because if they did they would be defiled and unable to eat the passover. Therefore Pilate summoned Jesus inside and asked Him, "Art thou the king of the Jews?" Jesus asked, *Dost thou say this of thyself, or have others told thee of Me? . . . My kingdom is not of this world. If My kingdom were of this world, My followers would have*

---

128. *John 18:1-11;* 129. *Matthew 26:55;* 130. *Mark 14:43-49;* 131. *Mark 14:60-62;* 132. *Luke 22:66-71*

fought that I might not be delivered to the Jews. But, as it is, My Kingdom is not from here. Pilate therefore said to Him, "Thou art then a king?" Jesus answered, *Thou sayest it; I am a King. This is why I was born, and why I have come into the world, to bear witness to the Truth. Everyone who is of the Truth hears My voice.* Pilate asked Him, "What is truth?" John 18:28-38

203. PILATE QUESTIONED JESUS FURTHER but could find nothing unlawful upon which to convict Him to death. So he went out to the mob gathered in front of the praetorium and proclaimed, "I find no guilt in him. Do you wish, therefore, that I release to you the king of the Jews?" The Jews shouted, "Not this man!" Pilate then gave Jesus over to the torturers who scourged Him. Then the soldiers made sport of Him by putting a crown of plaited thorns upon His head and a robe of purple over His shoulders. . . . Even after the scourging and the crowning of thorns, Pilate had misgivings, for he went again back into the praetorium, and asked Jesus, "Where art thou from?" Jesus made no answer. Pilate therefore said to Him, "Dost thou not speak to me? Dost thou not know that I have power to crucify thee, and that I have power to release thee?" Jesus answered, *Thou wouldst have no power at all over Me were it not given thee from above. Therefore, he who betrayed Me to thee has the greater sin.* John 19:1-11

204. AND THEY LED JESUS through the city and beyond its wall. When the executioners came to the Place of the Skull, called Golgotha, they crucified Jesus with the two robbers, one on His right hand and the other on His left. In His torment, nailed to the infamous cross, the compassionate Son of God made Man, implored, *Father, forgive them, for they do not know what they are doing.* Luke 23:33-34

205. ONE OF THOSE ROBBERS who were hanged was abusing Jesus, saying, "If thou art Christ, save thyself and us!" But the other in answer rebuked him and said, "Dost not even thou fear God, seeing that thou art under the same sentence? And we indeed justly, for we are receiving what our deeds deserved; but this man has done nothing wrong." And he said to Jesus, "Lord, remember me when Thou comest into Thy kingdom." And Jesus said to him, *Amen I say to thee, this day thou shalt be with Me in Paradise,* (that is, the abode of the just souls under the old dispensation, who were waiting in limbo for the coming of the Messias to lead them to Heaven.) Luke 23:39-43

206. THERE WAS DARKNESS over the whole land on that first Good Friday from the sixth hour (noon) until the ninth hour (three o'clock in the afternoon). But about the ninth hour Jesus cried out with a loud voice, *Eli, Eli, lema sabacthani,* that is, *My God, My God, why hast Thou forsaken Me?*[133] Matthew 27:45-46

207. AND THE CURTAIN OF THE TEMPLE was torn in two from top to bottom. Jesus cried out with a loud voice, *Father, into Thy hands I commend My spirit.* And having said this, He expired. Then the earth quaked; the rocks were rent; the tombs were opened, and many bodies of the saints who had fallen asleep arose. . . . Now when the centurion, and those who were with him keeping guard over Jesus, saw the earthquake and the things that were happening, they were very much afraid, and he said, "Truly this man was the Son of God."[134,135] Luke 23:45-46

208. AS THE FIRST DAY OF THE WEEK began to dawn, Mary Magdalene, Mary the mother of James, and Salome, came to the tomb. They found that an angel of the Lord had rolled away the stone in front of the tomb, and was sitting upon it. He said to the women, "Do not be afraid; for I know that you seek

133. *Mark 15:33-34;* 134. *Matthew 27:51-54;* 135. *Mark 15:38-39*

Jesus, Who was crucified. He is not here, for He has risen even as He said. Come, see the place where the Lord was laid. Go quickly, tell His disciples that He has risen." And they departed quickly from the tomb in fear and great joy, and ran to tell the disciples. Behold, Jesus met them, saying, *Do not be afraid; go, take word to My brethren that they are to set out for Galilee; there they shall see Me.*[136,137,138] Matthew 28:1-10

209. Saint John in his twentieth chapter renders his account of the resurrection of Jesus. When Mary Magdalene came early to the tomb and saw the stone had been rolled away from its entrance, she became alarmed and rushed to tell the Apostles, crying, "They have taken the Lord from the tomb, and we do not know where they have laid Him." Hearing this, Simon Peter and John ran to the tomb. When they saw that it was empty, they believed what Mary Magdalene had told them. Then they departed. But Mary was standing outside weeping at the tomb. . . . Then turning around she beheld Jesus standing there. She did not know that it was Jesus. . . . Then He said to her, *Mary!* Recognizing Him, she said, "Rabboni!" (that is to say, "Master!") Jesus said to her, *Do not touch Me, for I have not yet ascended to My Father, but go to My brethren and say to them, "I ascend to My Father and your Father, to My God and your God."* John 20:1-17

210. When it was late that same day, the first of the week, though the doors where the disciples gathered had been closed for fear of the Jews, Jesus came and stood in their midst and said to them, *Peace be to you!* And when He had said this, He showed them His hands and His side. The disciples therefore rejoiced at the sight of the Lord. He said to them again, *Peace be to you! As the Father has sent Me, I also send you.* When He had said this, He breathed upon them, and said to them, *Receive the Holy Spirit; whose sins you shall forgive, they*

136. *Mark 16:1-8;* 137. *Luke 24:1-11;* 138. *John 20:12*

are forgiven them; and whose sins you shall retain, they are re-tained.[139] John 20:19-23

211. Two of the disciples were returning from Jerusalem on the day of resurrection of Jesus to a village, about seven miles from it, named Emmaus. While in their perplexity they were discussing the crucifixion and pondering the news of the resurrection, Jesus Himself also drew near and went along with them. But their eyes were held, that they should not recognize Him. . . . Finally Jesus said to them, *O foolish ones and slow of heart to believe in all that the Prophets have spoken! Did not the Christ have to suffer these things before entering into His glory?* . . . Jesus went home with them. At the table He took bread and blessed and broke and began handing it to them. Suddenly their eyes were opened and they recognized Him. Then He vanished from their sight. . . . Rising up that very hour, they returned to Jerusalem, where they found the Eleven gathered together. Those who were with them, said, "The Lord has risen indeed, and has appeared to Simon." Then they themselves began to relate what had happened on the journey, and how they recognized Him in the breaking of the bread. Luke 24:13-35

212. Now Thomas, one of the Twelve, called the Twin, was not with them when Jesus came. The other disciples therefore said to him, "We have seen the Lord." But he said to them, "Unless I see in his hands the print of the nails, and put my finger into the place of the nails, and put my hand into his side, I will not believe." After eight days, Jesus' disciples were again inside, and Thomas with them. Jesus came, the doors being closed, and stood in their midst, and said, *Peace be to you!* Then He said to Thomas, *Bring here thy finger, and see My hands; and bring here thy hand, and put it into My side; and be not unbelieving, but believing.* Then Thomas must have

---

139. *Luke 24:36-43*

fallen to his knees, and must have wept, as he worshipped Jesus, saying, "My Lord and My God!" Jesus said to him, *Because thou hast seen Me, thou hast believed. Blessed are they who have not seen, and yet have believed.* John 20:24-29

213. JESUS MANIFESTED HIMSELF again at the Sea of Galilee. Simon Peter, Thomas, Nathanael, James and his brother, John, and two other disciples had gone out to fish. It was night. When day was breaking, Jesus stood on the beach. It was John who recognized Him, exclaiming, "It is the Lord!" How overwhelmed with joy they must have been to behold Him! When, therefore, they had landed, they saw a fire ready, and a fish upon it. And there was also bread. . . . Jesus said to them, *Come and Breakfast.* Breakfast over, Jesus said to Simon Peter, *Simon, son of John, Dost thou love Me more than these do?* He said to Him, "Yes, Lord, Thou knowest that I love Thee." Jesus said to him, *Feed My lambs.* He said to him a second time, *Simon, son of John, dost thou love Me?* Simon Peter said to Him, "Yes, Lord, Thou knowest that I love Thee." Jesus said to him, *Feed My lambs.* A third time He said to him, *Simon, son of John, dost thou love Me?* Peter was grieved because Jesus said to him for the third time, *Dost thou love Me?* And he said to Him, "Lord, Thou knowest all things, Thou knowest that I love Thee." Then Jesus said to him, *Feed My sheep.* . . . And, *Follow Me.* What further proof do we need for the primacy of Saint Peter, or what further sign from God is needed for Christians to believe that on that day beside the northern shore of the Sea of Galilee, Jesus Christ made Simon Bar-Jona the first vicar of what is called today the Roman Catholic Church? John 21:1-19

214. JESUS CHRIST, OUR RISEN LORD, instructed His beloved Eleven further, saying, *These are the words which I spoke to you while I was yet with you, that all things must be fulfilled that are written in the law of Moses and the Prophets and the*

Psalms concerning Me. Then He opened their minds, that they might understand the Scriptures. And He said to them, *Thus it is written; and thus the Christ should suffer, and should rise again from the dead on the third day; and that repentance and remission of sins should be preached in His name to all nations, beginning from Jerusalem. And you yourselves are witnesses of these things. And I send forth upon you the promise of My Father. But wait here in the city* (Jerusalem), *until you are clothed with power from On High.* Luke 24:44-49

215. JESUS ALSO COMMANDED and said to His followers, *Go into the whole world and preach the Gospel* (of the Kingdom of God) *to every creature. He who believes and is baptized shall be saved, but he who does not believe shall be condemned. And these signs shall attend those who believe: in My name they shall cast out devils; they shall speak in new tongues; they shall take up serpents; and if they drink any deadly thing, it shall not hurt them; they shall lay hands upon the sick and they shall get well.* Mark 16:15-18

216. SAINT MATTHEW CLOSES HIS LAST CHAPTER of the first Gospel with these words which the Son of Man, Jesus Christ, uttered when He commissioned His chosen Apostles: *All power in Heaven and on earth has been given to Me. Go, therefore, and make disciples of all nations, baptizing them in the name of the Father, and of the Son, and of the Holy Spirit, teaching them to observe all that I have commanded you; and behold, I am with you all days, even unto the consummation of the world.* Matthew 28:16-20

CHAPTER IV

JESUS SAID
of the Crucifixion

217. MY HOUR *has not yet come.* These words prophetic of
the Passion and Crucifixion were uttered by Jesus to His
beloved mother, Mary, when at the wedding feast in Cana, she
whispered to Him, "They have no wine." This is not the usual
interpretation. Generally it is taken to mean that His time for
working the miracle had not yet arrived. However, Saint
Augustine and some of the Fathers did feel that it also referred
to the Passion.[140] Throughout His ministry Jesus often alluded
to His suffering and death on the cross as *hour.* John 2:1-4

218. THE PASSOVER OF THE JEWS was at hand, and Jesus went
up to Jerusalem. In the Temple He found men selling oxen,
sheep and doves, and money-changers at their tables. Making a
kind of whip of cords, he drove them all out of the Temple. . . .
The Jews said to Him, "What sign dost thou show us, seeing
that thou dost these things?" In answer Jesus said to them,

---

140. *Commentary on the New Testament, prepared by the Catholic Biblical Association of America, pp. 304f*

Destroy this Temple, and in three days I will raise it up. . . .
Jesus was speaking of the Temple of His own body. When accordingly, He had risen from the dead, His disciples remembered that He had said this. John 2:13-22

219. NICODEMUS, ONE OF THE FEW PHARISEES who believed in Jesus, came to Him at night. To him Jesus foretold the crucifixion, saying, *And as Moses lifted up the serpent in the desert, even so must the Son of Man be lifted up, that those who believe in Him may not perish, but may have Life Everlasting.* John 3:14-15

220. JESUS AND HIS CHOSEN APOSTLES were in Capharnaum. Some of the Jews there asked Jesus, "Why do the disciples of John fast often and make supplications, and likewise those of the Pharisees, whereas thy disciples eat and drink?" Jesus said to them, *Can the wedding guests fast as long as the Bridegroom is with them? As long as they have the Bridegroom with them they cannot fast. But the days will come when the Bridegroom shall be taken away from them, and then they will fast on that day.*[141] Mark 2:18-20

221. JESUS SAID, *The Son of Man must suffer many things, and be rejected by the elders and chief priests and Scribes, and be put to death, and on the third day rise again.* Peter taking Him aside, began to chide Him, saying, "Far be it from Thee, O Lord; this will never happen to Thee." Jesus turned and said to Peter, *Get behind Me, satan, thou art a scandal to Me; for thou dost not mind the things of God, but those of men.*[142,143] Luke 9:22

222. JESUS TOOK PETER AND JAMES AND JOHN with Him to the summit of a high mountain, known to us as Mount Thabor. Here Jesus was transfigured: His face shone as the sun,

141. *Luke 5:33-35;* 142. *Matthew 16:21-23;* 143. *Mark 8:31-33*

and His garments became white as snow. Moses and Elias appeared and talked with Jesus. . . . As the four of them were coming down the mountain side, Jesus cautioned them, saying, *Tell the vision to no one, till the Son of Man has risen from the dead.* Peter and James and John kept what He said to themselves, discussing with one another what the words, *"When He shall have risen from the dead,"* might mean. Then they asked Jesus, "Why then do the Scribes say that Elias must come first?" Jesus answered, *Elias indeed is to come and will restore all things. But I say to you that Elias has come already, and they did not know him, but did to him whatever they wished. So also shall the Son of Man suffer at their hands.* Then the disciples understood that He had spoken to them of John the Baptist.[144,145] Matthew 17:9-13

223. Now WHILE THEY WERE TOGETHER *in Galilee,* Jesus tells His Apostles that He is to be betrayed. In this, His second prediction of the Passion, He said, *The Son of Man is to be betrayed into the hands of men, and they will kill Him; and on the third day He will rise again.* They did not understand this saying, and it was hidden from them, that they might not perceive it; and they were afraid to ask Him about this saying.[146,147] Matthew 17:21-22

224. JESUS AND HIS DISCIPLES entered Samaria on their way to Jerusalem. They found the Samaritans very unfriendly. This was true because the Samaritans contended (and still contend) that their temple on Mount Garizim in Samaria was the only legitimate place for worship and thus were hostile to anyone going to the Temple of Jerusalem for worship. When His Apostles James and John became aware of this hostility, they said, "Lord, wilt Thou that we bid fire come down from Heaven and consume them?" Jesus rebuked them, saying, *You do not*

---

144. *Mark 9:8-12;* 145. *Luke 9:28-36;* 146. *Mark 9:29-31;* 147. *Luke 9:44-45*

know of what manner of Spirit you are; for the Son of Man did not come to destroy men's lives, but to save them. Luke 9:51-56

225. THE SOLEMN FEAST of the Tabernacles was at hand. Jesus commanded His disciples to go to the Feast, although He did not wish to go because He knew that the Jews were seeking to put Him to death. Therefore He said to them, *My time has not yet come, but your time is always at hand. The world cannot hate you, but it hates Me because I bear witness concerning it, that its works are evil. As for you, go up to this feast, for My time is not yet fulfilled.* When He had said these things He stayed on in Galilee. But as soon as His brethren had gone up to the Feast, then He also went up, not publicly, but as it were privately. John 7:1-10

226. THE PHARISEES AND THE SCRIBES were forever testing Jesus, yet did not want to believe in Him. So He said to them, *You are of this world. I am not of this world. Therefore I said to you that you will die in your sins; for if you do not believe that I am He* (the Messias), *you will die in your sin.* They then asked Him, "Who art thou?" Jesus replied, *When you have lifted up the Son of Man, then you will know that I am He, and that of Myself I do nothing: but that I preach only what the Father has taught Me. And He who sent Me is with Me; He has not left Me alone, because I do always the things that are pleasing to Him.* John 8:28-29

227. JESUS SAID TO THOSE who believed in Him, *The Truth shall make you free.* But the unbelievers among them did not understand what Jesus meant and retorted, "We are children of Abraham, and we have never yet been slaves to anyone. How sayest thou, 'You shall be free?'" Jesus answered, *Amen, amen, I say to you, everyone who commits sin is a slave of sin. . . . If therefore the Son makes you free, you will be free indeed. I know that you are the children of Abraham; but you*

*seek to kill Me because My word takes no hold among you. . . .
If you are the children of Abraham, do the works of Abraham.
But as it is, you are seeking to kill Me, One Who has spoken the
Truth to you which I have heard from God. That is not what
Abraham did.* John 8:31-40

228. JESUS SPOKE THE PARABLE of the good shepherd to the
people. How the good shepherd leads his own sheep out
of the sheephold and they follow him only because they know
his voice. *I am the Good Shepherd. The Good Shepherd lays
down His life for His sheep. . . . I am the Good Shepherd, and
I know Mine and Mine know Me, even as the Father knows
Me and I know the Father; and I lay down My life for My
sheep. And other sheep I have that are not of this Fold. Them
also I must bring, and they shall hear My voice, and there shall
be One Fold and One Shepherd. For this reason the Father loves
Me, because I lay down My life that I may take it up again.
No one takes it from Me, but I lay it down of Myself. I have the
power to lay it down, and I have the power to take it up again.
Such is the command I have received from My Father.* John
10:1-18

229. JESUS IS THE PRINCE OF PEACE. His salutation was *Peace
I give to you.* Yet He was aware that His coming to earth
from the Father would cause struggle. For He said, *I have come
to cast fire upon the earth, and what will I but that it be kindled?*
(Holy men have interpreted the image of fire as the purifying
and cleansing power which the Gospel, through the Holy Spirit,
will exercise upon mankind. But that this power is effective only
through Jesus' Passion and Death.) Then Jesus continued, *But
I have a baptism to be baptized with; and how distressed I am
until it is accomplished.* Luke 12:49-50

230. CERTAIN PHARISEES CAME UP TO JESUS, SAYING, "Depart
and be on thy way, for Herod wants to kill thee." To
them He said, *Go and say to that fox, "Behold, I cast out devils*

and perform cures today and tomorrow, and the third day I am to end My course. Nevertheless, I must go My way today and tomorrow and the next day, for it cannot be that a Prophet perish outside Jerusalem." Luke 13:31-33

231. JESUS USED THE WORD "CROSS" several times while instructing His followers. He said, *He who does not carry his cross and follow Me, cannot be My disciple.*[148,149,150,151] Luke 14:27

232. TO HIS DISCIPLES, JESUS SAID, *The days will come when you will long to see one day of the Son of Man and will not see it. . . . As the lightning when it flashes from one end of the sky to the other, so will the Son of Man be in His day. But first He must suffer many things and be rejected by this generation.* Luke 17:22-25

233. THEY WERE NOW ON THEIR WAY, going up to Jersusalem; and Jesus was walking on in front of them. They were in dismay, and those who followed were afraid. He took the twelve Apostles aside by themselves, and made His third prediction of the Passion, telling them what would happen to Him, saying, *Behold, we are going up to Jerusalem, and the Son of Man will be betrayed to the chief priests and the Scribes; and they will condemn Him to death, and will deliver Him to the Gentiles; and they will mock Him, and spit upon Him, and scourge Him, and put Him to death; and on the third day He will rise again.* The Apostles understood none of these things and they were hidden from them.[152,153] Luke 18:31-34

234. THE APOSTLES JAMES AND JOHN came to Jesus, saying, "Master, we want Thee to do for us whatever we ask. . . . Grant to us that we may sit, one at Thy right hand and the other at Thy left hand, in Thy glory." Jesus was astonished

---

148. *Matthew 10:38;* 149. *Matthew 16:24;* 150. *Mark 8:34;* 151. *Luke 9:23;* 152. *Matthew 20:17-19;* 153. *Mark 10:33-34*

120

and said to them, *You do not know what you are asking for. Can you drink of the cup which I drink, or be baptized with the baptism with which I am to be baptized?*[154] Mark 10:35-38

235. THE TEN APOSTLES became very indignant when James and John requested to sit next to Jesus in His Kingdom. Jesus said to them, *Whoever wishes to become great among you shall be your servant; and whoever wishes to be first among you shall be your slave; even as the Son of Man has not come to be served but to serve, and to give His life as a ransom for many.*[155] Mark 10:41-45

236. SIX DAYS BEFORE THE FEAST of the Unleavened Bread, which is called the Passover, Jesus and His Apostles came to Bethany. Bethany is where Jesus raised Lazarus, who had died, to life. One of His disciples, Simon the leper, made a supper for Jesus. Lazarus was there at table. Martha, his sister served. But Mary, their sister, took a pound of ointment, genuine nard of great value, and anointed the feet of Jesus, and with her hair wiped His feet dry. The house was filled with the odor of the ointment. Then one of His Apostles, Judas Iscariot, he who was about to betray Him, said, "Why was this ointment not sold for three hundred denarii (about fifty dollars), and given to the poor?" Now he said this, not that he cared for the poor, but because he was a thief, and holding the purse, used to take what was put in it. Jesus said, *Let her be. Why do you trouble her? She has done Me a good turn. For the poor you have always with you, and whenever you want you can do good to them; but you do not always have Me. She has done what she could; she has anointed My body in preparation for burial. Amen I say to you, wherever in the whole world this Gospel is preached, this also that she has done shall be told in memory of her.*[156,157] Mark 14:3-9

---

154. *Matthew 20:20-22;* 155. *Matthew 20:24-28;* 156. *Matthew 26:6-13;* 157. *John 12:1-8*

237. YES, JESUS' TASK in His Father's business here on earth was finally being consummated. He had made His triumphal entry into Jerusalem as was spoken of through the Prophet, "Tell the daughter of Sion: Behold, thy King comes to thee, meek and seated upon an ass, and upon a colt, the foal of a beast of burden."[158] The multitude that went before Him that day from Bethphage over the Mount of Olives and into Jerusalem by way of the Golden Gate, had cried out, "Hosanna! Blessed is He Who comes in the name of the Lord! Blessed is the Kingdom of our father David that comes! Hosanna in the highest!"[159] He had taught the Gospel of the Kingdom of God and the forgiveness and repentance of sins daily in the Temple. For a second time He cleansed it, saying, *Is it not written, "My House shall be called a House of prayer for all the nations?"*[160] *But you have made it a den of thieves.*[161,162,163] He had foretold the destruction of Jerusalem, the Day of Judgment and the ultimate end of the world.

238. NOW THE FEAST OF THE PASSOVER was near at hand. The chief priests and Scribes were seeking how they might seize Jesus by stealth and put Him to death before the Feast. Jesus knew His hour had come, for He said, *You know that after two days the Passover will be here; and the Son of Man will be delivered up to be crucified.*[164,165,166] Matthew 26:2

239. THE HOUR *has come for the Son of Man to be glorified. Amen, amen, I say to you, unless the grain of wheat falls into the ground and dies, it remains alone. But if it dies it brings forth much fruit. He who loves his life, loses it; and he who hates his life in this world, keeps it unto Life Everlasting. If anyone serves Me, let him follow Me; and where I am there also shall My servants be. If anyone serves Me, My Father*

---

158. *Matthew 21:5, Isaias 62:11, Zacharias 9:9; 159. Matthew 21:9, Psalm 117:26; 160. Isaias 56:7, Jeremias 7:11; 161. Matthew 21:13; 162. Mark 11:17; 163. Luke 19:46; 164. Mark 11:1-11; 13:1-37; 165. Luke 19:29-48; 21:5-38; 166. John 11:1-44*

will honor him. Now My soul is troubled. And what shall I say? Father, save Me from this hour! No, this is why I came to this hour. Father glorify Thy name! There came a voice from Heaven, "I have both glorified it, and I will glorify it again." Then the crowd which was standing around and had heard, said that it had thundered. Others said, "An angel has spoken to Him." Jesus said, *Not for Me did this voice come, but for you. Now is the judgment of the world; now will the prince of the world be cast out. And I, if I be lifted up from the earth, will draw all things to Myself.* Now He said this signifying what death He was to die. The crowd answered Him, "We have heard from the Law that the Christ abides forever. And how canst thou say, 'The Son of Man must be lifted up,' Who is this Son of Man?" Jesus replied, *Yet a little while the Light is among you. Walk while you have the Light, that darkness may not overtake you. He who walks in the darkness does not know where he goes. While you have the Light, believe in the Light, that you may become sons of Light.* These things Jesus spoke, and He went away and hid Himself from them. John 12:23-36

240. ON THE FIRST DAY OF THE FEAST of the Unleavened Bread, when it was customary for the Jews to sacrifice the Passover, the disciples came to Jesus, asking Him, "Where dost Thou want us to go and prepare for Thee to eat the Passover?" Jesus called Peter and John and sent them, saying, *Go into the city* (of Jerusalem) *to a certain man, and say to him, "The Master says, 'My time is near at hand; at thy house I am keeping the Passover with My disciples.'"* The two disciples went, and found just as Jesus had told them; and they prepared the Passover.[167,168] Matthew 26:17-19

241. WHEN THE HOUR OF THE FEAST had come, Jesus being at table with the twelve Apostles, said to them, *I have greatly*

---

167. *Mark 14:12-16;* 168. *Luke 22:7-13*

desired to eat this Passover with you before I suffer; for I say to you that I will eat of it no more, until it has been fulfilled in the Kingdom of God. Luke 22:14-16

242. DURING THE PASSOVER SUPPER, Jesus said sadly, *Amen I say to you, one of you will betray Me.* The Apostles also became sad, and asked, "Is it I, Lord?" Jesus answered, *He who dips his hand into the dish with Me, he will betray Me. The Son of Man indeed goes His way, as it is written of Him; but woe to that man by whom the Son of Man is betrayed! It were better for that man if he had not been born.* Then Judas Iscariot, who a few hours later, would betray Jesus, asked, "Is it I, Rabbi?" And Jesus said to him, *Thou hast said it.*[169,170,171] Matthew 26:20-25

243. AND WHILE JESUS AND THE TWELVE were at supper, He took bread, and blessed and broke, and gave it to them, saying, *Take and eat; this is My body.* And taking a cup, He gave thanks, and gave it to them, saying, *All of you drink of this; for this is My blood of the New Covenant, which is being shed for many unto the forgiveness of sins. But I say to you, I will not drink henceforth of this fruit of the vine, until that day when I shall drink it new with you in the Kingdom of My Father.* [172,173] Matthew 26:26-29

244. JESUS' LAST SUPPER with His Apostles was over. It is known as the Holy Eucharist, the Holy Thanksgiving. After reciting a hymn, Jesus and His Eleven went out of the Cenacle on Mount Sion to the foot of the Mount of Olives. And as they were going along, Jesus said, *You will all be scandalized this night because of Me; for it is written, "I will smite the Shepherd, and the sheep of the flock will be scattered."*[174] *But after I have risen, I will go before you into Galilee.*[175] Matthew 26:30-31

---

169. *Mark 14:17-21;* 170. *Luke 22:21-23;* 171. *John 13:21-30;* 172. *Mark 14:22-25;* 173. *Luke 22:17-20;* 174. *Zacharias 13:7;* 175. *Mark 14:27-28*

245. JESUS QUOTED another prophesy, saying, *For I say to you that this which is written must yet be fulfilled in Me, "And He was reckoned among the wicked."*[176] *For that which concerns Me is at its end.* Luke 22:37

246. THE ELEVEN WERE FRIGHTENED, saddened and confused. Jesus said to them, *Let not your heart be troubled. You believe in God, believe also in Me. In My Father's House there are many mansions. Were it not so, I should have told you, because I go to prepare a place for you. And if I go and prepare a place for you, I am coming again, and I will take you to Myself; that where I am, there you also may be. And where I go you know, and the way you know.* John 14:1-4

247. THIS IS MY COMMANDMENT, *that you love one another as I have loved you. Greater love than this no one has, that one lay down his life for his friends.* John 15:12-13

248. PEACE I LEAVE WITH YOU. *My peace I give to you; not as the world gives do I give to you. Do not let your heart be troubled, or be afraid. You have heard Me say to you, "I go away and I am coming to you." If you loved Me, you would indeed rejoice that I am going to the Father, for the Father is greater than I. And now I have told you before it comes to pass, that when it has come to pass you may believe. I will no longer speak much with you, for the prince of the world* (the devil) *is coming, and in Me he has nothing. But he comes that the world may know that I love the Father, and that I do as the Father has commanded Me. Arise, let us go from here.* John 15:27-31

249. AND AS JESUS LED HIS ELEVEN APOSTLES down the slope of Mount Sion, then across the Brook Cedron, to the cave near the Garden of Gethsemani, He said, *Behold, the hour is coming, and has already come, for you to be scattered, each*

---

176. *Isaias 53:12*

one to his own house, and to leave Me alone. But I am not alone, because the Father is with Me. These things I have spoken to you that in Me you may have peace. In the world you will have affliction. But take courage, I have overcome the world. John 16:32-33

250. HAVING SPOKEN THUS, Jesus turns His attention from His beloved Eleven and raising His eyes to Heaven, said, *Father, the hour has come! Glorify Thy Son, that Thy Son may glorify Thee, even as Thou hast given Him power over all flesh, in order that to all Thou hast given Him He may give Everlasting Life. Now this is Everlasting Life, that they may know Thee, the only true God, and Him Whom Thou hast sent, Jesus Christ. I have accomplished the work that Thou hast given Me to do. And now do Thou, Father, glorify Me with Thyself, with the glory that I had with Thee before the world existed.* John 17:1-5

251. NOW THEY HAD REACHED THE GARDEN of Gethsemani near the road which led over the Mount of Olives to Bethany, where Mary and Martha and Lazarus lived. Also near the Garden, on the other side of the road, was (and still is) a large cave. The Gospels make no mention of it but tradition has it that Jesus and His disciples took shelter here often, and again on this Thursday night, when Jesus said to them, *Sit down here, while I go over yonder and pray.* But He took Peter and James and John with Him. Withdrawing a short distance from them, He fell prostrate upon the ground and prayed, *Father, if it is possible, let this cup pass away from Me; yet not as I will, but as Thou willest.* He arose and went to the three Apostles and found them asleep. . . . A second time He went aside and prayed, *My Father, if this cup cannot pass away unless I drink it, Thy will be done.* Jesus came again to the three and found them still asleep. Leaving them He went back and prayed a third time, saying the same words over again. Returning to them, He said, *Sleep on now, and take your rest! Behold, the hour is at hand when the Son of Man will be betrayed into the hands of sinners. Rise, let us go. Behold, he who betrays Me is at hand.*[177,178] Matthew 26:36-46

252. AND WHILE HE WAS STILL SPEAKING, Judas Iscariot, one of the Twelve, now turned traitor, came and with him a great mob brought together by the unbelieving chief priests and the Scribes and elders. Peter struck the servant of the high priest with his sword, cutting off his ear. But Jesus, even at this late hour, performed a miracle by touching the ear and healing it. To Peter He said, *Put back thy sword into its place; for all those who take the sword will perish by the sword. Or dost thou suppose that I cannot entreat My Father, and He will even now furnish Me with more than twelve legions of angels? How then are the Scriptures to be fulfilled, that thus it must take place?*[179] Matthew 26:47-54

253. THEN JESUS TURNED to the threatening mob and said, *As against a robber you have come out, with swords and clubs, to seize Me. I sat daily with you in the Temple teaching, and you did not lay hands on Me.* Now all this was done that the Scriptures of the Prophets might be fulfilled. Then all the disciples left Him and fled.[180,181] Matthew 26:55-56

254. THOSE WHO HAD TAKEN JESUS PRISONER, now led Him away to the Sanhedrin where Caiphas the high priest, the Scribes and the elders had gathered together. . . . Caiphas said to Him, "I adjure thee by the living God that thou tell us whether thou art the Christ, the Son of God." Jesus said to him, *Thou hast said it. Nevertheless, I say to you, hereafter you shall see the Son of Man sitting at the right hand of the Power* (of God) *and coming upon the clouds of Heaven.* Then

---

177. *Mark 14:32-42;* 178. *Luke 22:39-46;* **179.** *John 18:1-11;* 180. *Mark 14:48-49;* 181. *Luke 22:52-53*

Caiphas tore his garments, saying, "He has blasphemed; what further need have we of witnesses?" . . . "He is liable to death."[182,183] Matthew 26:57-66

255. THEN THE JEWS LED JESUS from the house of Caiphas to Pontius Pilate's praetorium. It was early morning. The Jews themselves did not enter, because if they did they would be defiled and unable to eat the Passover. Therefore, Pilate summoned Jesus inside and asked Him, "Art thou the king of the Jews?" Jesus asked, *Dost thou say this of thyself, or have others told thee of Me? . . . My Kingdom is not of this world. If My Kingdom were of this world, My followers would have fought that I might not be delivered to the Jews. But, as it is, My Kingdom is not from here.* Pilate therefore said to Him, "Thou art then a king?" Jesus answered, *Thou sayest it; I am a King. This is why I was born, and why I have come into the world, to bear witness to the Truth. Everyone who is of the Truth hears My voice.* Pilate asked Him, "What is truth?" John 18:28-38

256. PILATE QUESTIONED JESUS FURTHER but could find nothing unlawful upon which to convict Him to death. So he went out to the mob gathered in front of the praetorium and proclaimed, "I find no guilt in him. Do you wish, therefore, that I release to you the king of the Jews?" The Jews shouted, "Not this man!" Pilate then gave Jesus over to the torturers who scourged Him. Then the soldiers made sport of Him by putting a crown of plaited thorns upon His head and a robe of purple over His shoulders. . . . Even after the scourging and the crowning of thorns, Pilate had misgivings, for he went again back into the praetorium, and asked Jesus, "Where art thou from?" Jesus made no answer. Pilate therefore said to Him, "Dost thou not speak to me? Dost thou not know that I have power to crucify thee, and that I have power to release thee?"

---

182. *Mark 14:60-62;* 183. *Luke 22:66-71*

OF THE CRUCIFIXION

Jesus answered, *Thou wouldst have no power at all over Me were it not given thee from Above. Therefore, he who betrayed Me to thee has the greater sin.* John 19:1-11

257. THUS, JESUS CHRIST, THE GOD-MAN, was condemned to die by crucifixion. They led Him through Jerusalem and beyond its wall. When the executioners came to the Place of the Skull, called Golgotha, they crucified Jesus with the two robbers, one on His right hand and the other on His left. In His torment, nailed to the infamous cross, Jesus implored, *Father, forgive them, for they do not know what they are doing.* Luke 23:33-34

258. ONE OF THOSE ROBBERS WHO WERE HANGED was abusing Jesus, saying, "If thou art Christ, save thyself and us!" But the other in answer rebuked him and said, "Dost not even thou fear God, seeing that thou art under the same sentence? And we indeed justly, for we are receiving what our deeds deserved; but this man has done nothing wrong." And he said to Jesus, "Lord, remember me when Thou comest into Thy kingdom." And Jesus said to him, *Amen I say to thee, this day thou shalt be with Me in Paradise,* (that is, the abode of the just souls under the old dispensation, who were waiting in limbo for the coming of the Messias to lead them to Heaven.) Luke 23:39-43

259. THERE WAS DARKNESS OVER THE WHOLE LAND on that first Good Friday from the sixth hour (noon) until the ninth hour (three o'clock in the afternoon). But about the ninth hour Jesus cried out with a loud voice, *Eli, Eli, lema sabacthani,* that is, *My God, My God, why hast Thou forsaken Me?*[184] Matthew 27:45-46

260. AND THE CURTAIN OF THE TEMPLE was torn in two from top to bottom. Again Jesus cried out with a loud voice,

---

184. *Mark 15:33-34*

Father, into Thy hands I commend My spirit. And having said this, He expired. Then the earth quaked; the rocks were rent; the tombs were opened, and many bodies of the saints who had fallen asleep arose. . . . Now when the centurion, and those who were with him keeping guard over Jesus, saw the earthquake and the things that were happening, they were very much afraid, and he said, "Truly, this man was the Son of God."[185,186] Luke 23:45-46

261. Now WHEN IT WAS EVENING, Joseph of Arimathea and Nicodemus, who had come to Jesus by night, took the body of Jesus down from the cross, wrapped it in a clean linen cloth and laid it in the tomb. At dawning of the first day of the week, several women who were followers of Jesus, came to the tomb. Behold, two men stood beside them clad in dazzling white raiments. They said, "Why do you seek the living one among the dead? He is not here, but has risen. Remember how He spoke to you while He was yet in Galilee, saying that the Son of Man must be betrayed into the hands of sinful men, and be crucified, and on the third day rise." Luke 24:1-7

262. AFTER HE HAD RISEN FROM THE DEAD, Jesus appeared to His disciples on several occasions. The afternoon of the resurrection two of the disciples were returning from Jerusalem to a village named Emmaus, a distance of some seven miles. While in their perplexity they were discussing the crucifixion and pondering the news of the resurrection, Jesus Himself drew near and went along with them. But their eyes were held, that they should not recognize Him. . . . Finally Jesus said to them, *O foolish ones and slow of heart to believe in all that the Prophets have spoken! Did not the Christ have to suffer these things before entering into His glory?* . . . Jesus went home with them. At the table He took bread and blessed and broke and began handing it to them. Suddenly their eyes were opened and

185. *Matthew 27:51-54;* 186. *Mark 15:38-39*

130

they recognized Him. Then He vanished from their sight. . . .
Luke 24:13-31

263. WHEN JESUS AND THE ELEVEN met in Galilee, He said to
them, *These are the words which I spoke to you while I
was yet with you, that all things must be fulfilled that are written in the Law of Moses and the Prophets and the Psalms concerning Me.* Then He opened their minds, that they might
understand the Scriptures. And He said to them, *Thus it is
written; and thus the Christ should suffer, and should rise again
from the dead on the third day; and that repentance and remission of sins should be preached in His name to all nations,
beginning from Jerusalem.* Luke 24:44-47

CHAPTER V

JESUS SAID
of the Resurrection
of Jesus

264. JESUS CAME WITH HIS APOSTLES to the Temple in Jerusalem. There He found that those who had to do with the buying and selling of necessities of the Temple worship had carried things too far. So making a sort of whip out of cords, He drove them out of the Temple. To those who were selling doves, He said, *Take these things away, and do not make the House of My Father a house of business.* The officials of Judaism who were in authority in the Temple asked a sign of Jesus in justification of His apparent usurpation of their authority, saying, "What sign dost thou show us, seeing that thou dost these things?" In answer Jesus said to them, *Destroy this Temple, and in three days I will raise it up.* When Jesus had risen from the dead, His disciples remembered that He had said this, and was speaking of the Temple of His body. John 2:13-22

265. EVEN EARLY IN HIS MINISTRY, Jesus performed many miracles. One day there was brought to Him a possessed man who was blind and dumb. Jesus cured him so that he spoke and saw. The multitude marvelled and were amazed. But the Scribes and Pharisees, who hated Him, learning of this cure, said, "This man does not cast out devils except by Beelzebub, the prince of devils." So they came to Jesus, and even called Him "Master", and said, "We would see a sign from thee." Jesus, knowing the hatred in their hearts, responded, *An evil and adulterous generation demands a sign, and no sign shall be given it but the sign of Jonas the Prophet. For even as Jonas was in the belly of the fish three days and three nights, so will the Son of Man be three days and three nights in the heart of the earth.* Matthew 12:38-40

266. ONE DAY JESUS ASKED HIS APOSTLES THIS QUESTION, *Who do you say that I am?* Simon Peter spoke up, "Thou art the Christ, the Son of the living God." Jesus strictly charged them, and commanded them not to tell this to anyone. Then He made the first prediction of His resurrection from the dead, saying, *The Son of Man must suffer many things, and be rejected by the elders and chief priests and Scribes, and be put to death, and on the third day rise again.*[187,188] Luke 9:18-22

267. JESUS TOOK PETER, JAMES AND JOHN and went up Mount Thabor to pray. And as He prayed, the appearance of His countenance was changed, and His raiment became a radiant white. Moses and Elias appeared and spoke of Jesus' death, which He was to fulfill in Jerusalem. Coming down the mountain, Jesus cautioned the three Apostles with these words, *Tell the vision to no one, till the Son of Man has risen from the dead.*[189,190] Matthew 17:9

268. FROM MOUNT THABOR, Jesus and His Apostles were passing through Galilee on their way to Capharnaum. Jesus did not want anyone to know it because He was teaching His disciples, and made the second prediction of His resurrection,

187. *Matthew 16:21-28;* 188. *Mark 8:31-33;* 189. *Mark 9:8-9;* 190. *Luke 9:36*

saying, *The Son of Man is to be betrayed into the hands of men, and they will kill him; and having been killed, He will rise again on the third day.* But they did not understand the saying, and were afraid to ask Him.[191] Mark 9:29-31

269. JESUS SAID, *I am the Good Shepherd. I lay down My life for My sheep. . . . For this reason, the Father loves Me, because I lay down My life that I may take it up again. No one takes it from Me, but I lay it down of Myself. I have the power to lay it down, and I have the power to take it up again. Such is the command I have received from My Father.* John 10:14-18

270. LAZARUS AND MARY AND MARTHA, who lived in Bethany a short distance from Jerusalem, were very good friends of Jesus. Lazarus became ill and died. In their sorrow, his sisters sent word to Jesus to come. When Jesus arrived in Bethany, Martha met Him. He said to her, *Thy brother shall rise. . . . I am the Resurrection and the Life; he who believes in Me, even if he dies, shall live; and whoever lives and believes in Me, shall never die.* John 11:23-26

271. JESUS WAS RETURNING TO JERUSALEM. This time He took the Twelve aside by themselves and made the third prediction of His passion and resurrection, saying, *Behold, we are going up to Jerusalem, and the Son of Man will be betrayed to the chief priests and the Scribes; and they will condemn Him to death, and will deliver Him to the Gentiles to be mocked and scourged and crucified; and on the third day He will rise again.*[192,193] Matthew 20:17-19

272. WHEN JESUS PREACHED about the end of the world and the Last Judgment of mankind, He was seeing far beyond His resurrection from the dead. For He said, *But when the Son of Man shall come in His majesty, and all the angels with Him,*

---

191. *Matthew 17:21-22;* 192. *Mark 10:32-34;* 193. *Luke 18:31-33*

134

then He will sit on the Throne of His glory; and before Him will be gathered all the nations, and He will separate them one from another, as the shepherd separates the sheep from the goats; and He will set the sheep on His right hand but the goats on the left. Matthew 25:31-33

273. DURING THE LAST SUPPER which Jesus had with His Apostles, when He instituted Holy Communion, the Holy Eucharist, He foretold His resurrection from the dead by these words, *For I say to you that I will eat of it* (the passover) *no more, until it has been fulfilled in the Kingdom of God. . . . For I say to you that I will not drink of the fruit of the vine, until the Kingdom of God comes.*[194,195] Luke 22:14-20

274. THE PASSOVER SUPPER HAD COME TO AN END. After reciting a hymn, the Eleven followed Jesus as He led them from the Upper Room (the Cenacle) on Mount Sion down to and across the Brook Cedron to the grotto at the foot of the Mount of Olives. And as they were going along, Jesus said, *You will all be scandalized this night because of Me; for it is written, "I will smite the Shepherd, and the sheep of the flock will be scattered." But after I have risen, I will go before you into Galilee.*[196] Matthew 26:31-32

275. THE ELEVEN WERE VERY MUCH SADDENED to learn from Jesus Himself that He was to be betrayed and that He was to be put to death. Something else bewildered them possibly more, for He said, *A little while and you shall see Me no longer; and again a little while and you shall see Me, because I go to the Father.* Some of His disciples therefore said to one another, "What is this He says to us, 'A little while and you shall not see Me, and again a little while and you shall see Me'; and, 'I go to the Father'?" Jesus knew that they wanted to ask Him, and He said to them, *You inquire about this among yourselves*

---

194. *Matthew 26:26-29;* 195. *Mark 14:22-25;* 196. *Mark 14:27-28*

because I said, "A little while and you shall not see Me, and and again a little while and you shall see me." Amen, amen, I say to you, that you shall weep and lament, but the world shall rejoice; and you shall be sorrowful, but your sorrow shall be turned into joy. . . . And you therefore have sorrow now; but I will see you again, and your heart shall rejoice, and your joy no one shall take from you. . . . I came forth from the Father and have come into the world. Again I leave the world and go to the Father. John 16:16-28

276. NEAR THE EASTERN BANK of the Brook Cedron is a road leading up over the Mount of Olives to Bethany, the hometown of Mary, Martha and Lazarus, dear friends of Jesus. To the right of this road is the Garden of Gethsemani; to its left a very large cave, known as the Grotto of Betrayal. Here daily today a Franciscan Priest, assisted by a Brother, celebrates Holy Mass. Jesus and the eleven Apostles, coming from the Last Supper, must have stopped here as Jesus said, *Sit down here while I go over yonder* (the Garden of Gethsemani) *and pray.*[197] And prostrating Himself on the ground, He prayed, *Father, if it is possible, let this cup pass from Me, yet not as I will, but as Thou willest.*[197] Then Judas Iscariot, the betrayer, came. To him, Jesus spoke these soul-searching words, *Judas, dost thou betray the Son of Man with a kiss?*[198] . . . To those who seized Him, He said, *I was daily with you in the Temple, and you did not stretch forth your hands against Me. But this is your hour, and the power of darkness.*[199] . . . The capturers led the Captive to the Sanhedrin, before the chief priests, the Scribes, and the Pharisees. In answer to Caiphas', the high priest's, question, "Art thou the Christ, the Son of the Blessed One?" Jesus replied, *I am.*[200] For this answer, which Caiphas called blasphemy, Caiphas said, "He is liable to death." . . . Jesus was brought to the Roman praetorium, before the Procurator

---

197. *Matthew 26:36-39;* 198. *Luke 22:48;* 199. *Luke 22:53;* 200. *Mark 14:62*

Pontius Pilate, who condemned Him to death. To him, Jesus said, *Thou wouldst have no power at all over Me were it not given thee from Above.*[201] ... The dying Jesus, nailed to a cross of shame, cried out these words, *Father, forgive them, for they do not know what they are doing.*[202] ... To the repentant thief, *Amen, I say to thee, this day thou shalt be with Me in Paradise.*[203] ... To His sorrowing mother, *Woman, behold thy son.*[204] ... To His beloved Apostle John, *behold thy mother.*[204] To mankind, *I thirst.*[205] ... And to Him Who sent Him, *My God, My God, why hast Thou forsaken Me?*[206] and *Father, into Thy hands I commend My spirit.*[207] ... *It is consummated.*[208] And bowing His head, He gave up His spirit.

277. ONE OF JESUS' DISCIPLES, not an Apostle, Joseph of Arimathea, asked Pontius Pilate for the body of Jesus. With the help of Nicodemus, who had come to Jesus by night, Joseph took the body down from the cross, wrapped it in a linen cloth, and laid Him in a tomb which had been hewn out of a rock. Then they rolled a large stone to the entrance of the tomb. Several holy women came there at sunrise and found that the stone had been rolled away. Behold, two men stood by them in dazzling raiment. They said, "Why do you seek the living one among the dead? He is not here, but has risen. Remember how He spoke to you while He was yet in Galilee, saying that the Son of Man must be betrayed into the hands of sinful men, and be crucified, and on the third day rise." Luke 24:1-7

278. ACCORDING TO THE GOSPEL OF SAINT MATTHEW, these holy women departed quickly from the tomb in fear and great joy, and ran to tell the Apostles what they had seen and heard. And behold, Jesus met them, saying, *Hail!* And they came up and embraced His feet and worshipped Him. Then Jesus said to them. *Do not be afraid; go, take word to My*

201. *John 19:11;* 202. *Luke 23:34;* 203. *Luke 23:43;* 204. *John 19:26-27;* 205. *John 19:28;* 206. *Matthew 27:46;* 207. *Luke 23:46;* 208. *John 19:30*

brethren that they are to set out for Galilee; there they shall see Me. Matthew 28:8-10

279. ACCORDING TO THE GOSPEL OF SAINT JOHN, Mary Magdalene was standing outside weeping at the tomb. Turning round she beheld Jesus, but did not know that it was He. Jesus said to her, *Woman, why art thou weeping? Whom do you seek?* She thinking that He was the gardener, said to Him, "Sir, if thou hast removed Him, tell me where thou hast laid Him and I will take Him away." Jesus said to her, *Mary!* She said to Him, "Rabboni!" (that is to say, "Master!") Jesus said to her, *Do not touch Me, for I have not yet ascended to My Father, but go to My brethren and say to them, "I ascend to My Father and your Father, to My God and your God."* John 20:11-17

280. SAINT JOHN CONTINUES, When it was late that same day, the first of the week, though the doors where the disciples gathered had been closed for fear of the Jews, Jesus came and stood in the midst and said to them, *Peace be to you!* And when He had said this, He showed them His hands and His side. The disciples therefore rejoiced at the sight of the Lord. He therefore said to them again, *Peace be to you! As the Father has sent Me, I also send you.* When He had said this, He breathed upon them, and said to them, *Receive the Holy Spirit; whose sins you shall forgive, they are forgiven them; and whose sins you shall retain, they are retained.* John 20:19-23

281. LATER ON THAT SAME DAY, two of the disciples were returning from Jerusalem and nearing the village of Emmaus. As they were walking along sorrowfully and pondering the news of the resurrection, Jesus Himself joined them. But their eyes were held, that they should not recognize Him, . . . Finally Jesus said to them, *O foolish ones and slow of heart to believe in all that the Prophets have spoken! Did not the Christ have to suffer these things before entering into His glory?* . . . Cleophas invited

Jesus to his home. Jesus went. At the table He took bread and blessed and broke and began handing it to them. Suddenly their eyes were opened and they recognized Him. Then He vanished from their sight. Luke 24:13-31

282. WHEN JESUS APPEARED to the ten Apostles the first time, Thomas was not present. Therefore, on seeing him, they said, "We have seen the Lord." But Thomas being doubtful, said, "Unless I see in his hands the print of the nails, and put my finger into the place of the nails, and put my hand into his side, I will not believe." After eight days, the disciples were again inside, and Thomas with them. Jesus came, the doors being closed, and stood in their midst, and said, *Peace be to you!* Then He said to Thomas, *Bring here thy finger, and see My hands; and bring here thy hand, and put in into My side; and be not unbelieving, but believing.* Thomas answered and said to Him, "My Lord and my God." Jesus said to him, *Because thou hast seen Me, thou hast believed. Blessed are they who have not seen and yet have believed.* John 20:24-29

283. WHEN JESUS AND THE ELEVEN met in Galilee as foretold, He said to them, *These are the words which I spoke to you while I was yet with you, that all things must be fulfilled that are written in the Law of Moses and the Prophets and the Psalms concerning Me.* Then He opened their minds, that they might understand the Scriptures. And He said to them, *Thus it is written; and thus, the Christ should suffer, and should rise again from the dead on the third day; and that repentance and remission of sins should be preached in His name to all nations, beginning from Jerusalem.* Luke 24:44-47

CHAPTER VI

JESUS SAID
of the Resurrection of Man

284. FOR GOD *so loved the world that He gave His only-begotten Son, that those who believe in Him may not perish, but may have Life Everlasting.* John 3:16

285. THE PHARISEES AND SCRIBES did not want to believe in Jesus and hated Him because He called God His own Father, making Himself equal to God. But Jesus justified His claim to divinity even more so when He said, *For as the Father raises the dead and gives them Life, even so the Son also gives Life to whom He will. . . . Amen, amen, I say to you, he who hears My word, and believes Him Who sent Me, has Life Everlasting, and does not come to judgment, but has passed from death to Life. Amen, amen, I say to you, the hour is coming, and now is here, when the dead shall hear the voice of the Son of God, and those who hear shall live. . . . Do not wonder at this, for the hour is coming in which all who are in the tombs shall hear the voice of the Son of God. And they who have done good shall come forth unto resurrection of Life; but they who have done evil unto resurrection of judgment.* John 5:21-29

286. A<small>FTER</small> J<small>ESUS</small> <small>HAD</small> <small>FED</small> the five thousand people miraculously with five loaves of barley bread and two fish, He went that evening alone to the nearby mountain. But the next day the multitude returned. To them Jesus said, *All that the Father gives to Me shall come to Me, and him who comes to Me I will not cast out. For I have come down from Heaven not to do My own will, but the will of Him Who sent Me. Now this is the will of Him Who sent Me, the Father, that I should lose nothing of what He has given Me, but that I should raise it up on the last day. For this is the will of My Father Who sent Me, that whoever beholds the Son, and believes in Him, shall have Everlasting Life, and I will raise him up on the last day.* John 6:37-40

287. T<small>HE</small> J<small>EWS</small> <small>MURMURED</small> <small>ABOUT</small> J<small>ESUS</small> because He had said, "I am the Bread that has come down from Heaven." In answer therefore Jesus said to them, *Do not murmur among yourselves. No one can come to Me unless the Father Who sent Me draw him, and I will raise him up on the last day.* John 6:41-44

288. J<small>ESUS</small> <small>HAD</small> <small>MORE</small> <small>TO</small> <small>SAY</small> about the Bread of Life. *I am the Bread of Life. This is the Bread that comes down from Heaven, so that if anyone eat of It he will not die. I am the Living Bread that has come down from Heaven. If anyone eat of this Bread he shall live forever; and the Bread that I will give is My flesh for the Life of the world. . . . Amen, amen, I say to you, unless you eat the flesh of the Son of Man, and drink His blood, you shall not have Life in you. He who eats My flesh and drinks My blood has Life Everlasting and I will raise him up on the last day. For My flesh is food indeed, and My blood is drink indeed. He who eats My flesh, and drinks My blood, abides in Me and I in him. As the living Father has sent Me, and as I live because of the Father, so he who eats Me, he also shall live because of Me. This is the Bread that has come down* *from Heaven; not as your fathers ate the manna, and died. He who eats this Bread shall live forever.* John 6:53-59

289. ONE DAY JESUS WAS RESTING beside the northern shore of the Sea of Galilee. Soon great crowds gathered about Him. They must have been pressing Him backward into the water, for He had to get into a boat. There He sat down with the crowd facing Him on the shore. He spoke many things to them but in parables. *Just as the weeds are gathered up and burnt with fire, so will it be at the end of the world. The Son of Man will send forth His angels, and they will gather out of His Kingdom all scandals and those who work iniquity, and cast them into the furnace of fire, where there will be the weeping, and the gnashing of teeth. Then the just will shine forth like the sun in the Kingdom of their Father. He who has ears to hear, let him hear.* Matthew 13:39-43

290. AND AS JESUS WAS SITTING there in the boat rocked gently by the incoming waves of the Sea, He spoke to them of the parable of the fishing net. *Again, the Kingdom of Heaven is like a net cast into the sea that gathered in fish of every kind. When it was filled, they hauled it out, and sitting down on the beach, they gathered the good fish into vessels, but threw away the bad. So will it be at the end of the world. The angels will go out and separate the wicked from among the just, and will cast them into the furnace of fire, where there will be the weeping, and the gnashing of teeth.* Matthew 13:47-50

291. JESUS WAS PASSING THROUGH SAMARIA on His way to Jerusalem. He sent two of His disciples ahead to a town to make ready for Him. But the unfriendly Samaritans would not receive Jesus. When James and John saw this, they said, "Lord, wilt Thou that we bid fire come down from Heaven and consume them?" Jesus rebuked them, saying, *You do not know of what manner of spirit you are; for the Son of Man did not come to destroy men's lives, but to save them.* Luke 9:51-56

OF THE RESURRECTION OF MAN

292. THE RULER OF A SYNAGOGUE showed great indigation when Jesus cured the sick on the Sabbath. Jesus said to him, *Hypocrites! . . . There will be the weeping, and the gnashing of teeth, when you shall see Abraham and Isaac and Jacob and all the Prophets in the Kingdom of God but you yourselves cast forth outside. And they will come from the east and from the west, from the north and from the south, and will feast in the Kingdom of God.* Luke 13:28-29

293. JESUS ENTERED THE HOUSE of a ruler of the Pharisees as a dinner guest. While there He advised His host to invite poor guests and also gave the reason, saying, *When thou givest a dinner or a supper, do not invite thy friends, or thy brethren, or thy relatives, or thy rich neighbors, lest perhaps they also invite thee in return, and a recompense be made to thee. But when thou givest a feast, invite the poor, the crippled, the lame, the blind; and blessed shalt thou be, because they have nothing to repay thee with; for thou shalt be repaid at the resurrection of the just.* Luke 14:12-14

294. MARTHA AND MARY AND LAZARUS, three close friends of Jesus and the Apostles lived in Bethany to the east of the the Mount of Olives. Lazarus became ill and died. Martha sent word about it to Jesus. On the way to Bethany Jesus said to His Apostles, *Lazarus, our friend, sleeps. But I go that I may wake him from his sleep.* Now Jesus had spoken of his death, but the Apostles thought He was speaking of the repose of sleep. So then Jesus said to them plainly, *Lazarus is dead. . . .* Martha meeting Jesus as He approached, cried, "Lord, if Thou hadst been here my brother would not have died." Jesus said to her, *Thy brother shall rise.* John 11:11-22

295. WHEN JESUS SAID TO MARTHA, *Thy brother shall rise,* she replied, "I know that he will rise at the resurrection, on the last day." Then Jesus revealed to her as to no one else before, saying, *I am the Resurrection and the Life; he who believes in Me, even if he die, shall live; and whoever lives and believes in Me, shall never die. Dost thou believe this?* She said to Him, "Yes, Lord, I believe that thou art the Christ, the Son of God, Who hast come into the world." . . . Jesus asked the sisters, *Where have you laid him?* . . . They led Him to a cave where a stone was placed against it. Jesus said, *Take away the stone.* . . . Jesus raised His eyes and prayed to the Father. Then He cried out with a loud voice, *Lazarus, come forth!* And at once he who had been dead came forth, bound feet and hands with bandages, and his face was tied up with a cloth. Jesus said to them, *Unbind him, and let him go.* John 11:23-44

296. A RICH YOUNG RULER, who said that he obeyed the Ten Commandments, came to Jesus and asked Him what else he should do to have Eternal Life. Jesus told him to sell all that he had and give to the poor and follow Him. The young man became very sad, because he had great possessions, and walked away. Peter hearing this dialogue, said to Jesus, "Behold, we have left all and followed Thee; what then shall we have?" Jesus said to him, *Amen I say to you that you who have followed Me, in the regeneration when the Son of Man shall sit on the Throne of His glory, shall also sit on twelve thrones, judging the twelve tribes of Israel. And everyone who has left house, or brothers, or sisters, or father, or mother, or wife, or children, or lands, for My name's sake, shall receive a hundredfold, and shall possess Life Everlasting.*[209,210] Matthew 19:16-29

297. THERE CAME TO JESUS certain of the Sadducees, who said that there is no resurrection, and they questioned Him. Jesus said to them, *The children of this world marry and are given in marriage. But those who shall be accounted worthy of that world and of the resurrection from the dead, neither marry nor take wives. For neither shall they be able to die any more,*

209. *Mark 10:17-30;* 210. *Luke 18:18-30*

OF THE RESURRECTION OF MAN

for they are equal to the angels, and are sons of God, being sons of the resurrection. But that the dead rise, even Moses showed in the passage about the Bush, when he calls the Lord the God of Abraham, and the God of Isaac, and the God of Jacob. Now He is not the God of the dead, but of the living, for all live to Him.[211,212] Luke 20:27-38

298. JESUS BEGAN FORETELLING THE DESTRUCTION of Jerusalem, and the signs of the last day and the hatred of the world toward the believers in Him, *You will be hated by all for My name's sake; yet not a hair of your head shall perish. By your patience you will win your souls.*[213,214] Luke 21:17-19

299. IN THE TWENTY-FOURTH CHAPTER OF SAINT MATTHEW, Jesus foretells His second-coming to the earth, and the gathering of those who believed in Him. *But immediately after the tribulation of those days, the sun will be darkened, and the moon will not give her light, and the stars will fall from Heaven, and the powers of Heaven will be shaken. And then will appear the sign of the Son of Man in Heaven; and then will all tribes of the earth mourn, and they will see the Son of Man coming upon the clouds of Heaven with great power and majesty. And He will send forth His angels with a trumpet and a great sound, and they will gather His elect from the four winds, from one end of the heavens to the other.*[215,216] Matthew 24:29-31

300. THEN AT THE LAST JUDGMENT, Jesus *will sit on the Throne of His glory; and before Him will be gathered all the nations, and He will separate them one from another, as the shepherd separates the sheep from the goats; and He will set the sheep on His right hand but the goats on the left Then the King will say to those on His right hand, "Come, Blessed of My Father, take possession of the Kingdom prepared for you from*

---

211. *Matthew 22:23-32;* 212. *Mark 12:18-27;* 213. *Matthew 24:13;* 214. *Mark 13:13;* 215. *Mark 13:24-27;* 216. *Luke 21:25-28*

the foundation of the world; for I was hungry and you gave Me to eat; I was thirsty and you gave Me to drink; I was a stranger and you took Me in; naked and you covered Me; sick and you visited Me; I was in prison and you came to Me." Then the just will answer Him, saying, *"Lord, when did we see Thee hungry, and feed Thee; or thirsty, and give Thee drink? And when did we see Thee a stranger, and take Thee in; or naked, and clothe Thee? Or when did we see Thee sick, or in prison, and come to Thee?"* And answering the King will say to them, *"Amen, I say to you, as long as you did it for one of these, the least of My brethren, you did it for Me."* Then He will say to those on His left hand, *"Depart from Me, accursed ones, into the everlasting fire which was prepared for the devil and his angels. For I was hungry, and you did not give Me to eat; I was thirsty and you gave Me no drink; I was a stranger and you did not take Me in; naked, and you did not clothe Me; sick, and in prison, and you did not visit Me."* Then they also will answer and say, *"Lord, when did we see Thee hungry, or thirsty, or a stranger, or naked, or sick, or in prison, and did not minister to Thee?"* Then He will answer them, saying, *"Amen, I say to you, as long as you did not do it for one of these least ones, you did not do it for Me."* And these will go into everlasting punishment, but the just into Everlasting Life.* Matthew 25: 31-46

301. JESUS, KNOWING THAT HIS HOUR WAS DRAWING NEAR: that He must be crucified, die, rise again from the dead, and return to the Father, said to His Apostles, *The hour has come for the Son of Man to be glorified. Amen, amen, I say to you, unless the grain of wheat falls into the ground and dies, it remains alone. But if it dies, it brings forth much fruit. He who loves his life, loses it; and he who hates his life in this world, keeps it unto Life Everlasting. If anyone serves Me, let him follow Me; and where I am there also shall My servant be. If anyone serves Me, My Father will honor him.* John 12:23-26

302. IN RELATING THE HOLY EUCHARIST and the words Jesus employed at the Last Supper in the Cenacle, Saint Matthew quotes the words *new with you* implying resurrection. *And while they were at supper, Jesus took bread, and blessed and broke, and give it to His disciples, and said, Take and eat; this is My body.* And taking a cup, He gave thanks and gave it to them, saying, *All of you drink of this; for this is My Blood of the New Covenant, which is being shed for many unto the forgiveness of sins. But I say to you, I will not drink henceforth of this fruit of the vine, until that day when I shall drink it new with you in the Kingdom of My Father.* Matthew 26:26-29

303. WHEN JUDAS ISCARIOT LEFT the Passover Supper and went out quickly into the night, Jesus said to His Apostles, *Little children; yet a little while I am with you. You will seek Me, and, as I said to the Jews, "Where I go you cannot come," so to you also I say it now.* Peter said to Him, "Lord, where art Thou going?" Jesus answered, *Where I am going thou canst not follow now, but thou shalt follow later.* John 13:30-36

304. THE ELEVEN APOSTLES BECAME VERY SAD when told by Jesus that they could no longer follow Him. But He had these words of comfort: *Let not your heart be troubled. You believe in God, believe also in Me. In My Father's House there are many mansions. Were it not so, I should have told you, because I go to prepare a place for you. And if I go and prepare a place for you, I am coming again, and I will take you to Myself; that where I am, there you also may be.* John 14:1-3

305. All of the seventeenth chapter of the Gospel of Saint John is Jesus' prayer to the Father. In it He prays for His Apostles and their disciples and all who believe in Him down through the ages, even you and me. He prayed that we may have Everlasting Life with Him in glory. *Father, the hour has come! Glorify Thy Son, that Thy Son may glorify Thee, even*

as Thou hast given Him power over all flesh, in order that
to all Thou hast given Him He may give Everlasting Life. . . .
Those whom Thou hast given Me I guarded; and not one of
them perished except the son of perdition, in order that the
Scripture might be fulfilled. . . . Yet not for these only do
I pray, but for those also who through their word are to
believe in Me. . . . Father, I will that where I am, they also
whom Thou hast given Me may be with Me: in order that
they may behold My glory, which Thou hast given Me,
because Thou hast loved Me before the creation of the world.
John 17:1-3, 12, 20, 24

306. ON CALVARY HILL, at the Place of the Skull, also called
Golgotha, nailed to a cross of shame, Jesus hung in torment. Passers-by were jeering at Him, shaking their heads, and
saying, "Thou who destroyest the temple, and in three days
buildest it up again, save thyself! If thou are the Son of God,
come down from the cross!" In like manner, the chief priests
with the Scribes and the elders, mocking, said, "He saved
others, himself he cannot save! He trusted in God; let Him
deliver him now, if He wants him; for he said, 'I am the Son
of God.'" Two robbers were crucified with Jesus, one on His
right hand and one on His left. One of them reproached Jesus
in the same manner as the mob. But the other, Dismas by name,
rebuked him, saying, "Dost not even thou fear God, seeing that
thou art under the same sentence? And we indeed justly,
for we are receiving what our deeds deserved; but this man
has done nothing wrong." And he said to Jesus, "Lord, remember me when Thou comest into Thy Kingdom." Jesus
said to him, *Amen, I say to thee, this day thou shalt be with*
Me in Paradise. Matthew 27:39-43; Luke 23:40-43

CHAPTER VII

JESUS SAID
of the Ascension of Jesus

307. THERE WAS A CERTAIN MAN among the Pharisees, Nicodemus by name, a ruler of the Jews, who believed in Jesus. But he came to Jesus at night because he feared what the other Pharisees seeing him might say or do. Yet to him Jesus revealed much about Himself. When Jesus told him that unless a man be born again, he could not see the Kingdom of God, Nicodemus was confused. Jesus said to him, *If I have spoken of earthly things to you, and you do not believe, how will you believe if I speak to you of Heavenly things?* Then He spoke this mystery: *No one has ascended into Heaven except Him Who has descended from Heaven; the Son of Man Who is in Heaven.* Religious scholars have said that the Incarnation of Christ did not remove Him from the presence of the Father. John 3:1-13

308. THE PHARISEES FOUND FAULT with the disciples of Jesus because they did not observe the fasts. Jesus said to these critics, *Can you make the wedding guests fast as long as the*

Bridegroom is with them? But the days will come—and when the Bridegroom shall be taken away from them, then they will fast in those days.[217] Luke 5:33-35

309. SHORTLY AFTER JESUS HAD FED the five thousand miraculously with the five barley loaves and the two fish, He was in Capharnaum teaching in the synagogue. Here He proclaimed that He was the Living Bread that had come down from Heaven. . . . The Bread that He would give was His flesh for the Life of the world. . . That he who ate His flesh, and drank His blood had Life Everlasting and that He would raise him up on the last day. . . . Jesus, knowing in Himself that His disciples were murmuring at this, said to them, *Does this scandalize you? What then if you should see the Son of Man ascending where He was before?* John 6:48-63

310. JESUS, IN EXPLAINING THE PARABLE of the weeds to His disciples, said that just as the weeds are gathered up and burnt with fire, so will it be at the end of the world. *The Son of Man will send forth His angels, . . .* When Jesus said this, He saw beyond the crucifixion, beyond the resurrection, and even beyond the ascension, when in glory *the Son of Man will send forth His angels, and they will gather out of His Kingdom all scandals and those who work iniquity, and cast them into the furnace of fire, where there will be the weeping and the gnashing of teeth.* Matthew 13:37-42

311. THE SOLEMN FEAST of the Tabernacles was at hand. It lasted eight days. Jesus was in Galilee with His disciples. They entreated Him to go up to Jerusalem to the Feast and manifest Himself to the world. But Jesus said to them, *My time has not yet come, but your time is always at hand. The world cannot hate you, but it hates Me because I bear witness concerning it, that its works are evil. As for you, go up to the*

---

217. *Mark 2:18-20*

Feast, but I do not go up to this feast, for My time is not yet fulfilled. When Jesus said, *My time has not yet come,* and *My time is not yet fulfilled,* just what did He mean? Was He speaking of the passion and crucifixion, or of the resurrection, or of the ascension, or of all three fulfilling His time on earth? John 7:1-8

312. JESUS WAS TEACHING THE MULTITUDE about the coming of the Kingdom of God. On being asked by the Pharisees, "When is the Kingdom of God coming?" Jesus answered, *The Kingdom of God comes unawares,* and, *The Kingdom of God is within you.* Then to His disciples, He said, *The days will come when you will long to see one day of the Son of Man, and will not see it.* Luke 17:20-22

313. WHEN PETER ADDRESSED JESUS, saying, "Behold, we have left all and followed Thee; what then shall we have?" Jesus, again seeing beyond the ascension, said to His disciples, *Amen I say to you that you who have followed Me, in the regeneration when the Son of Man shall sit on the Throne of His glory, shall also sit on twelve thrones, judging the twelve tribes of Israel.* Matthew 19:27-28

314. JESUS FORETOLD THE DESTRUCTION OF JERUSALEM and the end of the world. Also His own re-appearance. *And then will appear the Sign of the Son of Man in Heaven; and then will all tribes of the earth mourn, and they will see the Son of Man coming upon the clouds of Heaven with great power and majesty.*[218,219] Matthew 24:30

315. IN FORETELLING THE END OF THE WORLD, Jesus gives His Apostles some idea of the Last Judgment of all mankind, *But when the Son of Man shall come in His majesty, and all the angels with Him, then He shall sit on the Throne of His glory; and before Him will be gathered all the nations and He will*

---

218. *Mark 13:26;* 219. *Luke 21:27*

separate them one from another, as the shepherd separates the sheep from the goats; and He will set the sheep on His right hand, but the goats on the left. Matthew 25:31-33

316. THE HOUR *has come for the Son of Man to be glorified. . . . If anyone serves Me, let him follow Me; and where I am there also shall My servant be.* John 12:23, 26

317. THE EVENING OF THE LAST SUPPER, the Holy Eucharist, Jesus said to His Apostles that He had greatly desired to eat that Passover with them before He suffered; *for I say to you that I will eat of it no more, until it has been fulfilled in the Kingdom of God.* Luke 22:14-16

318. AND WHILE JESUS AND HIS APOSTLES were at table during that last supper, He took a cup, gave thanks, and gave it to them, saying that all of them should drink of it, for it was His blood of the New Covenant, which was being shed for many unto the forgiveness of sins. *But I say to you, I will not drink henceforth of this fruit of the vine, until that day when I shall drink it new with you in the Kingdom of My Father.*[220,221] Matthew 26:26-29

319. WHEN JUDAS ISCARIOT, THE BETRAYER, had left the Upper Room, the Cenacle, where the Passover Supper had taken place, and gone out into the night, Jesus said to the Eleven, *Now is the Son of Man glorified, and God is glorified in Him. If God is glorified in Him, God will also glorify Him in Himself, and will glorify Him at once. Little children, yet a little while I am with you. You will seek Me, and, as I said to the Jews, "Where I go you cannot come," so to you also I say it now.* John 13:31-34

320. SIMON PETER SAID TO HIM, "Lord, where art Thou going?" Jesus answered, *Where I am going thou canst not follow Me now, but thou shalt follow later.* John 13:36

---

220. *Mark 14:22-25;* 221. *Luke 22:17-20*

OF THE ASCENSION OF JESUS

321. THE ELEVEN APOSTLES WERE FILLED WITH SORROW when
Jesus said to them that He was going away and that they
could not follow Him. But He had words of comfort, saying,
*Let not your heart be troubled. You believe in God, believe also
in Me. In My Father's House there are many mansions. Were
it not so, I should have told you, because I go to prepare a place
for you. And if I go and prepare a place for you, I am coming
again, and I will take you to Myself; that where I am, there
you also may be. And where I go you know, and the way you
know.* John 14:1-4

322. THOMAS, ONE OF THE ELEVEN, said to Jesus, "Lord, we do
not know where Thou art going, and how can we know
the way?" Jesus said to him, *I am the Way, and the Truth, and
the Life. No one comes to the Father but through Me. . . . Amen,
amen, I say to you, he who believes in Me, the works that I do
he also shall do, and greater than these he shall do, because I
am going to the Father.* John 14:5-7, 12

323. AND JESUS CONTINUED, *I will not leave you orphans; I
will come to you. Yet a little while and the world no longer
sees Me. But you see Me, for I live and you shall live. In that
day you will know that I am in My Father, and you in Me,
and I in you.* John 14:18-20

324. JESUS CONCLUDES HIS COMFORTING WORDS to His beloved
Eleven saying, *Peace I leave with you, My peace I give to
you; not as the world gives do I give to you. Do not let your
heart be troubled, or be afraid. You have heard Me say to you,
"I go away and I am coming to you." If you loved Me, you
would indeed rejoice that I am going to the Father, for the
Father is greater than I. And now I have told you before it
comes to pass, that when it has come to pass you may believe.
I will no longer speak much with you, for the prince of the*

world is coming, and in Me he has nothing. But he comes that the world may know that I love the Father, and that I do as the Father has commanded Me. John 14:27-31

325. AND NOW *I am going to Him Who sent Me, and no one of you asks Me, "Where art Thou going?"* The question had already been asked, but, in the opinion of scholars, not under present circumstances. Christ sought to evoke the thought of His return to the Father as consolation in the sadness of the Apostles over His departure. *But because I have spoken to you these things, sorrow has filled your heart. But I speak the truth to you; it is expedient for you that I depart. For if I do not go, the Advocate will not come to you; but if I go, I will send Him to you. And when He has come He will convict the world of sin, and of justice, and of judgment; of sin, because they do not believe in Me; of justice, because I go to the Father, and you will see Me no more; and of judgment, because the prince of this world has already been judged.* John 16:5-11

326. A LITTLE WHILE *and you shall see Me no longer; and again a little while and you shall see Me, because I go to the Father.* Some of His disciples therefore said to one another, "What is this He says to us, 'A little while and you shall not see Me, and again a little while and you shall see Me'; and, 'I go to the Father' "? They kept saying therefore, "What is this 'little while' of which He speaks? We do not know what He is saying." But Jesus knew that they wanted to ask Him, and He said to them, *You inquire about this among yourselves because I said, "A little while and you shall not see Me, and again a little while and you shall see Me." Amen, amen, I say to you, that you shall weep and lament, but the world shall rejoice; and you shall be sorrowful, but your sorrow shall be turned into joy. . . . And you therefore have sorrow now; but I will see you again, and your heart shall rejoice, and your joy no one shall take from you.* John 16:16-22

OF THE ASCENSION OF JESUS

327. I CAME FORTH *from the Father and have come into the world. Again I leave the world and go to the Father.* John 16:28

328. JESUS, IN THE EVENING before His betrayal by Judas, turns to the Father, saying, *Father, the hour has come! Glorify Thy Son, that Thy Son may glorify Thee. . . . I have glorified Thee on earth; I have accomplished the work that Thou hast given Me to do. And now do Thou, Father, glorify Me with Thyself, with the glory that I had with Thee before the world existed. I have manifested Thy name to the men whom Thou hast given Me out of the world. They were Thine, and Thou hast given them to Me, and they have kept Thy word. Now they have learnt that whatever Thou hast given Me is from Thee; because the words that Thou hast given Me I have given to them. And they have received them, and have known of a truth that I came forth from Thee, and they have believed that Thou didst send Me. . . . And I am no longer in the world, and I am coming to Thee. Holy Father, keep in Thy name those whom Thou hast given Me, that they may be one even as We are. . . . But now I am coming to Thee; and these things I speak in the world, in order that they may have My joy made full in themselves. . . . Father, I will that where I am, they also whom Thou hast given Me may be with Me; in order that they may behold My glory, which Thou hast given Me, because Thou hast loved Me before the creation of the world.* John 17:1-8, 11, 13, 24

329. NOW THOSE WHO HAD TAKEN JESUS PRISONER in the Garden of Gethsemani led Him to the Jewish council, the Sanhedrin. The high priest, Caiphas, stood up and said to Jesus, "I adjure thee by the living God that thou tell us whether thou art the Christ, the Son of God." Jesus said to him, *Thou hast said it. Nevertheless, I say to you, hereafter you shall see the Son of Man sitting at the right hand of the Power* (of God) *and coming upon the clouds of Heaven.* Then the high priest tore his garments, saying, "He has blasphemed; what further need have we of witnesses?" Those present in the Sanhedrin said, "He is liable to death."[222,223] Matthew 26:57-66

330. AND THEY CRUCIFIED JESUS. Two of His disciples, Joseph of Arimathea and Nicodemus took Him down from the cross, laid His body in a linen cloth, and placed Him in a new tomb hewn out of the rock. Now on the first day of the week Mary Magdalene came early to the tomb, while it was still dark, and she saw the stone taken away from the tomb. She told Peter and John. They rushed to the tomb and found it empty. Therefore the disciples went away to their homes. But Mary who had returned with Peter and John, stood outside the tomb weeping. Jesus stood beside her. She did not recognize Him until He said, *Mary!* Looking up, she cried, "Rabboni!" ("Master!") Jesus said to her, *Do not touch Me, for I have not yet ascended to My Father, but go to My brethren and say to them, "I ascend to My Father and your Father, to My God and your God."* John 20:1-17

331. THE DAY OF THE RESURRECTION OF JESUS, two of His disciples were returning to their village, Emmaus, some seven miles from Jerusalem. While they were conversing and arguing together, Jesus joined them. But their eyes were held that they should not recognize Him. Jesus asked them what they were talking about. They said to Him, "Concerning Jesus of Nazareth, who was a Prophet, mighty in work and word before God and all the people; and how our chief priests and rulers delivered Him up to be sentenced to death, and they crucified Him." *Jesus said to them, O foolish ones and slow of heart to believe in all that the Prophets have spoken! Did not the Christ have to suffer these things before entering into His glory?* Luke 24:13-26

---

222. *Mark 14:60-64;* 223. *Luke 22:66-71*

156

CHAPTER VIII

JESUS SAID
of Faith, Belief in God

332. ANDREW LED HIS BROTHER, Simon Peter, to Jesus; Jesus found Philip, and Philip found Nathanael. When Jesus saw Nathanael coming, He spoke of him as a true Israelite having no guile. Nathanael asked Him, "Whence knowest thou me?" Jesus replied that even before Philip had called him, when he was under the fig tree, He saw him. Nathanael exclaimed, "Rabbi, Thou art the Son of God, Thou art King of Israel." Answering him, Jesus said, *Because I said to thee that I saw thee under the fig tree, thou dost believe. Greater things than these shalt thou see. Amen, amen, I say to you, you shall see Heaven opened, and the angels of God ascending and descending upon the Son of Man.* John 1:40-51

333. To NICODEMUS, THE GOOD PHARISEE, who came to Him by night, Jesus said, *If I have spoken of earthly things to you, and you do not believe, how will you believe if I speak to you of Heavenly things? And no one has ascended into Heaven except Him who has descended from Heaven: the Son of Man*

157

Who is in Heaven. And as Moses lifted up the serpent in the desert, even so must the Son of Man be lifted up, that those who believe in Him may not perish, but may have Life Everlasting. For God so loved the world that He gave His only-begotten Son, that those who believe in Him may not perish, but may have Life Everlasting. . . . He who believes in Him is not judged; but he who does not believe is already judged, because he does not believe in the name of the only-begotten Son of God. John 3:12-18

334. SIMON PETER WITH JAMES AND JOHN had been out all night on the Sea of Galilee fishing but caught nothing. Jesus said to Simon that he should put out into the deep and lower their net for a catch. Simon said, "Master, the whole night through we have toiled and have taken nothing; but at Thy word I will lower the net." They did and enclosed a great number of fish so that their net was breaking. The men were astounded. Jesus said to Simon, *Do not be afraid; henceforth thou shalt catch men.* Luke 5:4-10

335. WHEN JESUS ENTERED CAPHARNAUM, a Roman official approached Him, saying, "Lord, my servant is lying sick in the house, paralyzed, and is grievously afflicted." Jesus said to him that He would come and cure him. But the centurion replied, "Lord, I am not worthy that Thou shouldst come under my roof; but only say the word, and my servant will be healed. . . . When Jesus heard this, He marvelled, and said to those who were following Him, *Amen I say to you, I have not found such great faith in Israel. And I tell you that many will come from the east and from the west, and will feast with Abraham and Isaac and Jacob in the Kingdom of Heaven. . . .* Then Jesus said to the centurion, *Go thy way; as thou hast believed, so be it done to thee.* And the servant was healed in that hour.[224,225] Matthew 8:5-13

---

224. *Luke 7:1-10;* 225. *John 4:46-51*

OF FAITH, BELIEF IN GOD

336. JESUS CAME TO THE GALILEEAN TOWN OF MAGDALA. A woman, named Mary, who was sorrowful for her many grave sins, learning that Jesus was at table in the house of a certain Pharisee, went there. Kneeling at His side, she bathed His feet with her tears, and wiped them dry with her hair. Then she kissed His feet and anointed them with ointment. . . . Noting the disapproval of the Pharisee, Jesus said to Him, *Dost thou see this woman? I came into thy house; thou gavest Me no water for My feet* (a custom of that time) ; *but she has bathed my feet with tears, and has wiped them with her hair. Thou gavest Me no kiss; but she, from the moment she entered, has not ceased to kiss My feet. Thou didst not anoint My head with oil; but she has anointed My feet with ointment. Wherefore I say to thee, her sins, many as they are shall be forgiven her, because she has loved much.* . . . And Jesus said to her, *Thy sins are forgiven.* . . . *Thy faith has saved thee; go in peace.* Luke 7:36-50

337. JESUS HAD SPENT THE DAY on the northern shore of the Sea of Galilee teaching the multitude about the Kingdom of God. When evening came He was tired. So He got into a boat with His Apostles and they put out to sea. Jesus was in the stern of the boat asleep. A great squall arose, and the waves were beating into the boat, so that it was filling. The frightened Apostles awakened Jesus saying, "Master, we are perishing!" Then rising up, Jesus rebuked the wind, and said to the sea, *Peace, be still!* The wind fell and there came a great calm. He said to them, *Why are you fearful? Are you still without faith?* The Apostles feared exceedingly and said to one another, "Who, then, is this that even the wind and the sea obey him?"[226,227] Mark 5:33-40

338. WHEN WORD SPREAD THAT JESUS was again at home in Capharnaum, four men came carrying a paralytic on a pallet. Since they could not bring him in to Jesus because of

226. *Matthew 8:23-26;* 227. *Luke 8:23-25*

the crowd standing outside the door, they went to the roof. Having stripped it, and made an opening, they let down the pallet. Jesus seeing their faith, said to the paralytic, *Take courage, son; thy sins are forgiven thee.* The Scribes and Pharisees, listening to this, said within themselves, "He blasphemes. Who can forgive sins, but God only?" Jesus knowing their thoughts, said, *Why do you harbor evil thoughts in your hearts? For which is easier, to say, "Thy sins are forgiven thee," or to say, "Arise, and walk"? But that you may know that the Son of Man has power on earth to forgive sins.* Then He said to the paralytic, *Arise, take up thy pallet and go to thy house.* And he arose, and went away to his house.[228,229] Matthew 9:1-7

339. ONE OF THE RULERS OF THE SYNAGOGUE at Capharnaum came to Jesus. Falling at His feet, he entreated Him, saying, "My daughter is at the point of death; come, lay Thy hands upon her, that she may be saved and live." Someone came from the house of Jairus, the ruler, saying, "Thy daughter is dead. Why dost thou trouble the Master further?" Jesus, having heard what was being said, said to Jairus, *Do not be afraid, only have faith.* . . . When Jesus came to the house, He took the father and the mother and Peter, James and John with Him, and entered in where the girl was lying. Taking the girl by the hand, He said to her, *Talitha cumi,* which is interpreted, *Girl, I say to thee, arise.* And the girl rose up immediately and began to walk.[230,231] Mark 5:22-23; 35-42

340. NOW AT THE SAME TIME a woman who for twelve years had been suffering from hemorrhage, came up behind Jesus and touched the tassel of His cloak, saying to herself, "If I touch but His cloak I shall be saved." But Jesus, turning and seeing her, said, *Take courage, daughter; thy faith has saved thee.* And

---

228. *Mark 2:1-12;* 229. *Luke 5:18-25;* 330. *Matthew 9:18-19; 23-25;* 231. *Luke 8:41-42; 49-50*

the woman was restored to health from that moment.[232,233] Matthew 9:20-22

341. NOW AS JESUS WAS PASSING ON FROM THERE, two blind men followed Him, crying out and saying, "Have pity on us, Son of David!" Jesus said to them, *Do you believe that I can do this to you?* They answered Him, "Yes, Lord." Then He touched their eyes, saying, *Let it be done to you according to your faith.* And their eyes were opened. Matthew 9:27-30

342. HAVING SUMMONED THE TWELVE APOSTLES, Jesus said to them, *Behold, I am sending you forth like sheep in the midst of wolves. . . . Do not be afraid of those who kill the body but cannot kill the soul. But rather be afraid of Him Who is able to destroy both soul and body in hell.*[234] Matthew 10:16, 28

343. THE SCRIBES AND PHARISEES PERSECUTED JESUS not only because He cured the sick on the Sabbath but because He called God His own Father, making Himself equal to God. But Jesus went on to say, *Amen, amen, I say to you, he who hears My word, and believes Him Who sent Me, has Life Everlasting, and does not come to judgment, but has passed from death to Life. . . . And you have not His word abiding in you, since you do not believe Him Whom He has sent. You search the Scriptures, because in them you think that you have Life Everlasting. And it is they that bear witness to Me, yet you are not willing to come to Me that you may have Life. . . . How can you believe who receive glory from one another, and do not seek the glory which is from the only God? Do not think that I shall accuse you to the Father. There is one who accuses you, Moses, in whom you hope. For if you believed Moses you would believe Me also, for he wrote of Me. But if you do not believe his writings, how will you believe My words?* John 5:24, 38-40, 44-47

---

232. *Mark 5:25-34;* 233. *Luke 8:43-48;* 234. *Luke 12:4-7*

344. IMMEDIATELY AFTER JESUS had miraculously fed the five
thousand with five barley loaves and the two fish He made
His disciples get into the boat and cross the sea ahead of Him
to Bethsaida, while He Himself dismissed the crowd. Then
Jesus went up the mountain by Himself to pray. The boat was
in the midst of the sea. In the fourth watch of the night, He
came to the Apostles, walking upon the water. They, seeing
Him, were greatly alarmed, and exclaimed, "It is a ghost!"
Then Jesus immediately spoke to them, saying, *Take courage; it
is I, do not be afraid.* Peter said, "Lord, if it is Thou, bid me
come to Thee over the water." And He said, *Come.* Then
Peter got out of the boat and walked on the water to come to
Jesus. But seeing the wind was strong, he was afraid; and as he
began to sink he cried out, saying, "Lord, save me!" And Jesus
at once stretched forth His hand and took hold of him, saying
to him, *O thou of little faith, why didst thou doubt?* [235,236] Matthew 14:22-31

345. JESUS SAID TO THE PEOPLE that they should not labor for
the food that perishes but for that which endures unto Life
Everlasting, which the Son of Man would give them. They
asked Him, "What sign, then, dost thou, that we may see and
believe thee? What work dost thou perform? Our fathers ate
the manna in the desert, even as it is written, "Bread from
Heaven he gave them to eat." Jesus then said to them, *Amen,
amen, I say to you, Moses did not give you the Bread from
Heaven, but My Father gives you the true Bread from Heaven.
For the Bread of God is that which comes down from Heaven
and gives Life to the world.* They said to Him, "Lord, give us
always this bread." Jesus said to them, *I am the Bread of Life.
He who comes to Me shall not hunger, and he who believes in
Me shall never thirst. But I have told you that you have seen
Me and you do not believe. . . . This is the will of My Father*

---

235. *Mark 6:45-51;* 236. *John 6:16-21*

OF FAITH, BELIEF IN GOD

Who sent Me, that whoever beholds the Son, and believes in Him, shall have Everlasting Life, and I will raise him up on the last day. John 6:27-40

346. THE JEWS THEREFORE MURMURED ABOUT JESUS because He had said that He was the Bread that had come down from Heaven. And they kept saying, "Is this not Jesus the son of Joseph, whose father and mother we know? How, then, does he say that he has come down from Heaven?" In answer Jesus said to them, *Do not murmur among yourselves. . . . Amen, amen, I say to you, he who believes in Me has Life Everlasting.* John 6:41-47

347. THEN JESUS WENT TO THE COASTAL DISTRICT of Tyre and Sidon. A Canaanite woman came to Him, saying, "Have pity on me, O Lord, Son of David! My daughter is sorely beset by a devil." Jesus answered her not a word. She kept following Him. Then He said, *I was not sent except to the lost sheep of the house of Israel.* Still she followed and worshipped Him, saying, "Lord, help me!" Jesus said, *It is not fair to take the children's bread and to cast it to the dogs.* She cried, "Yes, Lord; for even the dogs eat of the crumbs that fall from their master's table." Then Jesus said to her, *O woman, great is thy faith! Let it be done to thee as thou wilt.* And her daughter was healed from that moment.[237] Matthew 15:21-28

348. SOON AFTER JESUS HAD FED miraculously the five thousand and then the four thousand with a few loaves of bread and a few fish, He was with His Apostles in a boat on the Sea of Galilee. They found that they had forgotten to bring bread. Jesus cautioned them to beware of the leaven of the Pharisees and Sadducees. The Apostles began arguing among themselves, saying, "We have brought no bread." Jesus, knowing this,

---

237. *Mark 7:24-30*

said, *You of little faith, why do you argue among yourselves that you have no bread? Do you not yet understand, nor remember the five loaves among five thousand men, and how many baskets you took up? Nor the seven loaves among four thousand, and how many large baskets you took up? Why do you not understand that it was not of bread I said to you, "Beware of the leaven of the Pharisees and Sadducees?"* Then they understood that He bade them beware not of the leaven of bread, but of the teaching of the Pharisees and Sadducees.[238] Matthew 16:5-12

349. WHEN JESUS WAS TRANSFIGURED on Mount Thabor, Peter, James and John were with Him. A voice out of a bright cloud said, "This is My beloved Son, in Whom I am well pleased; hear Him." On hearing it the disciples fell on their faces and were exceedingly afraid. Jesus came near and touched them, saying, *Arise, and do not be afraid.* Matthew 17:1-7

350. AND WHEN JESUS AND THE THREE APOSTLES returned to the village at the foot of Mount Thabor, a man threw himself on his knees before Jesus, saying, "Lord, have pity on my son, for he is a lunatic and suffers severely. I brought him to Thy disciples, but they could not cure him." Jesus responded, *O unbelieving and perverse generation, how long shall I be with you? How long shall I put up with you? Bring him here to Me.* Jesus rebuked him; and the devil went out of the boy; and from that moment he was cured. Then the Apostles came to Jesus privately, saying, "Why could not we cast it out?" He said to them, *Because of your little faith; for amen I say to you, if you have faith like a mustard seed, you will say to this mountain, "Remove from here"; and it will remove. And nothing will be impossible to you.*[239,240] Matthew 17:14-19

238. *Mark 8:13-21;* 239. *Mark 9:16-28;* 240. *Luke 9:37-44*

351. WHOEVER CAUSES *one of these little ones who believe in me to sin, it were better for him to have a great millstone hung around his neck, and to be drowned in the depths of the sea.*[241] Matthew 18:5-6

352. IT WAS AUTUMN. The Feast of the Tabernacles was at hand. Jesus sent His Apostles to Jerusalem but remained in Galilee saying that He would not go because His time had not yet come. Then He went secretly to the Feast. On the last day of the great Feast Jesus stood up before the multitude and cried out, *If anyone thirst, let him come to Me and drink. He who believes in Me, as the Scripture says, "From within him there shall flow rivers of Living Water."* He said this of the Holy Spirit Whom they who believed in Him were to receive; for the Holy Spirit had not yet been given, since Jesus had not yet been glorified. John 7:38-39

353. JESUS WAS TEACHING THE PEOPLE about the Kingdom of God daily in the Temple. The unbelieving Pharisees and the Scribes were always present to test His every word hoping to be able to accuse Him and put Him to death. Jesus said to them, *You are from below, I am from above. You are of this world, I am not of this world. Therefore I say to you that you will die in your sins; for if you do not beleive that I am He* (the Messias), *you will die in your sin.* John 8:23-24

354. JESUS CONTINUED, *If God were your Father, you would surely love Me. For from God I came forth and have come; for neither have I come of Myself, but He sent Me. Why do you not understand My speech? Because you cannot listen to My word. The father from whom you are is the devil, and the desires of your father it is your will to do. He was a murderer from the beginning, and has not stood in the Truth because there is no Truth in him. When he tells a lie he speaks*

241. *Mark 9:41*

from his very nature, for he is a liar and the father of lies. But because I speak the Truth you do not believe Me. Which of you can convict Me of sin? If I speak the Truth, why do you not believe Me. He who is of God hears the words of God. The **reason** *why you do not hear is that you are not of God.* John 8:42-47

355. WHEN JESUS SAID TO THE PHARISEES that He had been in existence before Abraham came to be, they took up stones to cast at Him. But Jesus went out of the Temple from them. As He walked along, He saw a man blind from birth. . . . Jesus made clay with His spittle and put it on his eyes, and told him to wash in the near-by Pool of Siloe. The man went and returned seeing. . . . Jesus saw him later that day and asked him, *Dost thou believe in the Son of God?* He asked, "Who is He, Lord, that I may believe in Him?" Jesus revealed Himself, saying, *Thou hast both seen Him, and He it is Who speaks with thee.* The man, falling down at His feet, worshipped Jesus, saying, "I believe, Lord." John 9:1-38

356. JESUS GIVES ENCOURAGEMENT TO HIS DISCIPLES in times of persecution, saying, *My friends: Do not be afraid of those who kill the body, and after that have nothing more that they can do. But I will show you Whom you shall be afraid of; be afraid of Him Who, after He has killed, has power to cast into hell. Yes, I say to you, be afraid of Him. Are not five sparrows sold for two farthings* (about one cent)? *And yet not one of them is forgotten before God. Yes, the very hairs of your head are all numbered. Therefore do not be afraid, you are of more value than many sparrows.* . . . *And when they bring you before the synagogues and the magistrates and the authorities, do not be anxious how or wherewith you shall defend yourselves, or what you shall say, for the Holy Spirit will teach you in that very hour what you ought to say.* . . . *Therefore I say to you, do not be anxious for your life what you shall eat; nor yet for*

*your body, what you shall put on. The life is a greater thing
than the food, and the body than the clothing. Consider the
ravens; they neither sow nor reap, they have neither storeroom
nor barn; yet God feeds them. Of how much more value are
you than they! But which of you by being anxious about it can
add to his stature a single cubit? Therefore if you are not able
to do even a very little thing, why are you anxious concerning
the rest? Consider how the lilies grow; they neither toil nor
spin, yet I say to you that not even Solomon in all his glory was
arrayed like one of these. But if God so clothes the grass which
flourishes in the field today but tomorrow is thrown into the
oven, how much more you, O you of little faith!*[242] . . . *Do not
be afraid, little flock, for it has pleased your Father to give you
the Kingdom. Sell what you have and give alms. Make for
yourselves purses that do not grow old, a treasure unfailing in
Heaven, where neither thief draws near nor moth destroys. For
where your treasure is, there also will your heart be.* Luke
12:4-7, 11-12, 22-28, 32-34

357. WHO, DOST THOU THINK, *is the faithful and prudent
steward whom the Master will set over His household to
give them their ration of grain in due time? Blessed is that servant
whom his Master, when He comes, shall find so doing. Truly
I say to you, He will set him over all His goods. But if that
servant says to himself, "My Master delays His coming," and
begins to beat the menservants and the maids, and to eat and
drink, and to get drunk, the Master of that servant will come on
a day he does not expect, and in an hour he does not know, and
will cut him asunder and make him share the lot of the unfaithful.* Luke 12:42-46

358. IT WAS WINTER IN JERUSALEM and the time of the Feast
of the Dedication. Jesus was walking in that part of the
Temple called Solomon's portico. As always, Jews gathered

242. *Matthew 6:25-34*

round Him. This time they asked Him, "How long dost thou keep us in suspense? If thou art the Christ, tell us openly." Jesus answered them, *I tell you and you do not believe. The works that I do in the name of My Father, these bear witness concerning Me. But you do not believe because you are not of My sheep. My sheep hear My voice, and I know them and they follow Me. And I give them Everlasting Life; and they shall never perish, neither shall anyone snatch them out of My hand.* John 10:22-28

359. IN THEIR HATRED, THE UNBELIEVING JEWS took up stones to stone Jesus. He asked them, *Many good works have I shown you from My Father. For which of these works do you stone Me?* They retorted, "Not for a good work do we stone thee, but for blasphemy, and because thou, being a man, makest thyself God." Jesus answered them, *Is it not written in your Law, "I said you are gods?" If he called them gods to whom the word of God was addressed (and the Scripture cannot be broken), do you say of Him Whom the Father has made holy and sent into the world, "Thou blasphemest," because I said, "I am the Son of God"? If I do not perform the works of My Father, do not believe Me. But if I do perform them, and if you are not willing to believe Me, believe the works, that you may know and believe that the Father is in Me and I in the Father.* Full of rage, they sought to seize Jesus. His time had not yet come. He went forth out of their hands. John 10:33-38

360. THE APOSTLES ASKED JESUS, "Increase our faith." Then He told them of the efficacy of faith by saying, *If you have faith even like a mustard seed, you will say to this mulberry tree, "Be uprooted and be planted in the sea."*[243,244] Luke 17:5-6

361. JESUS WAS ON HIS WAY TO JERUSALEM, passing between Galilee and Samaria. Ten lepers met Him. Standing afar

---

243. *Matthew 17:19;* 244. *Mark 11:23*

off, they cried, "Jesus, Master, have pity on us." Jesus looked at them, then said merely that they should go and show themselves to the priests. As they went one of them—a Samaritan—noticed that all had been made clean. He rushed back to Jesus, falling on his face at His feet, and worshipped Him. Jesus wondered why the nine had not also returned to give thanks and glory to God. Then He said to the Samaritan, *Arise, go thy way, for thy faith has saved thee.* Luke 17:11-19

362. To impress upon the Apostles the efficacy of prayer, that they must always pray to God and not lose heart, Jesus told them this parable. A widow asked a judge to handle her case. He refused. But she never gave up coming to him again and again. The judge found her a nuisance and reflected, "Although I do not fear God, nor even respect man, but because this widow bothers me, I will do her justice, lest by her continual coming she finally wears me out." Jesus asked, *Will not God avenge His elect, who cry to Him day and night? And will He be slow to act in their case? I tell you that He will avenge them quickly. Yet when the Son of Man comes, will He find, do you think, faith on the earth?* Luke 18:1-8

363. Mothers were bringing their babies and little children to Jesus that He might touch them. When the disciples saw this, they rebuked them. Jesus called them together and said, *Let the little children come to Me, and do not hinder them, for of such is the Kingdom of God. Amen I say to you, whoever does not accept the Kingdom of God as a little child will not enter into it.*[245,246] Luke 18:15-17

364. Lazarus, a friend of Jesus, who lived with his sisters, Mary and Martha, in Bethany close to Jerusalem, became very sick. When Jesus heard of it, He said that the sickness was not unto death but for the glory of God that through it the Son

---

245. *Matthew 19:13-15;* 246. *Mark 10:13-16*

of God would be glorified. On the way to Bethany, Jesus said that He was going to wake Lazarus from his sleep. The Apostles thought that He was speaking of the repose of sleep, but Jesus had spoken of his death. Then Jesus said to them plainly that Lazarus was dead; and *I rejoice on your account that I was not there, that you may believe.* Martha met Jesus and cried, "Lord, if Thou hadst been here my brother would not have died. But even now I know that whatever Thou shalt ask of God, God will give it to Thee." Jesus said to her that Lazarus would rise. Martha replied, "I know that he will rise at the resurrection, on the last day." Then Jesus spoke out plainly, *I am the Resurrection and the Life; he who believes in Me, even if he die, shall live; and whoever lives and believes in Me shall never die. Dost thou believe this?* Martha said to Jesus, "Yes, Lord, I believe that Thou art the Christ, the Son of God, Who hast come into the world." John 11:1-27

365. MANY JEWS HAD COME FROM JERUSALEM to Mary and Martha in Bethany to comfort them. When they saw Jesus weeping at the death of Lazarus, they said, "Could not he who opened the eyes of the blind, have caused that this man should not die?" When Jesus came to the tomb, He commanded that the stone in front of it be taken away. Martha said, "Lord, by this time he is already decayed, for he is dead for four days." Jesus said to her, *Have I not told thee that if thou believe thou shalt behold the glory of God?* They removed the stone. Jesus, raising His eyes, said, *Father, I give Thee thanks that Thou hast heard Me. Yet I know that Thou always hearest Me; but because of the people who stand round, I spoke, that they may believe that Thou hast sent Me.* When He had said this, He cried out, *Lazarus, come forth!* At once he who had been dead came forth, bound feet and hands with bandages, and his face was tied up with a cloth. Jesus said, *Unbind him, and let him go.* John 11:35-44

OF FAITH, BELIEF IN GOD

366. As Jesus drew near to Jericho, a blind man, Bartimeus by name, was sitting by the wayside, begging. But when he learned from the crowd that Jesus was passing by, he cried, "Jesus, Son of David, have mercy on me." Jesus asked him, *What wouldst thou have Me do for thee?* The blind man said, "Lord, that I may see." Jesus said to him, *Receive thy sight, thy faith has saved thee.* And at once he received his sight, and followed Him, glorifying God.[247] Luke 18:35-43

367. Jesus was in Jerusalem, in the Temple when He said to the people, *And I, if I be lifted up from the earth, will draw all things to Myself.* Now He said this signifying by what death He was to die. Those in the crowd said to Him, "We have heard from the Law that the Christ abides forever. And how canst thou say, 'The Son of Man must be lifted up'? Who is this Son of Man?" Jesus therefore said to them, *Yet a little while the Light is among you. Walk while you have the light, that the darkness may not overtake you. He who walks in the darkness does not know where he goes. While you have the Light, believe in the Light, that you may become sons of Light.* These things Jesus spoke, and then He went away and hid Himself from them. John 12:32-36

368. It was morning and Jesus had hunger. Passing a fig tree, He went up to it to pluck some of its fruit. It had none. He said to the tree that henceforth no fruit should ever come from it. And immediately it withered up. The disciples marvelled, asking, "How did it come to wither up immediately?" Jesus said, *Amen I say to you, if you have faith and do not waver, not only will you do what I have done to the fig tree, but even if you shall say to this mountain* (Mount of Olives), *"Arise, and hurl thyself into the sea,"*[248] *it shall be done. And all things whatever you ask for in prayer, believing, you shall receive.*[249] Matthew 21:18-22

---

247. *Mark 10:46-52;* 248. *Matthew 17:19;* 249. *Mark 11:20-24*

369. EVEN AMONG THE RULERS OF THE JEWS, many believed in Jesus; but because of the Pharisees they did not acknowledge it, lest they should be put out of the synagogue. For they loved the glory of men more than the glory of God. Jesus said to all who were listening, *He who believes in Me, believes not in Me but in Him Who sent Me. And he who sees Me, sees Him Who sent Me. I have come a Light into the world, that whoever believes in Me may not remain in the darkness. And if anyone hears My words, and does not keep them, it is not I Who judge him; for I have not come to judge the world, but to save the world. He who rejects Me, and does not accept My words, has One to condemn him. The word that I have spoken will condemn him on the last day.* John 12:42-48

370. JESUS WAS RECLINING WITH HIS APOSTLES on the slope of the Mount of Olives facing the Temple. He had been foretelling the destruction of Jerusalem and the end of the world. And as He was foretelling these things, He said to them, *Whoever perseveres to the end, he shall be saved.* Matthew 24:13

371. IT WAS THE EVENING OF THE LAST SUPPER in the Cenacle on Mount Sion. Jesus had washed the feet of His Apostles. He asked them if they knew what it was that He had done. He commended them for calling Him Lord and Master for so He was. But if He as their Lord and Master had washed their feet, then He had given them an example that as He had done to them so they also should do to one another. Jesus continued, *Amen, amen, I say to you, no servant is greater than his master, nor is one who is sent greater than he who sent him. If you know these things, blessed shall you be if you do them. I do not speak of you all. I know whom I have chosen; but that the Scripture may be fulfilled, "He who eats bread with Me has lifted up his heel against Me." I tell you now before it comes to pass, that when it has come to pass you may believe that I am He* (the Messias). John 13:16-19

372. THE APOSTLES WERE STILL TOGETHER IN THE CENACLE.
Jesus' hour had come! He must have looked searchingly at
Simon Peter, for He knew that this very night he would deny
Him three times; would grieve, shed bitter tears, and have
deep sorrow for his denials; but despite Peter's weaknesses he
would emerge once more a devoted Apostle who loved his
Master more than anything else in the world. Jesus said to
him, *Simon, Simon, behold, Satan has desired to have you, that
he may sift you as wheat. But I have prayed for thee, that thy
faith may not fail; and do thou, when once thou hast turned
again, strengthen thy brethren.* Luke 22:31-32

373. IN THE FOURTEENTH, FIFTEENTH AND SIXTEENTH CHAP-
TERS of the Gospel according to Saint John, Jesus made a
long discourse. It was immediately after the Last Supper. To
the bewildered and saddened Apostles, He said, *Let not your
heart be troubled. You believe in God, believe also in Me. In
My Father's House there are many mansions. Were it not so,
I should have told you, because I go to prepare a place for
you. And if I go and prepare a place for you, I am coming
again, and I will take you to Myself; that where I am, there
you also may be. And where I go you know, and the way you
know. . . . I am the Way, the Truth, and the Life. No one
comes to the Father but through Me. If you had known Me,
you would also have known My Father. And henceforth you do
know Him, and you have seen Him.* Philip said to Him, "Lord,
show us the Father and it is enough for us." Jesus said to him,
*Have I been so long a time with you, and you have not known
Me? Philip, he who sees Me sees also the Father. How canst
thou say, "Show us the Father"? Dost thou not believe that I am
in the Father and the Father in Me? The words that I speak
to you I speak not on My own authority. But the Father dwelling in Me, it is He Who does the works. Do you believe that
I am in the Father and the Father in Me? Otherwise believe
because of the works themselves. Amen, amen, I say to you,*

he who believes in Me, the works that I do he also shall do, and greater than these he shall do, because I am going to the Father. John 14:1-12

374. PEACE I LEAVE WITH YOU, *My peace I give to you; not as the world gives do I give to you. Do not let your heart be troubled, or be afraid. You have heard Me say to you, "I go away and I am coming to you." If you loved Me, you would indeed rejoice that I am going to the Father, for the Father is greater than I. And now I have told you before it comes to pass, that when it has come to pass you may believe.* John 14:27-29

375. REMEMBER THE WORD *that I have spoken to you: No servant is greater than his master. If they have persecuted Me, they will persecute you also; if they have kept My word, they will keep yours also. But all these things they will do to you for My name's sake, because they do not know Him Who sent Me. If I had not come and spoken to them, they would have no sin. But now they have no excuse for their sin. He who hates Me hates My Father also.* John 15:20-23

376. BUT I SPEAK *the truth to you; it is expedient for you that I depart. For if I do not go, the Advocate will not come to you; but if I go, I will send Him to you. And when He has come He will convict the world of sin, and of justice, and of judgment: of sin, because they do not believe in Me; of justice, because I go to the Father, and you will see Me no more; and of judgment, because the prince of this world has already been judged.* John 16:7-9

377. AMEN, AMEN, *I say to you, if you ask the Father anything in My name, He will give it to you. . . . For the Father Himself loves you because you have loved Me, and have believed that I came forth from God.* John 16:23, 27

OF FAITH, BELIEF IN GOD

378. Do you now believe? *Behold, the hour is coming, and has already come, for you to be scattered, each one to his own house, and to leave Me alone. But I am not alone, because the Father is with Me. These things I have spoken to you that in Me you may have peace. In the world you will have affliction. But take courage, I have overcome the world.* John 16:31-33

379. During Jesus' priestly prayer to the Father for unity among all Christians, Jesus said, *I have manifested Thy name to the men whom Thou hast given Me out of the world. They were Thine, and Thou has given them to Me, and they have kept Thy word. Now they have learnt that whatever Thou has given Me is from Thee; because the words that Thou hast given Me I have given them. And they have received them, and have known of a truth that I came forth from Thee, and they have believed that Thou didst send Me.* John 17:6-8

380. Yet not *for these* (the Apostles) *only do I pray, but for those also who through their word are to believe in Me, that all may be one, even as Thou, Father, in Me and I in Thee; that they may be one in Us, that the world may believe that Thou hast sent Me.* John 17:20-21

381. Now late in the night of the Sabbath, as the first day of the week began to dawn, Mary Magdalene and the other Mary came to the sepulchre in which the body of Jesus had been laid. . . . An angel of the Lord which had come down from Heaven, spoke to them, saying, "Do not be afraid; for I know that you seek Jesus, Who was crucified. He is not here, for He has risen even as He said. Come, see the place where the Lord was laid. And go quickly, tell His disciples that He has risen; and behold, He goes before you into Galilee; there you shall see Him. Behold, I have foretold it to you." The women departed from the tomb in fear and great joy, and ran to tell the disciples. Behold, Jesus met them, saying, *Hail!* They came up and embraced His feet and worshipped Him. Then Jesus said to them, *Do not be afraid; go, take word to My brethren that they are to set out for Galilee; there they shall see Me.* Matthew 28:1-10

382. THE DAY OF THE RESURRECTION two of Jesus' disciples were returning from Jerusalem to their home in Emmaus. Jesus drew near and went along with them, but their eyes were held, that they should not recognize Him. And He said to them, *What words are these that you are exchanging as you walk and are sad?* One of them, named Cleophas, asked Him, "Art thou the only stranger in Jerusalem who does not know the things that have happened there in these days?" Jesus asked, *What things?* They said, "Concerning Jesus of Nazareth, who was a Prophet, mighty in work and word before God and all the people; and how our chief priests and rulers delivered him up to be sentenced to death, and crucified him. But we were hoping that it was he who should redeem Israel. Yes, and besides all this, today is the third day since these things came to pass. And moreover, certain women of our company, who were at the tomb before it was light, astounded us, and not finding his body, they came, saying that they had also seen a vision of angels, who said that he is alive. So some of our company went to the tomb, and found it even as the women had said, but him they did not see." Jesus said to them, *O foolish ones and slow of heart to believe in all that the Prophets have spoken! Did not the Christ have to suffer these things before entering into His glory?* Luke 24:13-26

383. WHEN IT WAS LATE THAT SAME DAY, the first of the week, though the doors where the disciples gathered had been closed for fear of the Jews, Jesus came and stood in their midst and said to them, *Peace to you! It is I, do not be afraid.* But they were startled and panic-stricken, and thought that they saw a spirit. He said to them, *Why are you disturbed, and why do doubts arise in your hearts? See My hands and feet, that it is I Myself. Feel Me and see; for a spirit does not have flesh and bones, as you see I have.* Luke 24:36-39

384. NOW THOMAS, ONE OF THE TWELVE, was not with them when Jesus came. The other disciples therefore said to him, "We have seen the Lord." But he said to them, "Unless I see in his hands the print of the nails, and put my finger into the place of the nails, I will not believe." After eight days, Jesus' disciples were again inside, and Thomas with them. Jesus came, the doors being closed, and stood in their midst, and said, *Peace be to you!* Then He said to Thomas, *Bring here thy finger, and see My hands; and bring here thy hand, and put it into My side; and be not unbelieving, but believing.* Thomas answered and said to Jesus, "My Lord and my God!" Jesus said to him, *Because thou hast seen Me, thou hast believed. Blessed are they who have not seen, and yet have believed.* John 20:24-29

385. THE ELEVEN APOSTLES WENT INTO GALILEE, to the mountain where Jesus had directed them to go. At length He appeared to them. He upbraided them for their lack of faith and hardness of heart, in that they had not believed those who had seen Him after He had risen. And He said to them, *Go into the whole world and preach the Gospel to every creature. He who believes and is baptized shall be saved, but he who does not believe shall be condemned. And these signs shall attend those who believe: in My name they shall cast out devils; they shall speak in new tongues; they shall take up serpents; and if they drink any deadly thing, it shall not hurt them; they shall lay hands upon the sick and they shall get well.* Mark 16:14-18

CHAPTER IX

JESUS SAID
of the Holy Spirit

386. NOW THERE WAS A CERTAIN MAN among the Pharisees, Nicodemus by name, a ruler of the Jews. This man came to Jesus at night, and said to Him, "Rabbi, we know that Thou hast come a teacher from God, for no one can work these signs that Thou workest unless God be with him." Jesus answered him, *Amen, amen, I say to thee, unless a man be born again, he cannot see the Kingdom of God.* Nicodemus said to Him, "How can a man be born when he is old? Can he enter a second time into his mother's womb and be born again?" Jesus answered, *Amen, amen, I say to thee, unless a man be born again of water and the Holy Spirit, he cannot enter into the Kingdom of God. That which is born of the flesh is flesh; and that which is born of the Spirit is spirit. Do not wonder that I said to thee, "You must be born again." The wind blows where it will, and thou hearest its sound but dost not know where it comes from or where it goes. So is everyone who is born of the Spirit.* John 3:5-8

387. JESUS WAS PASSING THROUGH SAMARIA on His way into Galilee. He came to a town called Sichar, near the field that Jacob gave to his son, Joseph. Jacob's well was there. Jesus being weary, was seated beside the well. A Samaritan woman, who came to draw water, recognizing Him to be a Jew, said, "Our fathers worshipped on this mountain (Gerizim), but you say that at Jerusalem is the place where one ought to worship." Jesus said to her, *Woman, believe Me, the hour is coming when neither on this mountain nor in Jerusalem will you worship the Father. You worship what you do not know; we worship what we know, for Salvation is from the Jews. But the hour is coming, and is now here, when the true worshippers will worship the Father in Spirit and in Truth. For the Father also seeks such to worship Him. God is Spirit, and they who worship Him must worship in Spirit and in Truth.*[250] John 4:21-24

388. IT WAS IN NAZARETH OF GALILEE, where He had been brought up, that Jesus began His ministry. According to His custom, He entered the synagogue on the Sabbath and stood up to read. And the volume of Isaias the Prophet was handed to Him. After He opened the volume, He found the place where it was written, *The Spirit of the Lord is upon Me because He has anointed Me; to bring good news to the poor He has sent Me, to proclaim to the captives release, and sight to the blind; to set at liberty the oppressed, to proclaim the acceptable year of the Lord, and the day of recompense.* Closing the volume, He gave it back to the attendant and sat down. The eyes of all in the synagogue were gazing on Him. He said, *Today this Scripture has been fulfilled in your hearing.* All

---

250. *The author is cognizant of variance in the interpretation of "in Spirit" with Saint Thomas who does not take spirit as a reference to the Holy Spirit. The author's interpretation is justified by Monsignor Michael Schmaus, Professor of Theology at the University of Munich, who, in commenting on this text, states, "The word 'in Spirit' we may not confuse with 'innerness' in the psychological sense in contrast to externalization. . . . The adoration in the Spirit and in Truth is therefore an adoration which is formed by the Spirit. . . ."* KATHOLISCHE DOGMATIK, Vol. I, p.313

bore Him witness, and marvelled at the words of grace that came from His mouth. They said, "Is not this Joseph's son?" Luke 4: 16-22

389. Soon after Jesus had chosen the Twelve Apostles, He summoned them together and gave them power over unclean spirits, to cast them out, and to cure every kind of disease and infirmity. Then before sending them out He foretold the opposition which they would meet from the Jews. He said, *Behold, I am sending you forth like sheep in the midst of wolves. Be therefore wise as serpents, and guileless as doves. But beware of men; for they will deliver you up to councils, and scourge you in their synagogues, and you will be brought before governors and kings for My sake, for a witness to them and to the Gentiles. But when they deliver you up, do not be anxious how or what you are to speak; for what you are to speak will be given you in that hour. For it is not you who are speaking, but the Spirit of your Father Who speaks through you.*[251,252] Matthew 10:16-20

390. Jesus cured a possessed man who was also blind and dumb so that he spoke and saw. The people were amazed. But the Pharisees belittled it, saying, "This man does not cast out devils except by Beelzebub, the prince of devils." Jesus knowing their thoughts, said, *But if I cast out devils by the Spirit of God, then the Kingdom of God has come upon you. Or, how can anyone enter the strong man's house, and plunder his goods, unless he first binds the strong man? Then he will plunder his house. He who is not with Me is against Me, and he who does not gather with Me scatters. Therefore I say to you, that every kind of sin and blasphemy shall be forgiven men; but the blasphemy against the Spirit will not be forgiven. And whoever speaks a word against the Son of Man, it shall be for-*

---

251. *Mark 13:10-11;* 252. *Luke 12:11-12*

*given him; but whoever speaks against the Holy Spirit, it will
not be forgiven him, either in this world or in the world to
come.*[253],[254] Matthew 12:28-32

391. JESUS SAID TO THE PEOPLE that He was the Living Bread
that had come down from Heaven. That unless they ate
the flesh of the Son of Man and drank His blood, they would
not have Life Everlasting, neither would He raise them up on
the last day. Many of His disciples said, "This is a hard saying.
Who can listen to it?" Jesus, knowing in Himself that His
disciples were murmuring at this, said to them, *Does this scandalize you? What then if you should see the Son of Man
ascending where He was before? It is the Spirit that gives life;
the flesh profits nothing. The words that I have spoken to you
are Spirit and Life.* Some of the disciples turned back and no
longer went about with Him. John 6:61-64

392. TRADITION HAS IT THAT JESUS gave His Apostles a second
lesson on prayer similar to the one recorded by Matthew
in the Sermon on the Mount in Galilee. This one took place
on the Mount of Olives overlooking the Temple in Jerusalem.
Jesus concluded, *For every one who asks receives; and he who
seeks finds; and to him who knocks it shall be opened. But if
one of you asks his father for a loaf, will he hand him a stone?
or for a fish, will he for a fish hand him a serpent? or if he asks
for an egg, will he hand him a scorpion? Therefore, if you, evil
as you are, know how to give good gifts to your children, how
much more will your Heavenly Father give the Holy Spirit to
those who ask Him!* Luke 11:13

393. THE PHARISEES WERE EVER READY TO TEST JESUS' WORDS
that they might lead to His conviction. One day while
teaching in the Temple, Jesus tested them, saying, *What do you
think of the Christ? Whose Son is He?* They answered, "David's"

---

253. *Mark 3:28-29;* 254. *Luke 12:8-10*

Then Jesus asked further, *How do the Scribes say that the Christ is the son of David? For David himself says, by the Holy Spirit, "The Lord said to my Lord: Sit Thou at My right hand, till I make Thy enemies Thy footstool." David himself, therefore, calls Him "Lord"; how, then, is He his son?* And no one could answer Him a word.[255] Mark 12:35-37

394. THE APOSTLES WERE VERY MUCH SADDENED and could not rejoice when Jesus told them that He was returning to the Father. In His words of comfort He said that He would not leave them orphans; that He was sending them a Comforter, another Advocate. *If you love Me, keep My Commandments. And I will ask the Father and He will give you another Advocate to dwell with you forever, the Spirit of Truth Whom the world cannot receive, because it neither sees Him nor knows Him. But you shall know Him, because He will dwell with you, and be in you. . . . These things I have spoken to you while yet dwelling with you. But the Advocate, the Holy Spirit, Whom the Father will send in My name, He will teach you all things, and bring to your mind whatever I have said to you.* John 14:15-17, 26

395. JESUS SPOKE TO THE ELEVEN about the world's hatred of Him. That if the Jews persecuted Him they would also persecute them because they bore witness to Him. *But when the Advocate has come, Whom I will send from the Father, the Spirit of Truth Who proceeds from the Father, He will bear witness concerning Me. And you also bear witness, because from the beginning you are with Me.* John 15:26-27

396. AND NOW *I am going to Him Who sent Me, and no one of you asks Me, "Where art Thou going?" But because I have spoken to you these things, sorrow has filled your heart. But I speak the truth to you; it is expedient for you that I depart.*

255. *Matthew 22:41-46*

OF THE HOLY SPIRIT

For if I do not go, the Advocate will not come to you; but if I go, I will send Him to you. And when He has come He will convict the world of sin, and of justice, and of judgment: of sin, because they do not believe in Me; of justice, because I go to the Father, and you will see Me no more; and of judgment, because the prince of this world has already been judged. Many things yet I have to say to you, but you cannot bear them now. But when He, the Spirit of Truth, has come, He will teach you all the Truth. For He will not speak on His own authority, but whatever He will hear He will speak, and the things that are to come He will declare to you. He will glorify Me, because He will receive of what is Mine and declare it to you. All things that the Father has are Mine. That is why I have said that He will receive of what is Mine, and will declare it to you. A little while and you shall see Me no longer; and again a little while and you shall see Me, because I go to the Father. John 16:5-16

397. AFTER THE CRUCIFIXION OF JESUS ON GOLGOTHA, His disciples hid themselves. However, late the day of the resurrection of Jesus, the first day of the week, though the doors where the disciples gathered had been closed for fear of the Jews, Jesus came and stood in the midst and said to them, *Peace be to you!* And when He had said this, He showed them His hands and His side. The disciples rejoiced at the sight of the Lord. He said to them again, *Peace be to you!* Despite Peter's denial and their desertion of Him, they remained His chosen Eleven. *As the Father has sent Me, I also send you.* When He had said this, He breathed upon them, and said, *Receive the Holy Spirit; whose sins you shall forgive, they are forgiven them; and whose sins you shall retain, they are retained.* John 20: 19-23

398. THE ELEVEN APOSTLES WENT INTO GALILEE, to the mountain where Jesus had directed them to go. When they saw

Him drawing near, they worshipped Him. Jesus said to them, *All power in Heaven and on earth has been given to Me. Go, therefore, and make disciples of all nations, baptizing them in the name of the Father, and of the Son, and of the Holy Spirit, teaching them to observe all that I have commanded you; and behold, I am with you all days, even unto the consummation of the world.* Matthew 28:16-20

399. JESUS AND HIS APOSTLES WERE GATHERED together for the last time on the Mount of Olives opposite the Temple in Jerusalem. Just before He blessed them, and was carried up into Heaven, He said, *These are the words which I spoke to you while I was yet with you, that all things must be fulfilled that are written in the Law of Moses and the Prophets and the Psalms concerning Me.* Then He opened their minds, that they might understand the Scriptures. And He said to them, *Thus it is written; and thus the Christ should suffer, and should rise again from the dead on the third day; and that repentance and remission of sins should be preached in His name to all the nations, beginning from Jerusalem. And you yourselves are witnesses of these things. And I send forth upon you the promise* (of the Advocate, the Holy Spirit) *of My Father. But wait here in the City, until you are clothed with power On High.* Luke 24:44-49

CHAPTER X

JESUS SAID
of the Soul

400. WHEN NICODEMUS, THE BELIEVING PHARISEE, heard Jesus say that a man cannot enter into the Kingdom of God unless he be born again of water and the Spirit, he was confused. But, in a few pertinent words Jesus explained man's soul in its relationship with the Holy Spirit. Jesus said, *That which is born of the flesh is flesh; and that which is born of the Spirit is spirit. Do not wonder that I said to thee, "You must be born again." The wind blows where it will, and thou hearest its sound but dost not know where it comes from or where it goes. So is everyone who is born of the Spirit.* John 3:5-8

401. JESUS WAS GOING ABOUT all the towns and villages of Galilee, teaching in their synagogues, and preaching the Gospel of the Kingdom of God, and curing every kind of disease and infirmity. Summoning His twelve Apostles, He gave them power over unclean spirits, to cast them out, and to cure every kind of disease and infirmity. Before sending them forth, He cautioned them, that if the Pharisees had called Him Beelzebub, the prince of the devils, how much more those of His household. But Jesus encouraged His disciples, saying, *Do not be afraid of them. . . . Do not be afraid of those who kill the body but cannot kill the soul. But rather be afraid of Him Who is able to destroy both soul and body in hell.*[256] Matthew 9:35, 10:25-28

402. COME TO ME, *all you who labor and are burdened, and I will give you rest. Take My yoke upon you, and learn from Me, for I am meek and humble of heart; and you will find rest for your souls. For My yoke is easy, and My burden light.* Matthew 11:28-30

403. JESUS AND HIS DISCIPLES went out also into the villages of Caesarea Philippi which is to the northeast of Galilee. While there Peter made his confession of faith. After several disciples had ventured to say who the Christ was, Peter said to Jesus, "Thou art the Christ, the Son of the living God." From that time on, Jesus began to show them that He must go to Jerusalem and suffer many things from the elders and Scribes and chief priests, and be put to death, and on the third day rise again. Then He said to His disciples, *If anyone wishes to come after Me, let him deny himself, and take up his cross, and follow Me. For he who would save his life will lose it; but he who loses his life for My sake will find it. For what does it profit a man, if he gain the whole world, but suffer the loss of his own soul? Or what will a man give in exchange for his soul?*[257,258] Matthew 16:24-26

404. NOW WHEN THE TIME APPROACHED for Jesus to be taken up to Heaven, He steadfastly set His face to go to Jerusalem. This particular time He sent two Apostles, James and John, before Him. They entered a Samaritan town to make ready for Jesus. But the Samaritans did not receive Jesus, because they contended that their place of worship on Mount

---

256. *Luke 12:4-5;* 257. *Mark 8:34-37;* 258. *Luke 9:24-25*

OF THE SOUL

Gerizim was the only legitimate place for worship, thus were hostile to anyone going on to the Temple of Jerusalem to worship. When James and John noticed this hostility, they said, "Lord, wilt Thou that we bid fire come down from Heaven and consume them?" Jesus rebuked the Apostles, saying, *You do not know of what manner of spirit you are; for the Son of Man did not come to destroy men's lives, but to save them.* And they went to another village. Luke 9:51-56

405. JESUS WARNED THE PEOPLE AGAINST AVARICE; that a man's life did not consist in the abundance of his possessions. He spoke this parable to them. *The land of a certain rich man brought forth abundant crops. And he began to take thought within himself, saying, "What shall I do, for I have no room to store my crops? I will do this: I will pull down my barns and build larger ones, and there I will store up all my grain and my goods. And I will say to my soul, 'Soul, thou hast many good things laid up for many years; take thy ease, eat, drink, be merry.' " But God said to him, "Thou fool, this night do they demand thy soul of thee; and the things that thou hast provided, whose will they be?" So is he who lays up treasure for himself, and is not rich as regards God.* Luke 12:13-21

406. THE PHARISEES SOUGHT ALWAYS TO PERSECUTE JESUS and to discredit His work in the eyes of the people. One of them, a doctor of the Law, put Him to the test, asking, "Master, which is the great commandment of the Law?" Jesus replied, *"Thou shalt love the Lord thy God with thy whole heart, and with thy whole soul, and with thy whole mind." This is the greatest and the first commandment. And the second is like it, "Thou shalt love they neighbor as thyself." On these two commandments depend the whole Law and the Prophets.*[259] Matthew 22:37

---

259. *Mark 12:30*

407. JESUS PREDICTED THAT BEFORE THE END OF THE WORLD, nation would rise against nation, there would be great earthquakes, pestilences and famines, and terrors and great signs from Heaven. But that before these things happened, the followers of Christ would be arrested and persecuted for bearing witness to Jesus. Some would be put to death. That they would be hated for His name's sake; yet not one hair of their heads would perish. Jesus concluded by saying, *By your patience you will win your souls.* Luke 21:19

408. JESUS' MINISTRY ON EARTH was drawing to a close. He was teaching daily in the Temple about the Kingdom of God and Life Everlasting with Him in Heaven. He had warned the people of the impending destruction of Jerusalem and the end of the world. Then His thoughts turned to Himself. He said that the hour had come for the Son of Man to be glorified: that unless the grain of wheat fell into the ground and died, it remained alone, but if it died, it brought forth much fruit. Anticipating the agony in the Garden and the crucifixion on Golgotha, being filled with fear and sadness, He said, *Now My soul is troubled. And what shall I say? "Father, save Me from this hour!" No, this is why I came to this hour. Father, glorify Thy name!* There came a voice from Heaven, "I have both glorified it, and I will glorify it again." John 12:23-28

409. AFTER THE LAST SUPPER IN THE UPPER ROOM, the Cenacle, on Mount Sion, Jesus foretold the world's hatred and persecution of His Apostles because they believed in Him. But He also had words of comfort. That when He had returned to the Father, He would send them an Advocate, the Spirit of Truth, Who would teach them all the Truth. So having said these things, Jesus went forth with the eleven Apostles, according to His custom, beyond the torrent of Cedron, to the Garden of Gethsemani at the foot of the Mount of Olives. When they arrived there, He told them to sit down, while He went over yonder to pray. He took with Him Peter and James and John. Jesus became saddened and exceedingly troubled. He said to the three, *My soul is sad, even unto death. Wait here and watch with Me.* And going forward a little, He fell prostrate and prayed, saying, *Father, if it is possible, let this cup pass away from Me; yet not as I will, but as Thou willest.*[260] Matthew 26:38

410. PETER AND JAMES AND JOHN whom Jesus had asked to watch with Him in the Garden of Gethsemani, fell asleep; Judas Iscariot, one of the chosen Twelve, betrayed Him; Simon Peter, whom Jesus called the Rock upon which He would build His church, denied Him; the priests, Annas and Caiphas, members of God's chosen race, condemned Him to death; Pontius Pilate, the Roman procurator, who found no guilt in Him, washed His hands of Him; the Jewish mob who had witnessed His innumerable good works, cried, "Crucify Him." Hanging, bleeding and covered with wounds, nailed to a cross of shame between two thieves, Jesus cried, *Father, forgive them, for they know not what they are doing;* to the penitent thief, He said, *Today thou shalt be with Me in Paradise;* to followers, who believe in Him, He gave His mother. His last words were, *Father, into Thy hands I commend My spirit.* And having said this, He expired. Luke 23:46

---

260. *Mark 14:34*

CHAPTER XI

JESUS SAID
of the Good Angels

411. PHILIP, THE THIRD APOSTLE, found Nathanael and said to him, "We have found Him of Whom Moses in the Law and the Prophets wrote, Jesus the son of Joseph of Nazareth." Nathanael said, "Can anything good come out of Nazareth?" Philip replied, "Come and see." Jesus saw Nathanael coming to Him and said of him that he was a true Israelite without guile. Nathanael said to Him, "Whence knowest thou me?" Jesus said that He had seen him under a fig tree before Philip called him. Nathanael was amazed and cried, "Rabbi, Thou art the Son of God, Thou art King of Israel!" Answering, Jesus said to him, *Because I said to thee that I saw thee under the fig tree, thou dost believe. Greater things than these shalt thou see. Amen, amen, I say to you, you shall see Heaven opened, and the angels of God ascending and descending upon the Son of Man.* John 1:45-51

412. JESUS SPOKE IN PARABLES TO THE PEOPLE. One day He
compared the Kingdom of Heaven to a man who sowed
good seed in the field; but while men were asleep, his enemy
came and sowed weeds among the wheat, and went away. Later
on that day the Apostles asked Jesus to explain this parable.
He said, *He Who sows the good seed is the Son of Man. The
field is the world; the good seed, the sons of the Kingdom; the
weeds, the sons of the wicked one; and the enemy who sowed
them is the devil. But the harvest is the end of the world, and
the reapers are the angels. Therefore, just as the weeds are
gathered up and burnt with fire, so will it be at the end of the
world. The Son of Man will send forth His angels, and they will
gather out of His Kingdom all scandals and those who work
iniquity, and cast them into the furnace of fire, where there will
be the gnashing of teeth. Then the just will shine forth like the
sun in the Kingdom of their Father. He who has ears to hear,
let him hear.* Matthew 13:37-43

413. JESUS WAS TEACHING IN THE SYNAGOGUE at Capharnaum
located on the northern shore of the Sea of Galilee. He
likened the Kingdom of God to a fisherman's net, saying, *Again,
the Kingdom of Heaven is like a net cast into the sea that
gathered in fish of every kind. When it was filled, they hauled it
out, and sitting down on the beach, they gathered the good fish
into vessels, but threw away the bad. So will it be at the end of
the world. The angels will go out and separate the wicked from
among the just, and will cast them into the furnace of fire, where
there will be the weeping, and the gnashing of teeth.* Matthew
13:47-50

414. IN TEACHING HIS DISCIPLES the doctrine of the cross, Jesus
said that if anyone wished to come after Him, he must
deny himself, and take up his cross, and follow Him; that he
who would save his life, would lose it; but he who lost his life

for Jesus' sake would find it. Also what profit would a man have, if he gained the whole world, but lost his own soul? Or what would a man give in exchange for his soul? Then Jesus foretold, *For the Son of Man is to come with His angels in the glory of His Father, and then He will render to everyone according to his conduct.*[261,262] Matthew 16:24-27

415. MOTHERS WERE BRINGING LITTLE CHILDREN to Jesus that He might touch them. The disciples rebuked those who brought them. Jesus, seeing this, became indignant, and said to them, *See that you do not despise one of these little ones; for I tell you, their angels in Heaven always behold the face of My Father in Heaven.* Matthew 18:10

416. JESUS OFFERED ENCOURAGEMENT TO HIS DISCIPLES in times of persecution, saying, *And I say to you, everyone who acknowledges Me before men, him will the Son of Man also acknowlege before the angels of God. But whoever disowns Me before men will be disowned before the angels of God.* Luke 12:8-9

417. THE PUBLICANS (MONEY-CHANGERS), AND SINNERS, were drawing near to Jesus to listen to Him. The Pharisees and the Scribes, who were very critical of Him, murmured, saying, "This man welcomes sinners and eats with them." Jesus rebuked them by telling a parable about a woman, having lost a coin, lit a lamp and swept the house and searched carefully until she found it. And when she found it, she called together her friends and neighbors, saying, "Rejoice with me, for I have found the coin that I lost." *Even so, I say to you, there will be joy among the angels of God over one sinner who repents.* Luke 15:8-10

418. JESUS SAW THROUGH THE PRETENSES of the sneering Pharisees and spoke this parable to them. A rich man

---

261. *Mark 8:38;* 262. *Luke 9:26*

clothed himself in purple and fine linen and feasted every day in splendid fashion. And a poor man lay at his gate, covered with sores, who longed to be filled with the crumbs that fell from the rich man's table. The rich man died and was buried in hell. The poor man died also. But he *was borne away by the angels into Abraham's bosom.* Luke 16:22

419. THE SADDUCEES, WHO DID NOT BELIEVE in the resurrection of the dead, came to Jesus and questioned Him regarding the marriage state of the risen dead. Jesus said to them, *The children of this world marry and are given in marriage. But those who shall be accounted worthy of that world and of the resurrection from the dead, neither marry nor take wives. For neither shall they be able to die any more, for they are equal to the angels, and are sons of God, being sons of the resurrection.*[263,264] Luke 20:34-36

420. JESUS WAS SITTING ON THE MOUNT OF OLIVES, opposite the Temple. He had been foretelling the destruction of Jerusalem, and the end of the world. Four of His disciples asked Him privately what would be the sign when all these things began to happen. Jesus said that the sun would be darkened, the moon would not give her light, and the stars would fall, and the powers of Heaven would be shaken. Then would appear the sign of the Son of Man in Heaven. *They will see the Son of Man coming upon clouds with great power and majesty. And then He will send forth His angels, with a trumpet and a great sound, and they will gather His elect from the four winds, from one end of the heavens to the other.*[265] Matthew 24:29-31

421. BUT OF *that day or hour* (of the end of the world) *no one knows, neither the angels in Heaven, nor the Son, but the Father only.*[266] Mark 13:32

---

263. *Matthew 22:30;* 264. *Mark 12:25;* 265. *Mark 13:24-27 ;* 266. *Matthew 24:36*

422. BUT WHEN *the Son of Man shall come in His majesty, and all the angels with Him, then He will sit on the Throne of His glory; and before Him will be gathered all the nations, and He will separate them one from another, as the shepherd separates the sheep from the goats; and He will set the sheep on His right hand, but the goats on the left.* Matthew 25:31-33

423. IT WAS THE NIGHT OF JESUS' AGONY in the Garden of Gethsemani. It was also the hour when Judas Iscariot, one of the Twelve Apostles, now turned traitor, betrayed Him. Judas came with soldiers and a huge mob. When they seized Jesus, Simon Peter drew his sword and cut off the ear of the servant of the high priest. Jesus said to him, *Put back thy sword into its place; for all those who take the sword will perish by the sword. Or dost thou suppose that I cannot entreat My Father, and He will even now furnish Me with more than twelve legions of angels? How then are the Scriptures to be fulfilled, that thus it must take place.* Matthew 26:52-54

CHAPTER XII

JESUS SAID
of the Kingdom of God

424. AFTER JOHN THE BAPTIST had been imprisoned by Herod Antipas of Galilee, Jesus came into Galilee, preaching the Kingdom of God, saying, *The time is fulfilled, and the Kingdom of God is at hand. Repent and believe in the Gospel.*[267] Mark 1:14-15

425. To NICODEMUS, A PHARISEE and a leader among the Jews, who believed in Jesus, Jesus said, *Amen, amen, I say to thee, unless a man be born again, he cannot see the Kingdom of God.* Nicodemus said to Him, "How can a man be born when he is old? Can one enter a second time into his mother's womb and be born again?" Jesus answered, *Amen, amen, I say to thee, unless a man be born again of water and the Holy Spirit, he cannot enter into the Kingdom of God. That which is born of the flesh is flesh; and that which is born of the Spirit is spirit.* John 3:1-7

---

267. *Matthew 4:12-17*

426. JESUS WENT ABOUT ALL GALILEE teaching in the synagogues, and healing every kind of disease. When He withdrew to a desert place to pray the crowds found Him. They
tried to detain Him so that He might not depart from them.
But Jesus said, *To the other towns also I must proclaim the
Kingdom of God, for this is why I have been sent.* Luke 4:42-43

427. JESUS AND HIS DISCIPLES were on the high rise of ground,
known to us as the Mount, on the northern shore of
Galilee. Before them was a great multitude of people. To them
all Jesus said, *Blessed are you poor, for yours is the Kingdom
of God.*[268] Luke 6:20

428. MATTHEW IN HIS SIXTH CHAPTER and Luke in his eleventh
chapter record Jesus' lessons on prayer. In both, Jesus
teaches, *Thy Kingdom come.*[269] Matthew 6:10

429. WE MUST HAVE COMPLETE TRUST IN GOD. For Jesus taught,
*Do not be anxious, saying, "What shall we eat?" or, "What
shall we drink?" or, "What are we to put on?" (for after all
these things the Gentiles seek); for your Father knows that
you need all these things. But seek first the Kingdom of God
and His justice, and all these things shall be given you
besides.*[270] Matthew 6:31-33

430. IN MAKING WITNESS TO JOHN THE BAPTIST, Jesus said,
*This is he of whom it is written, "Behold, I send My
messenger before Thy face, who shall make ready Thy way
before Thee." I say to you, among those born of women there
is not a greater Prophet than John the Baptist; yet the least
in the Kingdom of God is greater than he.*[271] Luke 7:27-28

431. JESUS WAS TEACHING BY THE WATER'S EDGE near Capharnaum. And as a great crowd gathered about Him, He
got into a boat and sat on board. The crowd remained on land

---

268. *Matthew 5:3;* 269. *Luke 11:2;* 270. *Luke 12:29-31;* 271. *Matthew 11:11*

facing the sea. Jesus taught them the parable of the sower who went out to sow. Some seed fell by the wayside, some on rocky ground, some among thorns, but some fell on good ground which grew up yielding much. Later, when the disciples were alone with Jesus they asked Him what the parable meant. He said to them, *To you it is given to know the majesty of the Kingdom of God; but to those outside all things are treated in parables, that "Seeing, they may see, but not perceive; and hearing they may hear, but not understand; lest perhaps at any time they should be converted, and their sins be forgiven them."*[272,273] Mark 4:10-12

432. The seed grows of itself. Jesus said, *Thus is the King-dom of God, as though a man should cast seed into the earth, then sleep and rise, night and day, and the seed should sprout and grow without his knowing it. For of itself the earth bears the crop, first the blade, then the ear, then the full grain in the ear. But when the fruit is ripe, immediately he puts in the sickle because the harvest has come.* Mark 4:26-29

433. Then Jesus makes the comparison of the tiny mustard seed. He said, *To what shall we liken the Kingdom of God; or to what parable shall we compare it? It is like a grain of mustard seed, which, when sown upon the earth, is the smallest of all the seeds upon the earth; yet when it is sown, it grows up and becomes larger than any herb, and puts out great branches, so that the birds of the air can dwell beneath its shade.*[274,275] Mark 4:30-32

434. Jesus must have watched His mother make bread. *To what shall I liken the Kingdom of God? It is like leaven, which a woman took and buried in three measures of flour, until all of it was leavened.*[276] Luke 13:20-21

---

272. *Matthew 13:11; 24-30;* 273. *Luke 8:9-10;* 274. *Matthew 13:31-32;* 275. *Luke 13:18-19;* 276. *Matthew 13:33*

435. THE APOSTLES ASKED JESUS TO EXPLAIN the parable of the weeds. He said to them, *He Who sows the good seed is the Son of Man. . . . Just as the weeds are gathered up and burnt with fire, so will it be at the end of the world. The Son of Man will send forth His angels, and they will gather out of His Kingdom all scandals and those who work iniquity, and cast them into the furnace of fire, where there will be the weeping, and the gnashing of teeth. Then the just will shine forth like the sun in the Kingdom of their Father. He who has ears to hear, let him hear.* Matthew 13:37-43

436. IN TEACHING THE DOCTRINE OF THE CROSS, Jesus said that he who loses his life for Jesus' sake, will save it. *I say to you truly, there are some of those standing here who will not taste death, till they have seen the Kingdom of God.*[277,278] Luke 9:27

437. MANY DESIRED TO FOLLOW CHRIST but could not make the sacrifice. One said, "Lord, let me first go and bury my father." But Jesus said to him, *Let the dead bury their dead, but do thou go and proclaim the Kingdom of God.* Another said, "I will follow Thee, Lord; but let me first bid farewell to those at home." Jesus said to him, *No one, having put his hand to the plow and looking back, is fit for the Kingdom of God.* Luke 9:59-62

438. WHEN JESUS SENT THE SEVENTY-TWO DISCIPLES out before Him, He said to them, *Whatever town you enter, and they receive you, eat what is set before you, and cure the sick who are there, and say to them, "The Kingdom of God is at hand for you." But whatever town you enter, and they do not receive you—go out into its streets and say, "Even the dust from your town that cleaves to us we shake off against you; yet know this, that the Kingdom of God is at hand." I say to*

---

277. *Matthew 16:28;* 278. *Mark 8:39*

198

you, that it will be more tolerable for Sodom in that day than for that town.[279] Luke 10:8-12

439. THE PHARISEES, WHO BLASPHEMED JESUS, said that He cast out devils by Beelzebub, the prince of the devils. Jesus rebuked them, saying, *But if I cast out devils by the finger of God, then the Kingdom of God has come upon you.*[280] Luke 11:20

440. JESUS WAS ASKED BY THE JEWS, "Lord, are only a few to be saved?" He said, *Strive to enter by the narrow gate; for many, I tell you, will seek to enter and will not be able. . . . There will be the weeping, and the gnashing of teeth, when you shall see Abraham and Isaac and Jacob and all the Prophets in the Kingdom of God, but you yourselves cast forth outside. And they will come from the east and from the west, from the north and from the south, and will feast in the Kingdom of God. And behold, there are those last who will be first, and those first who will be last.* Luke 13:24-30

441. ONE TIME WHEN JESUS WAS A DINNER GUEST of a ruler of the Pharisees, He observed how the guests as they entered took the first places at table. Therefore, He gave them a lesson on humility, saying that when they were invited they should go and recline at the last place. To the master of the house, He had a lesson on charity that when he gave a feast he should invite the poor, the crippled, the lame, and the blind. That by so doing he would be blessed, because they had nothing to repay him. However, the master would be repaid at the resurrection of the just. One of those at table, hearing this, said to Jesus, "Blessed is he who shall feast in the Kingdom of God." Then Jesus spoke a parable of a certain man who gave a great supper and invited many. But all of them being pre-occupied, declined the invitation; one had bought a farm, an-

---

279. *Matthew 10:5-15;* 280. *Matthew 12:28*

other five yoke of oxen, another had taken a wife. The master of the house became very angry and sent out his servant to invite the poor, the crippled, the lame, and the blind. And still there was room. Jesus concluded, *Then the master said to the servant, "Go out into the highways and hedges, and make them come in, so that my house may be filled. For I tell you that none of those who were invited shall taste of my supper.*[281] Luke 14:15-24

442. JESUS WAS PREACHING IN THE REGION OF PEREA east of the River Jordan. As usual in the crowd, were some Pharisees. When Jesus saw them sneering at Him, He said, *You are they who declare yourselves just in the sight of men, but God knows your heart; for that which is exalted in the sight of men is an abomination before God. Until John came, there were the Law and the Prophets; since then the Kingdom of God is being preached, and everyone is forcing his way into it. Yet it is easier for Heaven and earth to pass away than for one tittle of the Law to fail.*[282] Luke 16:15-17

443. ON BEING ASKED BY THE PHARISEES, "When is the Kingdom of God coming?" Jesus answered, *The Kingdom of God comes unawares. Neither will they say, "Behold, here it is," or "Behold, there it is." For behold the Kingdom of God is within you.* Theologians interpret that when Jesus used the words *within you* He was saying to the people that the Kingdom of God was in the midst of them and within their power to reach through faith, justice and love. That the Kingdom of God had already begun and the Pharisees might recognize it if they had eyes to see and ears to hear, that the Messias (Christ) is already reigning. Luke 17:20-21

444. MOTHERS WERE BRINGING THEIR BABES TO JESUS that He might touch them. When the disciples saw it, they re-

---

281. *Matthew 22:1-14;* 282. *Matthew 11:12*

buked them. But Jesus called them together and said, *Let the little children come to Me, and do not hinder them, for of such is the Kingdom of God. Amen I say to you, whoever does not accept the Kingdom of God as a little child will not enter into it.*[283] Luke 18:15-17

445. A RICH RULER, WHO KEPT THE TEN COMMANDMENTS OF GOD, knelt before Jesus, imploring, "Good Master, what shall I do to gain Eternal Life?" Jesus said that one thing was lacking to him. That he should sell whatever he had and give to the poor. Then he would have treasure in Heaven. Also that he should come and follow Jesus. When the ruler heard these things, he grieved, for he was very rich. Jesus, seeing him become sad, said, *With what difficulty will they who have riches enter the Kingdom of God! For it is easier for a camel to pass through the eye of a needle, than for a rich man to enter the Kingdom of God.* They who heard this said, "Who then can be saved?" Jesus said to them, *Things that are impossible with men are possible with God.*[284,285] Luke 18:22-27

446. THE MOTHER OF THE APOSTLES JAMES AND JOHN came with them to Jesus, requesting that her two sons might sit, one at Jesus' right hand and one at His left hand in His Kingdom. Jesus said, *To sit at My right hand and at My left, that is not mine to give you, but it belongs to those for whom it has been prepared by My Father.*[286] Matthew 20:20-23

447. WHEN SIMON PETER REMARKED that the disciples had left all and followed Him, Jesus said, *Amen I say to you, there is no one who has left house, or parents, or brother, or wife, or children, for the sake of the Kingdom of God, who shall not receive much more in the present time, and in the age to come Life Everlasting.*[287] Luke 18:28-30

---

283. *Mark 10:13-15;* 284. *Mark 10:17-27;* 285. *Matthew 19:16-26;* 286. *Mark 10:35-40;* 287. *Mark 10:28-30*

448. IF ANYONE *serves Me, let him follow Me; and where I am there also shall My servant be.* John 12:26-27

449. JESUS SPOKE THIS PARABLE to the unbelieving Jews, saying, *But what do you think? A man had two sons; and he came to the first and said, "Son, go and work today in my vineyard." But he answered, "I will not"; but afterwards he repented it and went. And he came to the other and spoke in the same manner. This one answered, "I go, sir"; but he did not go. Which of the two did the father's will?* They said, "The first." Jesus said to them, *Amen, I say to you, the publicans and the harlots are entering the Kingdom of God before you. For John came to you in the way of justice, and you did not believe him. But the publicans and the harlots believed him; whereas you, seeing it, did not even repent afterwards, that you might believe him.* Matthew 21:28-32

450. A SCRIBE, WHO HAD BEEN LISTENING TO JESUS, was very much impressed by His teaching and the answers that He made to questions asked by the Jews. Using the words which Jesus had just uttered, this Scribe said to Him, "Well answered, Master, Thou hast said truly that He (God) is one and that there is no other besides Him; and that He should be loved with the whole heart, and with the whole understanding, and with the whole soul, and with one's whole strength; and that to love one's neighbor as oneself is a greater thing than all holocausts and sacrifices." Jesus, seeing that the Scribe had answered wisely, said to him, *Thou art not far from the Kingdom of God.* Mark 12:28-34

451. To THE CHIEF PRIESTS AND ELDERS of the people gathered in the Temple, Jesus put this question, *Did you never read in the Scriptures, "The stone which the builders rejected, has become the corner stone; by the Lord this has been done, and it is wonderful in our eyes?" Therefore I say to you, that the*

Kingdom of God will be taken away from you and will be given to a people yielding its fruits. And he who falls on this stone will be broken to pieces; but upon whomever it falls, it will grind him to powder. Matthew 21:42-44

452. JESUS HAD BEGUN FORETELLING the destruction of Jerusalem, and the signs that would appear before the end of the world. He foretold that wars, rumors of wars, nation against nation, kingdom against kingdom, pestilences and famines and earthquakes, all these things would be the beginnings of sorrows. The disciples would be delivered up and put to death. They would be hated by all nations for Jesus' name's sake. Then He concluded, *But whoever perseveres to the end, he shall be saved. And this Gospel of the Kingdom shall be preached in the whole world, for a witness to all nations; and then will come the end.*[288,289] Matthew 24:4-14

453. EVEN SO, *when you see these things coming to pass, know that the Kingdom of God is near.*[290,291] Luke 21:31

454. THEN JESUS SAID OF THE LAST JUDGMENT, *But when the Son of Man shall come in His majesty, and all the angels with Him, then He will sit on the Throne of His glory; and before Him will be gathered all the nations, and He will separate them one from another, as the shepherd separates the sheep from the goats; and He will set the sheep on His right hand, but the goats on the left. Then the king will say to those on His right hand, "Come, blessed of My Father, take possession of the Kingdom prepared for you from the foundation of the world."* Matthew 25:31-34

455. IT WAS EARLY SPRING AND THE DAYS OF THE FEAST of the Unleavened Bread. The twelve Apostles went with Jesus to the Cenacle, the Upper Room, on Mount Sion, where Peter

---

288. *Mark 13:10-13;* 289. *Luke 21:13-19;* 290. *Matthew 24:33;* 291. *Mark 13:29*

and John had come earlier to prepare the Passover (the Pascal) Supper. And when the hour had come, Jesus reclined at table, and the twelve Apostles with Him. He said to them, *I have greatly desired to eat this Passover with you before I suffer; for I say to you that I will eat of it no more, until it has been fulfilled in the Kingdom of God.* Luke 22:14-16

456. WHILE THEY WERE EATING THE PASSOVER, Jesus took bread, and blessing it, He broke and gave it to His Apostles, saying, *Take; this is My body.* And taking a cup and giving thanks, He gave it to them, and they all drank of it; and He said to them, *This is My blood of the New Covenant, which is being shed for many. Amen I say to you, that I will drink no more of the fruit of the vine, until that day when I shall drink it new in the Kingdom of God.*[292,293] Mark 14:22-25

457. IN VERY TENDER WORDS, CALLING HIS APOSTLES "little children," Jesus told them that He would be with them but a little while and that where He was going they could not come. Simon Peter asked, "Lord, where art Thou going?" Jesus answered him, *Where I am going thou canst not follow Me now, but thou shalt follow later.* John 13:33-36

458. WHEN THE ELEVEN APOSTLES UNDERSTOOD that Jesus was really leaving them and going to the Father, they could not but grieve that they were not to see Him anymore. Jesus comforted them, saying, *Let not your heart be troubled. You believe in God, believe also in Me. In My Father's House there are many mansions. Were it not so, I should have told you, because I go to prepare a place for you. I am coming again, and I will take you to Myself; that where I am, there you also may be. And where I go you know, and the way you know.* John 14:1-4

---

292. *Matthew 26:29; 293. Luke 22:18*

459. Jesus, made prisoner by the unbelieving Jews, stood before Pontius Pilate. It was in the praetorium of Antonia Palace just across from the Temple in Jerusalem. The Roman procurator, finding no fault in Jesus, asked Him, "What hast thou done?" Jesus answered, *My Kingdom is not of this world. If My Kingdom were of this world, My followers would have fought that I might not be delivered to the Jews. But, as it is, My Kingdom is not from here.* Pilate therefore said to Him, "Thou art then a King?" Jesus answered, *Thou sayest it; I am a King. This is why I was born, and why I have come into the world, to bear witness to the Truth. Everyone who is of the Truth hears My voice.* John 18:36-37

CHAPTER XIII

JESUS SAID
of Heaven and the Kingdom of Heaven

460. As YOU KNOW, Andrew and Simon Peter and Philip were Jesus' first disciples. Then Philip brought Nathanael. When Jesus revealed by what He said that He already knew quite a bit about Nathanael, Nathanael was so filled with faith, that he exclaimed, "Rabbi, Thou art the Son of God, Thou art King of Israel." Jesus answered him, *Amen, amen, I say to you, you shall see Heaven opened and the angels of God ascending and descending upon the Son of Man.* John 1:51

461. NICODEMUS, A PHARISEE AND LEADER AMONG THE JEWS, came by night to learn from Jesus. In teaching him, Jesus used such words and phrases as: being born again of water and the Spirit; flesh, spirit; that the wind is heard, but no one knows where it comes from or where it goes. Summing it up, Jesus said to Nicodemus, *If I have spoken of earthly things to you, and you do not believe, how will you believe if I speak to you of Heavenly things? And no one has ascended into Heaven except Him Who has descended from Heaven: the Son of Man Who is in Heaven.* John 3:12-13

OF HEAVEN AND THE KINGDOM OF HEAVEN

462. JESUS CAME TO NAZARETH, HIS BOYHOOD TOWN. The people there wanted Him to perform miracles as He had in Capharnaum, His adopted city. But He would not, saying that no Prophet is acceptable in his own country. Then as He was preaching He told of the time *when Heaven was shut up for three years and six months, and a great famine came over all the land.* How the Lord protected Elias, the Prophet, by sending him to the home of a widowed woman living in Serepta of Sidon, beyond the northern Jewish border. When Jesus had concluded, the people of Nazareth were so enraged they wanted to destroy Him. Luke 4:25

463. NOW WHEN JESUS HEARD THAT JOHN THE BAPTIST had been delivered up to Herod, He withdrew into Galilee. And leaving the town of Nazareth, He came and dwelt in Capharnaum, which is by the sea, in the territory of Zabulon and Nephthalim; that what was spoken through Isaias the Prophet might be fulfilled: "Land of Zabulon and land of Nephthalim, by the way to the sea, beyond the Jordan, Galilee of the Gentiles: The people who sat in darkness have seen a great Light; and upon those who sat in the region and shadow of death, a Light has arisen." From that time Jesus began to preach, and to say, *Repent, for the Kingdom of Heaven is at hand.*[294,295] Matthew 4:12-17

464. JESUS HAD BEEN ALL NIGHT IN PRAYER on a mountain, the high slope, located on the northwest shore of the Sea of Galilee. In the morning He summoned His disciples, choosing from among them, the Twelve Apostles. Coming down with them, He took His stand on a level stretch, with a crowd of His disciples, and a great multitude of people from all Judea and Jerusalem, and the sea coast of Tyre and Sidon, who came to listen to Him and to be healed of their diseases. Opening His

---

294. *Mark 1:14;* 295. *Saint Matthew records the words of Jesus regarding the Kingdom as the* KINGDOM OF HEAVEN *whereas Saint Mark, Saint Luke and Saint John use the phrase* KINGDOM OF GOD.

mouth He taught them saying, *Blessed are the poor in spirit, for theirs is the Kingdom of Heaven. Blessed are they who suffer persecution for justice' sake, for theirs is the Kingdom of Heaven. Rejoice and exult, because your reward is great in Heaven; for so did they persecute the Prophets who were before you.*[296] Matthew 5:3,10,12

465. SPEAKING OF THE OLD LAW in its relation to the New, Jesus said, *Do not think that I have come to destroy the Law or the Prophets. I have not come to destroy, but to fulfill. For amen I say to you, till Heaven and earth pass away, not one jot or tittle shall be lost from the Law till all things have been accomplished. Therefore whoever does away with one of these least Commandments, and so teaches men, shall be called least in the Kingdom of Heaven; but whoever carries them out and teaches them, he shall be called great in the Kingdom of Heaven. For I say to you that unless your justice exceeds that of the Scribes and Pharisees, you shall not enter the Kingdom of Heaven.*[297] Matthew 5:17-20

466. THEN JESUS TAUGHT THEM CONCERNING OATHS, saying, *You have heard that it was said to the ancients, "Thou shalt not swear falsely, but fulfill thy oaths to the Lord." But I say to you not to swear at all: neither by Heaven, for it is the Throne of God; nor by the earth, for it is His footstool; nor by Jerusalem, for it is the City of the great King.* Matthew 5:33-35

467. JESUS COMMANDED THEM TO LOVE THEIR ENEMIES, saying, *You have heard that it was said, "Thou shalt love thy neighbor, and shalt hate thy enemy." But I say to you, love your enemies, do good to those who hate you, and pray for those who persecute and calumniate you, so that you may be children of your Father in Heaven, Who makes His sun to rise on the*

---

296. *Luke 6:22-23;* 297. *Luke 16:17*

good and the evil, and sends rain on the just and the unjust.
Matthew 5:43-45

468. JESUS CAUTIONED THEM AGAINST INSINCERITY OF INTEN-
TION, saying, *Take heed not to do your good before men, in
order to be seen by them; otherwise you shall have no reward
with your Father in Heaven.* Matthew 6:1

469. IT WAS THERE ON THE MOUNT that Jesus in His Sermon
gave us His Prayer, saying, *In this manner shall you
pray:*[298]

> *Our Father Who art in Heaven,*
> *Hallowed by Thy name.*
> *Thy Kingdom come*
> *Thy will be done on earth*
> *As it is in Heaven.*
> *Give us this day our daily bread.*
> *And forgive us our debts,*
> *As we also forgive our debtors.*
> *And lead us not into temptation,*
> *But deliver us from evil.*

*For if you forgive men their offenses, your Heavenly Father
will also forgive you your offenses.*[299] Matthew 6:9-14

470. Do NOT LAY *up for yourselves treasures on earth, where
rust and moth consumes, and where thieves break in and
steal; but lay up for yourselves treasures in Heaven, where
neither rust nor moth consumes, nor thieves break in and
steal.*[300] Matthew 6:19-20

471. IN EXPOUNDING THE POWER OF PRAYER, Jesus asked the
multitude what man among them, who, if his son asked for
a loaf of bread, would hand him a stone; or, if he asked for a
fish, would give him a serpent. Then He said, *Therefore, if you,*

---

298. *Luke 11:1-4;* 299. *Mark 11:25-26;* 300. *Luke 12:32-34*

evil as you are, know how to give good gifts to your children, how much more will your Father in Heaven give good things to those who ask Him![301] Matthew 7:8-11

472. NEAR THE CONCLUSION OF HIS SERMON on the Mount, regarding obstacles to virtue, Jesus said, *Not everyone who says to Me, "Lord, Lord," shall enter the Kingdom of Heaven; but he who does the will of My Father in Heaven shall enter the Kingdom of Heaven. Many will say to Me in that day, "Lord, Lord, did we not prophesy in Thy name, and cast out devils in Thy name, and work many miracles in Thy name?" And then I will declare to them, "I never knew you. Depart from Me, you workers of iniquity!"* Matthew 7:21-23

473. WHEN THE ROMAN CENTURION IN CAPHARNAUM, whose servant Jesus healed, said to Him, "Lord, I am not worthy that Thou shouldst come under my roof; but only say the word, and my servant will be healed," Jesus marvelled. Jesus said to those about Him, *Amen I say to you, I have not found such great faith in Israel. And I tell you that many will come from the east and from the west, and will feast with Abraham and Isaac and Jacob in the Kingdom of Heaven, but the children of the kingdom will be put forth into the darkness outside; there will be the weeping, and the gnashing of teeth.* Matthew 8:5-12

474. THE TWELVE APOSTLES WERE SENT BY JESUS to their own people. For Jesus instructed them thus: *Do not go in the direction of the Gentiles, nor enter the towns of Samaritans; but go rather to the lost sheep of the house of Israel. And as you go, preach the message, "The Kingdom of Heaven is at hand!"* Matthew 10:5-7

475. JESUS FORETOLD THE OPPOSITION which the Apostles would meet; that they should not be afraid to acknowledge Him

---

301. *Luke 11:11-13*

210

before men; to fear only God Who was able to destroy both body and soul in hell. He said, *Everyone who acknowledges Me before men, I also will acknowledge him before My Father in Heaven. But whoever disowns Me before men, I in turn will disown him before My Father in Heaven.* Matthew 10:32-33

476. IN CHRIST'S WITNESS CONCERNING JOHN THE BAPTIST, Jesus said, *Amen I say to you, among those born of women there has not risen a greater than John the Baptist; yet the least in the Kingdom of Heaven is greater than he. But from the days of John the Baptist until now the Kingdom of Heaven has been enduring violent assault, and the violent have been seizing it by force. For all the Prophets and the Law have prophesied until John. And if you are willing to receive it, he is Elias who was to come. He who has ears to hear, let him hear.*[302] Matthew 11:11-15

477. JESUS REPROACHED THE TOWNS in which most of His miracles were worked, because they had not repented: Corozain and Bethsaida to the north of the Sea of Galilee. To His adopted city, He cried, *And thou, Capharnaum, shalt thou be exalted to Heaven? Thou shalt be thrust down to hell! For if the miracles had been worked in Sodom that have been worked in thee, it would have remained to this day. But I tell you, it will be more tolerable for the land of Sodom on the day of judgment than for thee.*[303] Matthew 11:23-24

478. REJOICING, JESUS SAID, *I praise Thee, Father, Lord of Heaven and earth, that Thou didst hide these things from the wise and prudent, and didst reveal them to little ones. Yes, Father, for such was Thy good pleasure.* Theologians interpret "these things" as the truths of the Kingdom of God which are hidden from the worldly-wise and prudent, but revealed to the

---

302. *Luke 16:16;* 303. *Luke 10:15*

spiritually humble and docile. That the uniqueness of Christ's Sonship (that is, His equal power and perfection with the Father) is among these revealed truths.[304] Luke 10:21-22

479. THE PHARISEES SAID THAT JESUS cast out devils by Beelzebub. This was blasphemy against the Holy Spirit. Jesus said, *Whoever speaks a word against the Son of Man, it shall be forgiven him; but whoever speaks against the Holy Spirit, it will not be forgiven him, either in this world or in the world to come.* Matthew 12:31-32

480. JESUS SAID, *Whoever does the will of My Father in Heaven, he is My brother and sister and mother.* Matthew 12:50

481. GREAT CROWDS LISTENED TO JESUS as He spoke to them in parables. One day the disciples asked Him, "Why dost Thou speak to them in parables? He answered, *To you it is given to know the mysteries of the Kingdom of Heaven, but to them it is not given. . . . In them is being fulfilled the prophecy of Isaias, who says, "Hearing you will hear, but not understand; and seeing you will see, but not perceive. For the heart of this people has been hardened, and with their ears they have been hard of hearing, and their eyes they have closed; lest at any time they see with their eyes, and hear with their ears, and understand with their mind, and be converted, and I heal them."* Matthew 13:10-15

482. HOW THE DEVIL TAKES ADVANTAGE of our lack of understanding. Jesus said, *When anyone hears the word of the Kingdom (of Heaven), but does not understand it, the wicked one comes and snatches away what has been sown in his heart.* Matthew 13:19

---

304. *Matthew 11:25-26*

483. JESUS SET BEFORE THE PEOPLE another parable, saying, *The Kingdom of Heaven is like a man who sowed good seed in his field; but while men were asleep, his enemy came and sowed weeds among the wheat, and went away.* In time the good seed sprouted and so did the weeds. Instead of pulling out the weeds the householder let the wheat and the weeds grow together until the harvest. Jesus concludes the parable, saying, *At harvest time I will say to the reapers: Gather up the weeds first and bind them in bundles to burn; but gather the wheat into my barns.*[305] Matthew 13:24-30

484. ANOTHER PARABLE JESUS SET BEFORE THEM, saying, *The Kingdom of Heaven is like a grain of mustard seed, which a man took and sowed in his field. This indeed is the smallest seed of all the seeds; but when it grows up it is larger than any herb and becomes a tree, so that the birds of the air come and dwell in its branches.*[306,307] Matthew 13:31-32

485. HOUSEWIVES, LISTENING TO THIS PARABLE, could readily understand it. Jesus said, *The Kingdom of Heaven is like leaven, which a woman took and buried in three measures of flour, until all of it was leavened.*[308] Matthew 13:33

486. WHEN JESUS FINALLY LEFT THE CROWDS, His disciples came to Him, saying, "Explain to us the parable of the weeds." Jesus said that He Who sows the seed is the Son of Man. That the field is the world; *the good seed, the sons of the Kingdom;* the weeds, the sons of the wicked one; and the enemy who sowed them is the devil. That the harvest is the end of the world, and the reapers the angels. That therefore, just as the weeds are gathered up and burnt with fire, so will it be at the end of the world. That the Son of Man will send forth His angels, and *they will gather out of His Kingdom* all scandals and those who work iniquity, and cast them into the

---

305. *Mark 4:26-29;* 306. *Mark 4:30-32;* 307. *Luke 13:18-19;* 308. *Luke 13:20-21*

furnace of fire, where there will be the weeping, and the gnashing of teeth. *Then the just will shine forth like the son in the Kingdom of their Father.* Matthew 13:36-43

487. THEN WITH HIS DISCIPLES GATHERED ABOUT HIM, He spoke several more parables, saying, the *Kingdom of Heaven is like a treasure hidden in a field;* he who finds it hides it, and in his joy goes and sells all that he has and buys that field. Again, the *Kingdom of Heaven is like a merchant in search of fine pearls.* When he finds a single pearl of great price, he goes and sells all that he has and buys it. Matthew 13:44-46

488. THE FINAL PARABLE, SPOKEN BY JESUS in this series, was one which the fishermen of Galilee fully understood. It was the parable of the net. Jesus said, *Again, the Kingdom of Heaven is like a net cast into the sea that gathered in fish of every kind. When it was filled, they hauled it out, and sitting down on the beach, they gathered the good fish into vessels, but threw away the bad. So it will be at the end of the world. The angels will go out and separate the wicked from the just, and will cast them into the furnace of fire, where there will be the weeping, and the gnashing of teeth.* Matthew 13:47-50

489. WHEN JESUS HAD FINISHED THESE PARABLES, He asked His beloved Apostles if they understood them. They replied, "Yes." Jesus concluded, *So then every Scribe instructed in the Kingdom of Heaven is like a householder who brings forth from his storeroom things new and old.* Matthew 13:51-52

490. THE JEWS ASKED JESUS, "What are we to do that we may perform the works of God?" Jesus answered that the work of God was for them to believe in Him Whom God had sent. Then they asked Him for a sign that they might believe; that of Moses it was written, "Bread from Heaven he gave them to eat." Jesus replied that Moses did not give them Bread from

Heaven, but *My Father gives you the true Bread from Heaven. For the Bread of God is that Which comes down from Heaven and gives Life to the world.* They said therefore to Him, "Lord, give us always this bread." Jesus said, *I am the Bread of Life. He who comes to Me shall not hunger, and he who believes in Me shall never thrist. . . . For I have come down from Heaven, not to do My own will, but the will of Him Who sent Me. . . . I am the Bread of Life. Your fathers ate the manna in the desert, and have died. This is the Bread That comes down from Heaven, so that if anyone eat of It he will not die. I am the Living Bread that has come down from Heaven. If anyone eat of this Bread he shall live forever; and the Bread that I will give is My flesh for the Life of the world.* John 6:32-33, 38, 48-52

491. THE JEWS ON THAT ACCOUNT ARGUED with one another, saying, "How can this man give us his flesh to eat?" But Jesus repeated, *Amen, amen, I say to you, unless you eat the flesh of the Son of Man and drink His blood, you shall not have Life in you. . . . This is the Bread that has come down from Heaven; not as your fathers ate the manna, and died. He who eats this Bread shall live forever.* John 6:53-59

492. JESUS SAID TO THE SCRIBES AN PHARISEES that the Prophet Isaias had prophesied well about them, saying, "This people honors me with their lips, but their heart is far from me;" His disciples came up to Him later and said that the Pharisees had taken offense at what He had said. Jesus answered, *Every plant that My Heavenly Father has not planted will be rooted up.* Matthew 15:8-13

493. SEVENTY-TWO DISCIPLES HAD BEEN SENT OUT BY JESUS to spread His Gospel of the Kingdom of Heaven. Also, Jesus had given them the power to cure all diseases. They returned with joy, saying, "Lord, even the devils are subject to us in Thy name." Jesus rejoiced too that the powers of evil were being shaken, for He said, *I was watching Satan fall as lightning from Heaven. Behold, I have given you power to tread upon serpents and scorpions, and over all the might of the enemy; and nothing shall hurt you. But do not rejoice in this, that the spirits are subject to you; rejoice rather in this, that your names are written in Heaven.* Luke 10:18-20

494. THE DISCIPLES FELL TO ARGUING amongst themselves but finally came to Jesus, asking, "Who then is the greatest in the Kingdom of Heaven?" Jesus set a little child in their midst, and said, *Amen I say to you, unless you turn and become like little children, you will not enter into the Kingdom of Heaven. Whoever, therefore, humbles himself as this little child, he is the greatest in the Kingdom of Heaven.* Matthew 18:3-4

495. JESUS COUNSELLED HIS DISCIPLES STRONGLY to avoid scandal. He said that if one's hand, or foot, or eye was an occasion of sin, to cast it away. That it is better to enter the Kingdom of Heaven, maimed than be cast into hell-fire. Then calling their attention to the little child beside Him, He said, *See that you do not despise one of these little ones; for I tell you, their angels in Heaven always behold the face of My Father in Heaven.*[309] *. . . It is not the will of your Father in Heaven that a single one of these little ones should perish.* Matthew 18:7-14

496. GREAT POWERS OF FRATERNAL CORRECTION were conferred upon the Church by Jesus. Any wrong should be settled by the two persons concerned. If no reconciliation is made, to call in two or three witnesses. If the wrongdoer refuses to listen, appeal to the Church. If he refuses even to hear the Church, let him be as the heathen and the publican. Jesus said, *Amen*

---

309. *Mark 9:42-46*

216

I say to you, whatever you bind on earth shall be bound also in Heaven; and whatever you loose on earth shall be loosed in Heaven. I say to you further, that if two of you shall agree on earth about anything at all for which they ask, it shall be done for them by My Father in Heaven. Matthew 18:15-19

497. SIMON PETER THEN ASKED JESUS, "Lord how often shall my brother sin against me, and I forgive him? Up to seven times? Jesus replied, *I do not say to thee seven times, but seventy times seven. This is why the Kingdom of Heaven is likened to a king who desired to settle accounts with his servants.* One of them owed him a huge sum of money, ten thousand talents. The king demanded payment. Since the servant had no means of paying, he was ordered sold, with his wife and children and all that he had, and payment to be made. But because the servant, falling at his knees, implored him to be merciful and have patience, the king forgave him the debt. As this servant went out, he met a fellow-servant who owed him one hundred denarii, less than twenty dollars. He demanded payment of him but the man had no means of paying. Even so, he began strangling him, saying, "Pay what you owe." The fellow-servant pleaded for mercy and patience. But he would not. When the fellow-servants witnessed this cruelty, they informed the king. He became so enraged that he handed the unmerciful servant over to the torturers until he should pay all that he owed him. Jesus concluded, *So also My Heavenly Father will do to you, if you do not each forgive your brothers from your hearts.* Matthew 18:22-35

498. JESUS WARNED HIS DISCIPLES against avarice and covetousness of things material. Also that they should put their trust in God. He said, *Do not be afraid, little flock, for it has pleased your Father to give you the Kingdom. Sell what you have and give alms. Make for yourselves purses that do not* *grow old, a treasure unfailing in Heaven, where neither thief draws near nor moth destroys. For where your treasure is, there also will your heart be.*[310] Luke 12:32-34

499. THE MARRIAGE STATE WAS DISCUSSED BY JESUS and His disciples. Scholars have interpreted Jesus' teaching that chastity in view of the Kingdom of God (Heaven) is better than the married life. For Jesus said, *Not all can accept this teaching; but those to whom it has been given. For there are eunuchs who were born so from their mother's womb; and there are eunuchs who were made so by men; and there are eunuchs who have made themselves so for the sake of the Kingdom of Heaven. Let him accept it who can.* Matthew 19:10-12

500. LITTLE CHILDREN WERE BROUGHT TO JESUS that He might lay His hands on them and pray; but the disciples rebuked the mothers. Jesus said, *Let the little children be, and do not hinder them from coming to Me, for of such is the Kingdom of Heaven.*[311,312] Matthew 19:13-15

501. A RICH RULER, who obeyed the Ten Commandments, came to Jesus and asked Him, "Good Master, what shall I do to gain Eternal life? What is yet wanting in me?" Jesus replied, *If thou wilt be perfect, go, sell what thou hast, and give to the poor, and thou shalt have treasure in Heaven; and come, follow Me.* But when the young man heard the saying, he went away sad, for he had great possessions. Jesus said to His disciples, *Amen I say to you, with difficulty will a rich man enter the Kingdom of Heaven. And further I say to you, it is easier for a camel to pass through the eye of a needle, than for a rich man to enter the Kingdom of Heaven.* The astonished disciples asked, "Who then can be saved?" Jesus answered, *With men this is impossible, but with God all things are possible.*[313] Matthew 19:16-26

---

310. *Matthew 6:19-20;* 311. *Mark 10:13-16;* 312. *Luke 18:15-17;* 313. *Luke 18:22-25*

502. WHEN THE PHARISEES AND SCRIBES saw publicans (tax collectors), and sinners drawing near to Jesus to listen to Him, they murmured, "This man welcomes sinners and eats with them." Therefore Jesus spoke a parable to them of the shepherd who had lost one sheep. He left the ninety-nine to search for it. Great was his joy when he found it and returned it to the fold. Jesus concluded, *I say to you that, even so, there will be joy in Heaven over one sinner who repents, more than over ninety-nine just who have no need of repentance.* Luke 15:1-7

503. ON BEING ASKED BY THE PHARISEES, "When is the Kingdom of God coming?" Jesus answered, *The Kingdom of God* (Heaven) *comes unawares. Or as it came to pass in the days of Lot: they were eating and drinking, they were buying and selling, they were planting and building; but on the day that Lot went out from Sodom, it rained fire and brimstone from Heaven and destroyed them all. In the same wise will it be on the day that the Son of Man is revealed.* Luke 17:20-30

504. TO THOSE WHO TRUSTED IN THEMSELVES as being just and despised others, Jesus spoke this parable. *Two men went up to the Temple to pray, the one a Pharisee and the other a publican.* The Pharisee extolled himself in prayer and boasted of his many pious deeds. *But the publican, standing afar off, would not so much as lift up his eyes to Heaven, but kept striking his breast, saying, "O God, be merciful to me the sinner!" I tell you, this man went back to his home justified rather than the other; for everyone who exalts himself shall be humbled, and he who humbles himself shall be exalted.* Luke 18:9-14

505. JESUS SPOKE THIS PARABLE of laborers in a vineyard, saying, *The Kingdom of Heaven is like a householder who went out early in the morning to hire laborers for his vineyard.* Some he hired at nine o'clock, others at noon, at three, and even as late as five o'clock. He agreed to pay all of them the usual day's wage for field work of one denarius (about seventeen cents). At the end of the day, those who had worked all day, complained, when they noticed that even those who had worked but an hour received one denarius also. But the householder, who hired them, felt justified, saying that he chose to give these last the same reward. Thus in the supernatural life of the soul, God's grace may make one who has served Him but a short time as worthy of supernatural rewards as one who has borne the burden of the day's heat. Matthew 20:1-16

506. THE MOTHER OF THE APOSTLES JAMES AND JOHN came to Jesus with her sons, saying, "Command that these my two sons may sit, one at Thy right hand and one at Thy left in Thy Kingdom." Jesus replied, *As for sitting at My right hand and at My left, that is not Mine to give you, but it belongs to those for whom it has been prepared by My Father.*[314] Matthew 20:20-23

507. IF ANYONE *serves Me, let him follow Me; and where I am there also shall My servant be. If anyone serves Me, My Father will honor him.* John 12:26

508. ADDRESSING THE JEWS, Jesus spoke to them again in parables, saying, *The Kingdom of Heaven is like a king who made a marriage feast for his son. And he sent his servants to call in those invited to the marriage feast, but they would not come.* (This refers to the rejection of the Jews.) The king became very angry. Therefore when the marriage feast was indeed ready, and those invited no longer worthy, the king said to his servants, "Go, therefore, to the crossroads and invite whomever you shall find." And the marriage feast was filled with guests. Now the king saw there a man who had not on a wedding garment. The attendants were told to bind his hands

---

314. *Mark 10:35-40*

and feet and cast him forth into the darkness outside. *For many are called but few are chosen.*[315] Matthew 22:1-14

509. THE LEADERS OF THE JEWS BLASPHEMED JESUS and His works, and tried their worst to make naught of His teachings. Jesus said to them, *Woe to you, Scribes and Pharisees, hypocrites! because you shut the Kingdom of Heaven against men. For you yourselves do not go in, nor do you allow those going in to enter.* Matthew 23:13

510. THE JEWS WERE TOLD OF OLD NOT TO SWEAR FALSELY, but to fulfill the oaths to the Lord. But Jesus taught them not to swear at all.[316] He said, *He who swears by Heaven swears by the Throne of God, and by Him Who sits upon it.* Matthew 23:22

511. ON ONE OF THE DAYS, AS JESUS WAS TEACHING THE PEOPLE in the Temple and preaching the Gospel of the Kingdom of God, the chief priests and Scribes together with the elders came up and spoke to Him, saying, "Tell us, by what authority dost thou do these things? Or who is it that gave thee this authority?" He said to them, *I also ask you one question. Answer Me: Was the baptism of John from Heaven, or from men?* But they began to argue among themselves, saying, "If we say, 'From heaven,' he will say, 'Why then did you not believe him?' But if we say, 'From men,' all the people will stone us; for they are convinced that John (the Baptist) was a Prophet." And they answered that they did not know whence it was. Then Jesus said to them, *Neither do I tell you by what authority I do these things.*[317] Luke 20:1-8

512. SOME OF THE SADDUCEES, who did not believe in the resurrection, came to Jesus to test Him. So they asked Him this question: At the resurrection, whose wife will a woman be

315. *Luke 14:16-24;* 316. *Matthew 5:33-34;* 317. *Mark 11:27-33*

who during her lifetime, had had several husbands? For each had had her as wife. Jesus answered, *You err because you know neither the Scriptures nor the power of God. For at the resurrection they will neither marry nor be given in marriage, but will be as angels of God in Heaven.*[318,319] Matthew 22:23-30

513. JESUS HAD BEEN IN THE ENVIRONS OF JERUSALEM for some days. One day, after preaching to the people in the Temple, He left with His disciples for the Mount of Olives. As He was sitting there, facing Jerusalem, His disciples came to Him privately, saying, "Tell us, when are these things to happen, and what will be the sign of Thy coming and of the end of the world?"[320] He told them that they would be hated by all nations for His name's sake; they would be persecuted and even put to death. He prophesied the destruction of Jerusalem. And then He spoke of the signs preceding His coming, saying, *But immediately after the tribulation of those days, the sun will be darkened, and the moon will not give her light and the stars will fall from Heaven, and the powers of Heaven will be shaken. And then will appear the sign of the Son of Man in Heaven; and then will all tribes of the earth mourn, and they will see the Son of Man coming upon the clouds of Heaven with great power and majesty. And He will send forth His angels with a trumpet and a great sound, and they will gather His elect from the four winds, from one end of the Heavens to the other.*[321,322] Matthew 24:29-31

514. WHEN JESUS FORETOLD THE IMPENDING DESTRUCTION OF JERUSALEM and the end of the world, He did so with great authority and finality, saying, *Heaven and earth will pass away, but My words will not pass away. But of that day and hour no one knows, not even the angels of Heaven, nor the Son, but the Father only.*[323,324] Mark 13:31-32

---

318. *Mark 12:18-25;* 319. *Luke 20:27-36;* 320. *Luke 21:10-11;* 321. *Mark 13:24-27;* 322. *Luke 21:25-27;* 323. *Matthew 24:35-36;* 324. *Luke 21:32-33*

OF HEAVEN AND THE KINGDOM OF HEAVEN

515. To impress upon the minds of the disciples the great need for readiness and watchfulness when the Son of Man shall appear, Jesus spoke the parable of the ten virgins. He said, *Then will the Kingdom of Heaven be like ten virgins who took their lamps and went forth to meet the bridegroom. Five of them were foolish and five wise.* The five foolish virgins took no oil in their vessels with the lamps, the wise did. The bridegroom was long in coming; the foolish ones became drowsy and slept. When the bridegroom came the lamps of the foolish were going out and they had to go to purchase more oil. Since the wise virgins had oil in their vessels and were ready and watching, they went in with the bridegroom to the marriage feast. The door was then shut. Now the five foolish virgins came also to enter. But the bridegroom said, "Amen I say to you, I do not know you." Jesus concludes the parable by saying, *Watch therefore, for you know neither the day nor the hour.* Matthew 25:1-13

516. Because the people and even the disciples thought that the Kingdom of Heaven was going to appear immediately, Jesus spoke the parable of the ten gold pieces, saying, *For it* (the Kingdom of Heaven) *is like a man going abroad, who called his servants and handed over his wealth to them. To one he gave five talents, to another two, and to another one, to each according to his particular ability. Then he went on his journey.* After a long time the master of those servants came and settled accounts with them. He who had received five talents had gained five more; and likewise he who had received two talents gained two more. The master was very well pleased and rewarded them. But he was very disappointed with the servant who had received one talent, for he had buried it. Because he had done nothing with his talent, the master ordered him cast forth into the darkness outside where there would be the weeping, and the gnashing of teeth. Scholars have interpreted that through this parable Jesus intimated that considerable time would elapse before the establishment of the glorious phase of His Kingdom. Also that in the meantime His disciples should work for Him, and thus prepare for the judgment.[325] Matthew 25:14-30

517. THEN JESUS SPOKE PLAINLY TO HIS DISCIPLES of Himself and the Kingdom of Heaven, saying, *But when the Son of Man shall come in His majesty, and all the angels with Him, then He will sit on the Throne of His glory; and before Him will be gathered all the nations, and He will separate them one from another, as the shepherd separates the sheep from the goats; and He will set the sheep on His right hand, but the goats on the left. Then the King will say to those on His right hand, "Come, blessed of My Father, take possession of the Kingdom prepared for you from the foundation of the world.* Matthew 25:31-34

518. IT WAS AFTER THE PASSOVER (the Last Supper), in the Cenacle on Mount Sion that Jesus said to His Apostles, *You are they who have continued with Me in My trials. And I appoint to you a kingdom, even as My Father has appointed to Me, that you may eat and drink at My table in My Kingdom; and you shall sit upon thrones, judging the twelve tribes of Israel.* Luke 22:29-30

519. IT WAS DIFFICULT FOR THE APOSTLES to comprehend that their Friend and Master was leaving them to go . . . they knew not where. Then, Simon Peter spoke up, "Lord, where art Thou going?" Jesus answered, *Where I am going thou canst not follow Me now, but thou shalt follow later.* John 13:36

520. DURING THE LAST SUPPER JESUS HAD MUCH TO SAY to His Apostles which they then did not understand. It filled them with dismay and deep sorrow. Jesus had said that Judas

---

325. *Luke 19:11-27*

Iscariot would betray Him to the high priests; that Peter would deny Him three times; and that all of them would desert Him and be scattered. Then He had many words of comfort, saying, *Let not your heart be troubled. You believe in God, believe also in Me. In My Father's House there are many mansions. Were it not so, I should have told you, because I go to prepare a place for you. And if I go and prepare a place for you, I am coming again, and I will take you to Myself; that where I am, there you also may be. And where I go you know, and the way you know.* John 14:1-4

521. IN EXPLAINING THE ROLE OF THE HOLY SPIRIT, the Advocate, to His Apostles, Jesus said, *And now I am going to Him Who sent Me, and no one of you asks Me, "Where art Thou going?" But because I have spoken to you these things, sorrow has filled your heart. But I speak the truth to you; it is expedient for you that I depart. For if I do not go, the Advocate will not come to you; but if I go, I will send Him to you. And when He has come He will convict the world of sin, and of justice, and of judgment: of sin, because they do not believe in Me; of justice, because I go to the Father, and you will see Me no more; and of judgment, because the prince of this world has already been judged.* John 16:5-11

522. WHEN JESUS SAID, *I came forth from the Father and have come into the world. Again I leave the world and go to the Father,* His disciples said to Him, "Behold, now Thou speakest plainly, and utterest no parable. Now we know that Thou knowest all things, and dost not need that anyone should question Thee. For this reason we believe that Thou camest forth from God." John 16:28-30

523. SAINT JOHN IN HIS SEVENTEENTH CHAPTER does not tell us where Jesus was when He made His priestly prayer for unity. We know it was in or near Jerusalem. In my humble opinion it could have been somewhere along the way from the Cenacle down to the large cave, known to us as the Grotto of Betrayal, at the foot of Mount Olivet near the Garden of Gethsemani. Jesus was in profound communion with the Father when He prayed, *I pray for them* (His chosen Apostles); *not for the world do I pray, but for those whom Thou hast given Me, because they are Thine; and all things that are Mine are Thine, and Thine are Mine; and I am glorified in them. And I am no longer in the world, but these are in the world, and I am coming to Thee. Holy Father, keep in Thy name those whom Thou hast given Me, that they may be one even as We are. While I was with them, I kept them in Thy name. Those whom Thou hast given Me I guarded; and not one of them perished except the son of perdition, in order that the Scripture might be fulfilled. But now I am coming to Thee; and these things I speak in the world, in order that they may have My joy made full in themselves. . . . Father, I will that where I am, they also whom Thou hast given Me may be with Me; in order that they may behold My glory, which Thou hast given Me, because Thou hast loved Me before the creation of the world.* John 17:9-13, 24

524. JUDAS ISCARIOT, ONE OF THE TWELVE APOSTLES now turned traitor, came with soldiers and attendants of the Jews to the cave. There Judas betrayed Jesus with a kiss. Jesus was seized and made prisoner. They led Him bound first to Annas, who, although deposed as high priest, had great influence. Then they brought Him before the Sanhedrin, the highest ecclesiastical and civil court of the Jews. Caiphas, who was high priest that year, said to Jesus, "I adjure thee by the living God that thou tell us whether thou art the Christ, the Son of God." Jesus said to him, *Thou has said it. Nevertheless, I say to you, hereafter you shall see the Son of Man sitting at the right hand of the Power (of God) and coming upon the clouds of Heaven.*[326,327] *Matthew* 26:64-65

326. *Mark 14:62*; 327. *Luke 22:67-69*

525. THEN THE LEADERS OF THE JEWS caused Jesus to be brought from the Sanhedrin to the Roman praetorium, the Palace Antonia. There Pontius Pilate, the Roman governor of Judea, questioned Him. Since he could find no guilt in Jesus, Pilate asked Him, "What hast thou done?" Jesus replied, *My Kingdom is not of this world. If My Kingdom were of this world, My followers would have fought that I might not be delivered to the Jews. But, as it is, My Kingdom is not from here.* Pilate therefore said to Him, "Thou art then a king?" Jesus answered, *Thou sayest it; I am a King. This is why I was born, and why I have come into the world, to bear witness to the Truth. Everyone who is of the Truth hears My voice.* Pilate said to Him, "What is truth?" John 18:36-38

526. PONTIUS PILATE WENT BEFORE THE JEWISH MOB in front of the praetorium, and said, "Take Him (Jesus) yourselves and crucify Him, for I find no guilt in Him." The Jews answered, "We have a Law, and according to that Law he must die, because he has made himself Son of God." Now when Pilate heard this statement, he feared the more. He returned to Jesus and said, "Where art thou from?" Jesus made no answer. Pilate therefore said to Him, "Dost thou not know that I have power to crucify Thee, and that I have power to release Thee?" Jesus replied, *Thou wouldst have no power at all over Me were it not given thee from Above. Therefore, he who betrayed Me to thee has the greater sin.* John 19:6-11

527. IN THE EARLY MORNING OF HIS RESURRECTION from the dead, Jesus manifested Himself to the women who were returning from the empty tomb in which He had been laid. Jesus said to them, *Do not be afraid; go, take word to My brethren that they are to set out for Galilee; there they shall see Me.*[328] So the eleven Apostles went into Galilee, to the moun-

---

328. *Matthew 28:10*

tain where Jesus had directed them to go. And when they saw Him they worshipped Him; but some doubted. Jesus drew near and spoke to them saying, *All power in Heaven and on earth has been given to Me. Go, therefore, and make disciples of all nations, baptizing them in the name of the Father, and of the Son, and of the Holy Spirit, teaching them to observe all that I have commanded you; and behold, I am with you all days, even unto the consummation of the world.* Matthew 28:16-20

528. ACCORDING TO THE TWENTY-FOURTH CHAPTER OF SAINT LUKE, in His last instructions to the Apostles, Jesus said, *These are the words which I spoke to you while I was yet with you, that all things must be fulfilled that are written in the Law of Moses and the Prophets and the Psalms concerning Me.* Then He opened their minds, that they might understand the Scriptures. And He said to them, *Thus it is written; and thus the Christ should suffer, and should rise again from the dead on the third day; and that repentance and remission of sins should be preached in His name to all nations, beginning from Jerusalem. And you yourselves are witnesses of these things. And I send forth upon you the promise of My Father. But wait here in the city, until you are clothed with power from On High.* Then He led them out towards Bethany, but stopped on the summit of the Mount of Olives overlooking Jerusalem. Here He lifted His hands in benediction. During this farewell blessing He parted from them being carried up into Heaven. Luke 24:44-51

CHAPTER XIV

JESUS SAID
of Satan and the Bad Angels

529. IMMEDIATELY AFTER JESUS HAD BEEN BAPTIZED in the River Jordan by John the Baptist, He was led into the desert nearby by the Holy Spirit, to be tempted by the devil. Here He fasted for forty days and forty nights. He had great hunger. The tempter came and said to Him, "If Thou art the Son of God, command that these stones become loaves of bread." Jesus answered, *It is written, "Not by bread alone does man live, but by every word that comes forth from the mouth of God."* Then the devil took Him into the holy city, Jerusalem, and set Him on the pinnacle of the Temple, and said to Him, "If Thou art the Son of God, throw Thyself down; for it is written, 'He will give His angels charge concerning thee; and upon their hands they shall bear thee up, lest thou dash thy foot against a stone.'" Jesus said to him, *It is written further, "Thou shalt not tempt the Lord thy God."* Again, the devil took Him to a very high mountain, and showed Him all the kingdoms of the world and the glory of them. And he said to Him, "All these things will I give Thee, if Thou wilt fall down and worship me."

Then Jesus said to him, *Begone, Satan! for it is written, "The Lord thy God shalt thou worship and Him only shalt thou serve.* Then the devil left Him; and behold, angels came and ministered to Him.[329,330] Matthew 4:1-11

530. JESUS AND HIS NEWLY CHOSEN APOSTLES went through Samaria and into Galilee to Capharnaum on the northern shore of the Sea of Galilee, also known as Lake Tiberias or Lake Genesareth. Here at Capharnaum a Roman official had erected a beautiful synagogue for the Jews. It was the Sabbath. Jesus went into this synagogue to preach. A man was there possessed by an unclean devil. When the unclean devil saw Jesus, he cried out with a loud voice, "Let us alone! What have we to do with Thee, Jesus of Nazareth? Hast Thou come to destroy us? I know Thee, Who Thou art, the Holy One of God." Jesus rebuked him, saying, *Hold thy peace, and go out of him.* And when the devil had thrown the man down into their midst, he went out of him, without harming him at all. Amazement came upon all, and they discussed it with one another, saying, "What is this word? For with authority and power He commands the unclean spirits, and they come out." And rumor concerning Jesus went forth into every place roundabout Galilee.[331] Luke 4:33-37

531. A POSSESSED MAN WHO WAS BLIND AND DUMB was brought to Jesus. He cured the man so that he spoke and saw. The crowds were amazed but the Pharisees, hearing this, said, "This man does not cast out devils except by Beelzebub, the prince of devils. Knowing their thoughts, Jesus said to them, *If Satan casts out Satan, he is divided against himself; how then shall his kingdom stand? And if I cast out devils by Beelzebub, by whom do your children cast them out? Therefore they shall be your judges. But if I cast out devils by the Spirit of God, then*

329. *Mark 1:12-13;* 330. *Luke 4:1-13;* 331. *Mark 1:23-28*

230

the Kingdom of God has come upon you.[332,333] Matthew 12: 22-28

532. JESUS WARNED HIS LISTENERS THAT A DEVIL which has been cast out of a man may return. For He said, *When the unclean spirit has gone out of a man, he roams through dry places in search of rest, and finds none. Then he says, "I will return to my house which I left"; and when he has come to it, he finds the place unoccupied, swept and decorated. Then he goes and takes with him seven other spirits more evil than himself, and they enter in and dwell there; and the last state of that man becomes worse than the first. So shall it be with this evil generation also.*[334] Matthew 12:43-45

533. ACCORDING TO THE THIRTEENTH CHAPTER OF SAINT MATTHEW, Jesus spoke two parables on the Sower. In the first one, Jesus said, *The Sower went out to sow. And as he sowed, some seeds fell by the wayside.* That some fell on rocky ground, some fell among thorns, and some upon good ground which yielded much fruit. . . . *When anyone hears the word of the Kingdom* (of Heaven), *but does not understand it, the wicked one comes and snatches what has been sown in his heart. This is he who is sown by the wayside.* Matthew 13:18-19

534. ACCORDING TO THE FOURTH CHAPTER OF SAINT MARK, Jesus spoke this same parable, saying, *The Sower sows the Word* (of God). *Those by the wayside are they in whom the Word is sown. As soon as they have heard, Satan at once comes and takes away the Word that has been sown in their hearts.* Mark 4:14-15

535. ACCORDING TO THE EIGHTH CHAPTER OF SAINT LUKE, on this same parable, Jesus said, *Now the parable* (of the Sower) *is this: The seed is the Word of God. Those by the way-*

332. *Mark 3:20-26;* 333. *Luke 11:14-20;* 334. *Luke 11:24-26*

side are they who have heard. But the devil comes and takes away the Word from their heart, that they may not believe and be saved. Luke 8:11-12

536. IN HIS SECOND PARABLE OF THE SOWER (the parable of the weeds), Jesus said, *The Kingdom of Heaven is like a man who sowed good seed in his field; but while men were asleep, his enemy came and sowed weeds among the wheat, and went away. And when the blade sprang up and brought forth fruit, then the weeds appeared as well.* Seeing this, the servants of the sower asked him if they should gather up the weeds. He directed them not to, because in so doing they would uproot the wheat also; that at harvest time he would tell the reapers to gather the weeds up into bundles to burn; but put the wheat into his barn. . . . The disciples did not understand this parable. So when they were alone with Jesus, they asked Him to explain it. Jesus said, *He Who sows the good seed is the Son of Man. The field is the world; the good seed, the sons of the Kingdom* (of Heaven); *the weeds, the sons of the wicked one; and the enemy who sowed them is the devil.* Matthew 13:24-30;36-43

537. THESE PARABLES OF THE SOWER were spoken by Jesus near Capharnaum. Now He departed from there and went with His disciples to the other side of the Sea of Galilee southward to the country of the Gerasenes (Syria today). As soon as Jesus stepped out of the boat, there met Him from the tombs a man with an unclean spirit. This man lived in the tombs. No one could any longer bind him, even with chains. Often he had been bound with fetters and chains, and he rent the chains asunder and broke the fetters into pieces. No one was able to control him. Constantly, night and day, he was in the tombs and on the mountains, howling and gashing himself with stones. When he saw Jesus from afar, he ran and worshipped Him. Crying out with a loud voice, he said, "What have I to do with Thee, Jesus, Son of the most high God? I adjure

Thee by God, do not torment me!" For Jesus was saying to him, *Go out of the man, thou unclean spirit.* Jesus asked him, *What is thy name?* And he said to Jesus, "My name is Legion, for we are many." He entreated Jesus earnestly not to drive them out of the country. Now a great herd of swine was there on the mountain-side, feeding. The spirits kept entreating Him, saying, "Send us into the swine, that we may enter into them." Jesus immediately gave them leave, and the unclean spirits came out and entered the swine. The herd, in number about two thousand, rushed down with great violence into the sea and drowned. The swineherds, seeing this, fled and reported it in the town and in the country. The people came out to see what had happened. They came to Jesus. Then they saw the man who had been afflicted by the devil, sitting clothed and in his right mind. Those who had seen this miracle told how it had happened to the possessed man, also about the swine. They were afraid. So they entreated Him to depart from their district. As Jesus was getting into the boat, the man who had been afflicted by the devil began to entreat Him that he might remain with Him. But Jesus did not allow him, saying, *Go home to thy relatives, and tell them all that the Lord has done for thee, and how He has had mercy on thee.* The man departed and began publishing in the Decapolis all that Jesus had done for him. And all marvelled.[335],[336] Mark 5:1-20

538. Jesus returned to Capharnaum. From there He went north into the district of Tyre and Sidon along the Mediterranean seacoast. He entered a house and wanted no one to know it. But He could not keep that a secret. For immediately a woman, whose little daughter had an unclean spirit, on hearing of Him, came in and fell down at His feet. Now the woman was a Gentile, a Syrophoenician by birth. She besought Him to cast the devil out of her daughter. But He said to her,

---

335. *Matthew 8:28-34;* 336. *Luke 8:26-39*

Let the children first have their fill, for it is not fair to take the children's bread and to cast it to the dogs. She answered, "Yes, Lord; for even the dogs under the table eat of the children's crumbs." He said to her, *Because of this answer, go thy way; the devil has gone out of thy daughter.*[337] And when she went to her house, she found the girl lying upon the bed, and the devil gone. Mark 7:24-30

539. WHEN JESUS SAID THAT HE WHO ATE HIS FLESH and drank His blood had Life Everlasting and that He would raise him up on the last day, many of His disciples turned back and no longer went about with Him. Jesus therefore asked the Twelve if they also wished to go away from Him. Simon Peter answered, "Lord, to whom shall we go? Thou hast words of Everlasting Life, and we have come to believe and to know that Thou art the Christ, the Son of God." Then Jesus replied, *Have I not chosen you, the Twelve? Yet one of you is a devil.* Now He was speaking of Judas Iscariot; for he it was, though one of the Twelve, who would betray Him. John 6:71-72

540. FROM NOW ON JESUS BEGAN TO SHOW HIS DISCIPLES that He must go to Jerusalem and suffer many things from the elders and Scribes and chief priests, and be put to death, and on the third day rise again. Peter, taking Him aside, began to chide Him, saying, "Far be it from Thee, O Lord; this will never happen to Thee." Jesus turned to him and said, *Get behind Me, satan, thou art a scandal to Me; for thou dost not mind the things of God, but those of men.*[338] Matthew 16:21-23

541. JESUS WAS TRANSFIGURED ON MOUNT THABOR before the Apostles Peter and James and John. On the following day, when they came down from the mountain to the village below, a large crowd met them. A man in the crowd cried out, "Master, I have brought to Thee my son, who has a dumb spirit. I told

---

337. *Matthew 15:21-28;* 338. *Mark 8:31-33*

Thy disciples to cast it out, but they could not." Jesus said, *O unbelieving generation, how long shall I be with you? How long shall I put up with you? Bring him to Me.* And they brought the boy to Him. The spirit, when it saw Jesus, immediately threw the boy into convulsions. Jesus asked his father how long had this come upon him. The father replied, "From his infancy." . . . "If Thou canst do anything, have compassion on us and help us." Jesus said, *If thou canst believe, all things are possible to him who believes.* The father of the boy cried out, and said with tears, "I do believe; help my unbelief." Jesus then rebuked the unclean spirit, saying to it, *Thou deaf and dumb spirit, I command thee, go out of him and enter him no more.* It went out of the boy and he became like one dead, so that many said, "He is dead." Jesus took him by the hand, and he stood up. When Jesus came into the house, His disciples asked Him privately, "Why could not we cast it out?" He said to them, *This kind can be cast out in no way except by prayer and fasting.*[339,340] Mark 9:13-28

542. SOME OF THE JEWS WHO HAD COME to believe in Jesus could not understand Him when He said that if they abided in His word they would know the Truth, and the Truth *shall make you free.* When they said, "We have one Father, God," Jesus said that if God were their Father, they would surely love Him (Jesus). He told them that He came forth from God. That He had not come of Himself, but that God had sent Him. Continuing He said, *Why do you not understand My speech? Because you cannot listen to My word. The father from whom you are is the devil, and the desires of your father it is your will to do. He was a murderer from the beginning, and has not stood in the Truth because there is no Truth in him. When he tells a lie he speaks from his very nature, for he is a liar and the father*

---

339. *Matthew 17:14-20;* 340. *Luke 9:37-43*

of lies. But because I speak the Truth you do not believe Me.
John 8:42-45

543. THESE WERE STRONG WORDS COMING FROM JESUS and the
Jews retaliated by asking Him, "Are we not right in saying
that thou art a Samaritan, and hast a devil? *Jesus answered,*
I have not a devil, but I honor My Father, and you dishonor
Me. Yet I do not seek My own glory; there is One Who seeks
and Who judges. Amen, amen, I say to you, if anyone keep My
word, he will never see death. John 8:48-51

544. BESIDES THE TWELVE CHOSEN APOSTLES, Jesus had many
disciples. He sent out before Him seventy-two of them to
preach and declare that the Kingdom of God was at hand.
These disciples returned with joy, saying, "Lord, even the devils
are subject to us in Thy name." Jesus, rejoicing with them that
good was overcoming evil, said, *I was watching Satan fall as*
lightning from Heaven. Behold, I have given you power to
tread upon serpents and scorpions, and over all the might of the
enemy; and nothing shall hurt you. But do not rejoice in this,
that the spirits are subject to you; rejoice rather in this, that your
names are written in Heaven. Luke 10:17-20

545. ONE DAY JESUS WAS TEACHING in a synagogue on the
Sabbath. A woman was there who for eighteen years had
had a sickness by a spirit. She was bent over and utterly unable
to look upwards. When Jesus saw her, He called her to Him,
saying, *Woman, thou art delivered from thy infirmity.* He laid
His hands upon her, and instantly she was made straight, and
glorified God. But the ruler of the synagogue, indignant that
Jesus had cured on the Sabbath, addressed the crowd, saying,
"There are six days in which one ought to work; on these therefore come and be cured, and not on the Sabbath." Jesus rebuked
him, saying, *Hypocrites! does not each one of you on the Sabbath*
loose his ox or ass from the manger, and lead it forth to water?

OF SATAN AND THE BAD ANGELS

And this woman, daughter of Abraham as she is, whom Satan has bound, lo, for eighteen years, ought not she to be loosed from this bond on the Sabbath? Luke 13:10-17

546. CERTAIN PHARISEES IN THE DISTRICT OF PEREA, to the east of Judea, came up to Jesus and said to Him, "Depart and be on Thy way, for Herod wants to kill Thee." Jesus said to them, *Go and say to that fox, "Behold, I cast out devils and perform cures today and tomorrow, and the third day I am to end My course.* Luke 13:31-32

547. AFTER HIS TRIUMPHAL ENTRY INTO JERUSALEM, toward the close of His ministry on earth, Jesus still had many things to do and much to say to the multitude, to the Scribes and Pharisees, and to His Apostles. He was aware that His hour had come. Being the Son of Man (as well as the Son of God) He was human. He became sad. His soul was troubled. He asked His Apostles this rhetorical question: Should He ask the Father to save Him from this hour? No, that was why He had come to this hour. Turning His thoughts upward, He said, *Father, glorify Thy name!* Then a voice came from Heaven, saying, "I have both glorified it, and I will glorify it again." When Jesus heard these words, He said, *Now is the judgment of the world; now will the prince of the world be cast out. And I, if I be lifted up from the earth, will draw all things to Myself.* John 12:27-31

548. IN FORETELLING THE DAY OF THE LAST JUDGMENT, Jesus said, *When the Son of Man shall come in His majesty, . . . He will separate them* (all nations) *one from another, as the shepherd separates the sheep from the goats; and He will set the sheep on His right hand, but the goats on the left. Then the King will say to those on His right hand, "Come, blessed of My Father, take possession of the Kingdom prepared for you from*

237

the foundation of the world; . . . Then He will say to those on His left hand, "Depart from Me, accursed ones, into the everlasting fire which was prepared for the devil and his angels. . . ." And these will go into everlasting punishment, but the just into Everlasting Life. Matthew 25:31-46

549. THE PASSOVER OF THE FEAST OF THE UNLEAVENED BREAD, the Last Supper which Jesus and His Apostles were to have together, was over. At this Supper, Jesus had established the Holy Eucharist . . . *this is My body, . . . this is My blood, . . . do this in remembrance of Me.* Judas Iscariot had left their midst and was about the business of betraying his Lord for thirty pieces of silver. Jesus, as He looked at Simon Peter, knew that he was to deny his Master three times that very night. Yet to him, Jesus had these touchingly tender words, *Simon, Simon, behold, Satan has desired to have you, that he may sift you as wheat. But I have prayed for thee, that thy faith may not fail; and do thou, when once thou hast turned again, strengthen thy brethren.* Luke 22:31-32

550. JESUS BEGAN A LONG FAREWELL DISCOURSE to His eleven Apostles in the Cenacle after the Last Supper. The Apostle John has recorded these parting thoughts of Jesus in the fourteenth, fifteenth, sixteenth, and seventeenth chapters. The fourteenth chapter is full of words of comfort. But He said, *I will no longer speak much with you, for the prince of the world is coming, and in Me he has nothing. But he comes that the world may know that I love the Father, and that I do as the Father has commanded Me. Arise, let us go from here.* John 14:30-31

551. IN ACQUAINTING THE APOSTLES with the important role of the Holy Spirit, the Advocate (the Paraclete, the Comforter), Jesus said, *Now I am going to Him Who sent Me. . . .*

*If I do not go, the Advocate will not come to you; but if I go,
I will send Him to you. And when He has come, He will convict
the world of sin, and of justice, and of judgment: of sin, because
they do not believe in Me; of justice, because I go to the Father,
and you will see Me no more; and of judgment, because the
prince of this world* (the devil) *has already been judged.* John
16:5-12

552. IN HIS PRIESTLY PRAYER FOR UNITY, JESUS SAID, *Holy
Father, keep in Thy name those whom Thou hast given
Me, that they may be one even as We are. While I was with
them, I kept them in Thy name. Those whom Thou hast given
Me I guarded; and not one of them perished except the son of
perdition* (Judas Iscariot), *in order that the Scripture might be
fulfilled.* John 17:11-12

553. JUST BEFORE JESUS WAS SEIZED AND BOUND by the Roman
soldiers near the entrance to the Garden of Gethsemani,
Jesus said to the chief priests and captains of the Temple and
the elders, who had come against Him, *As against a robber have
you come out, with swords and clubs. When I was daily with
you in the Temple, you did not stretch forth your hands against
me. But this is your hour, and the power of darkness* (of the
devil). Luke 22:52-53

CHÁPTER XV

JESUS SAID
of hell

554. Nicodemus, a Pharisee and leader among the Jews, came to Jesus by night to learn from Him about the Kingdom of God and Life Everlasting. During the instruction Jesus must have refreshed Nicodemus' memory of the time when Moses led the Jews out of the captivity in Egypt toward the Promised Land. While passing through the desert the people became discouraged and discontented. One day they complained of God and of Moses. God was disappointed and chastised them by sending fiery serpents[341] to bite them. Many people died. Realizing that they had sinned against God, they were sorry. They asked Moses to pray to God to take away the fiery serpents. Obeying God's direction, Moses made a serpent of brass and set it upon a pole. When any man who had been bitten by a serpent beheld the serpent of brass, he lived. Jesus said, *And as Moses lifted up the serpent in the desert, even so must the Son of Man be lifted up, that those who believe in Him may not perish, but may have Life Everlasting.* John 3:14-15

---

341. *Old Testament, Numbers 21:5-9*

555. IN THE SEVENTH CHAPTER OF SAINT MATTHEW is recorded that part of the Sermon on the Mount regarding obstacles to virtue, in which Jesus said, *Enter by the narrow gate. For wide is the gate and broad is the way that leads to destruction, and many there are who enter that way. How narrow the gate and close the way that leads to Life! And few there are who find it.* . . . *Every tree that does not bear good fruit is cut down and thrown into the fire.* . . . *Not everyone who says to me, "Lord, Lord," shall enter the Kingdom of Heaven: but he who does the will of My Father in Heaven shall enter the Kingdom of Heaven. Many will say to Me in that day, "Lord, Lord, did we not prophesy in Thy name, and cast out devils in Thy name, and work many miracles in Thy name?" And then I will declare to them, "I never knew you. Depart from Me, you workers of iniquity."*[342] Matthew 7:13-23

556. AFTER THE SERMON ON THE MOUNT, Jesus came down from the Mount of Beautitudes (as it is now called) and walked along the shore of the Sea of Galilee toward Capharnaum. Now when He entered it, there came to Him a Roman official, a centurion, who entreated Him, saying, "Lord, my servant is lying sick in the house, paralyzed, and is grievously afflicted." Jesus said to him, *I will come and cure him.* But in answer the centurion said, "Lord, I am not worthy that Thou shouldst come under my roof; but only say the word, and my servant will be healed." . . . And when Jesus heard this, He marvelled, and said to those who were following Him, *Amen I say to you, I have not found such great faith in Israel. And I tell you that many will come from the east and from the west, and will feast with Abraham and Isaac and Jacob in the Kingdom of Heaven, but the children of the kingdom will be put forth into the darkness outside; there will be the weeping, and the gnashing of teeth.* Matthew 8:5-12

---

342. *Luke 13:24-30*

557. WHEN THE TWELVE APOSTLES WERE SENT OUT TO PREACH
the Kingdom of God, Jesus gave them definite instructions,
among them: *And whoever does not receive you, or listen to
your words—go forth outside that house or town, and shake
off the dust from your feet. Amen I say to you, it will be more
tolerable for the land of Sodom and Gomorrah in the day of
judgment than for that town.* Matthew 10:5-15

558. THAT THERE WAS TO BE MUCH OPPOSITION to this new
teaching of the Kingdom of God was foretold by Jesus to
the Apostles. But He said, *Do not be afraid of those who kill the
body but cannot kill the soul. But rather be afraid of Him Who
is able to destroy both soul and body in hell.* Matthew 10:28

559. SAINT LUKE HAS RECORDED JESUS' WORDS THUS: *But I
say to you, My friends: Do not be afraid of those who kill
the body, and after that have nothing more that they can do.
But I will show you Whom you shall be afraid of; be afraid of
Him Who, after He has killed, has power to cast into hell. Yes,
I say to you, be afraid of Him.* Luke 12:4-6

560. MANY, MANY MIRACLES JESUS HAD WORKED in the villages
and towns of Galilee, especially in Capharnaum, His
adopted city, and in Corozain, a short distance to the north of
it. He had also preached the Kingdom of God and the forgiveness of sins outside the district of Galilee, in Bethsaida east
of Capharnaum, in Caesarea Philippi some distance to the north,
and as far as Tyre and Sidon on the Mediterranean coast. Now
Jesus was set for Jerusalem. In departing, He said reproach-
fully, *Woe to thee, Corozain! woe to thee, Bethsaida! For if in
Tyre and Sidon had been worked the miracles that have been
worked in you, they would have repented long ago in sackcloth
and ashes. But I tell you, it will be more tolerable for Tyre
and Sidon on the day of judgment than for you. And thou,
Capharnaum, shalt thou be exalted to Heaven? Thou shalt be*

thrust down to hell! For if the miracles had been worked in Sodom that have been worked in thee, it would have remained to this day. But I tell you, it will be more tolerable for the land of Sodom on the day of judgment than for thee.[343] Matthew 11:21-24

561. THE SCRIBES AND PHARISEES AND ELDERS of the Jews refused to believe that Jesus was the Son of God. They blasphemed Him, saying that He drove out devils by Beelzebub, the prince of the devils. These Jesus warned, saying, *The men of Nineve will rise up in the judgment with this generation and will condemn it; for they repented at the preaching of Jonas, and behold, a greater than Jonas is here. The queen of the South* (Queen of Sheba) *will rise up in the judgment with this generation and will condemn it; for she came from the ends of the earth to hear the wisdom of Solomon, and behold, a greater than Solomon is here.*[344] Matthew 12:41-42

562. THERE WERE MANY PARABLES SPOKEN BY JESUS on the Kingdom of God or as Saint Matthew records them on the Kingdom of Heaven. One of them so understandable to the fishermen of the Sea of Galilee in which Jesus said, *The Kingdom of Heaven is like a net cast into the sea that gathered in fish of every kind. When it was filled, they hauled it out, and sitting down on the beach, they gathered the good fish into vessels, but threw away the bad. So will it be at the end of the world. The angels will go out and separate the wicked from among the just, and will cast them into the furnace of fire, where there will be the weeping, and the gnashing of teeth.* Matthew 13:47-50

563. THE DISCIPLES WERE WITH JESUS in the district of Caesarea Philippi. Jesus asked them, *Who do men say the Son of Man is?* They replied, "Some say, John the Baptist; and

---

343. *Luke 10:13-15;* 344. *Luke 11:24-26*

others, Elias; and others, Jeremias, or one of the Prophets."
He then asked, *But who do you say that I am?* Simon Peter
spoke up, "Thou art the Christ, the Son of the living God."
Then Jesus answered, *Blessed art thou, Simon Bar-Jona, for
flesh and blood has not revealed this to thee, but My Father in
Heaven. And I say to thee, thou art Peter, and upon this rock
I will build My Church, and the gates of hell shall not prevail
against it. And I will give thee the keys of the Kingdom of
Heaven; and whatever thou shalt bind on earth shall be bound
in Heaven, and whatever thou shalt loose on earth shall be
loosed in Heaven.* Matthew 16:13-19

564. WOE TO THE WORLD *because of scandals! For it must needs
be that scandals come, but woe to the man through whom
scandal does come.*[345] *Whoever causes one of these little ones
who believe in Me to sin, it were better for him if a great millstone were hung about his neck, and he were thrown into the
sea. If thy hand is an occasion of sin to thee, cut it off! It is
better for thee to enter into Life* (Everlasting) *maimed, than,
having two hands, to go into hell, into the unquenchable fire,
"Where their worm dies not, and the fire is not quenched."*[346]
*And if thy foot is an occasion of sin to thee, cut it off! It is
better for thee to enter into Life Everlasting lame, than, having
two feet, to be cast into the hell of unquenchable fire, "Where
their worm dies not, and the fire is not quenched." And if thy
eye is an occasion of sin to thee, pluck it out! It is better for
thee to enter into the Kingdom of God with one eye, than
having two eyes, to be cast into hell-fire, "Where their worm
dies not, and the fire is not quenched." For everyone shall be
salted with fire, and every victim shall be salted.*[347,348] Mark
9:41-48

565. PETER ASKED JESUS, "Lord, how often shall my brother
sin against me, and I forgive him? Up to seven times?"

---

345. *Matthew 18:7;* 346. *Isaias 66:24;* 347. *Matthew 18:7-9;* 348. *Matthew 5:27-30*

Jesus replied, *I do not say to thee seven times, but seventy times seven. This is why the Kingdom of Heaven is likened to a king who desired to settle accounts with his servants. And when he had begun the settlement, one was brought to him who owed him ten thousand talents. And as he had no means of paying, his master ordered him to be sold, with his wife and children and all that he had, and payment to be made. But the servant fell down and besought him saying, "Have patience with me and I will pay thee all!" And moved with compassion, the master of that servant released him, and forgave him the debt. But as that servant went out, he met one of his fellow-servants who owed him a hundred denarii, and he laid hold of him and throttled him, saying, "Pay what thou owest." His fellow-servant therefore fell down and began to entreat him, saying, "Have patience with me and I will pay thee all." But he would not; but went away and cast him into prison until he should pay what was due. His fellow-servants, therefore, seeing what had happened, were very much saddened, and they went and informed their master of what had taken place. Then his master called him, and said to him, "Wicked servant! I forgave thee all the debt, because thou didst entreat me. Shouldst not thou also have had pity on thy fellow-servant, even as I had pity on thee?" And his master, being angry, handed him over to the torturers until he should pay all that was due to him. So also My Heavenly Father will do to you, if you do not each forgive your brothers from your hearts.* Matthew 18:21-35

566. SAINT LUKE LIKE SAINT MATTHEW TELLS US about entering by the narrow gate. Jesus said, *Strive to enter by the narrow gate; for many, I tell you, will seek to enter and will not be able. But when the master of the house has entered and shut the door, you will begin to stand outside and knock at the door, saying, "Lord, open for us!" And He shall say to you in answer, "I do not know where you are from." Then you will begin to say, "We ate and drank in Thy presence, and Thou*

*didst teach in our streets." And He shall say to you, "I do not
know where you are from. Depart from Me, all you workers
of iniquity." There will be the weeping, and the gnashing of
teeth, when you shall see Abraham and Isaac and Jacob and
the Prophets in the Kingdom of God, but you yourselves cast
forth outside. And they will come from the east and from the
west, from the north and from the south, and will feast in the
Kingdom of God.*[349] Luke 13:24-29

567. No SERVANT *can serve two masters; for either he will hate
the one and love the other, or else he will stand by the*
one and despise the other. *You cannot serve God and mammon*
(worldly goods). Now the Pharisees, who were fond of money,
were listening to all these things, and they began to sneer at
Jesus. . . . He said to them, *There was a certain rich man who
used to clothe himself in purple and fine linen, and who feasted
every day in splendid fashion. And there was a certain poor
man, named Lazarus, who lay at his gate, covered with sores,
and longing to be filled with the crumbs that fell from the rich
man's table; even the dogs would come and lick his sores. And
it came to pass that the poor man died and was borne away
by the angels into Abraham's bosom; but the rich man also
died and was buried in hell. And lifting up his eyes, being in
torments, he saw Abraham afar off and Lazarus in his bosom.
He cried and said, "Father Abraham, have pity on me, and
send Lazarus to dip the tip of his finger in water and cool my
tongue, for I am tormented in this flame." But Abraham said
to him, "Son, remember that thou in thy lifetime hast received
good things, and Lazarus in like manner evil things; but now
here he is comforted whereas thou are tormented. And besides
all that, between us and you a great gulf is fixed, so that they
who wish to pass over from this side to you cannot, and they
cannot cross from your side to us." And he said, "Then, father,*

---

349. *Matthew 7:13-23*

I beseech thee to send him to my father's house, for I have five brothers, that he may testify to them, lest they too come into this place of torments." Abraham said to him, "They have Moses and the Prophets: let them hearken to them." But he answered, "No, father Abraham, but if someone from the dead goes to them, they will repent." But he said to him, "If they do not hearken to Moses and the Prophets, they will not believe even if someone rises from the dead." Luke 16:19-31

568. To THE PHARISEES, WHO SCOFFED at everything Jesus said, He declared, *You are from below, I am from above. You are of this world, I am not of this world. Therefore I said to you that you will die in your sins; for if you do not believe that I am He* (the Messias), *you will die in your sin.* John 8:23-24

569. SAINT MATTHEW'S TWENTY-THIRD CHAPTER records Jesus' condemnation of the Scribes and Pharisees. To quote a portion of it, Jesus said, *Woe to you, Scribes and Pharisees, hypocrites! because you traverse sea and land to make one convert; and when he has become one, you make him twofold more a son of hell than yourselves. . . . You also fill up the measure of your fathers. Serpents, brood of vipers, how are you to escape the judgment of hell?* Matthew 23:15, 32

570. IN SPEAKING OF THE LAST JUDGMENT TO HIS APOSTLES, Jesus said, *But when the Son of Man shall come in His majesty, and all the angels with Him, then He will sit on the Throne of His glory; and before Him will be gathered all the nations, and He will separate them one from another, as the shepherd separates the sheep from the goats; and He will set the sheep on His right hand, but the goats on the left. . . . Then He will say to those on His left hand, "Depart from Me, accursed ones, into the everlasting fire which was prepared for the devil and his angels. For I was hungry, and you gave Me* no drink; I was a stranger and you did not take Me in; naked, and you did not clothe Me; sick, and in prison, and you did not visit Me." Then they also will answer and say, "Lord, when did we see Thee hungry, or thirsty, or a stranger, or naked, or sick, or in prison, and did not minister to Thee?" Then He will answer them, saying, "Amen I say to you, as long as you did not do it for one of these least ones, you did not do it for Me." And these will go into everlasting punishment, but the just into Everlasting Life. Matthew 25:31-33, 41-46

571. TO THE ELEVEN APOSTLES (Judas Iscariot had left them), as they were gathered about Him in the evening before His passion and crucifixion, Jesus said, *I am the Vine, you are the branches. He who abides in Me, and I in him, he bears much fruit; for without Me you can do nothing.* But to these chosen ones He also said, *If anyone does not abide in Me, he shall be cast outside as the branch and wither; and they shall gather them up and cast them into the fire, and they shall burn.* John 15:5-6

572. THEN AFTER JESUS HAD TOLD THE ELEVEN that He was going to the Father, and that He would send them the Holy Spirit, the Advocate, to be with them and to tell them all things, Jesus turned to God the Father, saying, *While I was with them* (the Apostles), *I kept them in Thy name. Those whom Thou hast given Me I guarded; and not one of them perished except the son of perdition* (Judas Iscariot), *in order that the Scripture might be fulfilled.* John 17:12

573. BEFORE JESUS ASCENDED INTO HEAVEN He commissioned the Eleven to *go into the whole world and preach the Gospel to every creature. He who believes and is baptized shall be saved, but he who does not believe shall be condemned.* Mark 16:16

CHAPTER XVI

JESUS SAID
of Judgment

574. JESUS HAD BEEN ALL ABOUT THE DISTRICT of Galilee,
teaching in the synagogues, preaching the Gospel of the
Kingdom of God, and healing every kind of disease among the
people. He entered Capharnaum on the northern shore of the
Sea of Galilee. Throngs followed Him here from everywhere.
Therefore with His Apostles He led them out of the city. On
a high slope, a short distance of less than a mile away, they
rested. This high slope is called the "mountain" or the "mount."
From it Jesus delivered the Sermon on the Mount. It was a
long sermon. Saint Matthew records it in his fifth, sixth and
seventh chapters. After the Beatitudes, Jesus preached against
anger, saying, *You have heard that it was said to the ancients,
"Thou shalt not kill": and that whoever shall kill shall be
liable to judgment. But I say to you that everyone who is angry
with his brother shall be liable to judgment; and whoever says
to his brother, "Raca,"* (empty-headed), *shall be liable to the
Sanhedrin* (Jewish court of justice); *and whoever says, "Thou*

fool!", shall be liable to the fire of Gehenna.[350] *Therefore, if thou art offering thy gift at the altar, and there rememberest that thy brother has anything against thee, leave thy gift before the altar and go first to be reconciled to thy brother, and then come and offer thy gift.* Matthew 5:21-24

575. TOWARD THE CONCLUSION OF THE SERMON ON THE MOUNT, Jesus spoke to His disciples on avoiding judgments, saying, *Do not judge, that you may not be judged. For with what judgment you judge, you shall be judged; and with what measure you measure, it shall be measured to you. But why dost thou see the speck in thy brother's eye, and yet dost not consider the beam in thy own eye?*[351] Matthew 7:1-2

576. THEN JESUS CAUTIONED HIS DISCIPLES, SAYING, *Not everyone who says to Me, "Lord, Lord," shall enter the Kingdom of Heaven; but he who does the will of My Father in Heaven shall enter the Kingdom of Heaven. Many will say to Me in that day, "Lord, Lord, did we not prophesy in Thy name, and cast out devils in Thy name, and work many miracles in Thy name?" And then I will declare to them, "I never knew you. Depart from Me, you workers of iniquity!"*[352] Matthew 7:21-23

577. TO NICODEMUS, THE PHARISEE WHO CAME BY NIGHT, Jesus revealed many divine truths. Of judgment, He said, *For God did not send His Son into the world in order to judge the world, but that the world might be saved through Him. He who believes in Him is not judged; but he who does not believe is already judged, because he does not believe in the name of the Only-begotten Son of God. Now this is the judgment: The Light has come into the world, yet men have loved the darkness*

350. *Gehenna: originally the "Valley of Hinnom," outside Jerusalem, where the bodies of criminals were burnt after execution of sentence. In the New Testament the name is usually applied to hell.*
351. *Luke 6:37-38;* 352. *Luke 13:25-27*

rather than the Light, for their works were evil. For everyone who does evil hates the Light, and does not come to the Light, that his deeds may not be exposed. But he who does the truth comes to the Light that his deeds may be made manifest, for they have been performed in God. John 3:16-21

578. A ROMAN CENTURION IN CAPHARNAUM told Jesus that his servant was grievously afflicted. Jesus said that He would come and cure him. The official replied, "Lord, I am not worthy that Thou shouldst come under my roof; but only say the word, and my servant will be healed." When Jesus heard this, He marvelled, and said to those who were following Him, *Amen I say to you, I have not found such great faith in Israel. And I tell you that many will come from the east and from the west, and will feast with Abraham and Isaac and Jacob in the Kingdom of Heaven, but the children of the kingdom will be put forth into the darkness outside; there will be the weeping, and the gnashing of teeth.*[353,354,355] Matthew 8:5-12

579. THE SCRIBES AND PHARISEES BECAME VERY ANGRY with Jesus when He called God His own Father, making Himself equal to God. But Jesus had more to say of His claim to divinity, *For as the Father raises the dead and gives them Life, even so the Son also gives Life to whom He will. For neither does the Father judge any man, but all judgment He has given to the Son, that all men may honor the Son even as they honor the Father. He who does not honor the Son, does not honor the Father Who sent Him. Amen, amen, I say to you, he who hears My word, and believes Him Who sent Me, has Life Everlasting, and does not come to judgment, but has passed from death to Life. Amen, amen, I say to you, the hour is coming, and now is here, when the dead shall hear the voice of the Son of God, and those who hear shall live. For as the Father has Life in Himself, even so He has given to the Son also to have Life in Him-*

---

353. *Matthew* 22:13; 354. 24:51; 355. 25:30

self; and He has granted Him power to render judgment, because He is the Son of Man. Do not wonder at this, for the hour is coming in which all who are in the tombs shall hear the voice of the Son of God. And they who have done good shall come forth unto resurrection of Life; but they who have done evil unto resurrection of judgment. Of Myself I can do nothing. As I hear, I judge, and My judgment is just because I seek not My own will but the will of Him Who sent Me. John 5:22-30

580. AT THIS SAME TIME, JESUS SAID TO THE UNBELIEVING JEWS, *Do not think that I shall accuse you to the Father. There is one who accuses you, Moses, in whom you hope. For if you believed Moses you would believe Me also, for he wrote of Me. But if you do not believe his writings, how will you believe My words?* John 5:45-47

581. THAT THE APOSTLES WOULD MEET OPPOSITION when they preached the Kingdom of God and the forgiveness of sins, Jesus foretold. Also that they would be hated by all for Jesus' name's sake. . . . But Jesus said, *But I say to you, My friends: Do not be afraid of those who kill the body, and after that have nothing more that they can do. But I will show you Whom you shall be afraid of; be afraid of Him Who, after He has killed, has power to cast into hell. Yes, I say to you, be afraid of Him.*[356] Luke 12:4-5

582. JESUS REPROACHED THE TOWNS in which most of His Miracles were worked, because they had not repented. *Woe to thee, Corozain! woe to thee, Bethsaida! For if in Tyre and Sidon had been worked the miracles that have been worked in you, they would have repented long ago in sackcloth and ashes. But I tell you, it will be more tolerable for Tyre and Sidon on the day of judgment than for you. And thou, Capharnaum, shalt thou be exalted to Heaven? Thou shalt be thrust down to hell!*

---

356. *Matthew 10:28*

OF JUDGMENT

*For if the miracles had been worked in Sodom that have been
worked in thee, it would have remained to this day. But I tell
you, it will be more tolerable for the land of Sodom on the day
of judgment than for thee.*[357] Matthew 11:21-24

583. THE SCRIBES AND PHARISEES AND THE ELDERS of the
Jewish people did not want to believe that Jesus was the
Son of God. They found fault with everything that He did.
They even blasphemed Him when He cast out devils, saying He
did so by Beelzebub, the prince of the devils. Jesus rebuked
them, saying, *If I cast out devils by the Spirit of God, then the
Kingdom of God has come upon you. . . . Therefore I say to you,
that every kind of sin and blasphemy shall be forgiven to men;
but the blasphemy against the Spirit will not be forgiven. And
whoever speaks a word against the Son of Man, it shall be forgiven him; but whoever speaks against the Holy Spirit, it will
not be forgiven him, either in this world or in the world to come.
Either make the tree good and its fruit good, or make the tree
bad and its fruit bad; for by the fruit the tree is known. You
brood of vipers, how can you speak good things, when you are
evil? For out of the abundance of the heart the mouth speaks.
The good man from his treasure brings forth good things; and
the evil man from his evil treasure brings forth evil things. But
I tell you, that of every idle word men speak, they shall give
account on the Day of Judgment. For by thy words thou wilt be
justified, and by thy words thou wilt be condemned.*[358,359]
Matthew 12:31-37

584. DESPITE THE INNUMERABLE GOOD WORKS AND MIRACLES
that Jesus performed, the unbelieving Jews still clamored
for a sign from Him. To them He said, *This generation is an
evil generation: it demands a sign, and no sign shall be given it
but the sign of Jonas. For even as Jonas was a sign to the*

357. *Luke 10:13-15;* 358. *Mark 3:28-30;* 359. *Luke 12:10*

Ninevites, so will also the Son of Man be to this generation.[360]
*The men of Nineve will rise up in the judgment with this
generation and will condemn it; for they repented at the preaching of Jonas, and behold, a greater than Jonas is here.* The queen
of the South (queen of Sheba) *will rise up in the judgment with
this generation and will condemn it; for she came from the ends
of the earth to hear the wisdom of Solomon, and behold, a
greater than Solomon is here.* Matthew 12:41-42

585. JESUS SET A PARABLE OF THE WEEDS before the people.
How a man sowed good seed in his field. But during the
night his enemy came and sowed weeds among the wheat. When
the blade sprang up and brought forth fruit, the weeds appeared as well. The servants of the man asked him, "Do you
want us to gather up the weeds?" *"No," he said, "lest in
gathering the weeds you root up the wheat along with them.
Let both grow together until the harvest; and at harvest time
I will say to the reapers: Gather up the weeds first and bind
them in bundles to burn; but gather the wheat into my barn."*
Matthew 13:24-30

586. WHEN THE DISCIPLES WERE ALONE WITH JESUS, they
asked Him to explain this parable of the weeds in the field.
Answering them He said, *He Who sows the good seed is the Son
of Man. The field is the world; the good seed, the sons of the
Kingdom; the weeds, the sons of the wicked one; and the enemy
who sowed them is the devil. But the harvest is the end of the
world, and the reapers are the angels. Therefore, just as the
weeds are gathered up and burnt with fire, so will it be at the
end of the world. The Son of Man will gather out of His
Kingdom all scandals and those who work iniquity, and cast
them into the furnace of fire, where there will be the weeping,
and the gnashing of teeth. Then the just will shine forth like*

360. *Luke 11:29-32*

the sun in the Kingdom of their Father. He who has ears to hear, let him hear. Matthew 13:37-43

587. IN THE PARABLE OF THE NET, Jesus likens the Kingdom of Heaven to *a net cast into the sea that gathered in fish of every kind. When it was filled, they hauled it out, and sitting down on the beach, they gathered the good fish into vessels, but threw away the bad. So will it be at the end of the world. The angels will go out and separate the wicked from among the just, and will cast them into the furnace of fire, where there will be the weeping, and the gnashing of teeth.* Matthew 13:47-50

588. CALLING THE PEOPLE AND HIS DISCIPLES TOGETHER, Jesus proclaimed the doctrine of the cross. He said that if anyone wished to come after Him, he should deny himself, and take up his cross and follow Him. For he who saved his life would lose it; but he who lost his life for Jesus' sake would find it. *For what does it profit a man, if he gain the whole world, but suffer the loss of his own soul? Or what will a man give in exchange for his soul? For the Son of Man is to come with His angels in the glory of His Father, and then He will render to everyone according to his conduct.*[361,362] Matthew 16:26-27

589. SCANDAL GRIEVED JESUS. He had this to say about it. *Whoever causes one of these little ones who believe in Me to sin, it were better for him to have a great millstone hung around his neck, and to be drowned in the depths of the sea. Woe to the world because of scandals! For it must needs be that scandals come, but woe to the man through whom scandal does come! And if thy hand is an occasion of sin to thee, cut it off! It is better for thee to enter into Life maimed, than, having two hands, to go into hell, into the unquenchable fire, "Where their worm dies not, and the fire is not quenched." And if thy foot is an occasion of sin to thee, cut it off! It is*

---

361. *Mark 8:36-38;* 362. *Luke 9:25-26*

better for thee to enter into Life Everlasting lame, than, having two feet, to be cast into the hell of unquenchable fire, "Where their worm dies not, and the fire is not quenched." And if thy eye is an occasion of sin to thee, pluck it out! It is better for thee to enter into the Kingdom of God with one eye, than, having two eyes, to be cast into hell-fire, "Where their worm dies not, and the fire is not quenched."[363,364] Mark 9:41-47

590. BECAUSE JESUS SAID THAT HE WAS THE LIGHT OF THE WORLD, the Pharisees said to Him, "Thou bearest witness to thyself. Thy witness is not true." Jesus answered, *Even if I bear witness to Myself, My witness is true, because I know where I came from and where I go. But you do not know where I came from or where I go. You judge according to the flesh; I judge no one. And even if I do judge, My judgment is true, because I am not alone, but with Me is He Who sent Me, the Father. And in your law it is written that the witness of two persons is true. It is I Who bear witness to Myself, and He Who sent Me, the Father, bears witness to Me.* John 8:14-18

591. A YOUNG RULER, who said that he obeyed the Commandments, came to Jesus and asked Him, "Good Master, what shall I do to gain Eternal Life?" Jesus said that one thing was lacking to him: that he should sell all that he had and give to the poor and then he would have treasure in Heaven. *Come, follow Me!* But when the young man heard this, he went away sad, for he had great possessions. Turning to those about Him, Jesus said that with difficulty would a rich man enter the Kingdom of Heaven. Peter said, "Behold, we have left all and followed Thee; what then shall we have?" Jesus replied, *Amen I say to you that you who have followed Me, in the regeneration when the Son of Man shall sit on the Throne of His glory, shall also sit on twelve thrones, judging the twelve tribes of Israel. And everyone who has left house, or brothers, or sisters, or*

---

363. *Matthew 5:30;* 364. *18:5-9*

father, or mother, or wife, or children, or lands, for My name's sake, shall receive a hundredfold, and shall possess Life Everlasting. But many who are first now will be last, and many who are last now will be first.[365,366,367] Matthew 19:16-30

592. SAINT MATTHEW'S TWENTY-THIRD CHAPTER is a vehement condemnation by Jesus of the Scribes and Pharisees, the leaders of the Jewish people during His divine visitation on earth. *Woe to you, Scribes and Pharisees, hypocrites! you who build the sepulchres of the Prophets, and adorn the tombs of the just, and say, "If we had lived in the days of our fathers, we would not have been their accomplices in the blood of the Prophets." Thus you are witnesses against yourselves that you are the sons of those who killed the Prophets. You also fill up the measure of your fathers. Serpents, brood of vipers, how are you to escape the judgment of hell? Therefore, behold, I send you Prophets, and wise men, and scribes; and some of them you will put to death, and crucify, and some you will scourge in your synagogues, and persecute from town to town; that upon you may come all the just blood that has been shed on the earth, from the blood of Abel the just unto the blood of Zacharias the son of Barachias, whom you killed between the Temple and the altar. Amen I say to you, all these things will come upon this generation. Jerusalem, Jerusalem! thou who killest the Prophets, and stonest those who are sent to thee! How often would I have gathered thy children together, as a hen gathers her young under her wings, but thou wouldst not! Behold, your house is left to you desolate. For I say to you, you shall not see Me henceforth until you shall say, "Blessed is He Who comes in the name of the Lord!"*[368] Matthew 23:29-39

593. AND IN THE TWELFTH CHAPTER OF SAINT MARK, Jesus said to the people, *Beware of the Scribes, who like to walk about in long robes, and to be greeted in the market place, and*

---

365. *Mark 10:28-31;* 366. *Luke 18:18-30;* 367. *Luke 22:29-30;* 368. *Luke 11:46-52*

to have the front seats in the synagogues and the first places at suppers; who devour the houses of widows, making pretense of long prayers. These shall receive a heavier sentence.[369] Mark 12:38-40

594. BELIEVERS IN THE RETURN OF THE SON OF MAN must always be ready and ever watchful. Jesus said to His disciples, *Let your loins be girt about and your lamps burning, and you yourselves like men waiting for their master's return from the wedding; so that when he comes and knocks, they may straightway open to him. Blessed are those servants whom the master, on his return, shall find watching. Amen I say to you, he will gird himself, and will make them recline at table, and will come and serve them. And if he comes in the second watch, and if in the third, and finds them so, blessed are those servants! But of this be assured, that if the householder had known at what hour the thief was coming, he would certainly have watched, and not have let his house be broken into. You also must be ready, because at an hour that you do not expect, the Son of Man is coming.* Peter said to Him, "Lord, dost Thou speak this parable for us or for all alike?" Jesus replied thus, *Who, dost thou think, is the faithful and prudent steward whom the master will set over his household to give them their ration of grain in due time? Blessed is that servant whom his master, when he comes, shall find so doing. Truly I say to you, he will set him over his goods. But if that servant says to himself, "My master delays his coming," and begins to beat the menservants and the maids, and to eat and drink, and to get drunk, the master of that servant will come on a day he does not expect, and in an hour he does not know, and will cut him asunder and make him share the lot of the unfaithful. But that servant who knew his master's will, and did not make ready for him and did not act according to his will, will be beaten with many stripes. Whereas he who did not know it, but did things deserving*

369. *Luke 20:46-47*

of stripes, will be beaten with few. But of everyone to whom much has been given, much will be required; and of him to whom they have entrusted much, they will demand the more. Luke 12:35-48

595. JESUS HAD HIS FACE SET TOWARDS JERUSALEM, for His hour was approaching. He know that in Jerusalem—and only in Jerusalem—He was to suffer, to die redeeming mankind from sin, to rise from the dead, to be glorified, and then to return to God the Father in Heaven. Therefore, He passed through towns and villages, preaching the coming of the Kingdom of God, and making His way towards Jerusalem. He was asked, "Lord, are only a few to be saved?" His answer was, *Strive to enter by the narrow gate; for many, I tell you, will seek to enter and will not be able. But when the Master of the house has entered and shut the door, you will begin to stand outside and knock at the door, saying, "Lord, open for us!" And He shall say to you in answer, "I do not know where you are from." Then you shall begin to say, "We ate and drank in Thy presence, and Thou didst teach in our streets." And He shall say to you, "I do not know where you are from. Depart from Me, all you workers of iniquity." There will be the weeping, and the gnashing of teeth, when you shall see Abraham and Isaac and Jacob and all the Prophets in the Kingdom of God, but you yourselves cast forth outside. And they will come from the east and from the west, from the north and from the south, and will feast in the Kingdom of God. And behold, there are those last who will be first, and there are those first who will be last.*[370] Luke 13:24-30

596. JESUS HAD BEEN ABOUT HIS FATHER'S BUSINESS. It was being completed. Now *the hour has come for the Son of Man to be glorified. . . . My soul is troubled. And what shall I*

---

370. *Matthew 7:21-23*

say? Father, save Me from this hour! No, this is why I came to this hour. Then Jesus said, *Father, glorify Thy name.* There came therefore a voice from Heaven, "I have both glorified it and I will glorify it again." . . . Having heard these words Jesus said, *Now is the judgment of the world; now will the prince of the world* (the devil) *be cast out. And I, if I be lifted up from the earth, will draw all things to Myself.* . . . These things Jesus spoke, and He went away and hid Himself from them. John 12:23-32

597. To the sneering Pharisees, Jesus spoke this parable

There was a certain rich man who used to clothe himself in purple and fine linen, and who feasted every day in splendid fashion. And there was a certain poor man, named Lazarus who lay at his gate, covered with sores, and longing to be filled with the crumbs that fell from the rich man's table; even the dogs would come and lick his sores. And it came to pass that the poor man died and was borne away by the angels into Abraham's bosom; but the rich man also died and was buried in hell. And lifting up his eyes, being in torments, he saw Abraham afar off and Lazarus in his bosom. And he cried out and said "Father Abraham, have pity on me, and send Lazarus to dip the tip of his finger in water and cool my tongue, for I am tormented in this flame." But Abraham said to him, "Son, remember that thou in thy lifetime hast received good things, and Lazarus in like manner evil things; but now here he is comforted whereas thou art tormented. And besides all that, between us and you a great gulf is fixed, so that they who wish to pass over from this side to you cannot, and they cannot cross from your side to us." And he said, "Then, father, I beseech thee to send him to my father's house, for I have five brothers that he may testify to them, lest they too come into this place of torments." And Abraham said to him, "They have Moses and the Prophets: let them hearken to them." But he answered "No, father Abraham, but if someone from the dead goes to them, they will repent." But he said to him, "If they do not hearken to Moses and the Prophets, they will not believe even if someone rises from the dead." Luke 16:19-31

598. ON BEING ASKED BY THE PHARISEES, "When is the Kingdom of God coming?" Jesus answered, *The Kingdom of God comes unawares. Neither will they say, "Behold, here it is," or "Behold, there it is." For behold, the Kingdom of God is within you.* He said to the disciples, *The days will come when you will long to see one day of the Son of Man, and will not see it. And they will say to you, "Behold, here he is; behold, there he is." Do not go, nor follow after them. For as the lightning when it lightens flashes from one end of the sky to the other, so will the Son of Man be in His day. But first He must suffer many things and be rejected by this generation. And as it came to pass in the days of Noe, even so will it be in the days of the Son of Man. They were eating and drinking, they were marrying and giving in marriage, until the day when Noe entered the ark, and the flood came and destroyed them all. Or as it came to pass in the days of Lot: they were eating and drinking, they were buying and selling, they were planting and building; but on the day that Lot went out from Sodom, it rained fire and brimstone from Heaven and destroyed them all. In the same wise will it be on the DAY that the Son of Man is revealed. In that hour let him who is on the housetop and his goods in the house, not go down to take them away; and likewise let him who is in the field not turn back. Remember Lot's wife. Whoever tries to save his life will lose it; and whoever loses it will preserve it. I say to you, on that night there will be two on one bed; one will be taken, and the other will be left. Two women will be grinding together; one will be taken, and the other will be left. Two men will be in the field; one will be taken, and the other will be left.* And they asked Him, "Where, Lord?" He said to them, *Wherever the body is, there will the eagles be gathered together. Luke 17:20-35*

599. SAINT MATTHEW, SAINT MARK AND SAINT LUKE give a full account of the impending destruction of Jerusalem and the end of the world. According to Saint Matthew, Jesus left the Temple and was going away, when His disciples came forward to show Him the buildings of the Temple. Jesus said to them, *Do you see these things? Amen I say to you, there will not be left here one stone upon another that will not be thrown down.* And as He was sitting on the Mount of Olives, the disciples came to Him privately, saying, "Tell us, when are these things to happen, and what will be the sign of Thy coming and of the end of the world?" And in answer Jesus said to them, *Take care that no one leads you astray. For many will come in My name, saying, "I am the Christ," and they will lead many astray. For you shall hear of wars and rumors of wars. Take care that you do not be alarmed, for these things must come to pass, but the end is not yet. For nation will rise against nation, and kingdom against kingdom; and there will be pestilences and famines and earthquakes in various places. But all these things are the beginnings of sorrows. Then they will deliver you up to tribulation, and will put you to death; and you will be hated by all nations for My name's sake. And many will fall away, and will betray one another, and will hate one another. And many false prophets will arise, and will lead many astray. And because iniquity will abound, the charity of the many will grow cold. But whoever perseveres to the end, he shall be saved. And this Gospel of the Kingdom shall be preached in the whole world, for a witness to all nations; and then will come the end. Therefore when you see the abomination of desolation, which was spoken of by Daniel the Prophet, standing in the holy place— let him who reads understand—then let those who are in Judea flee to the mountains; and let him who is on the housetop not go down to take anything from his house; and let him who is in the field not turn back to take his cloak. But woe to those who are with child, or have infants at the breast in those days! But pray that your flight may not be in the winter, or on the*

OF JUDGMENT

Sabbath. For then there will be great tribulation, such as has not been from the beginning of the world until now, nor will be. And unless those days had been shortened, no living creature would be saved. But for the sake of the elect those days will be shortened. Then if anyone say to you, "Behold, here is the Christ," or, "There He is," do not believe it. For false christs and false prophets will arise, and will show great signs and wonders, so as to lead astray, if possible, even the elect. Behold, I have told it to you beforehand. If therefore they say to you, "Behold, he is in the desert," do not go forth; "Behold, he is in the inner chambers," do not believe it. For as the lightning comes forth from the east and shines even to the west, so also will the coming of the Son of Man be. Wherever the body is, there will the eagles be gathered together. But immediately after the tribulation of those days, the sun will be darkened, and the moon will not give her light, and the stars will fall from Heaven, and the powers of Heaven will be shaken. And then will appear the sign of the Son of Man in Heaven; and then will all tribes of the earth mourn, and they will see the Son of Man coming upon the clouds of Heaven with great power and majesty. And He will send forth His angels with a trumpet and a great sound, and they will gather His elect from the four winds, from one end of the Heavens to the other. Now from the fig tree learn this parable. When its branch is now tender, and the leaves break forth, you know that summer is near. Even so, when you see all these things, know that it is near, even at the door. Amen I say to you, this generation will not pass away till all these things have been accomplished. Heaven and earth will pass away, but My words will not pass away. But of that DAY and hour no one knows, not even the angels of Heaven, but the Father only. And as it was in the days of Noe, even so will be the coming of the Son of Man. For as in the days before the flood they were eating and drinking, marrying and giving in marriage until the day when Noe entered the ark, and they did not understand until the flood came and swept them all away;

even so will be the coming of the Son of Man. Then two men will be in the field; one will be taken, and one will be left. Two women will be grinding at the millstone; one will be left. Watch therefore, for you do not know at what hour your Lord is to come. But of this be assured, that if the house-holder had known at what hour the thief was coming, he would certainly have watched, and not have let his house be broken into. Therefore you also must be ready, because at an hour that you do not expect, the Son of Man will come. Who, dost thou think, is the faithful servant whom his master has set over his household to give them their food in due time? Blessed is that servant whom his master, when he comes, shall find so doing. Amen I say to you, he will set him over all his goods. But if that wicked servant says to himself, "My master delays his coming," and begins to beat his fellow-servants, and to eat and drink with drunkards, the master of that servant will come on a day he does not know, and will cut him asunder and make him share the lot of the hypocrites. There will be the weeping, and the gnashing of teeth.[371] Matthew 24:1-51

600. AND AS JESUS WAS GOING OUT OF THE TEMPLE, one of His disciples said to Him, "Master, look what wonderful stones and buildings!" Jesus said to him, *Dost thou see all these great buildings? There will not be left one stone upon another that will not be thrown down.* And as He was sitting on the Mount of Olives, opposite the temple, Peter and James and John and Andrew asked Him privately, "Tell us, when are these things to happen, and what will be the sign when all these things will begin to come to pass?" In answer He said, *Take care that no one leads you astray. For many will come in My name, saying, "I am He"* (the Messias); *and they will lead many astray. But when you hear of wars and rumors of wars, do not be alarmed; for they must come to pass, but the end is not yet. For nation*

371. *Matthew 8:11-12*

will rise against nation, and kingdom against kingdom; and there will be earthquakes in various places, and famines. These things are the beginning of sorrows. But be on your guard. For they will deliver you up to councils, and you will be beaten in synagogues, and you will stand before governors and kings for My sake, for a witness to them. And the Gospel must first be preached to all the nations. And when they lead you away to deliver you up, do not be anxious beforehand what you are to speak; but speak whatever is given you in that hour. For it is not you who are speaking, but the Holy Spirit. And brother will hand over brother to death, and the father his child; children will rise up against parents and put them to death. And you will be hated by all for My name's sake; but he who has persevered to the end will be saved. Jesus foretells the destruction of Jerusalem. *And when you see the abomination of desolation, standing where it ought not—let him who reads understand—then let those who are in Judea flee to the mountains; and let him who is on the housetop not go down and enter to take anything from his house; and let him who is in the field not turn back to take his cloak. But woe to those who are with child, or have infants at the breast in those days! But pray that these things may not happen in winter. For in those day will be tribulations, such as have not been from the beginning of the creation which God created until now, nor will be. And unless the Lord had shortened the days, no living creature would be saved. But for the sake of the elect whom He has chosen, He has shortened the days.* Of the signs of the last days, Jesus said, *And then, if anyone say to you, "Behold, here is the Christ; behold, there he is," do not believe it. For false christs and false prophets will arise, and will show signs and wonders, so as to lead astray, if possible, even the elect. Be on your guard, therefore; behold, I have told you all things beforehand. But in those days, after that tribulation, the sun will be darkened, and the moon will not give her light, and the stars of Heaven will be falling, and the powers that are in Heaven will be shaken. And then they*

*will see the Son of Man coming upon clouds with great power
and majesty. And then He will send forth His angels, and will
gather His elect from the four winds, from the uttermost parts
of the earth to the uttermost parts of Heaven. Now from the fig
tree learn this parable. When its branch is now tender, and the
leaves break forth you know that summer is near. Even so, when
you see these things coming to pass, know that it is near, even
at the door. Amen I say to you, this generation will not pass
away till all these things have been accomplished. Heaven and
earth will pass away, but My words will not pass away. But of
that DAY or hour no one knows, neither the angels in Heaven,
nor the Son, but the Father only. Take heed, watch and pray,
for you do not know when the time is; just as a man when he
leaves home to journey abroad, puts his servants in charge, to
each his work, and gives orders to the porter to keep watch.
Watch, therefore, for you do not know when the Master of the
house is coming, in the evening, or at midnight, or at cockcrow,
or early in the morning; lest coming suddenly He find you
sleeping. And what I say to you, I say to all.* Mark 13:1-37

601. AND THIS IS SAINT LUKE'S ACCOUNT of Jesus foretelling
the destruction of Jerusalem and the end of the world.
And as some (of the Apostles) were saying of the Temple that
it was adorned with beautiful stones and offerings, Jesus said,
*As for these things that you behold, the days will come in
which there will not be left one stone upon another that will
not be thrown down.* They asked Him, "Master, when are these
things to happen, and what will be the sign when these things
will begin to come to pass?" Jesus answered, *Take care not
to be led astray. For many will come in My name, saying, "I
am he* (the Messias)," *and,* "*The time is at hand." Do not
therefore, go after them. But when you hear of wars and insurrections, do not be terrified; these things must first come to pass,
but the end will not be at once.* Then He said to them, *Nation*

will rise against nation, and kingdom against kingdom; and there will be great earthquakes in various places, and pestilences and famines, and there will be terrors and great signs from Heaven. But before all these things they will arrest you and persecute you, delivering you up to the synagogues and prisons, dragging you before kings and governors for My name's sake. It shall lead to your bearing witness. Resolve therefore in your hearts not to meditate beforehand how you are to make your defense. For I Myself will give you utterance and wisdom, which all your adversaries will not be able to resist or gainsay. But you will be delivered up by your parents and brothers and relatives and friends; and some of you they will put to death. And you will be hated by all for My name's sake; yet not a hair of your head shall perish. By your patience you will win your souls. And when you see Jerusalem being surrounded by an army, then know that her desolation is at hand. Then let those who are in Judea flee to the mountains; and let those who are in her midst go out and let those who are in the country not enter her. For these are days of vengeance, that all things that are written may be fulfilled. But woe to those who are with child or have infants at the breast in those days! For there will be great distress over the land, and wrath upon this people. And they will fall by the edge of the sword, and will be led away as captives to all the nations. And Jerusalem will be trodden down by the Gentiles, until the times of the nations be fulfilled. And there will be signs in the sun and moon and stars, and upon the earth distress of nations bewildered by the roaring of sea and waves; men fainting for fear and for expectation of things that are coming on the world; for the powers of Heaven will be shaken. And then they will see the Son of Man coming upon a cloud with great power and majesty. But when these things begin to come to pass, look up, and lift up your hearts, because your redemption is at hand. And Jesus spoke to them the same parable. *Behold the fig tree, and all the trees. When they now put forth their buds, you know that summer is near. Even so,*

*when you see these things coming to pass, know that the King-
dom of God is near. Amen I say to you, this generation will not
pass away till all things have been accomplished. Heaven and
earth will pass away, but My words will not pass away. But
take heed to yourselves, lest your hearts be overburdened with
self-indulgence and drunkenness and the cares of this life, and
that DAY come upon you suddenly as a snare. For come it will
upon all who dwell on the face of all the earth. Watch, then,
praying at all times, that you may be accounted worthy to escape all these things that are to be, and to stand before the
Son of Man.* Now in the daytime Jesus was teaching in the
Temple. As for the nights, He would go out and pass them on
the Mount of Olives facing the Temple and Jerusalem. And
all the people came to Him early in the morning in the Temple,
to hear Him. Luke 21:1-37

602. IN THE PARABLE OF THE TEN VIRGINS, Jesus said, *The
Kingdom of Heaven will be like ten virgins who took their
lamps and went forth to meet the bridegroom. Five of them
were foolish and five wise. But the five foolish, when they took
their lamps, took no oil with them, while the wise did take oil
in their vessels with the lamps. Then as the bridegroom was
long in coming, they all became drowsy and slept. And at midnight a cry arose, "Behold, the bridegroom is coming, go forth
to meet him!" Then all those virgins arose and trimmed their
lamps. And the foolish said to the wise, "Give us some of your
oil, for our lamps are going out." The wise answered, saying,
"Lest there may not be enough for us and for you, go rather to
those who sell it, and buy some for yourselves." Now while they
were gone to buy it, the bridegroom came; and those who
were ready went in with him to the marriage feast, and the
door was shut. Finally ther came also the other virgins, who
said, "Sir, sir, open the door for us!" But he answered and said,
"Amen I say to you, I do not know you." Watch, therefore, for
you know neither the DAY nor the hour.* Matthew 25:1-13

268

603. IN THE PARABLE OF THE TALENTS (the gold pieces), Jesus
said, *It* (the Kingdom of Heaven) *is like a man going
abroad, who called his servants and handed over his goods to
them. And to one he gave five talents, to another two, and to
another one, to each according to his particular ability, and
then he went on his journey. And he who had received the
five talents went and traded with them, and gained five more.
In like manner, he who had received the two gained two more.
But he who had received the one went away and dug in the
earth and hid his master's money. Then after a long time the
master of those servants came and settled accounts with them.
And he who had received five talents came and brought five
other talents, saying, "Master, thou didst hand over to me five
talents; behold, I have gained five others in addition." His
master said to him, "Well done, good and faithful servant; because thou hast been faithful over a few things, I will set thee
over many; enter into the joy of thy master." And he also who
had received the two talents came and said, "Master, thou didst
hand over to me two talents; behold, I have gained two more."
His master said to him, "Well done, good and faithful servant;
because thou hast been faithful over a few things, I will set
thee over many, enter into the joy of thy master." But he who
had received the one talent came and said, "Master, I know that
thou art a stern man; thou reapest where thou hast not sowed
and gatherest where thou hast not winnowed; and as I was
afraid, I went away and hid thy talent in the earth; behold, thou
hast what is thine. But his master answered and said to him,
"Wicked and slothful servant! thou didst know that I reap where
I do not sow, and gather where I have not winnowed? Thou
shouldst therefore have entrusted my money to the bankers,
and on my return I should have got back my own with interest.
Take away therefore the talent from him, and give it to him
who has the ten talents. For to everyone who has shall be given,
and he shall have abundance; but from him who does not have,
even that which he seems to have shall be taken away. But as*

269

for the unprofitable servant, cast him forth into the darkness outside, where there will be the weeping, and the gnashing of teeth.[372] Matthew 25:14-30

604. THE LAST JUDGMENT! *But when the Son of Man shall come in His majesty, and all the angels with Him, then He will sit on the Throne of His glory; and before Him will be gathered all the nations, and He will separate them one from another, as the shepherd separates the sheep from the goats; and He will set the sheep on His right hand, but the goats on the left. Then the King will say to those on His right hand, "Come, blessed of My Father, take possession of the Kingdom prepared for you from the foundation of the world; for I was hungry and you gave Me to eat; I was thirsty and you gave Me to drink; I was a stranger and you took Me in; naked and you covered Me; sick and you visited Me; I was in prison and you came to Me." Then the just will answer Him, saying, "Lord, when did we see Thee hungry, and feed Thee; or thirsty, and give Thee drink? And when did we see Thee a stranger, and take Thee in; or naked, and clothe Thee? Or when did we see Thee sick, or in prison, and come to Thee?" And answering the King will say to them, "Amen I say to you, as long as you did it for one of these, the least of My brethren, you did it for Me." Then He will say to those on His left hand, "Depart from Me, accursed ones, into the everlasting fire which was prepared for the devil and his angels. For I was hungry, and you did not give Me to eat; I was thirsty and you gave Me no drink; I was a stranger and you did not take Me in; naked, and you did not clothe Me; sick, and in prison, and you did not visit Me." Then they also will answer and say, "Lord, when did we see Thee hungry, or thirsty, or a stranger, or naked, or sick, or in prison, and did not minister to Thee?" Then He will answer them, saying, "Amen I say to you, as long as you did not do it for one*

---

372. *Luke 19:12-27*

of these least ones, you did not do it for Me." And these will go into everlasting punishment, but the just into Everlasting Life. Matthew 25:31-46

605. EVEN AMONG THE RULERS, MANY BELIEVED IN JESUS; but because of the Pharisees they did not acknowledge it, lest they should be put out of the synagogue. For they loved the glory of men more than the glory of God. Jesus cried out, *He who believes in Me, believes not in Me but in Him Who sent Me. And he who sees Me, sees Him Who sent Me. I have come a Light into the world, that whoever believes in Me may not remain in the darkness. And if anyone hears My words, and does not keep them, it is not I Who judge him; for I have not come to judge the world, but to save the world. He who rejects Me, and does not accept My words, has One to condemn him. The word that I have spoken will condemn him on the last day. For I have not spoken on My own authority, but He Who sent Me, the Father, has commanded Me what I should say, and what I should declare. And I know that His commandment is Everlasting Life. The things, therefore, that I speak, I speak as the Father has bidden Me.* John 12:42-50

606. IT WAS THE EVENING OF THE PASSOVER of the Feast of the Unleavened Bread. (On the morrow the Lamb of God would let Himself be sacrificed, on Calvary Hill nailed to an infamous cross of wood, to atone for the sins of mankind.) Jesus came with the Twelve to the Cenacle on Mount Sion, a part of the Holy City. Here they would eat the Passover Supper. While they were at table, Jesus said, *Amen I say to you, one of you will betray Me.* And being very much saddened they began each to say, "Is it I, Lord?" Jesus replied, *He who dips his hand into the dish with Me, he will betray Me. The Son of Man indeed goes His way, as it is written of Him; but woe to that man*

*by whom the Son of Man is betrayed! It were better for that man
if he had not been born.*[373,374] Matthew 26:20-24

607. AFTER THE LAST SUPPER, JESUS TELLS THE APOSTLES of
the role of the Holy Spirit, Whom He calls the Advocate.
He said, *And now I am going to Him Who sent Me, and no
one of you asks Me "Where art Thou going?" But because I
have spoken to you these things, sorrow has filled your heart.
But I speak the truth to you; it is expedient for you that I
depart. For if I do not go, the Advocate will not come to you;
but if I go, I will send Him to you. And when He has come He
will convict the world of sin, and of justice, and of judgment:
of sin, because they do not believe in Me; of justice, because
I go to the Father, and you will see Me no more; and of judgment, because the prince* (the devil) *of this world has already
been judged.* John 16:5-11

608. JESUS COMMISSIONED THE APOSTLES TO *go into the whole
world and preach the Gospel to every creature. He who
believes and is baptized shall be saved, but he who does not
believe shall be condemned.* Mark 16:15

---

373. *Mark 14:17-21;* 374. *Luke 22:21-22*

CHAPTER XVII

JESUS SAID
of Life Everlasting

609. IT WAS FROM THE HIGH SLOPE above the northern shore of
the Sea of Galilee that Jesus preached the Sermon on the
Mount. Visible to the left lay His adopted city, the seaport
town of Capharnaum. Jesus began with the Beatitudes, saying
to His disciples, *Blessed are the poor in spirit, for theirs is the
Kingdom of Heaven. . . . Blessed are the clean of heart, for they
shall see God. . . . Blessed are they who suffer persecution for
justice' sake, for theirs is the Kingdom of Heaven. Blessed are
you when men reproach you, and persecute you, and, speaking
falsely, say all manner of evil against you, for My sake. Rejoice
and exult, because your reward is great in Heaven; for so did
they persecute the Prophets who were before you.*[375] Matthew
5:3-12

610. WHAT A SIGHT IT MUST HAVE BEEN: Jesus standing there
(on the Mount of Beatitudes), facing the shimmering ex-
panse of the Sea of Galilee, and preaching to His disciples and
the multitudes gathered around and below Him! Toward the
close of His Sermon, Jesus warned them of the obstacles to vir-

---

375. *Luke 6:20-26*

tue, saying, *Enter by the narrow gate. For wide is the gate and broad is the way that leads to destruction, and many there are who enter that way. How narrow the gate and close the way that leads to Life! And few there are who find it. . . . Not everyone who says to Me, "Lord, Lord," shall enter the Kingdom of Heaven; but he who does the will of My Father in Heaven shall enter the Kingdom of Heaven. Many will say to Me in that day, "Lord, Lord, did we not prophesy in Thy name, and cast out devils in Thy name, and work many miracles in Thy name?" And then I will declare to them, "I never knew you. Depart from Me, you workers of iniquity."*[376] Matthew 7:13-14, 21-23

611. To Nicodemus, the Pharisee, Jesus said, *As Moses lifted up the serpent in the desert, even so must the Son of Man be lifted up, that those who believe in Him may not perish, but may have Life Everlasting. For God so loved the world that He gave His only-begotten Son, that those who believe in Him may not perish, but may have Life Everlasting.* Of this Pharisee, Saint John wrote, ["And there also came Nicodemus (who at first had come to Jesus by night), bringing a mixture of myrrh and aloes, in weight about a hundred pounds. They (Joseph of Arimathea and Nicodemus) therefore took the body of Jesus and wrapped it in linen cloths with the spices, after the Jewish manner of preparing for burial. Now in the place where He was crucified there was a garden, and in the garden a new tomb in which no one had yet been laid. There, accordingly, because of the Preparation Day of the Jews, for the tomb was close at hand, they laid Jesus."[377]] John 3: 14-16

612. Jesus came to a town of Samaria, called Sichar, near the field that Jacob gave to his son Joseph. Now Jacob's

---

376. *Luke 13:24-30;* 377. *John 19:39-42*

well was there. Jesus, therefore, wearied as He was from the journey, was sitting at the well. His disciples had gone away into the town to buy food. It was about the sixth hour (noon). There came a Samaritan woman to draw water. Jesus said to her, *Give Me to drink!* The Samaritan woman therefore said to Him, "How is it that thou, although thou art a Jew, dost ask drink of me, who am a Samaritan woman?" For Jews did not associate with Samaritans. Jesus answered her, *If thou didst know the gift of God, and Who it is Who says to thee, "Give Me to drink," thou perhaps, wouldst have asked of Him, and He would have given thee Living Water.* The woman said, "Sir, thou hast nothing to draw with, and the well is deep. Whence then hast thou living water? Art thou greater than our father Jacob who gave us the well, and drank from it, himself, and his sons, and his flocks?" In answer Jesus said, *Everyone who drinks of this water will thirst again. He, however, who drinks of the Water that I will give him shall never thirst; but the Water that I will give him shall become in him a Fountain of Water, springing up unto Life Everlasting.* John 4:5-14

613. THE DISCIPLES, WHEN THEY RETURNED FROM THE TOWN, wondered that Jesus was speaking to a woman, but said nothing. They brought Him food, saying, "Rabbi, eat." He replied, *I have food to eat of which you do not know.* They said to one another, "Has someone brought Him something to eat?" Then Jesus said, *My food is to do the will of Him Who sent Me, to accomplish His work. Do you not say, "There are yet four months, and then comes the harvest?" Well, I say to you, lift up your eyes and behold that the fields are already white for the harvest. And he who reaps receives a wage, and gathers fruit unto Life Everlasting, so that the Sower and the reaper may rejoice together. For herein is the proverb true, "One sows, another reaps." I have sent you to reap that on which you have not labored. Others have labored, and you have entered into their labors.* John 4:34-38

614. EVEN EARLY IN HIS MINISTRY JESUS FORETOLD the opposition which His disciples would meet when they preached
the Gospel of Jesus Christ. He said, *Behold, I am sending you
forth like sheep in the midst of wolves.*[378] . . . *And you will be
hated by all for My name's sake; but he who has persevered to
the end will be saved.*[379,380] Matthew 10:22

615. JESUS BEGAN TO TEACH THAT THE SON OF MAN must
suffer many things, and be rejected by the elders and
chief priests and Scribes, and be put to death, and after three
days rise again. Calling the people together with His disciples,
He said, *He who does not take up his cross and follow Me, is
not worthy of Me. He who finds his life will lose it, and he who
loses his life for My sake, will find it. He who receives you,
receives Me; and he who receives Me, receives Him Who sent
Me. He who receives a Prophet because he is a prophet, shall
receive a prophet's reward; and he who receives a just man,
shall receive a just man's reward. And whoever gives to one of
these little ones but a cup of cold water to drink because he is
a disciple, amen I say to you, he shall not lose his reward.*[381,382]
Matthew 10:38-42

616. THE UNBELIEVING JEWS PERSECUTED JESUS because He
performed works of mercy on the Sabbath. But they were
the more anxious to put Him to death when He called God His
own Father, making Himself equal to God. Answering them,
Jesus put forth His claim to divinity. In part He said, *For as the
Father raises the dead and gives them Life, even so the Son also
gives Life to whom He will.* . . . *Amen, amen, I say to you, he
who hears My word, and believes Him Who sent Me, has Life
Everlasting, and does not come to judgment, but has passed from
death to Life. Amen, amen, I say to you, the hour is coming,
and now is here, when the dead shall hear the voice of the Son*

---

378. *Matthew 10:16;* 379. *Matthew 24:9,13;* 380. *Luke 21:17-19;* 381. *Mark
8:34-39;* 382. *Luke 9:23-27*

of God, and those who hear shall live. For as the Father has Life in Himself, even so He has given to the Son also to have Life in Himself; and He has granted Him power to render judgment, because He is Son of Man. Do not wonder at this, for the hour is coming in which all who are in the tombs shall hear the voice of the Son of God. And they who have done good shall come forth unto resurrection of Life; but they who have done evil unto resurrection of judgment. . . . If I bear witness concerning Myself, My witness is not true. There is another who bears witness concerning Me, and I know that the witness that he bears concerning Me is true. You have sent to John, and he has borne witness to the Truth. I however do not receive the witness of man, but I say these things that you may be saved. . . . You search the Scriptures, because in them you think that you have Life Everlasting. And it is they that bear witness to Me, yet you are not willing to come to Me that you may have Life.
John 5:21-40

617. JESUS CAST OUT DEVILS BY THE SPIRIT OF GOD WITHIN HIM.[383] So when the Pharisees said that He cast out devils by Beelzebub, the prince of the devils, they blasphemed against the Holy Spirit. Of this blasphemy, Jesus said, *Therefore I say to you, that every kind of sin and blasphemy shall be forgiven to men: but the blasphemy against the Spirit will not be forgiven. And whoever speaks a word against the Son of Man, it shall be forgiven him; but whoever speaks against the Holy Spirit, it will not be forgiven him, either in this world or in the world to come.*[384,385] Matthew 12:31-32

618. AFTER THE MIRACULOUS FEEDING OF THE FIVE THOUSAND from the five barley loaves and two fish, Jesus retired to near-by Capharnaum. The people followed Him. Therefore He said to them, *Amen, amen, I say to you, you seek Me, not because you have seen signs, but because you have eaten of the*

383. *Matthew 12:28;* 384. *Mark 3:28-30;* 385. *Luke 12:10*

loaves and have been filled. Do not labor for the food that perishes, but for that which endures unto Life Everlasting, which the Son of Man will give you. For upon Him the Father, God Himself, has set His seal. . . . I am the Bread of Life. . . . For this is the will of My Father Who sent Me, that whoever beholds the Son, and believes in Him, shall have Everlasting Life, and I will raise him up on the last day. . . . Amen, amen, I say to you, he who believes in Me has Life Everlasting. I am the Bread of Life. . . . Amen, amen, I say to you, unless you eat the flesh of the Son of Man, and drink His blood, you shall not have Life in you. He who eats My flesh and drinks My blood has Life Everlasting and I will raise him up on the last day. . . . He who eats this Bread shall live forever. These things Jesus said when teaching in the synagogue at Capharnaum. Many of His disciples therefore, when they heard this, said, "This is a hard saying. Who can listen to it?" Some of them turned back and no longer went about with Him. Jesus, knowing in Himself that His disciples were murmuring at this, said to them, *Does this scandalize you? What then if you should see the Son of Man ascending where He was before? It is the Spirit that gives Life; the flesh profits nothing. The words that I have spoken to you are Spirit and Life.* John 6:26-64

619. WHEN JESUS WAS PASSING THROUGH A TOWN IN SAMARIA on His way to Jerusalem, the unfriendly Samaritans would not receive Him. The Apostles James and John seeing this, said, "Lord, wilt Thou that we bid fire come down from Heaven and consume them?" Jesus rebuked them, saying, *You do not know of what manner of Spirit you are; for the Son of Man did not come to destroy men's lives, but to save them.*[386] Luke 9:55-56

620. AVOID SCANDAL! JESUS SAID, *Whoever causes one of these little ones who believe in Me to sin, it were better for him*

---

386. *John 3:17*

278

if a great millstone were hung about his neck, and he were thrown into the sea. If thy hand is an occasion of sin to thee, cut it off! It is better for thee to enter into Life maimed, than, having two hands, to go into hell, into the unquenchable fire, "Where their worm dies not, and the fire is not quenched." And if thy foot is an occasion of sin to thee, cut it off! It is better for thee to enter Life Everlasting lame, than, having two feet, to be cast into the hell of unquenchable fire, "Where their worm dies not, and the fire is not quenched." And if thy eye is an occasion of sin to thee, pluck it out! It is better for thee to enter into the Kingdom of God with one eye, than having two eyes, to be cast into hell-fire, "Where their worm dies not, and the fire is not quenched."[387,388,389] Mark 9:41-47

621. TO THE UNBELIEVING JEWS WHO SAID JESUS HAD A DEVIL, He offered the key to salvation and Life Everlasting, saying, *Amen, amen, I say to you, if anyone keep My word, he will never see death.* John 8:51

622. SEVENTY-TWO DISCIPLES HAD BEEN SENT OUT BY JESUS into the towns and villages to preach the Gospel of the Kingdom of God and the forgiveness of sins. They returned with joy, saying, "Lord, even the devils are subject to us in Thy name." Jesus said, *But do not rejoice in this, that the spirits are subject to you; rejoice rather in this, that your names are written in Heaven.* Luke 10:20

623. A LAWYER GOT UP TO TEST JESUS, SAYING, "Master, what must I do to gain Eternal Life?" Jesus answered with a question, *What is written in the Law* (of Moses)? *How dost thou read?* The lawyer replied, "Thou shalt love the Lord thy God with thy whole heart, and with thy whole soul, and with thy whole strength, and with thy whole mind; and thy neighbor

---

387. *Matthew 5:30;* 388. *Matthew 18:6-9;* 389. *Luke 17:2*

as thyself." Jesus said, *Thou hast answered rightly; do this and thou shalt live.*[390,391] Luke 10:25-28

624. IN HIS SERMON ON THE MOUNT JESUS spoke of the entrance by the narrow gate. Much later, as He was on His way toward Jerusalem, He was asked, "Lord, are only a few to be saved?" He replied, *Strive to enter by the narrow gate; for many, I tell you, will seek to enter and will not be able. But when the Master of the house has entered and shut the door, you will begin to stand outside and knock at the door, saying, "Lord, open to us!" And He shall say to you in answer, "I do not know where you are from." Then you shall begin to say, "We ate and drank in Thy presence, and Thou didst teach in our streets." And He shall say to you, "I do not know where you are from. Depart from Me, all you workers of iniquity." There will be the weeping, and the gnashing of teeth, when you shall see Abraham and Isaac and Jacob and all the Prophets in the Kingdom of God, but you yourselves cast forth outside. And they will come from the east and from the west, from the north and from the south, and will feast in the Kingdom of God.*[392] Luke 13:22-30

625. A RULER OF THE PHARISEES IN PEREA, across the River Jordan, invited Jesus to a feast. As the guests were coming in, Jesus noticed that they were choosing the first places at table. He said to them, *When thou art invited, go and recline in the last place; that when he who invited thee comes in, he may say to thee, "Friend, go up higher!"* Then Jesus said to the ruler, *When thou givest a dinner or a supper, do not invite thy friends, or thy brethren, or thy relatives, or thy rich neighbors, lest perhaps they also invite thee in return, and a recompense be made to thee. But when thou givest a feast, invite the poor, the crippled, the lame, the blind: and blessed shalt thou be, because they have nothing to repay thee with; for thou shalt be repaid at the resurrection of the just.* Luke 14:7-14

390. *Matthew 22:34-39;* 391. *Mark 12:28-34;* 392. *Matthew 7:13-14*
280

626. IN THE FOURTEENTH CHAPTER OF SAINT LUKE, Jesus
spoke the parable of a great supper. He places it before
Jesus' triumphal entry into Jerusalem and His cleansing of the
Temple. Saint Matthew has a similar parable of a marriage
feast but records it after the triumphal entry of Jesus and after
His cleansing of the Temple. Whether this is one and the same
parable is a moot question. The parable according to Saint
Luke is milder in tone, in which Jesus said, *A certain man gave a
great supper, and he invited many. And he sent his servant at
supper time to tell those invited to come, for everything is now
ready. And they all with one accord began to excuse themselves. The first said to him, "I have bought a farm and I must
go out and see it; I pray thee hold me excused." And another
said, "I have bought five yoke of oxen, and I am on my way
to try them; I pray thee hold me excused." And another said,
"I have married a wife, and therefore I cannot come." And the
servant returned, and reported these things to his master. Then
the master of the house was angry and said to the servant, "Go
out quickly into the streets and lanes of the city, and bring in
here the poor, and the crippled, and the blind, and the lame."
And the servant said, "Sir, thy order has been carried out, and
still there is room." Then the master said to the servant, "Go
out into the highways and hedges, and make them come in, so
that my house may be filled. For I tell you that none of those
who were invited shall taste of my supper."*[393] Luke 14:16-24

627. Now THERE TOOK PLACE AT JERUSALEM the Feast of the
Dedication: a joyous commemoration of the rededication
of the Temple by Judas Machabeus. It was winter. Jesus was
walking in the Temple, in Solomon's portico. The Jews gathered
around and said to Him, "How long dost thou keep us in suspense? If thou art the Christ (the Messias), tell us openly."
Jesus answered, *I tell you and you do not believe. The works
that I do in the name of My Father, these bear witness con-*

---

393. *Matthew 22:1-14*

cerning Me. But you do not believe because you are not of My sheep. My sheep hear My voice, and I know them and they follow Me. And I give them Everlasting Life; and they shall never perish, neither shall anyone snatch them out of My hand. What My Father has given Me is greater than all; and no one is able to snatch anything out of the hand of My Father. Jesus added, *I and the Father are One!* John 10:22-30

628. THE PUBLICANS (TAX COLLECTORS), AND SINNERS, were drawing near to Jesus to listen to Him. The Pharisees and Scribes murmured, saying, "This man welcomes sinners." Therefore Jesus spoke this parable, saying, *What man of you having a hundred sheep, and losing one of them, does not leave the ninety-nine in the desert, and go after that which is lost, until he finds it? And when he has found it, he lays it upon his shoulders rejoicing. And on coming home he calls together his friends and neighbors, saying to them, "Rejoice with me, because I have found my sheep that was lost." I say to you that, even so, there will be joy in Heaven over one sinner who repents, more than over ninety-nine just who have no need of repentance.* Luke 15:1-7

629. CONTINUING WITH THE PARABLE OF THE LOST COIN, Jesus said, *Or what woman, having ten drachmas, if she loses one drachma, does not light a lamp and sweep the house and search carefully until she finds it? And when she has found it, she calls together her friends and neighbors, saying, "Rejoice with me, for I have found the drachma that I had lost." Even so, I say to you there will be joy among the angels of God over one sinner who repents.* Luke 15:8-10

630. THEN JESUS SPOKE TO THEM THE PARABLE OF THE PRODIGAL SON, SAYING, *A certain man had two sons. And the younger of them said to his father, "Father, give me the share of the property that falls to me." And he divided his means* *between them. And not many days later, the younger son gathered up all his wealth, and took his journey into a far country; and there he squandered his fortune in loose living. And after he had spent all, there came a grievous famine over that country, and he began to suffer want. And he went and joined one of the citizens of that country, who sent him to his farm to feed swine. And he longed to fill himself with the pods that the swine were eating, but no one offered to give them to him. But when he came to himself, he said, "How many hired men in my father's house have bread in abundance, while I am perishing here with hunger! I will get up and go to my father, and will say to him, "Father, I have sinned against Heaven and before thee. I am no longer worthy to be called thy son; make me as one of thy hired men." And he arose and went to his father. But while he was yet a long way off, his father saw him and was moved with compassion, and ran and fell upon his neck and kissed him. And the son said to him, "Father, I have sinned against Heaven and before thee. I am no longer worthy to be called thy son." But the father said to his servants, "Fetch quickly the best robe and put it on him, and give him a ring for his finger and sandals for his feet; and bring out the fattened calf and kill it, and let us eat and make merry; because this my son was dead, and has come to life again; he was lost, and is found." And they began to make merry. Now his elder son was in the field; and as he came and drew near to the house, he heard music and dancing. And calling one of the servants he inquired what this meant. And he said to him, "Thy brother has come, and thy father has killed the fattened calf, because he has got him back safe." But he was angered and would not go in. His father, therefore, came out and began to entreat him. But he answered and said to his father, "Behold, these many years I have been serving thee, and have never transgressed one of thy commands; and yet thou hast never given me a kid (goat) that I might make merry with my friends. But when this thy son comes, who has devoured his means with harlots, thou hast*

283

killed for him the fattened calf." But he said to him, "Son, thou art always with me, and all that is mine is thine; but we were bound to make merry and rejoice, for this thy brother was dead, and has come to life; he was lost, and is found." Luke 15:11-32

631. In rebuking the Pharisees, who were fond of money, Jesus said that no servant could serve two masters; that either he would hate the one and love the other, or else he would stand by the one and despise the other. That one cannot serve God and mammon (worldly riches). The Pharisees began to sneer at Him. Therefore Jesus spoke this parable to them, saying, *There was a certain rich man who used to clothe himself in purple and fine linen, and who feasted every day in splendid fashion. And there was a certain poor man, named Lazarus, who lay at his gate, covered with sores, and longing to be filled with the crumbs that fell from the rich man's table; even the dogs would come and lick his sores. And it came to pass that the poor man died and was borne away by the angels into Abraham's bosom; but the rich man also died and was buried in hell. And lifting up his eyes, being in torments, he saw Abraham afar off and Lazarus in his bosom. And he cried out and said, "Father Abraham, have pity on me, and send Lazarus to dip the tip of his finger in water and cool my tongue, for I am tormented in this flame." But Abraham said to him, "Son, remember that thou in thy lifetime hast received good things, and Lazarus in like manner evil things; but now here he is comforted whereas thou art tormented. And besides all that, between us and you a great gulf is fixed, so that they who wish to pass over from this side to you cannot, and they cannot cross from your side to us." And he said, "Then, father, I beseech thee to send him to my father's house, for I have five brothers, that he may testify to them, lest they too come into this place of torments." And Abraham said to him, "They have Moses and the Prophets; let them harken to them." But he answered, "No, father Abraham, but if someone from the dead goes to them, they* *will repent."* But he said to him, *"If they do not harken to Moses and the Prophets, they will not believe even if someone rises from the dead."* Luke 16:19-31

632. A RICH RULER CAME TO JESUS AND ADDRESSED HIM, "Good Master, What good work shall I do to have Eternal Life?" He answered, *If thou wilt enter into Life, keep the Commandments.* The young man said, "All these I have kept; what is yet wanting in me?" Jesus said, *If thou wilt be perfect, go, sell what thou hast, and give to the poor, and thou shalt have treasure in Heaven; and come, follow Me.* But the young ruler did not accept His invitation. Rather he went away sad for he had great possessions. Jesus, seeing him become sad, said to His Disciples, *Amen I say to you, with difficulty will a rich man enter the Kingdom of Heaven. . . .* The disciples, hearing this, were exceedingly astonished, and said, "Who then can be saved?" Jesus responded, *With men this is impossible, but with God all things are possible.*[394,395] Matthew 19:16-26

633. THE APOSTLES HAD BEEN LISTENING TO ALL THIS. Peter addressed Jesus, saying, "Behold, we have left all and followed Thee; what then shall we have?" Jesus said to them, *Amen I say to you who have followed Me, in the regeneration when the Son of Man shall sit on the Throne of His Glory, shall also sit on twelve thrones, judging the twelve tribes of Israel. And everyone who has left house, or brothers, or sisters, or father, or mother, or wife, or children, or lands, for My name's sake, shall receive a hundredfold, and shall possess Life Everlasting. But many who are first now will be last, and many who are last now will be first.*[396,397] Matthew 19:27-30

634. JESUS WAS IN THE DISTRICT OF PEREA, on the other side of the River Jordan, when word reached Him, that His friend, Lazarus, the brother of Mary Magdalene and Martha in Bethany, was grievously ill. Jesus said, *This sickness is not*

---

394. *Mark 10:17-21;* 395. *Luke 18:18-22;* 396. *Mark 10:28-31;* 397. *Luke 18:28-30*

unto death, but for the glory of God, that through it the Son of God may be glorified. . . . Lazarus, our friend, sleeps. But I go that I may wake him from sleep. . . . Jesus had spoken of his death, but the disciples thought He was speaking of the repose of sleep. Then Jesus said plainly, *Lazarus is dead; and I rejoice on your account that I was not there, that you may believe. But let us go to him. . . .* Jesus came to Bethany and found him four days in the tomb. . . . Martha said to Jesus, "Lord, if Thou hadst been here my brother would not have died. But even now I know that whatever Thou shalt ask of God, God will give it to Thee." Jesus said to her, *Thy brother shall rise.* Martha said, "I know that he will rise at the resurrection, on the last day." Jesus said to her, *I am the Resurrection and the Life; he who believes in Me, even if he die, shall live; and whoever lives and believes in Me shall never die. Dost thou believe this?* Martha said to Jesus, "Yes, Lord, I believe that Thou art the Christ, the son of God, Who hast come into the world." . . . Jesus was led to the entrance of the tomb. He wept. Some of the Jews said, "Could not he who opened the eyes of the blind, have caused that this man should not die?" . . . Jesus said, *Take away the stone.* Martha said, "Lord, by this time he is already decayed." Jesus said to her, *Have I not told thee that if thou believe thou shalt behold the glory of God?* They removed the stone. Jesus, raising His eyes, said, *Father, I give Thee thanks that Thou hast heard Me. Yet I knew that Thou always hearest Me; but because of the people who stand around, I spoke, that they may believe that Thou hast sent Me.* When He had said this, He cried out with a loud voice, *Lazarus, come forth!* And at once he who had been dead came forth, bound feet and hands with bandages, and his face was tied up with a cloth. Jesus said to them, *Unbind him, and let him go.* John 11:1-44

635. THE CHIEF PRIESTS AND PHARISEES knew that many of the parables spoken by Jesus referred to them. Here is the parable of the marriage feast. Jesus said, *The Kingdom of*

Heaven is like a king who had a marriage feast for his son. And he sent his servants to call in those invited to the marriage feast, but they would not come. Again he sent out other servants, saying, "Tell those who are invited, 'Behold, I have prepared my dinner; my oxen and fatlings are killed, and everything is ready; come to the marriage feast'." But they made light of it, and went off, one to his farm, and another to his business; and the rest laid hold of his servants, treated them shamefully, and killed them. But when the king heard of it, he was angry; and he sent his armies, destroyed those murderers, and burnt their city. Then he said to his servants, "The marriage feast indeed is ready, but those who were invited were not worthy; go therefore to the crossroads, and invite to the marriage feast whomever you shall find." And his servants went out into the roads, and gathered all whom they found, both good and bad; and the marriage feast was filled with guests. Now the king went in to see the guests, and he saw there a man who had not on a wedding garment. And he said to him, "Friend, how didst thou come in here without a wedding garment?" But he was speechless. Then the king said to the attendants, "Bind his hands and feet and cast him forth into the darkness outside, where there will be the weeping, and the gnashing of teeth." For many are called but few are chosen.[398] Matthew 22:1-14*

636. ALTHOUGH THE SADDUCEES SAID THERE WAS NO RESUR-
RECTION, they presented this case to Jesus: A woman had
been married and widowed several times during her lifetime.
Whose wife would she be at the resurrection? Jesus answered,
*The children of this world marry and are given in marriage. But
those who shall be accounted worthy of that world and of the
resurrection from the dead, neither marry nor take wives. For
neither shall they be able to die any more, for they are equal to
the angels, and are sons of God, being sons of the resurrection.*

---

398. *Luke 14:16-24*

But that the dead rise, even Moses showed in the passage about the Bush, when he calls the Lord the God of Abraham, and the God of Isaac, and the God of Jacob. Now He is not the God of the dead, but of the living, for all live to Him.[399] Luke 20:34-38

637. SAINT MATTHEW, SAINT MARK AND SAINT LUKE record Jesus' predictions of the persecution of His disciples, the destruction of Jerusalem, the signs of the last days, and the end of the world. To His disciples, Jesus said, *You will be hated by all for My name's sake; but he who has perservered to the end will be saved.*[400,401] Mark 13:13

638. IN FORETELLING THE SIGNS OF THE LAST DAY, JESUS SAID, *But in those days, after that tribulation, the sun will be darkened, and the moon will not give her light, and the stars of Heaven will be falling, and the powers that are in Heaven will be shaken. Then they will see the Son of Man coming upon clouds with great power and majesty. Then He will send forth His angels, and gather His elect from the four winds, from the uttermost parts of the earth to the uttermost parts of Heaven.*[402,403] Mark 13:24-27

639. KNOWING THAT HIS HOUR HAD COME, JESUS SAID TO HIS APOSTLES, *The hour has come for the Son of Man to be glorified. Amen, amen, I say to you, unless the grain of wheat falls into the ground and dies, it remains alone. But if it dies, it brings forth much fruit. He who loves his life, loses it; and he who hates his life in this world, keeps it unto Life Everlasting. If anyone serves Me let him follow Me; and where I am there also shall My servants be. If anyone serves Me, My Father will honor him.*[404] John 12:23-26

640. EVEN AMONG THE RULERS OF THE SYNAGOGUES, many believed in Jesus; but because of the Pharisees they did not

---

399. *Mark 12:24-27;* 400. *Matthew 24:9,13;* 401. *Luke 21:17-19;* 402. *Matthew 24:29-31;* 403. *Luke 21:25-28;* 404. *John 14:19*

acknowledge it, lest they should be put out of the synagogue. For they loved the glory of men more than the glory of God. Jesus cried out, *He who believes in Me, believes not in Me but in Him Who sent Me. And he who sees Me, sees Him Who sent Me. I have come a Light into the world, that whoever believes in Me may not remain in the darkness. And if anyone hears My words, and does not keep them, it is not I who judge him; for I have not come to judge the world, but to save the world. He who rejects Me, and does not accept My words, has One to condemn him. The words that I have spoken will condemn him on the last day. For I have not spoken on My own authority, but He Who sent Me, the Father, has commanded Me what I should say, and what I should declare. And I know that His commandment is Everlasting Life. The things, therefore, that I speak, I speak as the Father has bidden Me.* John 12:44-50

641. EVERLASTING LIFE IS LIVING FOREVER WITH GOD in the Kingdom of Heaven. In the parable of the ten virgins, Jesus said, *Then will the Kingdom of Heaven be like ten virgins who took their lamps and went forth to meet the bridegroom. Five of them were foolish and five wise. But the five foolish, when they took their lamps, took no oil with them, while the wise did take oil in their vessels with the lamps. Then as the bridegroom was long in coming, they all became drowsy and slept. And at midnight a cry arose, "Behold, the bridegroom is coming, go forth to meet him!" Then all those virgins arose and trimmed their lamps. And the foolish said to the wise, "Give us some of your oil, for our lamps are going out." The wise answered, saying, "Lest there may not be enough for us and for you, go rather to those who sell it, and buy some for yourselves." Now while they were gone to buy it, the bridegroom came; and those who were ready went in with him to the marriage feast, and the door was shut. Finally there came also*

289

the other virgins, who said, "Sir, sir, open the door for us!" But he answered and said, "Amen I say to you, I do not know you." Watch therefore, for you know neither the DAY nor the hour.[405]
Matthew 25:1-13

642. Not only the crowds but also the disciples thought Jesus would immediately establish in Jerusalem the temporal messianic Kingdom and proclaim His royalty publicly. Through the parable of the talents (gold pieces), Jesus intimated that considerable time would elapse before the establishment of the glorious phase of His Kingdom. In the meantime His disciples should work for Him, and thus prepare for judgment. So scholars interpret this parable, in which Jesus said, *For it* (the Kingdom of Heaven) *is like a man going abroad, who called his servants and handed over his goods to them. And to one he gave five talents, to another two, and to another one, to each according to his particular ability, and then He went on his journey. And he who had received the five talents went and traded with them, and gained five more. In like manner, he who had received the two gained two more. But he who had received the one talent went away and dug in the earth and hid his master's money. Then after a long time the master of those servants came and settled accounts with them. And he who had received the five talents came and brought five other talents, saying, "Master, thou didst hand over to me five talents; behold, I have gained five others in addition." His master said to him, "Well done, good and faithful servant; because thou hast been faithful over a few things, I will set thee over many; enter into the joy of thy master." And he also who had received the two talents came and said, "Master, thou didst hand over to me two talents; behold, I have gained two more." His master said to him, "Well done, good and faithful servant; because thou hast been faithful over a few things, I will set thee over many;*

---

405. *Luke 12:35-40*

290

---

enter into the joy of thy master." But he who had received the one talent came and said, "Master, I know that thou art a stern man; thou reapest where thou hast not sowed and gatherest where thou hast not winnowed; and as I was afraid, I went away and hid thy talent in the earth; behold, thou hast what is thine." But his master answered and said to him, "Wicked and slothful servant!" thou didst know that I reap where I do not sow, and gather where I have not winnowed? Thou shouldst therefore have entrusted my money to the bankers, and on my return I should have got back my own with interest. Take away therefore the talent from him, and give it to him who has the ten talents. For everyone who has shall be given, and he shall have abundance; but from him who does not have, even that which he seems to have shall be taken away. But as for the unprofitable servant, cast him forth into the darkness outside, where there will be the weeping, and the gnashing of teeth.[406] Matthew 25:14-30

643. OF THE LAST JUDGMENT, JESUS SAID, But when the Son of Man shall come in His majesty, and all the angels with Him, then He will sit on the Throne of His glory; and before Him will be gathered all the nations, and He will separate them one from another, as the shepherd separates the sheep from the goats; and He will set the sheep on His right hand, but the goats on the left. Then the King will say to those on His right hand, "Come, blessed of My Father, take possession of the Kingdom prepared for you from the foundation of the world; for I was hungry and you gave Me to eat; I was thirsty and you gave Me to drink; I was a stranger and you took Me in; naked and you covered Me; sick and you visited Me; I was in prison and you came to Me." Then the just will answer Him, saying, "Lord, when did we see Thee hungry, and feed Thee; or thirsty, and give Thee drink? And when did we see Thee a stranger, and

---

406. *Luke 19:11-27*

*take Thee in; or naked, and clothe Thee? Or when did we see
Thee sick, or in prison, and come to Thee?" And answering the
King will say to them, "Amen I say to you, as long as you did
it for one of these, the least of My brethren, you did it for Me."*
. . . These *the just* will go *into Everlasting Life.* Matthew
25:31-40, 46

644. CONTENTION AROSE AMONG THE APOSTLES. Strangely
enough it was after the Passover Supper in the Cenacle;
after the first Holy Eucharist when Jesus had offered bread,
saying, *This is My body,* and offered the cup of wine, saying,
This is My blood! Yes, there arose a dispute: which of them was
reputed to be the greatest! Jesus said to them, *The kings of the
Gentiles lord it over them, and they who exercise authority over
them are called Benefactors. But not so with you. On the con-
trary, let him who is greatest among you become as the youngest,
and him who is the chief as the servant. For which is the
greater, he who reclines at table, or he who serves? Is it not he
who reclines? But I am in your midst as He Who serves. But you
are they who have continued with Me in My trials. And I
appoint to you a kingdom, even as My Father has appointed to
Me, that you may eat and drink at My table in My Kingdom;
and you shall sit upon thrones, judging the twelve tribes of
Israel.*[407,408] Luke 22:24-30

645. A LITTLE LATER THAT SAME HOLY THURSDAY EVENING,
just after Judas Iscariot had left the Cenacle and gone out
into the dark to betray his Lord to the chief priests, Jesus said,
Now is the Son of Man glorified, God is glorified in Him. . . .
*Little children, yet a little while I am with you. You will seek
Me, and, as I said to the Jews, "Where I go you cannot come,"
so to you also I say it now.* . . . Simon Peter said to Him, "Lord,
where art Thou going?" Jesus answered, *Where I am going thou*

---

407. *Mark 10:28-31;* 408. *Luke 18:28-30*

canst not follow Me now, but thou shalt follow later. John
13:31-36

646. THE ELEVEN APOSTLES WERE VERY MUCH SADDENED AND
CONFUSED. They understood and yet they did not understand. *I go . . . I am coming again!* Then Jesus offered
these words of comfort, saying, *Let not your heart be troubled.
You believe in God, believe also in Me. In My Father's House
there are many mansions. Were it not so, I should have told you,
because I go to prepare a place for you. And if I go and prepare
a place for you, I am coming again, and I will take you to
Myself; that where I am, there you also may be. And where
I go you know, and the way you know. . . . But you see Me
*(i.e., the world will not see Me, but you will see Me), *for I live
and you shall live.* John 14:1-4, 19

647. IN HIS PRIESTLY PRAYER FOR UNITY, that His disciples be
one, even as They (God the Father and God the Son) are
One, Jesus began, *Father, the hour has come! Glorify Thy Son,
that Thy Son may glorify Thee, even as Thou hast given Him
power over all flesh, in order that to all Thou hast given Him
He may give Everlasting Life. Now this is Everlasting Life, that
they may know Thee, the only true God, and Him Whom Thou
hast sent, JESUS CHRIST. . . . Father, I will that where I am,
they also whom Thou hast given Me may be with Me; in order
that they may behold My glory, which Thou hast given Me,
because Thou hast loved Me before the creation of the world.*
John 17:1-4, 24

648. AFTER HIS RESURRECTION FROM THE DEAD, Jesus manifested Himself to His chosen Eleven during forty days.[409]
Once while at table in Galilee, He upbraided them for their
lack of faith and hardness of heart, in that they had not believed

---
409. *Acts 1:3*

those who had seen Him after He had risen. Then He com
missioned them, saying, *Go into the whole world and preach
the Gospel to every creature. He who believes and is baptized
shall be saved, but he who does not believe shall be condemned*
Mark 16:15-16

O SACRED HEART OF JESUS!
To know Thee more intimately,
To love Thee more ardently,
To serve Thee more perfectly.

Concordant Index

(Aside from the words in parenthesis, all words in this concordant index are the very words of Jesus Himself.)

PAGE NO.

Abel the just, the blood of..................257

Abiather was high priest. What
David did when.............................. 21

Abide in Me and I in you..................102

abide in Me. If anyone does not........248

abide in My love. If you keep
My commandments you..................102

Abraham
afar off. (The rich man) he saw....246

as she is. This woman daughter of..236

came to be I AM. Before............... 60

I am the God of............................ 40

in the Kingdom of God. You
shall see...................................199

in the Kingdom of Heaven. Many
will come and feast with..................210

rejoiced that he was to see My
day. He saw it................................. 60

You (the Jews) are children of...... 29

(Zaccheus) He is a son of............... 95

Abraham's bosom. He (Lazarus)
was borne away by the angels into..193

accept the Kingdom of God as a
little child will not enter into it.
Whoever does not............................169

Accursed ones, depart from Me
into the fire everlasting...................247

accuses you (Pharisees and Scribes)
Moses in whom you hope. There
is one who...252

acknowledges Me before men I also
will acknowledge him before My
Father in Heaven. Everyone who..211

Advocate
the Holy Spirit Whom the Father
will send in My name. The............182

the Spirit of Truth Who proceeds
from the Father. The.....................182

to dwell with you forever . . . .
I will ask the Father and He will
give you another............................182

PAGE NO.

Advocate (continued)
will bear witness concerning Me.
The 182

will bring to your mind whatever
I have said to you. The..................182

will not come to you. For if I
do not go the....................................182

will bring to your mnid what-
ever I have said to you. The............182

will not come to you. For if
I do not go the 182

will teach you all things. The........182

afraid
Arise and do not be........................164

Do not be...158

Do not let your heart be..................174

go take word to My breathren
that they are to set out for Galilee
there they shall see Me. Do not be..176

it is I. Do not be.............................176

little flock. Do not be........................167

of Him (God) Who after He has
killed has the power to cast into
hell. Be 166

of Him (God) Who is able to
destroy both soul and body in hell.
But rather be.....................................161

of those who kill the body but
cannot kill the soul. Do not be......161

only have faith. Do not be..............160

you are of more value than many
sparrows. Do not be.........................166

angels
and are sons of God being sons
of the resurrection. For they are
equal to the......................................193

Depart from Me accursed ones
into the everlasting fire prepared
for the devil and his........................237

295

angels (continued)

Dost thou suppose I cannot entreat My Father and He will even now furnish Me with more than twelve legions of.......................194

He (the Son of Man) will send forth His 193

in Heaven always behold the face of My Father. Their (the children's)... 27

in Heaven nor the Son but the Father only. But of that day or hour no one knows neither the........193

in the glory of His Father. For the Son of Man is to come with His......192

into Abraham's bosom. He (Lazarus) was borne away by the..193

of God ascending and descending upon the Son of Man. You shall see the...190

of God over one sinner who repents. There will be joy among the........... 35

of God. Everyone who acknowledges Me before men, him will the Son of Man also acknowledge before the..192

of God. Whoever disowns Me before men will be disowned before the...192

The reapers are the...........................191

The son of Man is to come with His..192

The Son of Man will send forth His..191

they will gather His elect. The......193

will go out and separate the wicked from among the just. The................191

with a trumpet and a great sound. And then He will send forth His....193

with Him. But when the Son of Man shall come in His majesty and the...193

angry

with his brother shall be liable to judgment. Everyone who is............249

anointed

Me. The Spirit of the Lord is upon Me because He has.........................179

anxious

for your life. Do not be..................166

ascend to

My Father. I...................................... 52

My God. I.. 52

your Father. I.................................. 52

your God. I...................................... 52

ascended into Heaven except Him Who has descended from Heaven. No one has..149

ascended to My Father. Do not touch Me for I have not yet...................... 52

ascending where He was before? What then if you should see the Son of Man..150

Ask and you shall receive that your joy may be full..................................105

Ask Him, your Father in Heaven........210

ask it shall be done for them by My Father in Heaven. Whatever they..217

authority. I have not spoken on My own 271

baptism

of John from Heaven or from men? Answer Me was the..........................221

to be baptized with. I have a..........119

with which I am to be baptized? Can you be baptized with the........121

baptized shall be saved. He who is....272

Baptizing them in the name of the Father and of the Son and of the Holy Spirit 53

Barachias, the blood of Zacharias, the son of..257

Beelzebub by whom do your children cast them out? If I cast out devils by..230

believe

also in Me. You believe in God,....173

because I said I saw thee (Nathanael) under a fig tree. Thou dost......................................157

because of the works themselves. Otherwise...173

because you are not of My sheep. You (Pharisees) do not....................168

But I have told you (Pharisees) that you have seen Me (the Son) and you do not..................................162

Do you (the Apostles) now............175

believe (continued)

his (Moses') writings how will you (Pharisees) believe My word. If you do not.....................................161

if I speak of Heavenly things? If I have spoken of earthly things and you do not believe how will you....157

I rejoice on your account that I was not there (in Bethany) that you may 170

is already judged. He who does not..158

I tell you (I am the Christ) and you (Pharisees) do not.....................168

it. If anyone say to you "behold here is the christ," do not.................263

Me. Because I speak the Truth you (Pharisees) do not............................166

Me. If I do not perform the works of My Father do not.........................168

Me. If you are not willing to..........168

My word? If you (Pharisees) do not believe his (Moses') writings, how will you...............................161

shall be condemned. He who does not 177

that I am HE (the MESSIAS). That you (Apostles) may.................172

that I am HE (the MESSIAS) you (Pharisees) will die in your sins. If you do not.....................................165

that I am in the Father and the Father in Me.................................... 45

that the Father is in Me and I in the Father.................................... 32

that Thou hast sent Me. That the world may.....................................175

that Thou hast sent Me. That they (the people) may.....................170

that when it (ascension) has come to pass. You (Apostles) may..........153

that you shall receive. Whatever you ask for in prayer........................ 39

the works that I do...........................168

thou shalt behold the glory of God? Have I not told thee (Martha) that if you.................................... 38

who receive glory from one another? How can you (Pharisees)..................161

believe in

all that the Prophets have spoken. O foolish ones and slow of heart to..176

God, believe also in Me.................. 44

Him (Son of Man) may not perish but may have Life Everlasting. Those who 158

Me. The Advocate (Holy Spirit) will convict the world of sin because they do not..........................174

Me that they may be one. I pray for those also who through their word are to..175

Me to sin . . . . Whoever causes one of these little ones who............165

My name they shall cast out devils; they shall speak in new tongues; they shall take up serpents; and if they drink any deadly thing it shall not hurt them; they shall lay hands upon the sick and they shall get well. And these signs shall attend those who.......................................177

the Gospel 195

the Light. While you have the Light...171

the Son of God? Dost thou..............166

the Son of Man Whom He (God) has sent. This is the work of God that you 25

the Son of Man may not perish. That those who...............................158

believed

Because thou (Thomas) hast seen Me thou hast 177

Blessed are they who have not seen (Me) and yet have..........................177

so be it done to thee (centurion). As thou hast.....................................158

that I came forth from God. The Father Himself loves you because you have loved Me and have.......... 48

that Thou didst send Me. They (Apostles) have...............................175

believes

and is baptized shall be saved. He who..177

Him (God) Who sent Me—does not come to judgment. He who hears My word and......................................161

believes (continued)

Him (God) Who sent Me, has Life Everlasting. He who..........................161

in Him (Son of Man) is not judged. He who...158

in Him (Son of Man) shall have Everlasting Life. That he who........163

believes in Me

as the Scripture says, "From within him there shall flow rivers of living waters," he who..............................165

believes not in Me but in Him Who sent Me. He who............................ 44

even if he die shall live. He who..170

has Life Everlasting. He who........163

may not remain in the darkness. That whoever......................................172

shall never die. Whoever lives and..170

shall never thirst. He who...............162

the works that I do he also shall do and greater than these he shall do .... He who.....................................174

believes in the Son shall have Life Everlasting. Whoever.......................278

believes shall be saved. He who........177

believing. Bring here thy (Thomas') finger and see My hand and be not unbelieving but.................................139

believing. Bring here thy hand and put it into My side and be not unbelieving but.................................139

believing you shall receive. All things whatever you ask for in prayer........171

Bethsaida. Woe to thee......................242

(Bethsaida) you. It will be more tolerable for Tyre and Sidon on the day of judgment than for.................252

betray Me. One of you will.................124

betray the Son of Man with a kiss? Judas, dost thou................................108

betrayed

into the hands of sinners. The hour is at hand when the Son of Man will be...127

Me to thee (Pilate) has the greater sin. Therefore he who.....................129

The Son of Man is to be..................117

to the Scribes and to the chief priests. The Son of Man will be....120

betrayed (continued)

Woe to the man by whom the Son of Man is..124

betrays Me is at hand. He who..........127

bind on earth shall be bound in Heaven. Whatever thou (Peter) shalt..216

blasphemy against the Son of Man shall be forgiven men. Every kind of...180

Blasphemy against the (Holy) Spirit will not be forgiven...........................180

Blessed are

the clean in heart for they shall see God... 17

the poor in spirit for theirs is the Kingdom of Heaven.........................208

they who have not seen (Me) and yet have believed..............................177

they who hear the word of God and keep it....................................... 33

they who suffer persecution for justice' sake for theirs is the Kingdom of Heaven......................208

you poor for yours is the Kingdom of God..196

Blessed is He Who comes in the name of the Lord............................. 35

blessed of My Father. Come................291

blind and blessed shalt thou be. When thou givest a feast invite the..........280

blind. Bring in to the great supper the..281

(blind men, two)...................................161

blood of the New Covenant. This is My...124

blood of the Son of Man you shall not have life in you. Unless you drink the 90

body but cannot kill the soul. Do not be afraid of those who kill the........161

body in hell. But rather be afraid of Him Who is able to destroy both soul and..242

body. Take and eat. This is My........124

born again he cannot see the Kingdom of God. Unless a man be................195

born again of water and the Holy Spirit he cannot enter the Kingdom of God. Unless a man be........178

born of the Spirit is spirit. That
which is 185

born of the Spirit, so is
everyone who is........................178

bound in Heaven. Whatever thou
(Peter) shalt bind on earth shall be 90

branches. I am the true Vine and you
(Apostles) are the....................102

Bread from Heaven. Moses did not
give you 89

Bread from Heaven. My Father gives
you the true.................... 89

Bread of God gives Life to the world.
For the 25

Bread of Life. I am the.............. 57

Bread shall live forever. He who eats
this 142

Bread that comes down from Heaven.
This is the........................ 58

Bread that has come down from
Heaven. I am the Living............. 58

Bread that has come down from
Heaven. This is the.................. 58

Bread that I will give is My flesh for
the Life of the world. The........... 58

Bridegroom shall be taken away from
them. The.............................116

brother for the sake of the Kingdom
of God who shall not receive in the
age to come Life Everlasting. There
is no one who has left.................201

brothers for My name's sake shall
receive a hundredfold and shall
possess Life Everlasting. And
everyone who has left....................285

burial. She (Mary Magdalene) has
anointed My body in preparation
for 121

burn. Gather up the weeds first and
bind them in bundles to.................254

burnt with fire. Just as weeds are......254

Bush. But that the dead rise even
Moses showed in the passage of the.145

business. But they made light of it
(invitation to the marriage feast)
and went off one to his...............287

Caesar the things that are Caesar's.
Render to 40

camel to pass through the eye of a
needle than for a rich man to enter
the Kingdom of God. It is easier
for a.....................................201

Capharnaum shalt thou be exalted to
Heaven? Thou shalt be thrust down
to hell.................................211

(Capharnaum) thee it would have
remained to this day. For if the
miracles had been worked in Sodom
that have been worked in...............211

cast forth outside. But you yourselves
(Pharisees)...............................246

Cast him (the unfaithful servant)
forth into the darkness outside
where there will be the weeping....270

cast into hell. Be afraid of Him Who
after He has killed has power to....242

cast into the fire as the branch.
Anyone who does not abide in Me
shall be................................248

cast out. Now will the prince of the
world be................................260

cast outside as the branch. Anyone
who does not abide in Me shall be..248

chief priests. The Son of Man must
be rejected by the.....................116

child he is the greatest in the Kingdom of Heaven. Whoever humbles
himself as this little.................216

child will not enter into it.
Whoever does not accept the Kingdom of God as a little...............169

children
be and do not hinder them from
coming to Me. Let the little..........218

come to Me of such is the Kingdom
of God. Let the little...................201

for My name's sake shall receive a
hundredfold and shall possess Life
Everlasting. And everyone who
has left 285

for the sake of the Kingdom of God
who shall not receive in the age to
come Life Everlasting. There is no
one who has left...........................201

of God. Peacemakers shall be
called 17

of the kingdom will be put forth
outside. But the......................251

children (continued)
of your Father in Heaven. Pray for those who persecute you so that you may be.......................208

them from coming to Me for of such is the Kingdom of Heaven. Let the little children be and do not hinder...................218

together as a hen gathers her young but thou (Jews) wouldst not. How often I would have gathered thy (Jerusalem's) 257

you will not enter the Kingdom of Heaven. Unless you turn and become like little............................216

Christ
and you (Pharisees) do not believe. I tell you (that I am the Christ)....168

do not believe it. If anyone say to you, "behold here is the christ,".......265

have to suffer these things before entering into His glory? Did not the 81

He his (David's) Son? How is (the Christ)...................................... 64

he." Many will say, "I am (the christ) 64

He. That you (Apostles) may believe that I am (the Christ)........172

He. Then you (Pharisees) will know that I am (the Christ)..........118

He? Whose Son is............................ 41

He you will die in your sins. If you do not believe that I am.................. 92

or "there he is" do not believe it. Then if anyone say "Behold here is the..263

should rise again from the dead on the third day. Thus it is written that the..113

should suffer. Thus it is written and thus the......................................131

What do you think of the............... 64

(Christ's) His name to all nations beginning from Jerusalem. That repentence and remission of sins should be preached in.....................131

christs will arise. For false.................265

(Church) it. And the gates of hell shall not prevail against (the)........244

Church. Upon this rock (Peter) I will build My.................................... 90

clean of heart for they shall see God. Blessed are the...............................273

clothe Me. I was naked and you did not 270

cloud. The Son of Man coming upon a 267

clouds of Heaven. They will see the Son of Man coming upon the..........263

cock will not crow before thou (Peter) dost deny Me thrice. The..100

Come and breakfast...............................113

Come, blessed of My Father, take possession of the Kingdom prepared for you from the foundation of the world 291

Come, follow Me. If thou wilt be perfect, go, sell what thou (a rich young ruler) hast and give to the poor and thou shalt have treasure in Heaven and.................................218

come in His majesty. But when the Son of Man shall.............................270

come. My time has not yet................118

Come to Me all you who labor and are burdened 186

come to Me and drink. If anyone thirst let him......................................165

come to Me of such is the Kingdom of God. Let the little children........169

come to Me that you may have Life Everlasting. Yet you (Pharisees) are not willing to..............................277

come with His angels. The Son of Man is to...192

come. You will seek Me and where I go you cannot..............................152

Commandment
is Life Everlasting. I know His (the Father's) 289

of God you (Pharisees) hold fast to the tradition of men. Letting go of the.. 24

that you (Apostles) love one another as I have loved you. This is My..102

The greatest and first........................ 41

The second...................................... 41

Commandments. I have kept My
Father's 46

(Commandments) them out and
teaches them he shall be called
great in the Kingdom of Heaven.
Whoever carries (the)....................208

condemn him. He who rejects My
word has One to................................271

condemn him on the last day. The
word that I have spoken will..........271

condemn the Son of Man to death.
They will..120

condemned by thy words. Thou wilt
be 253

condemned. He who does not believe
shall be 248

consummated. It is....................137

consummation of the world. I am
with you all days even unto the......114

converted and their (the unbelieving
Jews) sins may be forgiven them.
Lest perhaps at any time they
should be 197

convict the world of sin because they
do not believe in Me. The Holy
Spirit will 272

Corban (given to God). Any support
thou mightest have had is................ 24

cornerstone"? Did you never read in
the Scripture, "The stone which the
builders rejected has become the....202

Corozain. Woe to thee........................252

(Corozain) you. It will be more
tolerable for Tyre and Sidon on the
day of judgment than for................252

courage daughter thy faith has saved
thee. Take..160

courage I have overcome the world.
Take 175

courage thy sins are forgiven thee.
Take 160

Covenant. This is My blood of the
New 124

creation of the world. Thou hast
loved Me before the........................ 49

creation of the world. Which (My
glory) Thou hast given Me before
the 49

Creator made male and female. The.. 37

creature. Preach the Gospel to every..294

crippled and blessed shalt thou be.
When thou givest a feast invite
the 280

crippled. Bring in here (to the great
supper) the..281

cross and follow Me
cannot be My disciple. He who
does not carry his..............................120

If anyone wishes to follow Me, let
him take up his................................ 91

is not worthy of Me. He who does
not take up his..................................276

crucified. The Son of Man will be
delivered up to be............................122

cup pass away from Me. Father, if it
is possible, let this............................126

cup which I drink? Can you drink
of the..121

cures. Go and say to that fox
(Herod) I perform.......................... 63

Daniel the Prophet. Which (the
abomination of desolation) was
spoken of by......................................262

darkness. But this is the power of......239

darkness outside. But the children of
the kingdom will be put forth into
the 241

darkness outside where there will be
the weeping. Cast him (the unprofitable servant) forth into the....270

David call Him (the Christ) Lord?
How does 64

David did? Have you never read
what 21

David? How do the Scribes say that
the Christ is the son of....................182

David in the Spirit call Him (the
Christ his son), Lord? How then
does 96

(David's) his son? How is He (the
Christ) 64

day or hour (the Last Day) no one
knows neither the angels in Heaven
nor the Son but the Father only.
But of that 263

day he (the servant) does not expect.
The master will come on a..............258

Day. I will raise him (who believes in the Son) up on the Last..............278

Day of Judgment. That every idle word men speak they shall give account on the....................................253

Day. The word that I have spoken will condemn him on the Last........271

day when I shall drink it new in the Kingdom of God. I will drink no more of the fruit of the vine until that 204

dead

and gives them Life (Everlasting) even so the Son gives Life to whom He will. For as the Father raises the..140

bury their dead but do thou go and proclaim the Kingdom of God. Let the 198

He is not the God of the............... 40

neither marry nor take wives. Those who shall be accounted worthy of that world and of the resurrection from the........................144

on the third day. That the Christ should rise from the..........................131

rise. The 145

shall hear the voice of the Son of God and those who hear shall live. When the..................................276

Tell the vision to no one till the Son of Man has risen from the........133

death

If anyone keep My word he will never see.. 60

The Son of Man must be put to....116

They (the Gentiles) will put the Son of Man to..................................120

till they have seen the Kingdom of God. There are those standing here who will not taste....................198

to Life. He who believes Him (God) Who sent Me has passed from 276

deliver the Son of Man to the Gentiles. They (the Jews) will......120

den of thieves. You have made it (My House of prayer, the Temple) a.. 39

Depart from Me, accursed ones, into everlasting fire which was prepared for the devil and his angels...........237

Depart from Me all you workers of iniquity..246

depart. It is expedient for you (Apostles) that I..............................154

destroy both soul and body in hell. But rather be afraid of Him who is able to....................................186

destroy men's lives but to save them. For the Son of Man did not come to..142

destroy the soul and body in hell. Be afraid of God Who is able to..........186

Destroy this Temple and in three days I will raise it up......................132

destruction. For wide is the gate and broad is the way that leads to........241

devil

and his angels. Depart from Me accursed ones into the everlasting fire which was prepared for the......237

comes and takes away the word from their heart. But Satan (the)..231

has gone out of thy daughter. Because of this answer, go thy way the..234

Have I not chosen you the Twelve, yet one of you is a............................234

he is a liar. (The)............................235

he was a murderer from the beginning. (The) 235

I have not a..236

The enemy who sowed them (the weeds) is the..................................232

The father from whom you (Pharisees) are is the......................235

devils

by Beelzebub by whom do your children cast them out? If I cast out 230

by the finger of God then the Kingdom of God has come upon you. But if I cast out......................199

by the Spirit of God. I cast out....230

Go and say to that fox (Herod) I cast out..237

die
any more for they (those accounted
worthy) are equal to the angels.
Neither 144

He who believes in Me shall never..144

in your sins, if you do not believe
that I am HE (the MESSIAS).
You will...247

If anyone eat of it (Bread, My
Body), he will not............................141

shall live. He who believes in
Me even if he.....................................170

Whoever lives and believes in
Me shall never 170

died. Your (Pharisees') fathers ate
the manna in the desert and have..215

dies not and the fire is not
quenched." It is better for thee to
enter Life maimed than having two
hands go into hell into the
unquenchable fire "where their
worm 244

disciple. He who does not carry his
cross and follow Me cannot be My..120

disciple shall not lose his reward.
Whoever gives but a cup of cold
water to drink to a............................276

disciples of all nations. Go
therefore and make 184

dishonor Me. You (the
unbelieving Jews) 236

disowns Me before men I in turn
will disown him before My Father
in Heaven. Whoever........................211

disowns Me before men will be
disowned before the angels
of God. Whoever...............................192

do it for one of these least ones you
did not do it for Me." Then the
King will say to them (those on
His left hand), "as long as you
did not 270

doubt? O thou (Peter) of little faith
why didst thou...................................162

doubts arise in your (Apostles')
hearts? Why do..................................177

drachma that I have lost. Rejoice
with me for I have found the........282

drink. I was thirsty and you gave
Me no 270

earth has been given to Me. All
power in Heaven and on.................228

earth will pass away but My words
will not pass away. Heaven and....263

earthquakes but the end is not yet.
There will be 262

eat. For I was hungry and you did
not give Me to....................................270

elders. The Son of Man must be
rejected by the...................................116

elect
from the four winds. His (Son of
Man's) angels will gather the..........263

from the uttermost parts of the
earth. The Son of Man will
gather His...288

They (the angels) will gather
His (Son of Man's)............................145

Eli, Eli lema sabacthani (Jesus
on the cross cries out), My
God, My God, Why hast Thou
forsaken Me? 129

Elias has come already. But I
say to you that.................................. 92

Elias who was to come. If you
are willing to receive it he
(John the Baptist) is.........................211

end of the world. But the harvest
is the...254

end of the world. So it (as the
weeds are burnt with fire) will
be at the...254

enemy came and sowed weeds among
the wheat. But while men were
asleep, his (the sower's).................232

enemy (the devil). I have given you
(Apostles) power over all the
might of the 236

enemy who sowed them (the weeds)
is the devil. The...............................232

eunuchs who have made themselves
so for the sake of the Kingdom
of Heaven. There are.......................218

Everlasting Life (See also Life
Everlasting.)

Everlasting Life. I give them
(My sheep) 62

Everlasting Life. I know that His
(the Father's) commandment is...... 44

PAGE NO.

Everlasting Life. In order that to all
Thou (Father) hast given Him
(Son of Man) He may give...........293

Everlasting Life. The just will
go into................................271

everlasting punishment. These (those
who did not do it to the least
ones) will go into......................271

evil unto resurrection of judgment.
They who have done...................252

Exult, when men persecute you
because your reward is great in
Heaven 273

eye is an occasion of sin to thee,
pluck it out! . . . If thy..............244

face of My Father in Heaven. Their
(children's) angels always
behold the............................. 27

faith
and do not waiver it shall be
done. If you have......................171
Are you (disciples) still without....159
Do not be afraid; only have...........160
even like a mustard seed. If
you have..............................168
has saved thee. Arise go thy
way thy...............................169
has saved thee. Go in peace, thy....159
has saved thee. Receive thy
sight, thy.............................171
has saved thee. Take courage
daughter thy..........................160
in Israel. I have not found
such great............................158
Let it be done to you according
to your...............................161
Let it be done to thee as thou
wilt. O woman, great is thy...........163
may not fail. I have prayed for
thee (Peter) that thy..................173
on the earth? When the Son of
Man comes will He find................169
O you of little.......................167
Why didst thou doubt? O thou
of little 162
why do you argue among
yourselves that you have no
bread? You of little..................163

PAGE NO.

faith (continued)
you will do what I have done to
the fig tree. If you have..............171

faithful steward? Who is the..........167

false christs will arise. For..........263

famines but the end is not yet.
There will be.........................262

farm. But they (those invited to the
marriage feast) made light of it
and went off one to his................287

farm. I have bought a (man
invited to a great supper but
excused himself) 281

father, for My name's sake shall
receive a hundredfold and shall
possess Life Everlasting. Everyone
who has left 285

Father
also. He who hates Me hates My.... 46
and He will even now furnish Me
with more than twelve legions of
angels? Dost thou (Peter) suppose
that I cannot entreat My.............. 50
and of the Son and of the Holy
Spirit. Baptizing them (all
nations) in the name of the.......... 53
and the Father in Me? Do you
believe that I am in the.............. 45
and your Father. I ascend to My.... 52
anything in My name He will give
it to you. If you ask the............. 47
are one. I and the................... 32
bears witness to Me. The............. 29
Believe that I am in the............. 32
But it (sitting at Jesus' right or
left) belongs to those for whom it
has been prepared by My.............. 38
but through Me. No one comes
to the............................... 45
didst send Me. They (Apostles)
have believed that Thou..............175
doing. The Son can do nothing of
Himself but only what He sees the.. 22
dwelling in Me. It is He Who
does the works, the.................. 45
except Him (the Son) Who is
from God, He has seen the Father.
Not that anyone has seen the......... 25
except the Son. No one knows the.. 21

Father (continued)

forgive them for they do not know what they are doing. (Jesus on the cross.)....................129

gives to Me shall come to Me. All that the........................ 25

glorify Me with Thyself.................... 48

glorify Thy name............................ 44

God Himself has set His seal upon the Son of Man. The.............. 25

has appointed to Me. I appoint to you (the twelve) a kingdom even as My.. 43

has are Mine. All things that the.. 47

has bidden Me. I speak the things that the................................. 44

has commanded Me. I do as the.... 46

has commanded Me what I should declare. The........................... 44

has given Me to accomplish. The works the.................................... 22

has not planted will be rooted up. Every plant that My Heavenly.. 24

has sent Me. The........................... 25

has sent Me. I also send you as the 53

has taught Me. I preach only what the 29

He has given to the Son. Neither does the Father judge any man but all judgment......................251

He has granted Him (the Son) power to render judgment. The....252

He who loves Me will be loved by My... 45

He who sees Me sees also the........ 45

He Who sent me. Even if I do judge, My judgment is true because I am not alone but with Me is the..256

He Who sent Me. It is I Who bear witness to Myself and the........256

He will bear witness concerning Me. But when the Advocate has come Whom I will send from the Father the Spirit of Truth Who Proceeds from the............................182

Him Who sent Me does not come to judgment. He who hears My word and believes the......................276

Father (continued)

Him Who sent Me has Life Everlasting. He who hears My word and believes the......................276

Him Who sent Me. He who believes in Me believes not in Me but in the....................................172

Him Who sent Me. He who receives Me receives the.................276

Him Who sent Me. He who sees Me sees the..271

Himself loves you because you have believed that I came forth from God. The................................. 48

Himself loves you because you have loved Me. The........................ 48

I am going to the............................ 45

I ascend to My................................ 52

I ascend to your................................ 52

I do always the things that are pleasing to Him, the........................ 29

I go to the.. 47

I give Thee thanks that Thou hearest Me 38

I have come in the name of My.... 23

I have not yet ascended to My (to Mary Magdalene)...................... 52

I send forth upon you (Apostles) the promise of My........................... 53

I will that where I am they (the Apostles) also whom Thou hast given Me may be with Me.............. 49

If it is possible let this cup pass away from Me (Agony in the Garden of Gethsemani), My...........126

if this cup cannot pass away unless I drink it Thy will be done. (Agony in the Garden of Gethsemani) My...............................126

If you had known Me you would also have known the........................ 45

If you knew Me you (Pharisees) would know My.............................. 29

in Heaven. For their (children's) angels always behold the face of My 27

in Heaven has revealed this (Who I AM) to thee (Peter). My........... 26

Father (continued)

in Heaven may also forgive your
offenses. Forgive whatever you
have against anyone that your........ 39

in Me and I in Thee. That all
may be one even as Thou............... 49

in Me. Believe that I am in
the Father and the........................... 45

in My name He may give you.
That whatever you ask the............. 46

into Thy hands I commend My
spirit. (Jesus' last words on
the Cross.)..130

is greater than I. The...................... 46

is in Me and I in the Father.
Believe that the............................... 32

is merciful. Your............................. 20

is the Vine-dresser. My................... 46

is with Me. I am not alone
because the.. 48

judge any man but all judgment
He has given to the Son.
Neither does the............................... 22

keep in Thy name those whom
(Apostles) Thou hast given
Me. Holy.. 49

knows that you need these things
(what to eat and drink). Your...... 35

loves me. The.................................... 61

loves the Son. The........................... 22

Many good works have I shown
you (the Jews) from My................... 32

My judgment is true because I
am not alone but with Me is
He (God) Who Sent Me the.......... 29

No one can come to Me unless he
is enabled to do so by My.............. 26

nor Me. They (Pharisees) have
known neither the............................. 47

Not anyone except Him Who (the
Son) is from God He has seen the.. 25

ONE is your...................................... 41

only. But of that Day (Judgment)
and hour no one knows but the...... 42

Philip! He who sees Me sees
also the 45

Rejoice that I am going to the...... 46

raises the dead. The........................ 22

Father (continued)

shall enter the Kingdom of
Heaven. He who does the will
of My 274

take possession of the Kingdom
prepared for you from the
foundation of the world. Come
Blessed of My.................................... 42

That all men may honor the
Son as they honor the...................... 22

that I should lose nothing. This
is the will of the............................... 25

that speaks through you. It is
the Spirit of your (Apostles').......... 20

The Advocate Whom I will send
you from the..................................... 47

The hour has come!........................... 48

The Son of Man is to come in
the glory of His................................ 26

the Spirit of Truth Who proceeds
from the Father He will bear
witness concerning Me. But when
the Advocate has come Whom
I will send from the...........................182

these (Apostles) have known that
Thou hast sent Me. Just................. 49

these bear witness concerning Me.
The works that I do in the
name of My....................................... 32

Thou hast sent me. That the
world may believe that (the)........175

to give you (Apostles) the
Kingdom. It has pleased your........ 35

Who glorifies Me. It is My............ 30

Who sent Me bears witness to Me.
It is I who bear witness to
Myself and He (the)........................256

Who sent Me. He who receives
Me receives the.................................276

will give the Good Spirit to those
who ask Him. Your Heavenly........ 32

will honor him. If anyone
serves Me My.................................... 43

will send in My name He will
teach you all things. But the
Advocate the Holy Spirit
Whom My 46

Worship the 16

Father (continued)
you would surely love Me. If God
were your (unbelieving Jews')........ 30

Father's business? Did you not
know that I must be about My...... 13

Father's commandments. I have
kept My 46

(Father's) commandment is
Everlasting Life. His (the)............ 44

Father's House. There are many
mansions in My................................159

fearful? Why are you.........................159

feast in the Kingdom of God.
They (the elect) will......................143

Feed (to Peter) My lambs................ 82

Feed (to Peter) My sheep................ 82

fig tree. If you have faith you will
do what I have done to the............171

finger of God then the Kingdom of
God has come upon you. But if
I cast out devils by the...................199

fire
Angels will cast them (the
wicked) into the furnace of............243

Angels will separate the wicked
from among the just, and cast
them into the furnace of.................243

as the branch. Anyone who does
not abide in Me shall be cast
into the..248

Cast them (who work iniquity)
into the furnace of............................254

Depart from Me into the
everlasting 247

Every tree that does not bear
good fruit is cut down and
thrown into the 241

is not quenched." Than having
two hands go into hell into the
unquenchable fire "where their
worm dies not and the.....................244

Just as weeds are burnt with..........254

which was prepared for the devil
and his angels. Depart from Me
accursed ones into the everlasting..247

fish of every kind. The Kingdom
of Heaven is like a net cast into
the sea that gathered in.................214

flesh of the Son of Man. You shall
not have Life (Everlasting)
in you unless you eat the................ 90

Fold and One Shepherd. There
shall be One..................................... 61

Follow Me (to Peter)........................113

follow Me cannot be My disciple.
He who does not carry his
cross and...120

foot is an occasion of sin to thee,
cut it off! If thy.............................244

forgive
men their offenses your Heavenly
Father will also forgive you your
offenses. For if you........................209

seventy times seven........................245

sins. The Son of Man has
power on earth to............................160

them for they know not what
they are doing. Father, (Jesus
on the Cross)...................................129

whatever you have against anyone
that your Father in Heaven may
also forgive you your offenses......... 39

forgive your brothers from your
hearts. So also your Heavenly
Father will do to you if you do not..217

forgiven
her (Mary Magdalene) because
she has loved much. Her sins
many as they are shall be............. 159

him. Whoever speaks against the
Holy Spirit it will not be................180

men. Every kind of sin and
blasphemy against the Son of
Man shall be....................................180

thee. Take courage thy sins are......160

them (the (unbelieving Jews).
Lest they perhaps at any time
should be converted and their
sins may be......................................197

forgiveness of sins. This is My blood
of the New Covenant which
is being shed for many unto the....124

forsaken Me? My God, My God,
Why hast Thou (Jesus on the
Cross) 129

foundation of the world. Come
blessed of My Father take
possession of the Kingdom
prepared for you from the............. 43

fox (Herod), "Behold, I cast out
devils. . . ." Go and say to that......237

fulfilled
All things concerning Me must be..131
in Me. That this which is
written must yet be............................125
in your hearing. Today this
Scripture has been.............................179
My time is not yet...........................118
that are written in the Law of
Moses and the Prophets and the
Psalms concerning Me. That
all things must be............................131
That the Scripture may be..............172
that thus it must take place?
How then are the Scriptures to be..127

furnace of fire. The angels will
go out and separate the wicked
from among the just and will
cast them into the...........................243

gain the whole world but suffer
the loss of his own soul? For
what does it profit a man if he......186

Galilee
after I have risen. I will go
before you into....................................135
there they will see Me. Take
word to My brethren (Apostles)
that they are to set out for..............138

gate
Strive to enter by the narrow..........280
that leads to destruction. For
wide is the..241
that leads to Life (Everlasting).
How narrow the..................................274

gathers fruit unto Life Everlasting.
He who reaps receives a wage and..275

generation! O unbelieving....................164

Gentiles
Do not go in the direction of the....210
for My sake. You will be brought
before governors and kings for a
witness to them and to the..............180
He (the Son of Man) will be
delivered to the................................ 95
Jerusalem will be trodden down
by the 267
lord it over them. But not so you
(Apostles). The kings of the..........292

Gentiles (continued)
multiply words. In praying the...... 18
seek. For after all these things
(what to eat and what to
put on) the..196

glorified
But for the glory of God that
through it (Lazarus' resurrection
from the dead) the Son of God
may be 38
in Him (the Son of Man). God is.. 44
in the Son. That the Father
may be...100
The hour has come for the Son
of Man to be....................................122
Thee (Father) on earth. I have....105

glorifies
Me. It is My Father Who.............. 30

glorify
Me because He will receive of
what is Mine and declare it to
you (Apostles). The Advocate will..104
Me. The Holy Spirit will...............183
Me with Thyself. And now do
Thou, Father,....................................105
Myself My glory is nothing. If I.... 30
Thee. That Thy Son may...............105
Thy name. Father............................ 44
Thy Son. Father...............................105

glory
Did not the Christ have to
suffer these things before
entering into His...............................138
of God? Have I not told thee
(Martha) that if you believe
thou shalt behold the........................170
of God that through it (Lazarus'
resurrection from the dead) the
Son of God may be glorified.
But for the.. 38
of His Father. The Son of Man
is to come in the.............................. 26
that I had with Thee (Father)
before the world existed. With the..105
that Thou hast given me. I have
given to them (Apostles) the..........106
The Son of Man will sit on the
Throne of His.................................... 97

glory (continued)
  When the Son of Man shall
  come in His.................................270
  When the Son of Man shall sit
  on the Throne of His...................... 94
  which Thou hast given Me. I
  will that they (Apostles) may
  be with Me (to) behold My..........226

glutton." The Son of Man came
  eating and drinking and you
  (Pharisees) say, "Behold a
  man who is a.................................... 87

gnashing of teeth
  Many will come from the east and
  from the west and will feast with
  Abraham and Isaac and Jacob in
  the Kingdom of Heaven but the
  children of the kingdom will be
  put forth into the darkness
  outside; there will be the
  weeping and the..............................241
  The Son of Man will gather out
  of His Kingdom all scandals and
  those who work iniquity and cast
  them into the furnace of fire
  where there will be the
  weeping and the................................254
  when you (the unbelieving Jews)
  shall see Abraham and Isaac and
  Jacob and all the Prophets in the
  Kingdom of God, but you yourselves cast forth outside. There
  will be the weeping and the...........199

Go into the whole world and preach
  the Gospel to every creature............294

goats. He (the Son of Man) will
  separate them (all the nations)
  one from another as a shepherd
  separates the sheep from the..........145

goats on the left. He (the Son
  of Man) will set the.......................270

God
  All things are possible with............ 38
  and Him Whom Thou hast sent
  JESUS CHRIST. Now this is
  Everlasting Life that they may
  know Thee the only true.................. 48
  and keep it. Blessed are they
  who hear the word of...................... 33
  and mammon. You cannot serve.... 19
  and your God. I ascend to My...... 52

God (continued)
  Angels of... 14
  avenge His elect? And will not...... 36
  Blessed are the clean of heart
  for they shall see............................... 17
  Blessed are the peacemakers for
  they shall be called the children of.. 17
  did not send His Son into the
  world to judge the world. For........ 15
  feeds the ravens................................. 34
  gives Life to the world. For
  the Bread of....................................... 25
  has joined together let no man
  put asunder. What........................... 37
  has killed has power to cast
  into hell. Be afraid of Him
  Who after He..................................... 34
  Have faith in..................................... 39
  hears the words of God. He
  who is of... 30
  Himself has set His seal. For
  upon the Son of Man....................... 25
  "I am the God of Abraham"?
  Have you not read what was
  spoken to you (the Jews) by.......... 40
  I ascend to My God and to your.... 52
  I came forth from............................. 30
  I cast out devils by the Spirit of....230
  If thou (Martha) believe thou
  shalt behold the glory of.................. 38
  in Heaven. They (man) will
  be as angels of.................................. 40
  in Spirit and in Truth.
  Worship Him...................................... 16
  in you. But I know that you
  (Pharisees) have not the love of.... 23
  is Everlasting Life. . . . To
  know the only true............................ 48
  is glorified in Him (Son of Man).... 44
  is not the God of the dead but
  of the living. He............................... 40
  is SPIRIT 16
  It is written in the Prophets
  "And they shall be taught of.......... 25
  Kingdom of (see Kingdom of God)
  Not by bread alone does man
  live but by every word that
  comes forth from the mouth of........ 14

God (continued)
of Abraham. I am the.................... 40
of Isaac. I am the............................ 40
of Jacob. I am the........................... 40
of the living. He is not the
God of the dead but........................145
One there is Who is good
and He is.. 37
over one sinner who repents.
There will be joy among the
angels of.. 35
so clothes the grass of the field
how much more you. But if.......... 19
That through it (Lazarus'
resurrection from the dead) the
Son of God may be glorified
but for the glory of.......................... 38
That which is exalted in the sight
of men is an abomination before.... 36
that you believe in Him (Son of
Man) Whom He has sent. This
is the work of................................... 25
The Father Himself loves you
(Apostles) because you have
loved Me and have believed that
I came forth from............................ 48
The hour is coming for everyone
who kills you (Apostles) to think
that he is offering worship to.......... 47
the things that are God's.
Render to 40
then the Kingdom of God has
come upon you. But if I cast out
devils by the finger of..................... 33
Things that are impossible with
men are possible with......................201
Thou (Peter) dost not mind
the things of.................................... 26
Thou shalt love the Lord thy.......... 41
Thou shalt not tempt the Lord thy 14
were to be made manifest in him.
Neither has this man (blind)
sinned not his parents but that
the works of.................................... 31
were your Father you (Pharisees)
would surely love Me. If................ 30
Who is able to destroy both soul
and body in hell. But rather
be afraid of Him..............................161

God (continued)
Who after He has killed has
power to cast into hell. Be
afraid of Him....................................166
Who sent Me . . . does not come
to judgment. He who hears My
word and believes in Him................251
Who sent me. He who sees
Me sees Him..................................... 44
Whoever disowns Me before men
will be disowned before the
angels of...192
Why hast Thou forsaken Me?
My God, My...................................... 52
with thy whole soul. Thou shalt
love the Lord thy..............................187
You believe in................................... 44
You (Pharisees) err because you
know neither the Scriptures
nor the power of.............................. 40
You (Pharisees) say He (My
Father) is your.................................. 30
You shall see the Son of Man
sitting at the right hand of
the Power (of)................................... 51
good seed in his field. The
Kingdom of Heaven is like a
man who sowed................................213
good seed is the sons of the
Kingdom (of Heaven). The..........213
Good Shepherd. I am the.................... 61
Good Shepherd lays down His life
for His sheep. The........................... 61
Gospel. Believe in the...........................195
Gospel is preached. This that she
(Mary Magdalene) has done shall
be told wherever in the
whole world this...............................121
Gospel of the Kingdom (of
Heaven) shall be preached in the
whole world for a witness to all
nations. . . . This..............................203
Gospel to every creature.
Preach the...294
grain of mustard seed. The
Kingdom of God is like a................197
grain of mustard seed. The
Kingdom of Heaven is like a..........213

grain of wheat falls into the ground
and dies it remains alone.
Unless the...........................122

grass how much more you. If
God so clothes the........................... 35

greatest Commandment. Thou shalt
love the Lord thy God . . . is the.. 41

greatest in the Kingdom of
Heaven. Whoever humbles himself
as this little child he is the............. 27

hand is an occasion of sin to thee,
cut it off! If thy...................244

hand. The Kingdom of God is at......195

hands go into hell into the
unquenchable fire "where their
worm dies not and the fire is not
quenched." It is better for thee
to enter into Life maimed
than having two.................................255

Harlots are entering the Kingdom
of God before you (Pharisees)........202

harvest is the end of the world. The..254

hated by all for My name's sake.
You will be.............................265

hated Me before you. If the world
hates you know that it has..............103

hated Me without cause." "They
have 103

hates his life in this world keeps
it unto Life Everlasting. He who....288

hates Me hates My Father also.
He who..............................174

He (the Christ) his (David's)
son? How is........................ 64

he (the christ)." Many will come
in My name, saying. "I am.............. 64

He (the Christ). That you
(Apostles) may believe that I am..172

He (the Christ). When you
(Pharisees) have lifted up the
Son of Man then you will
know that I am.................................118

He (the Christ)? Whose Son is........ 64

He (the Christ) you will die
in your sins. If you do not
believe that I am.............................247

He (the Father) has given to the
Son. Neither does the Father
judge any man but all judgment....251

He (the Father) has granted Him
(the Son of Man) power to
render judgment....................252

He (the Father) Who sent Me
bears witness to Me. It is I Who
bear witness to Myself and...........256

He (the Father) Who sent Me.
Even if I do judge My judgment
is true because I am not alone
but with Me is.................................256

He (God) has killed has power to
cast into hell. Be afraid of
Him Who after................................ 34

He (the Son of Man) will send
forth His angels...............................193

heart be afraid. Do not let your......174

heart be. For where your treasure
is there also will your.....................167

heart be troubled. Let not your........173

heart for they shall see God.
Blessed are the clean of....................273

heart. Thou shalt love the Lord
thy God with thy whole................. 41

heart to believe in all that the
Prophets have spoken. O foolish
ones and slow of...............................138

hearts? Why do doubts arise in your..177

Heaven (See also Kingdom of
Heaven).

Heaven
and destroyed them all (in
Sodom). It rained fire and
brimstone from.................................219

and earth pass away. Not one
jot or tittle shall be lost till.............208

and earth that Thou didst hide
these things from the wise and
prudent. I praise Thee
Father Lord of................................211

and earth will pass away but
My words will not pass away.........222

and gives Life to the world.
The Bread of God is that
which comes down from.................215

and on earth has been given to
Me. All power in.............................114

But of that day and hour
(Judgment) no one knows not
even the angels of...........................263

Heaven (continued)

But the publican would not so
much as lift his eyes to.....................219

But wait here in the City until
you (Apostles) are clothed
with power from On High..............228

Do not despise one of these
little ones for I tell you their
angels always behold the face
of My Father in................................192

Everyone who acknowledges Me
before men I also will acknowledge
him before My Father in..................211

except Him (the Son of Man)
Who has descended from Heaven.
No one has ascended into.................149

for it is the Throne of God.
Do not swear at all neither by........208

give good things to those who
ask Him. If you (Pharisees) know
how to give good gifts to your
children, how much more will
your Father in.................................210

Go sell what thou (rich ruler)
hast and give to the poor and
thou shalt have treasure in..............218

has revealed this (Who I Am)
to thee (Peter). My Father in...... 58

He who does the will of My
Father in Heaven shall enter
the Kingdom of................................210

I am the Living Bread that has
come down from.............................215

If two of you shall agree on
earth about anything at all for
which they ask it shall be done
for them by My Father in.............217

I have come down from...................215

is at hand. Repent for the
Kingdom of.....................................207

is My brother. Whoever does
the will of My Father in.................212

is my mother. Whoever does
the will of My Father in.................212

is My sister. Whoever does
the will of My Father in.................212

I was watching Satan fall as
lightning from 216

Make for yourselves a treasure
unfailing in.....................................217

Heaven (continued)

Moses did not give you
Bread from...162

My Father gives you the true
Bread from...215

nor the Son but the Father only.
But of that day and hour
(Judgment) no one knows not
even the angels of.............................222

opened and the angels of God
ascending and descending upon
the Son of Man. You shall see........190

or from men? Was the baptism
of John from......................................221

Our Father Who art in.....................209

over one sinner who repents.
There will be joy in...........................219

Pray for those who persecute
you so that you may be children
of your Father in...............................208

Rejoice and exult because
your reward is great in.....................273

Rejoice that your names are
written in 279

shall enter the Kingdom of
Heaven. He who does the will
of My Father in................................210

Stars will fall from...........................263

swears by the Throne of God.
He who swears by...........................221

Take heed not to do your good
before men in order to be seen
by them otherwise you shall
have no reward with your
Father in...209

The sign of the Son of Man
will appear in....................................263

The tribes of the earth will
see the Son of Man coming
upon the clouds of............................263

This is the Bread that has
come down from..............................215

Thy will be done on earth
as it is in...209

was shut up for three years and
six months. When...........................207

Whatever you (Peter) bind on
earth shall be bound also in............217

Whatever you (Peter) loose on
earth shall be loosed in...................217

Heaven (continued)
where neither rust nor moth
consumes nor thieves break in and
steal. Lay up for yourselves
treasure in..209

Whoever disowns Me before men
I in turn will disown him
before My Father in.......................211

will be shaken after the
tribulation. The powers of..............263

with great power and majesty.
They will see the Son of Man
coming upon the clouds of..............222

Heavenly Father
has not planted will be rooted
up. Every plant that My................215

is perfect. You therefore are to
be perfect even as your................... 17

will also forgive you your
offenses. If you forgive men
their offenses your...........................209

will do to you. If you do not
forgive your brothers from your
hearts so also My..............................217

Heavenly things? How will you
(Nicodemus) believe if I speak of..206

Heavens to the other. The angels
will gather His elect from one
end of the..222

hell
Be afraid of Him Who after
He has killed has power to
cast into 242

But rather be afraid of Him Who
is able to destroy both soul
and body in.......................................242

But the rich man also died
and was buried in...........................246

Capharnaum shalt thou be
exalted to Heaven? Thou
shalt be thrust down to....................242

into the unquenchable fire "where
their worm dies not and the fire
is not quenched." It is better
for thee to enter into Life
Everlasting maimed than having
two hands go into............................255

Serpents! Brood of vipers! How
are you (Scribes and Pharisees)
to escape the judgment of................247

hell (continued)
shall not prevail against it (the
Church). The gates of....................244

than yourselves. You (Pharisees)
make him (a convert) twofold
more a son of...................................247

hell-fire
It is better for thee to enter into
the Kingdom of God with one
eye than having two eyes
to be cast into...................................244

hen gathers her young under her
wings but thou (Jerusalem)
wouldst not! How often I would
have gathered thy children as a......257

hide these things (truths of the
Kingdom) from the wise and
prudent. I praise Thee Father
that Thou didst................................211

Him (God the Father) Who
after He has killed has power to
cast into hell. Be afraid of..............166

is able to destroy both soul
and body in hell. But rather
be afraid of......................................242

sent Me . . . does not come to
judgment. He who hears My
Word and believes in......................251

sent Me has Life Everlasting.
He who hears My word and
believes in.......................................251

sent Me. He who believes in Me
believes not in Me but in...............172

sent Me. He who receives me
receives 276

sent Me. He who sees Me sees......271

His (Christ's) name to all nations.
That repentance and remission
of sins should be preached in......... 83

Holy Father keep in Thy name
those whom Thou hast given Me....155

Holy Ghost (see Holy Spirit)

Holy Spirit
Baptizing them (all nations) in
the name of the Father and of
the Son and of the............................184

he cannot enter the Kingdom
of God. Unless a man be born
again of water and the....................178

He will teach you all things. The....182

Holy Spirit (continued)
  it will not be forgiven him either
  in this world or in the world to
  come. Whoever speaks against the..181
  Receive (to the Apostles) the........183
  "The Lord said to my Lord: Sit
  down at My right hand till I
  make Thy enemies Thy footstool."
  For David himself says by the........182
  to those who ask him. If you
  know how to give good gifts
  to your children, how much
  more will your Heavenly
  Father give the...................................181
  Whom the Father will send in
  My name He will teach you all
  things and bring to your mind
  whatever I have said to you.
  The Advocate the.............................182
  will convict the world of
  judgment. The...................................183
  will convict the world of
  justice. The 183
  will convict the world of sin
  because they do not believe
  in Me. The..183
  will glorify Me. The........................183

honor My Father. You (Pharisees)
  dishonor Me; but I.............................236

hour
  But this is your (the evil ones)......239
  (end of the world) no one knows
  neither the angels in Heaven nor
  the Son but the Father only. But
  of that Day or...................................263
  has come! The...................................126
  has come for the Son of Man
  to be glorified. The...........................122
  has not yet come. My......................115
  he (the servant) does not know.
  The master will come in an............258
  is at hand when the Son of Man
  will be betrayed into the hands
  of sinners. The...................................127
  that you do not expect. The
  Son of Man will come at an............258
  What shall I say? "Father save
  Me from this.....................................123

house
  for My name's sake shall receive
  a hundredfold and shall possess
  Life Everlasting. Everyone
  who has left......................................285
  for the sake of the Kingdom of
  God who shall not receive in the
  age to come Life Everlasting.
  There is no one who has left..........201
  of God? Have you never read
  what David did when he
  entered the...................................... 21
  of prayer" but you (sellers) have
  made it a den of thieves. "My
  House shall be called a.................. 39
  There are many mansions in
  My Father's 204

householder. Every Scribe
  instructed in the Kingdom of
  Heaven is like a...............................214
householder who went out . . . to
  hire laborers for his vineyard.
  The Kingdom of Heaven is like a.. 219
humble of heart. Learn from Me
  I am meek and................................. 55
hungry and you
  did not give Me to eat. I was......270
  gave Me to eat. I was....................270

hypocrites!
  Does not each one of you on
  the Sabbath loose his ox or
  ass from the manger?......................236
  Show Me the coin of tribute.......... 40
  The master will cut him (the
  unfaithful servant) asunder
  and make him share the lot of
  the unfaithful...................................264
  Woe to you! Pharisees and Scribes..247

I abide in His (My Father's) love.... 46
I also have loved you. As the
  Father has loved Me....................... 46
I also have sent them (Apostles).
  Even as Thou hast sent Me
  into the world................................... 49
I also send you as the Father
  has sent Me....................................... 81
I also will acknowledge him before
  My Father in Heaven. Everyone
  who acknowledges Me be men....... 21

PAGE NO.

I am a King............................... 78

I am a liar. If I say that I do not
know Him (My Father)................... 30

I AM. Before Abraham came to be.... 60

I am? But who do you say that........ 58

I am coming again..............................100

I am coming to you.............................101

I am coming to Thee (Father).......... 49

I am distressed until it (passion,
death and resurrection) is
accomplished 119

I am from Him (God). I know
Him because.. 28

I am from above (Heaven)................ 59

I am going thou (Peter) canst not
follow Me now, but thou shalt
follow later. Where...........................152

I am going to the Father. If you
loved Me you would indeed
rejoice that 46

I am going to Him Who sent Me
(the Father)...................................... 47

I am HE (the MESSIAS). When
you have lifted up the Son of
Man then you will know that..........118

I am HE (the MESSIAS) you
will die in your sin. If you
do not believe that............................165

"I am he." Many will come in
My name saying,................................ 64

I am in the Father and the
Father in Me? Do you
(Philip) believe that......................... 45

I am in the Father. Believe (to
the Pharisees) that the Father
is in Me and....................................... 32

I am in the midst of them. Where
two or three are gathered together.. 27

I am in your midst as He Who
serves 292

I am keeping the Passover with My
disciples. At thy house....................123

I am meek and humble of heart.
Learn from Me................................... 55

I am no longer in the world.............. 75

I am not alone because the
Father is with Me............................. 48

I am not alone but with Me is He
Who sent Me. Even if I do
judge My judgment is true because 29

PAGE NO.

I am not of this world........................ 59

I am sending you forth like sheep
in the midst of wolves......................180

I am the Bread of Life........................ 57

(I am the CHRIST) and you
(Pharisees) do not believe.
I tell you...168

(I am the CHRIST, the Son of God).
Thou (Caiphas) hast said it............127

"I am the christ." For many will
come in My name saying.................262

I am the Good Shepherd...................... 61

I am the Life...................................... 63

I am the Light of the world............. 59

I am the Living Bread that has
come down from Heaven................. 58

I am the Resurrection..........................134

I am the Son of God............................. 32

I am the true Vine..............................102

I am the Truth.................................... 69

I am the Way...................................... 69

I am there also shall My
servant be. And where....................220

I am there you also may be. Where..204

I am they (the Apostles) also whom
Thou (Father) hast given Me may
be with Me. I will that where........226

I am to be baptized? Can you
(Apostles James and John) be
baptized with the baptism with
which 121

I am to end My course the third day.
(in message to Herod)....................120

I am? Who do you (Apostles) say
that...58

I am with you all days even to the
consummation of the world............114

I am with you (Pharisees). Yet a
little while 28

I am you (Pharisees) cannot come.
Where.. 28

I and the Father are One.................... 32

I appoint to you (the Twelve
Apostles) a kingdom.......................224

I ascend to My Father........................156

I ascend to My God............................156

I ascend to your Father......................156

I ascend to your God..........................156

I bear witness concerning it. The
world hates Me because...................118

I bear witness to Myself...................... 59

I be lifted up from the earth I will
draw all things to Myself. If............123

I be with you? O unbelieving and
perverse generation! How long
shall..164

I came forth from God (said to the
Pharisees). 30

I came forth from God. The Father
Himself loves you (Apostles)
because you have loved Me and
have believed that............................174

I came forth from Thee (Father).
They (the Apostles) have known
of a truth that....................................106

I came to this hour. This is why (to
die for sins of mankind)...................123

I cannot entreat My Father and He
will even now furnish Me with more
than twelve legions of angels? Dost
thou suppose that...............................127

I cast out devils by Beelzebub, by
whom do your (the Jews) children
cast them out? If...............................230

I cast out devils by the finger of God
then the Kingdom of God has come
upon you. But if.............................. 33

I cast out devils by the Spirit of
God. If...180

I cast out devils. Go and say to that
fox (Herod).......................................237

I command you (Apostles) that you
love one another...............................102

I command thee go out of him (a
boy) . . . . Thou deaf and dumb
spirit 235

I command you. You are My friends
if you (Apostles) do the things......102

I commend My spirit. Father into
Thy hands (Jesus on the Cross)......130

I depart (and go to the Father). It
is expedient for you (Apostles)
that 154

I do always the things that are pleasing
to Him (My Father)...................... 29

I do as the Father has commanded
Me. 125

I do bear witness concerning Me. The
works that... 62

I do. Believe the works that................168

I do he also shall do and greater than
these He shall do. . . . He who
believes in Me the works that..........174

I do in the name of My Father these
bear witness concerning Me. The
works that... 32

I do judge My judgment is true because
I am not alone but with Me is He
(My Father) Who sent Me. Even if..256

I. Do not be afraid it is....................176

I do not go the Advocate (the Holy
Spirit) will not come to you. If......154

"I do not know where you are from."
(On Judgment Day the Master will
say), ...259

I do not perform the works of My
Father do not believe Me. If..........168

I do nothing of Myself...........................93

I do not seek My own glory................ 30

I drink? Can you (Apostles James and
John) drink of the cup...................121

I drink it Thy will be done Father. If
this cup cannot pass away unless
(Jesus' agony in the Garden of
Gethsemani)......................................126

I give Thee thanks that Thou hearest
Me. Father,...................................... 38

I give them (My sheep) Everlasting
Life..282

I give to you My peace........................101

I glorify Myself My glory is nothing.
If.. 60

"I go away and I am coming to you."
You (Apostles) have heard Me say..153

I go I will send Him (the Advocate)
to you. If..154

I go to prepare a place for you
(Apostles)...153

I go to the Father and again a little
while and you shall see Me............135

I go to the Father and you will see
Me no longer....................................154

I go yonder and pray. Sit down here
while (in the Garden of
Gethsemani)......................................126

I go you (the Apostles) cannot come (now). You will seek Me and where..152

I go and the way you (the Apostles) know. Where 153

I guarded those (the Apostles) whom Thou hast given Me......106

I had not come and spoken to them (the Jews) they would have no sin. If 103

I had with Thee before the world existed. With the glory that......105

I have a baptism to be baptized with...119

I have accomplished the work that Thou hast given Me to do. 48

I have appointed you (Apostles) to go and bear fruit......102

I have been sent to proclaim the Kingdom of God......196

I have called you (Apostles) friends...102

I have chosen you (Apostles) out of the world......103

I have come down from Heaven......215

I have come in the name of My Father. 23

I have come into the world to bear witness to the Truth......109

I have come to save the world......271

I have commanded you (Apostles). Teaching them (all nations) to observe all that......114

I have done to the fig tree. If you (Apostles) have faith you will do what 171

I have food to eat of which you do not know. 275

I have gathered thy (Jerusalem's) children together as a hen gathers her young but thou wouldst not. How often would......257

I have given to them (Apostles) the glory that Thou hast given to Me... 49

I have given them (Apostles) Thy word. 49

I have given to them (Apostles) the words that Thou hast given Me...... 48

I have given you (Apostles) power over all the might of the enemy (the devil)......236

I have glorified Thee on earth...... 48

I have greatly desired to eat this Passover with you (Apostles) before I suffer...... 99

I have kept My Father's commandments. 46

I have known Thee, Just Father...... 49

I have loved you. This is My Commandment that you (Apostles) love one another as......102

I have made known to them (Apostles) Thy name...... 49

I have made known to you (Apostles) all things that I have heard from My Father 46

I have manifested Thy name to the men (the Apostles) whom Thou hast given Me out of the world......105

I have not a devil......236

I have not come to judge the world but to save the world......271

I have not found such great faith (the centurion's) in Israel......158

I have not spoken on My own authority......271

I have not yet ascended to My Father. Do not touch Me (to Mary Magdalene) 138

I have other sheep that are not of this Fold...... 61

I have overcome the world. Take courage......105

I have prayed for thee (Peter) that thy faith may not fail......173

I have risen. I will go before you (Apostles) into Galilee after......135

I have said to you. The Advocate (the Holy Spirit) will bring to your (Apostles') mind whatever......182

I have sent you to reap that on which you have not labored......275

I have spoken of earthly things to you (Nicodemus) and you do not believe; how will you believe if I speak of Heavenly things? If...... 85

I have spoken will condemn him (he who does not believe) on the Last Day. The word that......271

I have told you (Apostles) all things (regarding Himself) beforehand. Behold......265

PAGE NO.

I have the power to take My life up
again..134

I have the power to lay it (My life)
down...119

I heard from Him (the Father) these
I speak in the world. The things
that 29

I honor My Father and you
(Pharisees) dishonor Me................ 30

I in him. He who drinks My blood
abides in Me and.............................. 90

I in him. He who eats My flesh
abides in Me and.............................. 90

I in Thee that all may be One. Even
as Thou Father in Me and.............. 49

I in them (Apostles) and Thou in Me..106

I in turn will disown him before My
Father in Heaven. Whoever disowns
Me before men...................................211

I in you. Abide in Me and...................102

I judge no one.......................................256

I keep His (My Father's) word......... 30

I kept them (the Apostles) in Thy
name...106

I know Him (God the Father) because
I am from Him................................... 28

I know Mine and Mine know Me........ 61

I know them (My sheep).................... 62

I know that His (the Father's) Commandment is Everlasting Life.......... 44

I lay it down of Myself. No one takes
it (My life) from Me.........................119

I lay down My life for My sheep......119

I lay down My life that I may take it
up again 134

I lay it (My life) down of Myself......119

I leave the world and go to the Father.
Again 155

I live and you shall live. For..............293

I love the Father. That the world
may know that.................................. 46

I might not be delivered to the Jews.
My followers would have fought
that 128

I must bring them also. Other sheep I
have that are not of this Fold (and) 61

I must do the works of Him (My
Father) Who sent Me....................... 31

PAGE NO.

I must go My way................................. 63

I must proclaim the Kingdom of God..196

I Myself. See (to Thomas) My hands
and feet that it is..............................177

I Myself will give you utterance and
wisdom 267

"I never knew you." I will declare to
them (workers of iniquity)..............250

I not chosen you the Twelve yet one
of you is a devil? Have....................234

I not told thee (Martha) that if you
believe thou shalt behold the glory
of God? Have....................................170

I perform cures. Go and say to that
fox (Herod)....................................... 62

I praise Thee Father Lord of Heaven
and earth that Thou didst hide
these things (about the Kingdom)
from the wise and prudent and didst
reveal them to little ones................211

I pray for them (the Apostles)..........226

I pray for those also who through their
(the Apostles') word are to believe
in Me 175

I pray (Jesus in Gethsemani). Sit
down here while................................126

I pray that Thou keep them (the
(Apostles) from evil.........................106

I preach only what the Father has
taught Me... 29

I put up with you! O unbelieving and
perverse generation how long shall..164

I sanctify Myself for them (the
Apostles) 106

I sat daily in the Temple and you did
not lay hands on Me.........................127

I say, "Save Me from this hour?"
What shall 123

I say to you be afraid of Him (God)
Who after He has killed has power
to cast into hell................................242

I send forth upon you (the Apostles)
the promise (sending of the Holy
Spirit) of My Father.........................184

I send also you. As the Father has
sent Me...138

I shall drink it new with you . . . in
the Kingdom of God. I will drink
no more of the fruit of the vine
until 204

318

PAGE NO.

I should declare. The Father has commanded Me what...................... 44

I should lose nothing of what He has given Me but that I should raise it up on the Last Day. This is the will of Him (the Father) Who sent Me that...................141

I speak as the Father has bidden Me.. 44

I speak in the world the things that I heard from Him (the Father)........ 29

I speak the Truth. You (Pharisees) do not believe Me because...............166

I suffer. I have greatly desired to eat this Passover with you before..........123

I take it (My life) up again................ 61

I tell you (Pharisees) (that I am the CHRIST) and you do not believe.. 62

I. The Father (God) is greater than.. 46

I thirst. (Jesus on the Cross cried,)..137

I was a stranger and you did not take Me in 270

I was a stranger and you took Me in..291

I was born to bear witness to the Truth..205

I was daily with you (the Jews) in the Temple teaching and you did not lay hands on Me.........................108

I was hungry and you did not give Me to eat..270

I was hungry and you gave Me to eat..291

I was in prison and you did not visit Me..270

I was in prison and you came to Me..291

I was naked and you covered Me......291

I was naked and you did not clothe Me..270

I was sick and you did not visit Me....270

I was sick and you visited Me............291

I was thirsty and you gave Me no drink 270

I was thirsty and you gave Me to drink 291

I Who bear witness to Myself and He (My Father) Who sent Me bears witness to Me. It is............................ 29

I Who judge him. If anyone hears My words and does not keep them it is not.. 44

PAGE NO.

I will ask the Father and He will send you another Advocate the Spirit of Truth Whom the world cannot receive because it neither sees nor knows Him....................................182

I will build MY CHURCH. Thou art Peter and upon this rock................. 58

I will but as Thou willest. Yet not as (Jesus in the Garden prays)............126

I will come to you (Apostles)............153

I will declare to them (workers of iniquity), "I never knew you.".......241

I will do it. If you ask Me anything in My name....................................100

I will do. Whatever you ask in My name that....................................100

I will draw all things to Myself. If I be lifted up (crucified) from the earth 123

I will eat of it (the Passover) no more until it has been fulfilled in the Kingdom of God...............................152

I will give him (who drinks of this Water) shall become in him a Fountain of Water springing up unto Life Everlasting. The Water..275

I will give is My flesh for the Life of the world. The Bread that............. 58

I will give My Flesh for the Life of the world 58

I will give thee (Peter) the keys of the Kingdom of Heaven................. 90

I will give you rest................................186

I will go before you (Apostles) into Galilee. After I have risen..............135

I will manifest Myself to him (who loves Me)......................................101

I will no longer speak much with you (Apostles) 125

I will not cast out. All that the Father gives Me...141

I will not cast out him who comes to Me 141

I will not leave you (Apostles) orphans...101

I will raise it (My body) up in three days..132

I will raise him up on the Last Day. No one can come to Me unless the Father Who sent Me draw him and..141

I will raise him up on the Last Day. Whoever believes in the Son shall have Everlasting Life and................141

I will see you (Apostles) again and your heart shall rejoice....................154

I will send you (Apostles) from the Father will bear witness concerning Me. The Advocate (Holy Spirit) Whom...103

I will take you (Apostles) to Myself..100

I will that where I am they (the Apostles) also whom Thou hast given Me may be with Me..............107

I will but as Thou willest. (Jesus prays in the Garden) Yet not as.................126

I work. My Father works even until now and 55

I would have gathered thy (Jerusalem's) children as a hen gathers her young but thou wouldst not...... 63

iniquity and cast them into the furnace of fire. The Son of Man will gather out of His Kingdom all scandals and those who work...............................254

iniquity. The angels will gather out of His Kingdom all those who work....198

iniquity. Depart from Me you workers of..246

insurrections . . . the end (of the world) will not come at once. When you hear of wars and............266

Isaac. I am the God of........................ 40

Isaac in the Kingdom of God. You (unbelieving Jews) shall see............199

Isaac in the Kingdom of Heaven. Many will come and feast with......210

Isaias. In them (the unbelieving Jews) is being fulfilled the prophecy of 212

Israel. Go rather to the lost sheep of..210

Israel. I have not found such great faith (centurion's) in......................158

Israel. You (the Apostles) who have followed Me shall sit on twelve thrones judging the twelve tribes of..256

It is consummated. (Words of Jesus on the Cross.)................................137

Jacob. I am the God of...................... 40

Jacob in the Kingdom of God. You (Pharisees) shall see........................199

Jacob in the Kingdom of Heaven. Many will come and feast with......210

Jerusalem and the Son of Man will be betrayed. . . . We are going up to..120

Jerusalem being surrounded by an army then know that her desolation is at hand. When you see................267

Jerusalem. For it cannot be that a Prophet perish outside....................120

Jerusalem for it is the city of the great king. I say to you not to swear at all by...208

Jerusalem. Repentance and remission of sins should be preached in His (CHRIST'S) name to all nations beginning from.................................131

Jerusalem! Thou who killest the Prophets 257

Jerusalem will be trodden down by the Gentiles 267

JESUS CHRIST. Now this is Everlasting Life that they may know Thee the only true God and Him (Thy ONLY-BEGOTTEN SON) Whom Thou hast sent,.................... 48

Jews. If My Kingdom were of this world My followers would have fought that I might not be delivered to the................................128

Jews. Salvation is from the................179

John the Baptist
Among those born of women there has not risen a greater than............211

came neither eating bread nor drinking wine...................................... 87

came there were the Law (Moses') and the Prophets; since then the Kingdom of God is being preached. Until 200

came to you in the way of justice and you (Pharisees) did not believe him. For.............................202

from Heaven or from men? Answer Me was the baptism of....................221

is Elias who was to come. If you are willing to receive it he.............211

There is not a greater Prophet than..196

The witness that I have is greater than that of... 56

John the Baptist (continued)
until now the Kingdom of Heaven
has been enduring violent assaults.
From the days of............................211

what you have heard and seen.
Report to.. 55

Jonas (the Prophet) is here. A
greater than.................................. 93

Jonas. No sign shall be given it (this
generation) but the sign of..............133

Jonas was a sign to the Ninevites so
the Son of Man will be to this
generation. As 253

joy among the angels over one sinner
who repents. There will be............192

Judas dost thou betray the Son of
Man with a kiss?.............................108

Judea flee to the mountains. Then
(Jerusalem's desolation) let those
who are in..262

judge him. If anyone hears My words
and does not keep them it is not
I who 271

judge My judgment is true because I
am not alone but with Me is He
Who sent Me. Even if I do............256

judge that you may not be judged.
Do not..250

judge the world. For God did not
send His Son into the world to........250

judge the world. I have not come to..271

judge you shall be judged. For with
what judgment you............................250

judged. He who believes in Him (Son
of Man) is not..................................250

judged. He who does not believe is
already 250

judged. The prince of this world
(Satan) has already been................238

judging the twelve tribes of Israel.
(The twelve Apostles) shall sit on
twelve thrones 256

judgment
because He is the Son of Man. He
(God) has granted Him power to
render...252

Everyone who is angry with his
brother shall be liable to................249

judgment (continued)
He has given to the Son. For
neither does the Father judge any
man but all.....................................251

He who hears My word and believes
Him Who sent Me . . . does not
come to.. 56

is just. My.......................................252

of hell. Serpents! Brood of vipers!
(Scribes and Pharisees) How are
you to escape the............................247

of the world. Now will the prince
of the world (the devil) be cast
out. Now is the................................260

than for that town (which does not
receive disciples). It will be more
tolerable for the land of Sodom and
Gomorrah in the Day of..................242

than for you (Corozain and Bethsaida). It will be more tolerable for
Tyre and Sidon on the Day of........252

That of every idle word men speak
they shall account on the Day of....253

The Holy Spirit will convict the
world of..183

the Light has come into the world.
Now this is the................................250

They who have done evil shall come
forth unto resurrection of................252

with this generation. The men of
Nineve (who repented) will rise
up in the..254

with this generation. The queen of
the South (who came to Solomon)
will rise up in the............................254

you judge you shall be judged. For
with what...250

just and will cast them into the furnace
of fire. The angels will separate the
wicked from among the....................255

just. Invite the poor (to the feast who
cannot repay and) thou shalt be
repaid at the resurrection of the....280

just man's reward. He who receives a
just man will receive a....................276

just. My judgment is..........................252

just will go into Life Everlasting.
The...271

just will shine forth like the sun in
the Kingdom of their Father. The..142

justice and all these things (to eat and to wear) shall be given you besides. Seek first the Kingdom of God and His...196

justice and you did not believe him. For John (the Baptist) came to you (the Jews) in the way of................202

justice because I go to the Father and you (Apostles) will see Me no more. The Advocate (the Holy Spirit) will convict the world of................183

justice exceeds that of the Scribes and Pharisees you (Apostles) shall not enter the Kingdom of Heaven. Unless your 208

justice. The Holy Spirit will convict the world of......................................183

justice' sake for theirs is the Kingdom of Heaven. Blessed are they who suffer persecution for........................273

keep My words. He who does not love Me does not..............................101

keys of the Kingdom of Heaven. I will give thee (Peter) the................ 58

kill Me because My word takes no hold among you. You seek to..........119

kill Me. You (Scribes and Pharisees) are seeking to.....................................119

kill the Son of Man. They will..........117

kill the soul. Do not be afraid of those who kill the body but cannot..186

killed has power to cast into hell. Be afraid of Him Who after He has....242

killest the Prophets! Jerusalem thou who...257

KING. I am a (to Pontius Pilate)....128

king who desired to settle accounts with his servants. The Kingdom of Heaven is likened to a......................217

king who had a marriage feast for his son. The Kingdom of Heaven is like a...287

king who made a marriage feast for his son. The Kingdom of Heaven is like a..220

KING (the Son of Man) will say to them (on His left hand) "As long as you did not do it for one of these least ones you did not do it for Me." Then the..........................248

KING (the Son of Man) will say to those on His left hand, "Depart from Me accursed ones . . .". Then He (the)..247

KING (the Son of Man) will say to those on his Right hand, "Come, blessed of My Father take possession of the Kingdom prepared for you from the foundation of the world." The 291

Kingdom (See also Kingdom of God, and Kingdom of Heaven.)

Kingdom come, Thy (from the Lord's Prayer)... 18

kingdom even as My Father has appointed to Me. I appoint to you (the Twelve) a....................................224

Kingdom is not of this world. My......227

Kingdom of My Father. I shall drink it (the fruit of the vine) new with you (Apostles) in the......................124

Kingdom prepared for you from the foundation of the world. Come blessed of My Father take possession of the 291

Kingdom will rise against kingdom (one of the signs of the Last Day)..262

Kingdom of God
and His justice and all these things (to eat and to wear) shall be given you besides. Seek first the.............196

as a little child will not enter it. Whoever does not accept the..........169

as though a man should cast seed into the earth. . . . Thus is the........197

before you (Pharisees). Harlots are entering the 202

Blessed are you poor for yours is the..196

but you yourselves (unbelieving Jews) cast forth outside. There will be the weeping and the gnashing of teeth when you shall see Abraham and Isaac and Jacob and all the Prophets in the..................................246

comes unawares. The......................200

for this is why I have been sent. To the other towns I must proclaim the..196

Kingdom of God (continued)
has come upon you. But if I cast out devils by the finger of God then the 199
is at hand. The................................195
is being preached. Until John (the Baptist) came there were the Law and the Prophets; since then the....200
is greater than he (John the Baptist). Yet the least in the..........196
is like a grain of mustard seed. The..197
is like leaven which a woman took and buried in three measures of flour. The 197
is near. Even so when you see these things (signs of the last days) coming to pass know that the..........203
is within you. The.............................200
It is easier for a camel to pass through the eye of a needle than for a rich man to enter the.............201
I will drink no more of the fruit of the vine until that day when I shall drink it new in the...........................204
I will eat of it (the Passover) no more until it has been fulfilled in the...152
Let the dead bury their dead but do thou go and proclaim the..........198
Let the little children come to Me and do not hinder them for of such is the..201
No one having put his hand to the plow and looking back is fit for the..198
There are those standing here who will not taste death till they have seen the..198
They will come from the east, west, north, and south and will feast in the..199
To you (Apostles) it is given to know the majesty of the..................197
Unless a man be born again of water and the Holy Spirit he cannot enter into the..178
who shall not receive much more in the present time and in the age to come Life Everlasting. There is no one who has left house, or parents, or brothers, or wife, or children, or lands, for the sake of the..................201

Kingdom of God (continued)
will be taken away from you (the unbelieving Jews) and will be given to a people yielding its fruits. The..203
with one eye than having two eyes to be cast into hell-fire. It is better for thee to enter the........................279
With what difficulty will they who have riches enter the........................201
You shall see Abraham in the..........199
You shall see Isaac in the................199
You shall see Jacob in the................199
You shall see the Prophets in the....199
Kingdom of Heaven
against men. You (Scribes and Pharisees) shut the......................221
all scandals and those who work iniquity. They (the angels) will gather out of His (the Son of Man's)...213
be like the ten virgins who took their lamps. Then the......................289
Blessed are the poor in spirit for theirs is the......................................208
Blessed are they who suffer persecution for justice' sake for theirs is the......................................273
but does not understand it the wicked one (the devil) comes and snatches away what has been sown in his heart. When anyone hears the word of the...............................212
but to them (non-believing Jews) it is not given. To you (Apostles) it is given to know the mysteries of the...212
Come blessed of My Father take possession of the...........................291
has been enduring violent assaults. From the days of John the Baptist until now the...................................211
He who does the will of My Father in Heaven shall enter the...............210
is at hand." Preach the message, "the...210
is greater than he (John the Baptist). Yet the least in the..........211
is like a grain of mustard seed. The..213
is like a householder who brings forth from his storeroom things new and old...214

Kingdom of Heaven (continued)
  is like a householder who went out
  to hire laborers for his vineyard.
  The 219

  is like a king who made a marriage
  feast for his son. The........................220

  is like a man going abroad who
  called his servants. The...................223

  is like a man who sowed good seed
  in his field. The................................213

  is like a net cast into the sea that
  gathered in fish of every kind. The..214

  is like a treasure hidden in a field.
  The 214

  is like a merchant in search of fine
  pearls. The 214

  is like leaven which a woman took
  and buried in three measures of
  flour. The 213

  is likened to a king who desired to
  settle accounts with his servants....217

  It has pleased your (the Apostles')
  Father to give you the...................... 35

  It is easier for a camel to pass
  through the eye of a needle than
  for a rich man to enter the..............218

  I will give thee (Peter) the keys
  of the... 58

  Let the little children be and do
  not hinder them from coming to
  Me for of such is the........................218

  Many will come and feast with
  Abraham and Isaac and Jacob
  in the..210

  Not everyone who says, "Lord,
  Lord," shall enter the......................274

  of their Father. Then the just will
  shine forth like the sun in the........214

  prepared for you from the foundation
  of the world. Come blessed of My
  Father take possession of the..........224

  shall be preached in the whole
  world for a witness to all nations.
  . . . This Gospel of the...................203

  The good seed is the sons of the....213

  Then the just will shine forth like
  the sun in the...................................214

  There are eunuchs who have made
  themselves so for the sake of the....218

Kingdom of Heaven (continued)
  Unless your justice exceeds that of
  the Scribes and Pharisees you
  (Apostles) shall not enter the........208

  Unless you turn and become like
  little children you will not enter
  the...216

  With difficulty will a rich man
  enter the..218

  will be like ten virgins. The............268

  Whoever carries them (the
  Commandments) out and teaches
  them he shall be called great in
  the...208

  Whoever humbles himself as this
  little child he is the greatest in the..216

laborers for his vineyard. The
  Kingdom of Heaven is like a
  householder who went out to hire..219

lambs. Feed (to Peter) My................113

lands for My name's sake shall receive
  a hundredfold and shall possess Life
  Everlasting. Everyone who has left..285

Last Day (Day of Judgment). I should
  lose nothing of what He (the
  Father) has given Me but that I
  should raise it up on the.................141

Law (of Moses)
  and the Prophets and the Psalms
  concerning Me. That all things must
  be fulfilled that are written in the..131

  and the Prophets. On these two
  Commandments depend the whole..41

  has prophesied until John (the
  Baptist). The.....................................211

  it is written that the witness of two
  persons is true. In your.................. 59

  may be fulfilled: "They have hated
  Me without cause." That the word
  written in their...................................103

  till Heaven and earth pass away.
  Not one jot or tittle shall be lost
  from the 208

  to fail. It is easier for Heaven and
  earth to pass away than for one
  tittle of the.......................................200

lawyers because you load men with
  oppressive burdens. Woe to you......33

lay down his life for his friends.
Greater love than this no man
has that he...125

lay down My life for My sheep. I......119

lays down His life for His sheep. The
Good Shepherd 119

Lazarus come forth!..............................144

Lazarus. There was a certain poor man
. . . covered with sores named........246

least of My brethren you did it for
Me. As long as you did it for one
of these...292

least in the Kingdom of God is greater
than he (John the Baptist). Yet the ..196

leaven. The Kingdom of God is like..197

leaven. The Kingdom of Heaven is
like 213

leaven of the Pharisees. Beware of
the...164

life. But we were bound to make
merry for this thy brother (prodigal
son) was dead and has come to......284

Life Everlasting
Do not labor for the food that
perishes but for that which
endures unto.....................................278

Everyone who has left house, or
brothers, or sisters, or father, or
mother, or wife, or children, or lands,
for My name's sake shall receive a
hundredfold and shall possess........285

He who believes Him Who sent
Me has 276

He who believes in Me has..............278

He who believes in My word and
in Him Who sent Me has passed
from death to.....................................276

He who drinks My blood has..........278

He who eats My flesh has................278

He who hates his life in this world
keeps it unto.....................................288

He who hears My word and believes
Him Who sent Me has.....................276

He who reaps receives a wage and
gathers fruit unto..............................275

Himself. He (the Father) has given
to the Son also to have....................277

How narrow the gate and close the
way that leads to..............................274

Life Everlasting (continued)
I give them...282

I know that His (the Father's)
Commandment is...............................289

in you. Unless you drink His (the
Son of Man's) blood you shall not
have 278

in you. Unless you eat the flesh of
the Son of Man you shall not have..278

It is the (Holy) Spirit that gives....181

lame than having two feet to be
cast into hell. It is better to enter 279

maimed than having two hands to
go into hell. It is better to enter
into 279

The just will go into........................292

The Son of Man will give you........278

The Water that I will give him shall
become in him a Fountain of Water
springing up unto.............................275

They who have done good shall
come forth unto.................................277

Those who believe in Him (the Son
of Man) may not perish but may
have 274

Thou hast given Him (the Son of
Man) power that He may give......293

To know JESUS CHRIST is..........293

To know the only true God is........293

to whom He will. The Son of Man
also gives..276

Whoever believes in the Son shall
have 293

with one eye than having two eyes
to be cast into hell-fire. If thy eye
is an occasion of sin to thee, pluck
it out! It is better for thee to enter
into 279

You (Scribes) search the Scriptures
because in them you think that you
have 23

life for My sake will find it. He who
loses his...276

Life. He who follows Me will have
the Light of...................................... 59

Life. I am the Resurrection and the..134

Life of the world. The Bread that I
will give is My flesh for the.............90

Life. The words that I have spoken to you are Spirit and............................278

Life to the world. The Bread of God is that which comes down from Heaven and gives............................ 89

lifted up. As Moses lifted up the serpent so must the Son of Man be..116

lifted up from the earth I will draw all things to Myself. If I be..............123

lifted up his heel against Me. He (Judas) who eats bread with Me has 172

lifted up the Son of Man then you (Pharisees) will know that I am HE (the Messias). When you have 59

Light believe in the Light. While you have the 171

Light has come into the world. Now this is the judgment: the..................250

Light is among you (Jews). Yet a little while the....................................123

Light of the world. I am the.............. 61

Light that you may become sons of Light. Believe in the........................171

lilies grow. Consider how the............167

little ones but a cup of cold water to drink because he is a disciple he shall not lose his reward. Whoever gives to these....................................276

little ones for I tell you their angels behold the face of My Father in Heaven. Do not despise one of these 192

little ones. I praise Thee Father that Thou didst reveal these things (of the Kingdom) to..............................211

little ones who believe in Me to sin, it were better . . . if he were thrown into the sea. Whoever causes one of these..165

live. Do this (love the Lord thy God with thy whole heart, . . . whole soul, . . . whole strength, . . . whole mind) and thou shalt......................280

live. For I live and you (Apostles) shall................................293

live forever. He who eats this Bread shall 142

live. He who believes in Me shall......144

lives and believes in Me shall never die. Whoever............................170

Living Bread that has come down from Heaven. I am the.................... 58

living. He is not the God of the dead but of the................................ 40

Living Water. He (Son of Man) would have given thee (a Samaritan woman) 275

Living Water." He who believes in Me, as the Scripture says, "from him shall flow rivers of....................165

loose on earth shall be loosed in Heaven. Whatever you (Peter)......217

loosed in Heaven. Whatever thou (Peter) shalt loose on earth shall be..217

Lord. Blessed is He Who comes in the name of the................................ 35

Lord is to come. You do not know at what hour your............................ 96

"Lord, Lord," shall enter the Kingdom of Heaven. Not everyone who says to Me,........................210

Lord of Heaven and earth. I praise Thee Father............................ 21

Lord of the harvest. Pray therefore the................................... 20

Lord thy God with thy whole heart and with thy whole soul and with thy whole mind. Thou shalt love the....................................187

Lord's Prayer. The............................209

loses his life for My sake will find it. He who................................276

loss of his own soul. For what does it profit a man if he gain the whole world but suffer the..............186

lost sheep of Israel. Go rather to the 210

lost. The Son of Man came to seek and to save what was...................... 95

Lot. So it came to pass (rained fire and brimstone) in the days of........ 94

love. Abide in My..............................102

love. I abide in His (My Father's).... 46

love. If you keep My commandments you will abide in My........................102

love Me does not keep My word.
He who does not...............................101

love Me he will keep My words.
If anyone 101

love Me? Simon son of John
(Peter) dost thou...............................113

love Me, We (the Father and I)
will come to him. If anyone............101

love Me, We will make Our abode
with him. If anyone........................101

love one another as I have loved
you. This is My commandment
that you..102

love than this no one has than
that one lay down his life for
his friends. Greater......................125

love the Father. I...............................101

Love the Lord with thy whole soul.... 41

love thy neighbor as thyself.
Thou shalt 41

love with which Thou hast loved
Me may be in them (Apostles).
That the 107

loved by My Father. He who
loves Me will be................................101

loved Me and have believed that
I came forth from God. The
Father Himself loves you
because you have..............................174

loved Me before the creation of
the world. Thou hast......................107

loved Me I also have loved you
(Apostles). As the Father has........102

loved Me may be in them. In
order that the love with which
Thou hast 107

loved Me. The Father Himself
loves you because you have............105

loved much. Her (Mary Magdalene's) sins many as they are shall
be forgiven her because she has....159

loved them (Apostles) as Thou hast
loved Me. That the world may
know that Thou hast........................106

loved you (Apostles). As the Father
has loved Me I also have................102

loves Me. He who has My commandments and keeps them he it is who..101

loves Me will be loved by My Father.
He who 101

loves you because you have
believed that I came forth from
God. The Father Himself...............105

loves you because you have loved
Me. The Father Himself..................105

majesty of the Kingdom of God.
To you it is given to know the......197

majesty. The Son of Man shall
come in His.......................................270

mammon. You cannot serve God and.. 19

Man, Son of (See Son of Man)

manna in the desert and have died.
Your fathers ate the........................215

mansions. In My Father's House
there are many.................................204

marriage feast for his son. The
Kingdom of Heaven is like a
king who had a.................................220

marry nor take wives. Those of
the resurrection neither...................193

(Mary Magdalene) has loved much.
Her sins many as they are shall
be forgiven her because she...........159

Master. One is your........................... 41

Me accursed ones into the everlasting
fire which was prepared for the
devil and his angels. Depart from..247

Me. A little while and the world
no longer sees...................................153

Me. All power in Heaven and on
earth has been given to...................114

Me. All that the Father gives to
Me shall come to.............................. 89

Me. All things (which I spoke to
you, Apostles) must be fulfilled
that are written in the Law of
Moses and the Prophets and the
Psalms concerning 131

Me all you who labor and are
burdened and I will give you
rest. Come to.................................... 55

Me all you workers of iniquity.
Depart from 259

Me alone. He (the Father) has
not left 29

Me alone. The hour has already
come for you to leave......................126

Me and drink. If anyone thirst
let him come to.................................165

Me and have believed that I came forth from God. The Father Himself loves you because you have loved 48

Me and I am in the Father. Believe that the Father is in 32

Me and I in him. He who drinks My blood abides in 90

Me and I in him. He who eats My flesh abides in 90

Me and I in Thee. That all may be one even as Thou Father in 106

Me and I in you. Abide in 102

Me and does not accept My words has One to condemn him. He who rejects 271

Me and as I said to the Jews, "Where I go you cannot come" (now). You (Apostles) will seek....152

Me and if My words abide in you ask whatever you will and it shall be done to you. If you abide in....102

Me and will not find Me and where I am you cannot come. You (Jews) will seek.................................. 28

Me and yet have believed. Blessed are they who have not seen............177

Me and you do not believe. I have told you (I am the Christ) that you (the Jews) have seen.................162

Me anything in My name I will do it. If you ask...............................100

Me. As against a robber you have come out to seize.............................127

Me. As long as you did it for one of these the least of My brethren you did it for....................292

Me. As long as you did not do it for one of these least ones you did not do it for........................248

Me as the Scripture says, "from him there shall flow rivers of Living Water." He who believes in..165

Me bears witness to Me. It is I who bear witness to Myself and He Who sent.............................256

Me because He has annointed Me. The Spirit of the Lord is upon........179

Me because He will receive of what is Mine and declare it to you. The Advocate will glorify......183

Me because I bear witness concerning it. The world hates............................118

Me because I go to the Father. Again a little while and you shall see......154

Me because I speak the Truth. You (Pharisees) do not believe.............166

Me because My word takes no hold among you (Pharisees). You seek to kill 119

Me before men him will the Son of Man acknowledge before the angels of God. Everyone who acknowledges 192

Me before men I also will acknowledge him before My Father in Heaven. Everyone who acknowledges...........................211

Me before men I in turn will disown before My Father in Heaven. Whoever disowns.............211

Me before men will be disowned before the angels of God. Whoever disowns...............................192

Me before the creation of the world. Thou hast loved....................107

Me before you. If the world hates you know that it has hated.............103

Me. Believe in.....................................100

Me. Believe that the Father is in...... 32

Me believes not in Me but in Him Who sent Me. He who believes in..172

Me but I lay it down of Myself. No one takes it (My life) from............119

Me, believe the works. If you are not willing to believe.........................168

Me but I should raise it up on the Last Day. This is the will of My Father that I should lose nothing of what He has given......................141

Me. But when the Advocate has come Whom I will send from the Father the Spirit of Truth Who proceeds from the Father He will bear witness concerning............182

Me by My Father. All things have been delivered to............................. 55

Me cannot be My disciple. He who does not carry his cross and follow..120

Me. Come to......... 55

Me . . . does not come to judgment. He who hears My word and believes Him Who sent............251

Me does not keep my words. He who does not love........101

Me even if he die shall live. He who believes in............170

Me. Even if I do judge My judgment is true because I am not alone but with Me is He Who sent.........256

Me. Father, if it is possible let this cup pass away from (Jesus prays in the Garden)............126

Me. Follow..........91

Me. Follow (to Peter)........113

Me for I have not yet ascended to My Father. Do not (to Mary Magdalene) touch.........156

Me for I live and you shall live. But you see.........293

Me for of such is the Kingdom of Heaven. Let the little children be and do not hinder them from coming to............218

Me from this hour." What shall I say? "Father, save............123

Me. Get thee behind Me satan. Thou (Peter) art a scandal to........234

Me has Life Everlasting. He who believes in............278

Me has Life Everlasting. He who believes Him (God) Who sent......276

Me has One Who condemns him. He who rejects............271

Me has passed from death to Life. He who hears My word and believes Him Who sent............140

Me hates My Father also. He who hates 46

Me he also shall live because of Me. He who eats............ 90

Me he has nothing. The prince of the world (Satan) is coming and in............101

Me he shall be cast outside as the branch . . . into the fire and shall burn. If anyone does not abide in..248

Me. He who does not take up his cross and follow Me is not worthy of 276

Me. He who has My commandments and keeps them loves............101

Me. He who is not with Me is against 180

Me. He who receives Me receives Him Who sent............276

Me. He who receives you receives....276

Me he will keep My word. If anyone love............101

Me henceforth until you say, "Blessed is He Who comes in the name of the Lord." You (the unbelieving Jews) shall not see......257

Me. Holy Father keep in Thy name those whom (Apostles) Thou hast given............106

Me I also have loved you (Apostles). As the Father has loved.........102

Me I also send you. As the Father has sent............111

Me I am meek and humble of heart. Learn from......... 55

Me. I am not alone because the Father is with............126

Me. I do as the Father has commanded 125

Me. I go to Him (God the Father) Who sent......... 28

Me. I guarded those whom (Apostles) Thou hast given............106

Me. I have given to them (Apostles) the glory that Thou hast given........106

Me. I have given to them (Apostles) the words that Thou hast given......106

Me I have not yet ascended to My Father. Do not (to Mary Magdalene) touch............138

Me. If anyone serves Me let him follow 288

Me. If anyone wishes to come after Me let him deny himself and take up his cross and follow............186

Me. If God were your Father you (Pharisees) would surely love........ 30

Me. If I do not perform the works of My Father do not believe............168

Me. If thou, (a rich young ruler) wilt be perfect go sell what thou hast and give to the poor and thou shalt have treasure in Heaven and come follow..................................218

Me. I in Thee and Thou in................ 49

Me in. I was a stranger and you did not take......................................270

Me in. I was a stranger and you took 291

Me in My trials. You (Apostles) are they who have continued with..292

Me in Paradise. Thou (the repentent thief) shalt be with........148

Me in the regeneration when the Son of Man shall sit on the Throne of His glory shall also sit on twelve thrones judging the twelve tribes of Israel. You (Apostles) who have followed............................285

Me into the world so I also have sent them. Even as Thou hast sent..106

Me. I know Mine and Mine know.... 61

Me. I pray for those also who through their (Apostles') word are to believe in................................106

Me. I preach only what the Father has taught.. 29

Me is against Me. He who is not with 180

Me is at its end. That which concerns 125

Me is at hand. He (Judas) who betrays 127

Me is from Thee. They (Apostles) have learnt that whatever Thou hast given................................ 48

Me is He Who sent Me. Even if I do judge My judgment is true because I am not alone but with.... 29

Me is not worthy of Me. He who does not take up his cross and follow..276

Me is with Me. He (the Father) Who sent 93

Me. It is I Who bear witness to Myself and He Who sent Me bears witness to.......................... 59

Me. It is My Father Who glorifies.... 30

Me. It is the Scriptures that bear witness to.................................. 57

Me. I should lose nothing of what He (the Father) has given.............. 89

Me. I was daily with you (the Jews) in the Temple and you did not lay hands on........................127

Me. I was in prison and you came to..291

Me. I was in prison and you did not come to....................................270

Me. I was naked and you did not clothe 270

Me. I was sick and you did not visit..270

Me I will not cast out. All that the Father gives to............................ 57

Me. I will not cast out him who comes to....................................141

Me. I will that where I am they also whom Thou hast given Me may be with................................107

Me keep My commandments. If you love 100

Me later. Thou (Peter) shalt follow 147

Me. Learn from.................................... 55

Me let him deny himself. If anyone wishes to come after......................182

Me let him follow Me. If anyone serves...................................288

Me let him take up his cross and follow Me. If anyone wishes to come after.................................... 91

Me. Let the little children come to....169

Me "Lord, Lord" shall enter the Kingdom of Heaven. Not everyone who says to........................210

Me may be in them (the Apostles). That the love with which Thou hast loved..107

Me may be with Me. I will that where I am they also whom Thou hast given...............................107

Me may not remain in the darkness. That whoever believes in.................172

Me. Moses wrote of...........................252

Me. My Father glorifies..................... 30

Me. My food is to do the will of Him Who sent.................................275

Me. My glory that Thou hast given....107

Me! My God, My God, Why hast Thou forsaken (Cry of Jesus on the Cross).....................................129

Me. My sheep hear My voice and they follow 62

Me no drink. You gave.........................270

Me no longer. A little while and you will see...104

Me no longer. I go to the Father and you will see...............................154

Me no more. The Advocate (Holy Spirit) will convict the world of justice because I go to the Father and you will see..................104

Me. No one comes to the Father but through 45

Me. Now I am going to Him Who sent 154

Me now but thou shalt follow later. Where I am going thou (Peter) canst not follow...................147

Me of such is the Kingdom of God. Let the little children come to........201

Me. One of you (Apostles) will betray 124

Me out of the world. I have manifested Thy name to the men (Apostles) whom Thou hast given...106

Me receives Him Who sent Me. He who receives.................................276

Me satan thou (Peter) art a scandal to Me. Get thee behind......234

Me scatters. He who does not gather with...180

Me sees also the Father. He who sees 45

Me sees Him Who sent Me. He who sees 44

Me shall come to Me. All that the Father gives to...........................141

Me shall live because of Me. So he who eats................................... 90

Me shall never die. He who believes in...162

Me shall never die. Whoever lives and believes in...................................170

Me shall never thirst. He who believes in...162

Me shall sit on twelve thrones judging the twelve tribes of Israel. You who have followed......256

Me. They (My sheep) follow............ 62

Me? Simon, son of John, dost thou love...113

Me. Take word to My brethren (the Apostles) that they are to set out for Galilee; there they will see........138

Me that bears no fruit My Father will take away. Every branch in.... 46

Me. That the world may believe that Thou hast sent.......................... 49

Me. That the world may know that Thou hast sent.................................. 49

Me. That all things must be fulfilled that are written in the Law of Moses and the Prophets and the Psalms concerning.....................131

Me. That they (Apostles) may believe that Thou hast sent...........170

Me that they may be one. I pray for those also who through their (Apostles') word are to believe in..175

Me. That this which is written, "And He was reckoned among the wicked," must yet be fulfilled in..125

Me. That where I am they also whom Thou hast given Me may be with.......................................293

Me that you may have Life (Everlasting). You (the Jews) are not willing to come to.....................277

Me. The Advocate will bear witness concerning............................182

Me. The Advocate (Holy Spirit) will convict the world of sin because they do not believe in........174

Me. The Father bears witness to...... 29

Me. The Father dwelling in............. 45

Me. The Father Himself loves you (Apostles) because you have loved 48

Me. The Father is in........................... 45

Me. The Holy Spirit will glorify........183

Me. The living Father has sent.......... 25

Me. The prince of the world (Satan) has nothing in...................238

Me. The Scriptures bear witness to.... 57

Me. The Spirit of the Lord is upon
Me because He has anointed..........179

Me. The things that I speak I
speak as the Father has bidden...... 44

Me. The works that I do in the
name of My Father these bear
witness concerning............................ 32

Me the works that I do he also
shall do and greater than these he
shall do. . . . He who believes in....174

Me. Then the King will say to them,
"As long as you did not do it for
one of these least ones you
did not do it for................................271

Me. These (the Apostles) have
known that Thou hast sent.............. 49

Me. They (the Apostles) have
believed that Thou didst send........ 49

Me. They will expel you (Apostles)
from the synagogues because they
have not known................................103

Me. They will kill you (Apostles)
because they have not known........103

Me they will persecute you also.
If they have persecuted...................103

Me. Thou (Father) always hearest.... 38

Me thou hast believed. Because
thou (Thomas) hast seen...............139

Me. Thou hast loved them (Apostles)
even as Thou hast loved..................107

Me thrice. The cock will not crow
before thou (Peter) dost deny........100

Me to bring good news to the poor.
He (God) has sent........................... 16

Me to death? Why do you seek to put 28

Me to do. I have accomplished the
work that Thou hast given...............105

Me to drink. You gave.........................291

Me to eat. You did not give..............270

Me to eat. You gave.............................291

Me to sin it were better for him
. . . to be drowned in the depths
of the sea. Whoever causes one
of these little ones who believe in....165

Me to thee (Pilate) has the greater
sin. He who betrayed.......................129

Me unless he is enabled to do so by
My Father. No one can come to.... 26

Me unless the Father Who Sent
Me draw him and I will raise
him up on the Last Day.
No one can come to...........................141

Me until the time comes when you
(the Jews) shall say, "Blessed is
He Who comes in the name of
the Lord." You shall not see.......... 35

Me were it not given thee from
above. Thou (Pilate) wouldst
have no power over...........................129

Me what I should say and what I
should declare. The Father
has commanded 44

Me. Where I am going thou (Peter)
canst not (now) follow.................... 99

Me. When I was daily with you
(the Jews) in the Temple
you did not stretch forth
your hands against............................239

Me. Whoever receives this little
child for My sake receives.............. 58

Me will be loved by My Father.
He who loves.................................... 45

Me will have the Light of Life.
He who follows................................ 59

Me? Wilt thou (Peter) lay down
thy life for..100

Me with more than twelve legions
of angels? Dost thou (Peter)
suppose that I cannot entreat
My Father and He will even
now furnish 194

Me with Thyself. And now do
Thou Father glorify...........................126

Me without cause." But that the
word written in their (Jews') Law
may be fulfilled, "They have hated..103

Me. Yet a little while and the
world no longer sees.........................101

Me yet have believed. Blessed are
those who have not seen..................139

Me. You (Apostles) also (with the
Holy Spirit) bear witness
because from the beginning
you are with.....................................103

Me. You are seeking to kill................119

Me. You believe in God, believe
also in... 44

Me. You came to.................................291

Me you can do nothing. For without..102

Me you cannot bear fruit. Unless
you abide in....................................102

Me. You covered.................................291

Me. You did it for.............................292

Me. You did not clothe......................270

Me. You do not always have............ 67

Me. You (Apostles) have not chosen..102

Me. You (Apostles) in........................101

Me. You may have peace in..............105

Me. You visited..................................291

Me. You will all be scandalized
this night (Judas' betrayal in the
Garden) because of...........................124

Me. You will seek.............................. 92

Me you workers of iniquity.
Depart from 241

Me you would indeed rejoice
that I am going to the
Father. If you loved.....................153

Me you would then know My
Father also. If you knew................ 29

Meek. Learn from Me I am..............186

MESSIAS). That you (Apostles)
may believe that I am HE (the......172

MESSIAS). When you (the Jews)
have lifted up the Son of Man then
you will know that I am HE (the..118

MESSIAS) you will die in your
sin. If you do not believe
that I am HE (the............................ 92

mind. Thou shalt love the Lord
thy God with thy whole.................. 41

Mine. All things that are Thine
(Father) are.....................................106

Mine. All things that the
Father has are..................................104

Mine and declare it to you. The
Advocate will glorify Me because
He will receive of what is..............104

Mine and Mine know Me. I know.... 61

miracles had been worked in Sodom
that have been worked in thee
(Capharnaum) it would have
remained to this day. If the..........211

miracles that have been worked in
you (Bethsaida) they would have
repented long ago. If in Sidon
and Tyre had been worked the......242

mocked. The Son of Man will be...... 95

moon. There (in the last days)
will be signs in the..........................267

moon will not give her light (end
of the world). The............................263

Moses and the Prophets and the
Psalms concerning Me. All
things must be fulfilled that
are written in the Law of................131

Moses did not give you (children of
Israel) the Bread from Heaven........ 25

Moses give you the Law? Did not...... 28

Moses lifted up the serpent in the
desert even so must the Son of
Man be lifted up. And as..............116

Moses showed in the passage of the
Bush. But that the dead rise even..145

Moses. There is one who accuses
you (the Jews):................................252

Moses. They (brothers of the
rich man suffering torments in
hell) have...247

Moses' writings? How will you
(Scribes and Pharisees) believe
My word if you do not believe........161

Moses wrote of Me..............................252

moth consumes. Do not lay up
for yourselves treasures on
earth where 209

mother. Behold thy (Jesus' words
to John standing with Mary
at the foot of the cross)....................137

mother for My name's sake shall
receive a hundredfold and
shall possess Life Everlasting.
Everyone who has left......................285

mother. Whoever does the will of
My Father in Heaven is My............212

mountain, "hurl thyself into the
sea." (If you have faith you
will say to this)................................. 39

mulberry tree, "Be uprooted and be
planted in the sea." If you have
faith you will say to this..................168

mustard seed. If you have faith
even like a...168

mustard seed. . . . The Kingdom
of God is like a grain of..................197

mustard seed. The Kingdom of
Heaven is like a grain of..................213

My blood abides in Me and I in him. He who drinks........................ 90

My blood which is being shed for many unto the forgiveness of sins. This is..........................124

My blood has Life Everlasting. He who drinks................................278

My blood is drink indeed.................... 90

My blood of the New Covenant. This is..124

My body in preparation for burial. She (Mary Magdalene) has anointed.......................................121

My body. Take and eat. This is........124

My brethren (Apostles) and say to them, "I ascend to My Father and your Father." Go to...................156

My brethren (Apostles) that they are to set out for Galilee; there they shall see Me. Take word to....138

My brethren you did it for Me. As long as you did it for one of these the least of..........................292

My brother. Whoever does the will of My Father is................................. 23

My burden light. For My yoke is easy and 55

My burial. She (Mary Magdalene) has done it for.................................... 67

MY CHURCH. The gates of hell shall not prevail against it..............244

MY CHURCH. Thou art Peter and upon this rock I will build.............. 90

My Commandment that you love one another as I have loved you. This is..102

My Commandments. If you love Me, keep..100

My Commandments. You will abide in My love if you keep....................102

My course the third day. I am to end (Jesus foretells His resurrection in message to the fox, Herod)...............................120

My day and he saw it. Abraham rejoiced that he was to see.............. 60

My disciple. He who does not carry his cross and follow Me cannot be..120

My disciples. In this is My Father glorified that you become..............102

My Father
a house of business. Take these things away and do not make the House (the Temple) of........... 15

All things have been delivered to Me by.. 21

also. He who hates Me hates.......... 46

also. If you knew Me you would then know................................... 29

and He will even now furnish Me with more than twelve legions of angels? Dost thou (to Peter) suppose that I cannot entreat.........194

and your Father. I ascend to........156

But it (to sit at My right hand and left) belongs to those for whom it has been prepared by........ 38

Come blessed of................................ 42

Do not believe Me if I do not perform the works of........................ 32

gives you the true Bread from Heaven. 25

He who loves Me will be loved by.. 45

If this cup cannot pass away unless I drink it Thy will be done. (in the Garden of Gethsemani)....126

I have come in the name of............ 23

I have made known to you (Apostles) all things that I have heard from................................ 46

I have not yet ascended to (Jesus said to Mary Magdalene)................156

I honor 30

I send forth upon you (Apostles) the promise (Holy Spirit) of..........184

My Father in Heaven
Do not despise these little ones (children) for their angels always behold the face of........................... 27

Everyone who acknowledges Me before men I also will acknowledge him before................. 21

has revealed this (Who I am) to thee, Simon Bar Jona (Peter)........ 26

If two of you (who believe in Jesus) shall agree on earth about anything at all for which they ask, it shall be done for them by........... 27

My Father in Heaven (continued)
is My brother and sister and
mother. Whoever does the will of.. 23

shall enter the Kingdom of
Heaven. He who does the will of.. 20

Whoever disowns Me before men I
in turn will disown him before...... 21

My Father is the Vine-dresser. I
am the true Vine and...................... 46

My Father. No one can come to Me
unless he is enabled to do so by.... 26

My Father shall enter the Kingdom
of Heaven. He who does the will of 20

My Father take possession of the
Kingdom prepared for you from
the foundation of the world.
Come blessed of............................... 42

My Father these bear witness
concerning Me. The works that
I do in the name of.......................... 32

My Father Who glorifies Me. It is.... 30

My Father Who sent Me. For I
have come down from Heaven
not to do My own will but to do
the will of Him............................... 25

My Father will honor him. If
anyone serves Me............................ 43

My Father will love him. If
anyone love Me............................... 45

My Father's business? Did you not
know that I must be about.............. 13

My Father's commandments. I
have kept 46

My Father's House. There are
many mansions in 44

My Father's love. I abide in............. 46

My Father's will Who Sent Me.
To do 25

My feet that it is I Myself. See
(to Apostles) My hands and..........177

My flesh abides in Me and I in
Him. He who eats............................ 90

My flesh for the Life of the world.
The Bread that I will give is.......... 90

My flesh has Life Everlasting.
He who eats.....................................278

My flesh is food indeed...................... 90

My followers would have fought
that I might not be delivered to
the Jews. If My Kingdom
were of this world.............................128

My food is to accomplish His
(the Father's) work...........................275

My food is to do the will of
Him Who sent Me..............................275

My friends. If you do the things
I command you are...........................102

My glory is nothing. If I
glorify Myself..................................... 60

My glory which Thou hast given
Me. I will that they (Apostles)
may behold.......................................107

My God and to your God.
I ascend to...156

My God! My God! Why hast Thou
forsaken Me? (Jesus cries on
the Cross)..129

My hands and feet that it is I
Myself (to the Apostles). See........177

My Heavenly Father has not planted
will be rooted up. Every plant that 24

My Heavenly Father will do to you
if you do not forgive your
brothers from your hearts. So also.. 27

My hour has not yet come.................115

My House (the Temple) shall be
called a House of prayer. It
is written:.. 39

My judgment is just...........................252

My judgment is true........................... 29

My Kingdom is not from here.
(to Pilate) 128

My Kingdom is not of this world.
(to Pilate) 128

My Kingdom. That you (Apostles)
may eat and drink at My table in....292

My Kingdom were of this world
My followers would have fought
that I might not be delivered to
the Jews (to Pilate). If...................128

My lambs. Feed (to Peter)...............113

My life for My sheep. I lay down....119

My life that I may take it up
again. I lay it down........................134

My life up again. I have the
power to take it...............................134

My love. If you keep My Commandments you will abide in......................102

My mother. Whoever does the will of My Father is................................. 23

My name He may give you. That whatever you ask the Father in......102

My name He will give it to you. If you ask the Father anything in........105

My name He will teach you all things and bring to your mind whatever I have said to you. The Advocate the Holy Spirit Whom the Father will send in....................182

My name I will do it. If you (Apostles) ask anything in...............100

My name saying, "I am he." Many will come in............................264

My name saying, "I am the christ." For many will come in....................262

My name that I will do. Whatever you (Apostles) ask in......................100

My name they (disciples) shall cast out devils. In............................114

My name they (disciples) shall lay hands upon the sick and they shall get well. In......................114

My name they (disciples) shall speak in new tongues. In.................114

My name's sake. They will be dragging you up before kings for....267

My name's sake. You (disciples) will be hated by all for.................... 64

My name's sake shall possess Life Everlasting. Everyone who has left house, or brothers, or sisters, or father, or mother, or wife, or children, or lands, for......................285

My own authority. I have not spoken on 271

My peace I give to you.......................101

My sake for a witness to them and to the Gentiles. You will be brought before governors and kings for.....................................180

My sake will find it. He who loses his life for..............................276

My servants be. Where I am there also shall..................................288

My sheep. But you (Pharisees) do not believe because you are not of..168

My sheep. Feed (to Peter)................113

My sheep hear My voice and they follow me................................. 62

My sheep. I know................................. 62

My sheep. I lay down My life for....119

My sheep shall never perish................282

My side and be not unbelieving but believing. Bring here thy (Thomas') hand and put it into......139

My sister. Whoever does the will of My Father is................................. 23

My soul is troubled and what shall I say? "Father, save Me from this Hour?".....................................188

My speech? Why do you (Pharisees) not understand..............................235

My spirit. Father into Thy hands I commend (Jesus on the Cross)....130

My table in My Kingdom. That you (Apostles) may eat and drink at....292

My teaching is not My own................ 27

My time has not yet come................118

"My time is near at hand." Go into the city (Jerusalem) to a certain man and say,.....................................123

My time is not yet fulfilled.................118

My trials. But you (Apostles) are they who have continued with Me in......................................292

My voice and they follow Me. My sheep hear.............................. 62

My voice. Everyone who is of the Truth hears...............................109

My way today and tomorrow and the next day for it cannot be that a Prophet perish outside Jerusalem. I must go......................120

My witness is true because I know where I came from and where I go. 59

My word and believes Him Who sent Me . . . does not come to judgment. He who hears.................276

My word he will never see death. If anyone keep.............................279

My word. If anyone love Me he will keep.....................................101

My word takes no hold among you. You seek to kill Me because...........119

My words abide in you ask whatever
you will and it shall be done
to you. If you (Apostles) abide
in Me and if......................................102

My words and does not keep them
it is not I Who judge him.
If anyone hears..................................271

My words has One to condemn him.
He who does not accept...................271

My words. He who does not love
Me does not keep..............................101

My words? If you do not believe
his (Moses') writings how will
you (Scribes) believe......................161

My words will not pass away.
Heaven and earth will pass
away but..263

My yoke is easy and My burden light.. 55

Myself for them (the Apostles).
I sanctify (Jesus says to
the Father)..106

Myself. I bear witness to................... 59

Myself I can do nothing. Of............. 56

Myself. I will take you to...................293

Myself. If I be lifted up from
the earth (crucified), I will
draw all things to...............................123

Myself My glory is nothing. If
I glorify... 60

Myself. No one takes it (My life)
from Me but I lay it down of........119

Myself. See My hands and feet
that it is I..177

Myself to him who loves Me. I
will manifest......................................101

Myself will give you (disciples)
utterance and wisdom. I,.................267

Mysteries of the Kingdom of
Heaven but to them (the
unbelieving Jews) it is not given.
To you (Apostles) it is given
to know the..212

naked and you covered Me. I was....291

naked and you did not clothe
Me. I was...270

narrow gate. Strive to enter by the....199

Nation will rise against nation . . .
but the end (the Last Day) will
not be at once....................................262

nations beginning from Jerusalem.
Repentance and remission of sins
should be preached to all................228

nations. But when the Son of Man
shall come in His majesty . . .
before Him will be gathered all......270

nations for My name's sake. You
(Apostles) will be hated by all......262

nations. Go (to Apostles) therefore
and make disciples of all.................228

nations. . . . This Gospel of the
Kingdom (of Heaven) shall be
preached in the whole world
for a witness to all............................203

needle than for a rich man to enter
the Kingdom of Heaven. It is
easier for a camel to pass
through the eye of a........................218

neighbor as thyself. Thou shalt
love thy... 41

net cast into the sea that gathered
in fish of every kind. The
Kingdom of Heaven is like a..........214

New Covenant which is being shed
for many unto the forgiveness of
sins. This is My blood of the..........124

(Nicodemus—although Jesus never
spoke his name—into the index
because to him, a Pharisee, Jesus
revealed much. The author feels
moved to insert the name).............. 54

ninety-nine just who have no need
of repentance. There will be joy
in Heaven over one sinner who
repents more than over....................219

Nineve will rise up in the judgment
with this generation and will
condemn it. The men of..................254

Ninevites so will also the Son of Man
be to this generation. For even
as Jonas was a sign to the............. 93

Noe, even so will it be in the days
of the Son of Man. They were
eating and drinking . . . until the
day Noe entered the ark and the
flood came and destroyed them
all. And as . . . in the days of...... 94

occasion of sin to thee, pluck it out!
If thy eye be an................................244

occasion of sin to thee, cut it off!
If thy foot be an...............................244

occasion of sin to thee, cut it off! If thy hand be an............244

On High (Heaven). But wait here in the City (Jerusalem) until you (Apostles) are clothed with power from 228

ONLY-BEGOTTEN SON. For God so loved the world that He gave His.. 15

Our Father Who are in Heaven (the Lord's Prayer)........................209

outside. Many will come . . . and feast with Abraham and Isaac and Jacob in the Kingdom of Heaven but the children of the kingdom will be put forth............................251

outside. You (unbelieving Jews) shall see Abraham and Isaac and Jacob in the Kingdom of God but you yourselves cast forth...............259

overcome the world. Take courage I have 175

oxen. . . . I pray thee hold me excused. . . ." A certain man gave a great supper and he invited many . . . they all began to excuse themselves. . . . (One said) "I have bought five yoke of..................281

(Parable of a prodigal son. Jesus spoke a) 282

parables. The hour is coming when I will no longer speak to you in....105

Paradise. This day thou (the repentent thief) shalt be with Me in 129

parents for the sake of the Kingdom of God who shall not receive much more in the present time and in the age to come Life Everlasting. There is no one who has left..........201

Passover will be here and the Son of Man shall be delivered up to be crucified. After two days the....122

Passover with you before I suffer. I have greatly desired to eat this....123

PEACE be to you!................................111

PEACE. I give to you, My................101

PEACE. I leave with you.................101

PEACE. These things (of God and the Son) I have spoken to you that in ME you may have...............105

peace thy faith has saved thee (to Mary Magdalene). Go in.................159

pearls. The Kingdom of Heaven is like a merchant in search of fine....214

perdition. Not one of them (Apostles) perished except (Judas) the son of............................239

perish but have Life Everlasting. For God so loved the world that He gave His ONLY-BEGOTTEN SON that those who believe in Him may not..................................274

perish. It is not the will of your Father in Heaven that a single one of these little ones (children) should 216

perish. Not a hair of your (Apostles') head shall......................145

perish outside Jerusalem. I must go My way . . . for it cannot be that a Prophet..................................119

perish. They (My sheep) shall never..282

perished except (Judas) the son of perdition. . . .Not one of them (Apostles)...............................148

perishes but for the food that endures unto Life Everlasting. Do not labor for the food that............278

persecute you so that you may be children of your Father in Heaven. Pray for those who..........208

persecution for justice' sake for theirs is the Kingdom of Heaven. Blessed are they who suffer...........273

persevered to the end will be saved. He who has.....................................288

pestilences (one of the signs of the Last Day). There will be........266

Peter and upon this rock I will build MY CHURCH. Thou art...... 90

Pharisee went up to the Temple to pray and boasted of his many pious deeds. The...................219

Pharisees are full of robbery and wickedness. You......................... 33

Pharisees. Beware of the leaven of the 164

Pharisees! Woe to you,......................247

Pharisees you shall not enter the Kingdom of Heaven. Unless your justice exceed that of the.................208

Philip, He who sees Me sees also the Father.. 45

place for you (Apostles). I go to prepare a...................................204

plow and looking back is fit for the Kingdom of God. No one having put his hand to the..............198

poor and thou shalt have treasure in Heaven. Go sell what thou (the rich young ruler) hast and give to the...................................218

poor . . . for I tell you none of those who were invited to the marriage feast shall taste of my supper. Bring in here the...............................281

poor for thou shalt be repaid at the resurrection of the just. But when thou givest a feast invite the..280

poor for yours is the Kingdom of God. Blessed are you.......................196

poor. He (the Father) has sent Me to bring good news to the........179

poor in spirit for theirs is the Kingdom of Heaven. Blessed are the...208

poor man named Lazarus . . . covered with sores. The..................246

poor you have always with you but you (Apostles) do not always have Me. The.................................. 67

possess Life Everlasting. Everyone who has left house, or brothers, or sisters, or father, or mother, or wife, or children, or lands, for My name's sake shall receive a hundredfold and shall.......................285

possession of the Kingdom prepared for you from the foundation of the world. Come blessed of My Father, take 291

power from On High. Wait here in the City (Jerusalem) until you (Apostles) are clothed with............184

power in Heaven and on earth has been given to Me. All...............114

Power (of God). You shall see the Son of Man sitting at the right hand of the.. 51

power (of the devil) of darkness. But this (Jesus' arrest in the Garden of Gethsemani) is your (unbelieving Jews) hour and the....239

power on earth to forgive sins. The Son of Man has........................160

power to cast into hell. Be afraid of Him (God) Who after He has killed has.................................. 34

power to render judgment. He (the Father) has granted Him (the Son of Man).....................................252

power to take My life up again. I have the..134

powers of Heaven will be shaken (on the Last Day). For the...........263

pray but for those who through their word are to believe in Me. . . . Yet not for these (the Apostles) only do I........................106

pray for them (the Apostles). I........106

Pray for those who persecute you so that you may be children of your Father in Heaven.....................208

pray forgive whatever you have against anyone that your Father in Heaven may also forgive your offenses. When you stand up to.... 39

pray: Our Father Who art in Heaven. . . . In this manner shall you...209

pray. Sit down here (to Peter, James and John) while I go yonder (into the Garden of Gethsemani) and..............................126

pray that Thou keep them (the Apostles) from evil. I.....................106

pray. The publican (tax collector) went up to the Temple to................219

prayed for thee (Peter) that thy faith may not fail. I have..............173

prayer believe that you shall receive. Whatever you (Apostles) ask for in 39

prayer, believing, you shall receive. All things whatever you ask for in..171

Prayer" but you have made it a den of thieves. "My House (the Temple) shall be called a House of 39

Prayer, the Lord's (The Our Father)..209

Preach the Gospel to every creature....294

Preach the message, "The Kingdom of Heaven is at hand."......................210

preached in His (Jesus') name to all nations beginning from Jerusalem. Repentance and remission of sins should be.............................131

preached in the whole world for a witness to all nations. . . . This Gospel of the Kingdom shall be......203

preached. Until John (the Baptist) came there were the Law and the Prophets; since then the Kingdom of God is being...................................200

prepared for you from the foundation of the world. Come blessed of My Father, take possession of the Kingdom.....................................291

prince of the world (the devil) be cast out. Now will the...............237

prince of the world (the devil) is coming and in Me he has nothing. The.....................................238

prince of this world (the devil) has already been judged. The........238

prison and you did not visit Me. I was in...270

prison and you came to Me. I was in..291

proclaim the Kingdom of God. Let the dead bury their dead but do thou (Apostles) go and......198

(prodigal son. Jesuse spoke a parable of a).....................................282

profit a man if he gain the whole world but suffer the loss of his own soul. For what does it.............186

promise (of the Holy Spirit) of My Father. I send forth upon you (Apostles) the...........................184

Prophet perish outside Jerusalem. It cannot be that a............................120

Prophet than John the Baptist. There is not a greater...................196

Prophet, standing in the Holy place (the Temple) . . . let him who reads understand . . . for then there will be great tribulation, such as has not been from the beginning of the world until now, nor will be. Therefore when you see the abomination of desolation, which was spoken of by Daniel the..........262

Prophets, "And they shall be taught of God." It is written in the.......... 25

Prophets. In the self-same manner (to hate and reject you) their fathers used to treat the.................. 86

Prophets have prophesied until John (the Baptist) 211

Prophets have spoken. O foolish ones and slow of heart to believe in all that the......................176

Prophets in the Kingdom of God. You (Pharisees) shall see.................280

Prophets! Jerusalem, thou who killest the 63

Prophets! Jerusalem, thou who stonest the... 63

Prophets must be fulfilled. All things that are written concerning Me in the.........................131

Prophets. On these Two Commandments (to love God, to love neighbor) depend the whole Law and the...................................... 41

Prophets; since then the Kingdom of God is being preached. Until John (the Baptist) came there were the Law and the.....................200

prophets will arise. False..................265

Psalms must be fulfilled. All things that are written concerning Me in the...131

publican went up to the Temple to pray and would not so much as lift his eyes to Heaven but kept striking his breast saying, "O God, be merciful to me the sinner." The..219

publicans." You Pharisees say (of the Son of Man), "Behold a man who is a friend of............................ 87

Publicans (tax collectors) are entering the Kingdom of God before you (Pharisees)...................202

punishment. These (who did not give Me to eat, to drink, take Me in, clothe Me, or visit Me) will go into everlasting...................271

queen of the South will rise up in the Judgment against this generation. The 254

quenched." "Where their worm dies not and the fire is not......................244

"Rabbi"; for One is your Master, and all you are brothers. Do not you be called................................ 41

raise him up on the Last Day. No one can come to Me unless the Father Who sent Me draw him and I will................................141

raise him up on the Last Day. Whoever believes in the Son shall have Everlasting Life and I will......141

raise it up on the Last Day. This is the will of My Father that I should lose nothing of what He has given Me but that I should......141

ransom for many. The Son of Man has come to give His Life as a......121

ravens. God feeds the.......................... 34

reap that on which you have not labored. I have sent you (Apostles) to 275

reapers are the angels. The................191

reaps." Herein is the proverb true, "One sows, another..........................275

reaps receives a wage and gathers fruit unto Life Everlasting so that Sower and the reaper may rejoice together. He who................275

regeneration when the Son of Man shall sit on the Throne of His glory, shall also sit on twelve thrones, judging the twelve tribes of Israel. Amen I say to you that you who have followed Me, in the..256

rejected by the elders and chief priests and Scribes. The Son of Man must be................................116

rejected has become the cornerstone?" Did you never read in the Scriptures "that the stone which the builders..........................202

rejects Me has One Who condemns him. He who..................271

Rejoice because your (Apostles') reward is great in Heaven; for so did they persecute the Prophets who were before you........................273

"Rejoice, for this thy brother (prodigal son) . . . was lost and is found." The father said.............284

Rejoice rather in this that your names are written in Heaven..........216

remission of sins should be preached in His (the Son of Man's) name to all nations beginning from Jerusalem. That repentance and....131

Repent for the Kingdom of Heaven is at hand............................207

Repentance of sins should be preached 131

repents. There will be joy in Heaven over one sinner who........................219

RESURRECTION. I am the..............134

resurrection. But those who shall be accounted worthy of that world and of the resurrection from the dead neither marry nor take wives; for neither shall they be able to die anymore for they are equal to the angels and are sons of God being sons of the......................287

resurrection of judgment. They who have done evil shall come forth unto..252

resurrection of Life. Those who have done good shall come forth unto....140

resurrection of the just. Invite the poor, the cripples, the lame, the blind: and blessed shalt thou be because they have nothing to repay thee with; for thou shalt be repaid at the......................................143

reveal these things (truths of the Kingdom of God) to little ones. I praise Thee, Father, that Thou didst 211

reward is great in Heaven for so did they persecute the Prophets who were before you. Rejoice and exult because your (Apostles')................273

reward. Whoever gives to one of these little ones but a cup of cold water because he is a disciple shall not lose his 276

reward with your Father in Heaven. Take heed not to do your good before men in order to be seen by them otherwise you shall have no..209

rich man enter the Kingdom of Heaven. With difficulty will a..........218

rich man to enter the Kingdom of God. It is easier for a camel to pass through the eye of a needle than for a 201

rich man who feasted every day in splendid fashion died and was buried in hell. . . . A certain............246

riches enter the Kingdom of God. With what difficulty will they who have...201

rise again from the dead on the third day. Thus it is written that the Christ should...................................139

rise again on the third day. The Son of Man will.......................................134

rise even Moses showed in the passage of the Bush. . . . But that the dead..145

rise. Thy (Martha's) brother shall......143

risen from the dead. Tell the vision to no one till the Son of Man has........133

risen. I will go before you into Galilee after I have...135

rock I will build MY CHURCH and the gates of hell shall not prevail against it. Thou art Peter and upon this 90

rust nor moth consumes. Lay up for yourselves treasures in Heaven where neither....................................209

Sabbath loose his ox or ass from the manger and lead it forth to water? Hypocrites (Pharisees)! Does not each one of you on the..................236

Sabbath. The Sabbath was made for man and not man for the.............. 21

Sabbath. The Son of Man is Lord of the 21

Sadducees (who did not believe in the resurrection of man from the dead). Beware of the leaven of the............164

Salvation has come to this (Zacchaeus') house........................... 95

Salvation is from the Jews................179

Samaritans. Do not go in the direction of the Gentiles nor enter the towns of...210

Sanctify them (the Apostles) in the Truth. . . . Thy word is Truth......106

Satan at once comes and takes away the word that has been sown in their (men's) hearts........................231

Satan casts out Satan? (Jesus questions Pharisees) How then shall his kingdom stand if.............................230

Satan fall as lightning from Heaven. I was watching.................................236

Satan! for it is written thou shalt not tempt the Lord thy God. Begone....230

Satan has bound. . . . This woman (bent over for eighteen years) whom 236

Satan has desired to have you, Simon (Peter). . . . but I have prayed for thee. . . . Behold................................238

satan, thou (Peter), art a scandal to Me. Get thee behind Me...................234

save Me from this hour! No, this is why I came to this hour. . . . Now My soul is troubled. And what shall I say? Father,.....................................123

save them. For the Son of Man did not come to destroy men's lives but to..142

save the world. I have come to..........289

save what was lost (God's chosen people). The Son of Man came to.. 95

saved. He who believes and is baptized shall be..............................177

saved. He who has persevered to the end will be..288

saved thee (blind Samaritan). Arise, go thy way thy faith has.................169

saved thee (Samaritan cured of leprosy). Go in peace thy faith has................159

saved thee (Bartimeus in Jericho). Receive thy sight, thy faith has....171

saved thee (woman with hemorrhages). Take courage daughter thy faith has......................160

scandal does come. Woe to the man through whom..................................255

scandal to Me. Get thee behind Me, satan, thou (Peter) art a................234

scandals and those who work iniquity and cast them into the furnace of fire. The Son of Man will send forth His angels and they will gather out of His Kingdom all.........................254

scandals. Woe to the world because of..244

scourge Him (the Son of Man). They will......................................120

scourged. The Son of Man will be...... 95

Scribe instructed in the Kingdom of Heaven is like a householder who brings forth from his store-room things new and old. Every..............214

Scribes, hypocrites! Woe to you. because you . . . make him (a convert) twofold more a son of hell than yourselves..........................247

because you shut the Kingdom of Heaven against men........................257

. . . You are the sons of those who killed the Prophets...........................257

Scribes say that the Christ is the Son of David? How do the....................182

Scribes. The Son of Man must be rejected by the.................................116

Scribes. . . . who devour the houses of widows, making pretense of long prayers. Beware of...........................258

Scribes you shall not enter the Kingdom of Heaven. Unless your justice exceeds that of the..............208

Scripture cannot be broken. The........ 32

Scripture might be fulfilled. Not one of them (Apostles) perished except the son of perdition (Judas) that the...148

Scripture says, "From within him there shall flow rivers of Living Waters." He who believes in Me as the........165

Scripture, "the Spirit of the Lord is upon Me because He has anointed Me," has been fulfilled in your hearing. Today this........................179

Scriptures because in them you think that you have Life Everlasting. You (unbelieving Jews) search the........277

Scriptures nor the power of God. You err because you (Saducees) know neither the 40

Scriptures that bear witness to Me. It is the... 57

Scriptures, "The stone which the builders rejected has become the cornerstone?" Did you never read in the 39

Scriptures to be fulfilled that thus (Jesus' passion, death, and resurrection) it must take place? How then are the.............................127

seal. For upon Him (the Son of Man) the Father, God Himself, has set His 25

seed in his field. The Kingdom of Heaven is like a man who sowed good 213

seed. The Kingdom of Heaven is like a grain of mustard.............................213

seed. The sons of the Kingdom are the good. 213

seek what was lost. The Son of Man came to.. 95

sell what thou hast and give to the poor and thou shalt have treasure in Heaven. Go, (to the rich young ruler)...218

separate the wicked from among the just, and will cast them into the furnace of fire. The angels will go out and...255

serpent in the desert even so must the Son of Man be lifted up. As Moses lifted up the.......................................116

Serpents, Brood of Vipers! How are you (Pharisees) to escape the judgment of hell?.............................257

servant! Wicked and slothful..............269

servants be. . . . Where I am there also shall My......................................288

servants and handed over his wealth to them. The Kingdom of Heaven is like a man going abroad who called his 223

servants. The Kingdom of Heaven is like a king who gave a marriage feast for his son; (some of those invited) killed his.............................287

sheep. Feed (to Peter) My..................113

sheep from the goats. The Son of Man will separate them (all nations) as the shepherd separates the..............270

sheep hear My voice and they follow Me. My.. 62

sheep I have that are not of this Fold them also I must bring. Other........ 61

sheep. I lay down My life for My.... 61

sheep in the midst of wolves. I am
sending you (Apostles) forth like..180

sheep of Israel. Go, (to the Apostles)
rather to the lost..............................210

sheep of the flock will be scattered."
It is written, "I will smite the
Shepherd and the............................124

sheep on His right hand. He (the Son
of Man) will set the........................270

sheep that was lost." (The man said)
"Rejoice with me because I have
found the 282

sheep. You (Pharisees) do not believe
because you are not of My..............168

Shepherd and the sheep of the flock
will be scattered." It is written, "I
will smite the....................................124

Shepherd. I am the Good................... 61

Shepherd lays down His life for His
sheep. The Good..............................119

shepherd separates the sheep from the
goats. The Son of Man will separate
them (all nations) as the................270

Shepherd. There shall be One Fold
and One 31

shine forth like the sun in the
Kingdom of their Father. The
just will..254

sick and you did not visit Me. I was..270

sick and you visited Me. I was..........291

Sidon had been worked the miracles
that have been worked in you
(Capharnaum), they would have
repented long ago in sackcloth
and ashes. If in..............................242

Sidon on the Day of Judgment than
for you (Capharnaum). It will be
more tolerable for............................252

sign of Jonas. An evil and adulterous
generation demands a sign, and no
sign shall be given it but the..........133

sign of the Son of Man in Heaven.
But immediately after the tribulation
. . . then will appear the...................263

sign to this generation. Even as Jonas
was a sign to the Ninevites so will
also the Son of Man be a................254

signs in the moon, stars and the sun
(when Jesus comes again). There
will be..267

signs shall attend those who believe.
(Many) 177

Siloe. (And he returned seeing.)
(Jesus said to the man blind from
birth), Go wash in the pool of........ 61

Simon (Peter) Bar-Jona, My Father
in Heaven has revealed this (Who
I am) to thee.................................. 26

Simon (Peter) behold Satan has
desired to have you . . . but I have
prayed for thee. 238

(Simon Peter) feed My lambs!..........113

(Simon Peter) feed My sheep!..........113

Simon (Peter), son of John, dost
thou love Me?..................................113

sin and blasphemy against the Son of
Man shall be forgiven men. . . .
Every kind of....................................180

sin because they do not believe in Me.
The Advocate (the Holy Spirit) will
convict the world of........................104

sin. If I had not come and spoken to
them (the Jews) they would have
no sin but now they have no excuse
for their 103

sin. If I had not done among them
works they (the Jews) would have
no 103

sin. If you do not believe that I am
HE (the Messias) you will die in
your...247

sin . . . it were better for him . . . to
be drowned. . . . Whoever causes
one of these little ones who believe
in Me to..165

sin. Therefore he who betrayed Me to
thee (Pontius Pilate) has the greater..129

sin to thee, cut it off! If thy foot is an
occasion of.......................................244

sin to thee, cut it off! If thy hand is
an occasion of..................................244

sin to thee, pluck it out! If thy eye is
an occasion of..................................244

sinned against Heaven. I (the
prodigal son) have...........................283

sinner." "O God be merciful to me
(the publican in the Temple) the..219

sinner who repents. There will be joy
among the angels of God over one.. 35

sinners. The hour is at hand when the Son of Man will be betrayed (in the Garden of Gethsemani) into the hands of 127

sinners." You (the Jews) say of the Son of Man, "friend of.................... 87

sins are forgiven thee (paralytic). Take courage thy.............................160

sins many as they are shall be forgiven her (Mary Magdalene) because she has loved much. Her..159

sins may be forgiven them." To those outside all things are treated as parables, "lest perhaps at any time they should be converted and their..197

sins should be preached to all nations beginning from Jerusalem. That repentance and remission of............131

sins. The Son of Man has power on earth to forgive................................160

sins. This is My blood of the New Covenant which is being shed for many unto the forgiveness of..........124

sins you (Apostles) shall forgive they are forgiven them and whose sins you shall retain they are retained. Whose..138

sister. Whoever does the will of My Father in Heaven is My..................212

sisters for My name's sake shall receive a hundredfold and shall possess Life Everlasting. Everyone who has left..285

Sodom in that day (Judgment) than for that town (which refuses disciples). It will be more tolerable for 253

Sodom it rained fire and brimstone from Heaven and destroyed them all. The day that Lot went out from....219

Sodom on the Day of Judgment than for thee (Capharnaum). It will be more tolerable for............................253

Solomon is here. A greater than........243

Solomon . . . was not arrayed like one of these (lilies)..............................167

Son (see Son of God, and Son of Man.)

Son and of the Holy Spirit. Go, therefore, and make disciples of all nations, baptizing them in the name of the Father and of the.................. 83

Son of God

All judgment He (the Father) has given to the..................................... 56

All who are in the tombs shall hear the voice of the................................140

and him to whom the Son chooses to reveal Him. No one knows the Father except the........................... 21

and those who hear shall live. When the dead shall hear the voice of the..276

but the Father only. But of that day or hour (the Last Day) no one knows neither the angels nor the.... 65

can do nothing of Himself but only what He sees the Father doing. The 22

Dost thou (blind man whose sight was restored at pool of Siloe) believe in the....................................166

even as they honor the Father. That all men may honor the.................... 56

except the Father. No one knows the... 21

For God so loved the world that He gave His only-begotten.............. 15

gives Life to whom He will. The....276

Glorify Thy 75

He who does not believe is already judged because he does not believe in the name of the only-begotten....158

I am the... 32

into the world that the world be saved through Him. God sent His.. 54

into the world to judge the world but that the world might be saved through Him. For God did not send His 54

is He (the Christ)? (Jesus asked the Pharisees) Whose...................... 41

makes you free. The......................... 60

may be glorified. That through it (death and resurrection of Lazarus) the.. 63

may give Everlasting Life. That to all Thou hast given Him the..........293

may glorify Thee. That Thy............ 75

may not perish. That those who believe in Him the............................158

Son of God (continued)

No one knows the Father except the.. 21

power over all flesh. Thou hast given the.. 75

shall have Everlasting Life. Whoever beholds and believes in Him the...278

The dead shall hear the voice of the...140

The Father has given all judgment to the 22

The Father loves the........................ 22

The ONLY-BEGOTTEN................ 15

"was reckoned among the wicked." The 125

Whatever you ask in My name, that I will do, in order that the Father may be glorified in the........100

Who is from God He has seen the Father. The 89

Whom Thou hast sent: JESUS CHRIST. Now this is Everlasting Life that they may know Him the..293

Son of Man (see also Son of God.)

Son of Man

acknowledge before the angels of God. Everyone who acknowledges Me before men him will the............192

All judgment He (the Father) has given to the Son that all men may honor the 22

All the nations will be gathered before the...270

ascending where He was before? What then if you should see the....150

be in His day. As the lightning when it flashes from one end of the sky to the other so will the..............261

be lifted up (crucified). As Moses lifted up the serpent in the desert even so must the...............................116

be three days and three nights in the heart of the earth. So will the..133

Blessed shall you be when men hate you and reproach you because of the 86

but the Father only. But of that day or hour (Last Day) no one knows neither the angels nor the.... 65

Son of Man (continued)

came eating and drinking. The...... 87

came to save men's lives. The........ 92

came to save what was lost. The.... 95

comes. You (Apostles) will not have gone through the towns of Israel before the............................... 86

comes will He find faith on the earth? Yet when the........................169

coming in His Kingdom. There are some of those standing here who will not taste death till they have seen the 91

coming upon a cloud with great power and majesty. They will see the...267

did not come to destroy men's lives but to save them. The....................187

Even so (as in the days of Noe) will be the coming of the................264

gives Life to whom He will. The....140

goes His way as it is written of Him. The 124

has come to give His life as a ransom for many. The......................121

has not come to be served but to serve. The... 95

has nowhere to lay His head. The.. 85

has power on earth to forgive sins. The...160

has risen from the dead. Tell the vision (on Mount Thabor) to no one till the.......................................133

He (God) has granted Him power to render judgment because He is the... 22

His elect from the four winds, from one end of the heavens to the other. The angels will gather......................263

in Heaven. Then will appear the sign of the......................................263

into the world in order to judge the world. For God did not send the.... 15

into the world that the world be saved through Him. God sent the.. 15

is betrayed. Woe to that man by whom the..124

is coming at an hour that you do not expect. The...............................258

Son of Man (continued)

is He (the Christ)? (Jesus asked the Pharisees) Whose......................... 41

is He Who sows the good seed. The 87

is Lord even of the Sabbath. The.. 86

is revealed. As it came in the days of Lot . . . in the same wise will it be on the day that the...................... 94

is to be betrayed into the hands of men. The 117

is to come with His angels in the glory of His Father. The.................255

is? (Jesus asked His Apostles) Who do men say the.................................. 90

it shall be forgiven him; but whoever speaks against the Holy Spirit it will not be forgiven him. Whoever speaks a word against the........ 87

may give Everlasting Life. That to all Thou hast given Him the............293

may glorify Thee. The hour has come . . . That Thy...........................126

may not perish but may have Life Everlasting. That those who believe in the.....................................274

must be lifted up (crucified). The..116

must be put to death. The..............116

must be rejected by this generation. The..120

must suffer many things. But first the...120

Neither does the Father judge any man but all judgment He has given to the 251

power over all flesh. Thou hast given the...105

power to render judgment. He (God) has granted Him the............252

(Pray) at all times that you may be accounted worthy . . . to stand before the...268

shall come in His majesty and all His angels with Him. The................270

shall come in His majesty . . . before Him will be gathered all nations. When the 270

shall have Everlasting Life. Whoever believes in the..................278

shall sit on the Throne of His glory. The...285

Son of Man (continued)

shall suffer at their (Jews') hands. The 117

sitting at the right hand of the Power (of God) and coming upon the clouds of Heaven. You (to Caiphas and the Sanhedrin) shall see the 127

that Thy Son may glorify Thee. Glorify Thy 105

The days will come when you will long to see one day of the............. 94

the Father God Himself has set His seal. For upon Him the.................... 25

The Father loves the......................... 22

then you will know that I am HE (the MESSIAS). When you have lifted up (crucified) the..................118

They (the Jews) will kill Him the..117

They (the Jews) will mock Him the...120

They will scourge Him the..............120

They will spit upon Him the..........120

to death. The chief priests and Scribes will condemn Him the........120

to death. They (the Gentiles) will put Him the......................................120

to the Gentiles. They (the Jews) will deliver Him the........................120

was reckoned among the wicked." "And He (the)................................125

Whatever you ask in My name, that I will do, in order that the Father may be glorified in the....................100

Who has descended from Heaven. No one has ascended into Heaven except Him the..............................149

Who is from God, He has seen the Father. Not anyone has seen the Father except Him the................... 25

Who is in Heaven. No one has ascended into Heaven . . . except Him the...149

Whom Thou hast sent: JESUS CHRIST. Now this is Everlasting Life that they may know Him the..293

will be a sign to this generation. The 93

Son of Man (continued)

will be accomplished. All things that have been written by the Prophets concerning the.................................. 95

will be betrayed into the hands of sinners. The hour is at hand (Jesus in the Garden of Gethsemani) when the..127

will be betrayed to the chief priests and Scribes. The............................120

will be delivered to the Gentiles. The 122

will be delivered up to be crucified. The 122

will be mocked. The........................ 95

will be scourged. The...................... 95

will be spit upon. The...................... 95

will be three days and three nights in the heart of the earth. The.......... 87

will come at an hour that you do not expect. The...............................264

will come in His majesty. The........134

will give you Life Everlasting. The..278

will render to everyone according to his conduct. Then He the............255

will rise again on the third day. The 134

will say to them (on His left hand), "As long as you did not do it for one of these least ones you did not do it for Me." Then He the..........270

will say to those on His left hand, "Depart from Me accursed ones into the everlasting fire. . . . He the..270

will say to them (on His right hand), "As long as you did it for one of these, the least of My brethren, you did it for Me." . . . The King, the....................................292

will say to those on His right hand, "Come blessed of My Father, take possession of the Kingdom prepared for you from the foundation of the world." Then the King, the.............291

will send forth His angels . . . and they will gather His elect . . . The 193

will separate them one from another as the shepherd separates the sheep from the goats. (At the Last Judgment) The 270

Son of Man (continued)

will set the goats on His left hand. (At the Last Judgment) The..........270

will set the sheep on His right hand. (At the Last Judgment) The..........270

will sit on the Throne of His glory. (At the Last Judgment) The..........270

with a kiss? Judas, Dost thou betray the..108

you shall not have Life in you. Unless you drink the blood of the..278

you shall not have Life in you. Unless you eat the flesh of the........278

son of perdition (Judas). Not one of them (Apostles) perished except the..148

son. Woman (Jesus to His mother at the foot of the Cross on Calvary) behold thy (meaning John the Apostle) 137

sons of God, being sons of the resurrection. Those accounted worthy of that world shall not be able to die anymore for they are equal to the angels and are...................................193

sons of Light. While you have the Light, believe in the Light, that you may become...............................171

sons of the Kingdom (of Heaven). The good seed is the......................213

sons of the resurrection. They are equal to the angels being................193

sons of the resurrection. They are sons of God being............................287

sons of the wicked one (the devil) are the weeds. The..........................232

soul and body in hell. Be afraid of Him Who is able to destroy both....242

soul and thy whole mind. Thou shalt love the Lord thy God with thy whole heart and with thy whole......187

soul. Do not be afraid of those who kill the body but cannot kill the....186

soul? For what does it profit a man if he gain the whole world but suffer the loss of his own...........................186

soul is sad even unto death." (Jesus anticipating His passion and crucifixion said,) "My...............................189

soul is troubled and what shall I say?
"Father save Me from this hour!"
No, this is why I came to this hour.
My 188

soul of thee." God said to him (a
rich man with abundant crops),
"Thou fool this night do they
demand thy..187

soul? What will a man give in
exchange for his..............................186

souls. By your patience you will win
your..188

souls. Learn from Me . . . and you
will find rest for your......................186

Sower (the Son of Man) and the
reaper (Apostle) may rejoice
together. So that the..........................275

Sower (the Son of Man) sows the
word (of God). The..........................231

Sower went out to sow . . . some seeds
fell upon good ground which
yielded much fruit. The..................231

sows another reaps." For herein is the
proverb true, "One............................275

sparrows. Do not be afraid, you are
of more value than many................166

Spirit (see also Holy Spirit)

Spirit
and in Truth. True worshippers
will worship God in..........................179

and Life. The words (eating His
flesh and drinking His blood) that
I have spoken to you (disciples)
are..278

and they who worship Him must
worship in Spirit and in Truth.
God is..179

he cannot enter the Kingdom of
God. Unless a man be born again
of water and the Holy....................178

is spirit. That which is born of the..185

of God then the Kingdom of God
has come upon you (Pharisees)....
But if I cast out devils by the........180

of the Lord is upon Me because
He has anointed Me. The................179

of Truth Who proceeds from the
Father, He will bear witness concerning Me. When the Advocate

Spirit (continued)
has come Whom I will send from
the Father, the..................................182

of Truth Whom the world cannot
receive because it neither sees Him
nor knows Him. I will ask the
Father and He will send you another
Advocate the 182

of Truth will teach you (Apostles)
all the Truth. He, the......................183

of your Father Who speaks through
you (Apostles). It is the.................. 20

that gives Life. It is the..................181

The wind blows where it will, and
thou hearest its sound but dost not
know where it comes from or where
it goes. So is everyone who is born
of the 178

to those who ask Him. Your
Heavenly Father will give the
Holy 179

will not be forgiven men either in
this world or in the world to come.
Blasphemy against the (Holy)........180

spirit. Father, into Thy hands I commend My (Having said this, Jesus
expired on the cross.)......................189

spirit for theirs is the Kingdom of
Heaven. Blessed are the poor in....273

spirit, go out of the man. Thou
unclean..233

spirit has gone out of a man . . . he
roams . . . (but returns) with seven
other evil spirits . . . (and) the last
state of that man becomes worse
than the first. When an unclean......231

spirit, I command thee, go out of him
(the boy) and enter him no more.
Thou deaf and dumb........................235

spirit. That which is born of the
Spirit is..178

spirits are subject to you. . . . Do not
rejoice that the..................................236

spirits more evil than himself. Then
he (the unclean spirit) goes and
takes with him seven other..............231

spit upon the Son of Man. They will..120

stars. There will be signs (on the Last
Day) in the......................................267

stars will fall (on the Last Day) from Heaven. The................................263

steward? Who is the faithful and prudent................................167

"stone which the builders rejected has become the cornerstone?" Did you never read in the Scripture that the..202

stone will be broken to pieces but upon whomever it falls it will grind him to powder. He who falls on this................................203

stranger and you did not take Me in. I was a................................270

stranger and you took Me in. I was a..291

suffer. Elias (John the Baptist) has come already and they (the Jews) did not know him but did to him whatever they wished. So shall the Son of Man................................117

suffer. I have greatly desired to eat the Passover with you (Apostles) before I................................123

suffer many things. As the lightning . . . flashes . . . so will the Son of Man be on His day. But first He must 120

suffer persecution for justice' sake for theirs is the Kingdom of Heaven. Blessed are they who................................273

suffer the loss of his own soul? For what does it profit a man if he gain the whole world but 186

suffer these things (passion and crucifixion) before entering into His glory? Did not the Christ have to..130

suffer. Thus it is written and thus the Christ should 131

sun. There will be signs (on the Last Day) in the................................267

sun will be darkened (on the Last Day). The 263

supper and invited many. A certain man gave a great................................281

supper. For I tell you that none of those who were invited (but offered excuses) shall taste of my................................281

synagogues. They will expell you (Apostles) from the................................ 47

take Me in. I was a stranger and you did not 270

take possession of the Kingdom prepared for you from the foundation of the world. Come, blessed of My Father 291

taken away from them (Apostles). But the days will come when the Bridegroom shall be................................150

talents, to another two, and to another one. . . . The Kingdom of Heaven is like a man going abroad who called his servants and handed over to them his goods, and to one he gave five 269

teaching them to observe all that I have commanded you. . . . Go and make disciples of all nations,..........184

Temple, and in three days I will raise it up. . . . Destroy this................................116

(The Our Father)................................209

thieves break in and steal. Lay up for yourselves treasures in Heaven where neither rust nor moth consumes nor 209

Thine. All things that are Mine are....106

third day I am to end My course (in message sent to Herod). The..........120

third day. The Son of Man will rise again on the................................133

thirst. He who believes in Me shall never................................162

thirst. I (Jesus on the Cross)..............137

thirst let him come to Me and drink. If anyone 165

thirsty and you gave Me no drink. I was................................270

thirsty and you gave Me to drink. I was................................291

three days and three nights in the heart of the earth. The Son of Man will be................................133

three days I will raise it (the Temple: My body) up. In................................132

Throne of His glory. The Son of Man will sit on the................................270

tombs shall hear the voice of the Son of God. . . . All who are in the........140

tradition of men. . . . Letting go the Commandment of God, you (Pharisees) hold fast the................................ 24

treasure hidden in a field. The
Kingdom of Heaven is like a..........214

treasure in Heaven. Go (to the rich
young ruler), sell what thou hast
and give to the poor and thou shalt
have 218

treasure is there also will your heart
be. For where your..........................218

treasure unfailing in Heaven. Make
for yourselves a.................................217

tree, mulberry 168

tree that does not bear good fruit is
cut down and thrown into the fire.
Every 241

tribes of Israel. You (Apostles) who
have followed Me . . . shall also sit
on twelve thrones judging the
twelve..256

tribulation. . . . They shall see the
Son of Man coming upon the clouds
with great power and majesty. After
the..265

troubled and what shall I say?
"Father, save Me from this hour!"
No, this is why I came to this hour.
My soul is..123

troubled. You believe in God, believe
also in Me. Let not your heart be..173

Truth
and the Life. I am the Way, and
the...100

has come He will teach you
(Apostles) all the Truth. But
when He the Spirit of.....................183

hears My voice. Everyone who is
of the 109

shall make you free. The................ 60

The true worshippers will worship
the Father in.....................................179

Thy (God the Father's) word is.... 49

I am a KING (to Pontius Pilate).
This is why I was born and why I
have come into the world to bear
witness to the....................................128

Who proceeds from the Father He
will bear witness concerning Me.
When the Advocate has come
Whom I will send from the Father,
the Spirit of......................................182

Truth (continued)
Whom the world cannot receive
because it neither sees nor knows
Him. I will ask the Father and He
will send you (Apostles) another
Advocate, the Spirit of....................182

Worship the Father in Spirit and in 16

You (Scribes and Pharisees) do not
believe Me because I speak the......166

twelve tribes of Israel. You (Apostles)
who have followed Me . . . shall sit
on twelve thrones judging the........256

Twelve, yet one of you (Judas) is a
devil? Have I not chosen you, the..234

Tyre had been worked the miracles
that have been worked in you
(Capharnaum). . . . If in................242

Tyre on the Day of Judgment than
for you (Corozain and Bethsaida).
It will be more tolerable for..........252

unbelieving and perverse generation,
how long shall I be with you? How
long shall I put up with you........164

unbelieving but believing. Bring here
thy (to Thomas) finger and see My
hands; bring here thy hand and
put it into My side; and be not....139

unclean spirit, go out of the man.
Thou..233

unclean spirit has gone out of a man,
he . . . (returns) . . . and takes
with him seven other spirits more
evil than himself. . . . When the....231

unfaithful. The master of that servant
(who says to himself, "My master
delays his coming." . . .) will come
on a day he does not expect, and in
an hour he does not know, and will
cut him asunder and make him
share the lot of the..........................258

unity. That they (who believe) may
be one, even as We are one: I in
them and Thou in Me, that they
may be perfected in..........................106

unprofitable servant, cast him forth
into the darkness outside, where
there will be the weeping, and the
gnashing of teeth. But as for the....270

unquenchable fire. If thy hand is an
occasion of sin to thee, cut it off!
. . . If thy foot is an occasion of sin
to thee, cut it off! . . . If thy eye is
an occasion of sin to thee, pluck it
out! . . .It is better for thee to enter
the Kingdom of God . . . maimed
. . . lame . . . with one eye than
having two hands . . . two feet . . .
two eyes to be cast into the hell of..244

Us. That they (who believe) may be
one in 106

Vine . . . and you (Apostles) are the
branches. I am the true...................102

Vine-dresser. My Father is the............ 46

vineyard. The Kingdom of Heaven is
like a householder who went out
early in the morning to hire laborers
for his 219

vipers, how are you to escape the
judgment of hell? Serpents, brood
(Scribes and Pharisees) of.............257

virgins who took their lamps and went
forth to meet the bridegroom: Five
of them were foolish and five wise.
Then will the Kingdom of Heaven
be like the ten..................................289

visit Me. I was in prison and you did
not..270

visit Me. I was sick and you did not..270

(visited) Me. I was in prison and
you came to......................................291

visited Me. I was sick and you............291

wars and rumors of wars . . . but the
end (of the world) is not yet. You
shall hear of.....................................262

Watch, therefore, for you do not know
at what hour your Lord is to come 96

water and the Holy Spirit he cannot
enter into the Kingdom of God.
Unless a man be born again of........195

Water." He who believes in Me, as
the Scripture says, "from within him
there shall flow rivers of Living......165

Water that I will give him (who
thirsts) shall become in him a
Fountain of Water springing up
unto Life Everlasting. The.............275

Way, and the Truth, and the Life.
I am the...100

way that leads to destruction. For
wide is the gate and broad is the....241

way that leads to Life Everlasting!
How close the..................................274

We are one. That they (who believe)
may be one even as..........................106

We will come to him and make Our
abode with him. If anyone love
Me..101

weeds among the wheat. But while
men were asleep his (the sower's)
enemy came and sowed..................232

weeds are gathered up and burnt with
fire, so will it be at the end of the
world. Just as...................................254

weeds first and bind them in bundles
to burn; but gather the wheat into
my barn. Gather up the...................254

weeds. The sons of the wicked one
(the devil) are the..........................232

weeping, and the gnashing of teeth,
when you (the unbelieving Jews)
shall see Abraham and Isaac and
Jacob and all the Prophets in the
Kingdom of God but you yourselves
cast forth outside. There will be
the..264

Where I am going thou (Peter) canst
not follow Me now..........................152

Where I am going thou (Peter) shalt
follow later.......................................292

where I am, there you (Apostles)
also may be. That............................293

where I am they (Apostles) also
whom Thou hast given Me may be
with Me. (Jesus prays to the
Father) I will that............................155

where I go you (Apostles) cannot
come (now). You will seek Me and..152

Where I go you (Apostles) know......204

while and you (Apostles) shall see
Me. And again a little......................135

wicked from among the just and cast
them into the furnace of fire. . . .
The angels will go out and separate
the..255

wicked." "He (the Son of God) was
reckoned among the........................125

wicked one (the devil) are the weeds.
The sons of the................................232

wicked one (the devil) comes and
snatches what has been sown in his
(the man's) heart. The..................231

widow has put in (to the treasury of
the Temple) more than all (the
others) . . . all that she had
to live on. This poor........................ 42

wife . . . for My name's sake, shall
receive a hundredfold, and shall
possess Life Everlasting.
Everyone who has left......................285

will of Him (the Father) Who sent
Me, to accomplish His work.
My food is to do the........................ 16

will of My Father in Heaven is
My brother, sister and mother.
Whoever does the............................212

will of My Father in Heaven shall
enter the Kingdom of Heaven.
He who does the.............................210

wine-drinker. . . ." The Son of Man
came eating and drinking, and
you (Pharisees) say, "Behold a
man who is a glutton and a............ 87

wise and prudent, and didst reveal
them to little ones. I praise Thee,
Father, Lord of Heaven and
earth, that Thou didst hide these
things (of the Kingdom of
God) from the..................................211

witness
because from the beginning
you (Apostles) are with Me.
You also bear....................................103

concerning it. The world
hates Me because I bear...................118

concerning Me. But when the
Advocate has come Whom I will
send from the Father the Spirit
of Truth Who proceeds from the
Father, He will bear.......................182

concerning Me. The works that
I do in the name of My Father
these bear...168

It (dragging you before kings and
governors for My name's sake)
shall lead to your bearing................267

to all nations. . . . This Gospel
of the Kingdom shall be preached
in the whole world for a.................203

witness (continued)
to Me. It is I Who bear witness
to Myself; and He Who
sent Me bears....................................256

to Me. It is they (the Scriptures)
that bear...277

to the Truth (to Pontius Pilate).
I am a KING. This is why I was
born and why I have come into
the world to bear..............................128

to them and to the Gentiles. You
will be brought before governors
and kings for My sake, for a..........180

witnesses of these things (the passion,
crucifixion, resurrection). You
yourselves (the Apostles) are..........184

wives. Those who shall be accounted
worthy of that world . . . neither
marry nor take..................................193

wolves. I am sending you forth
like sheep in the midst of.................180

Woman, Behold thy son. (Jesus said
to His mother, meaning John, the
young Apostle standing beside
Mary at the foot of the cross
on Calvary.).....................................137

word
and believes Him Who sent Me,
has Life Everlasting, and does
not come to judgment, but has
passed from death to Life.
He who hears My..............................276

he will never see death. If
anyone keep My.................................279

I have given them (Apostles) Thy..106

I keep His (the Father's).............. 60

is Truth. Thy (the Father's).......... 49

men speak they shall give account
on the Day of Judgment.
Every idle...253

of God and keep it. Blessed
are they who hear the...................... 33

takes no hold among you
(Pharisees). You seek to kill
Me because My.................................119

that has been sown in their
(men's) hearts. Satan at once
comes and takes away the...............231

word (continued)

that I have spoken will condemn him (unbeliever) on the Last Day. The 271

The Sower (the Son of Man) sows the 231

words

and does not keep them it is not I Who judge him. If anyone hears My..............................271

has One to condemn him. He who does not accept My..................271

He who does not love Me does not keep My............................101

I have spoken to you (to eat My flesh and drink My blood) are Spirit and Life. The.........................181

that Thou hast given Me. I have given to them (Apostles) the..........106

thou wilt be justified, and by thy words thou wilt be condemned. For by thy.......................................253

which I spoke to you (that all things must be fulfilled that are written . . . concerning Me) while I was yet with you. These are the..184

will not pass away. Heaven and earth will pass away but My..........266

workers of iniquity and cast them into the furnace of fire. . . . The Son of Man will gather out of His Kingdom all.............................254

workers of iniquity depart from Me. You 250

works

of My Father do not believe Me. If I do not perform the....................168

that I do, he also shall do and greater than these he shall do. . . . He who believes in Me, the............174

that I do in the name of My Father, these bear witness concerning Me. The........................ 62

The Father dwelling in Me, it is He Who does the...............................100

themselves. Believe because of the..173

which the Father has given Me to accomplish bear witness to Me that the Father has sent Me. The.... 56

world

and go to the Father. Again I leave the..225

and I am coming to Thee. I am no longer in the......................155

and preach the Gospel to every creature. Go into the whole............294

and the reapers are the angels. The harvest is the end of the..........254

be cast out. Now will the prince (the devil) of the.............................237

because of scandals! Woe to the....244

but suffer the loss of his own soul? For what does it profit a man if he gain the whole..............................186

cannot receive because it neither sees Him nor knows Him. I will ask the Father and He will send you another Advocate the Spirit of Truth Whom the.........................182

Come blessed of My Father take possession of the Kingdom prepared for you from the foundation of the..291

existed. And now do Thou, Father, glorify Me with Thyself, with the glory that I had with Thee before the...105

for a witness to all nations. . . . This Gospel of the Kingdom shall be preached in the whole................203

has already been judged. The prince (the devil) of this....................238

has not known Thee. Just Father the... 49

hates you know that it has hated Me before you. If the......................102

He Who sows the good seed is the Son of Man. The field is the.......... 87

I am the Light of the...................... 61

I am with you all days even unto the consummation of the........114

I have come to save the...................271

I have not come to judge the........271

I have overcome the.........................105

is coming and in Me he has nothing. The prince (the devil) of the.....................................238

keeps it unto Life Everlasting. He who hates his life in this..........288

world (continued)

may believe that Thou hast sent
Me. I pray . . . that they (who
believe) may be one in Us,
that the..175

may know that Thou hast sent Me.
I pray . . . that they may be perfected in unity, and that the..........106

My followers would have fought
that I might not be delivered to
the Jews (Jesus said to Pilate).
If My Kingdom were of this..........128

My Kingdom is not (to Pontius
Pilate) of this.....................................128

neither marry nor take wives.
Those who shall be accounted
worthy (of Heaven) of that............193

no longer sees Me. A little
while and the....................................153

Now will the prince (the devil)
of the world be cast out. Now
is the judgment of the......................260

of judgment. He (the Holy Spirit)
will convict the................................183

of justice because I go to the
Father and you will see Me no
more. The Advocate (the Holy
Spirit) will convict the....................104

of sin because they do not believe
in Me. The Advocate (the Holy
Spirit) will convict the....................174

or in the world to come (Heaven).
Whoever speaks against the Holy
Spirit it will not be forgiven him
either in this....................................181

so I also have sent them (the
Apostles). Even as Thou
hast sent Me into the......................106

Take courage I have overcome the..175

that He gave his ONLY-
BEGOTTEN SON that those who
believe in Him may not perish but
have Life Everlasting. For
God so loved the............................274

world (continued)

That they (Apostles) may behold
My glory which Thou hast given
Me before the creation of the.........293

The Bread of God is that which
comes down from Heaven and
gives Life to the................................215

The Bread that I will give is My
flesh for the Life of the.................. 90

Thou (Father) hast loved Me
before the creation of the............... 49

to bear witness to the Truth. I am
a KING (to Pontius Pilate). This
is why I was born and why I
have come into the...........................128

to judge the world, but that the
world might be saved through
him. For God did not send His
Son into the.....................................250

worm dies not, and the fire is not
quenched." It is better for thee
to enter into Life Everlasting
maimed . . . lame . . . with one
eye . . . than having two hands
. . . two feet . . . two eyes, to be
cast into hell-fire, "Where their......255

worship Him must worship in
Spirit and in Truth. God is
Spirit and they who........................179

You shall live for I LIVE....................293

Zacharias, the son of Barachias,
whom you (the Jews) killed
between the Temple and the Altar.
I send you Prophets . . . that
upon you may come all the just
blood that has been shed . . . from
the blood of Abel the just unto......257

Zacchaeus make haste and come
down (from the sycamore tree);
for I must stay in thy house today.. 95